Praise for

JOHNNY R

"I had to explain to my wife why I was laughing out loud."

"Full of adventure and soul-filled, full-bodied life."

"A wonderful storyteller."

"Palguta paints his narrative with a colorful exuberance. Using the irreverent language of our generation and creative simile and metaphor helps to create a richly textured read. But on a different level, the author explores the philosophical implications of his hiking experience. Thoroughly enjoyable."

"Read it in a weekend and wish there were more coming."

"Part societal dissection, part fairy tale, part bildungsroman.... It's unlike anything you'll ever read."

"Plenty of laugh out loud moments that kept me coming back for more!"

"You will think about it months later."

"Could not put this down and I don't read much. Laughed out loud in the airport and got some strange looks."

"I did NOT want Mount Guyot to be found as I wanted the search to go on and on and on."

"Maybe the best book I ever read."

Finding Mount Guyot

Finding Mount Guyot:

A Humorous Adventure Novel

Buddha Palguta

A Warning

I have tried to protect the majesty of Mount Guyot by intentionally confusing the directions to the top. Anyone who is inspired to try to summit Mount Guyot should not rely on the directions found in this book. You will get lost and suffer all the miseries described herein. You have to find Mount Guyot for yourself.

A Disclaimer

This is a work of fiction. Names, characters, places, and incidents are the products of the author's imagination or are used fictitiously. Any resemblance to actual persons, living or deceased, businesses, companies, events, or locations is entirely coincidental.

For Lori, with all my love. You made this book possible.

And to the friends with whom I've shared the experience of the Smokies, especially my brothers from another mother, you have my eternal thanks for some of the best and hardest days of my life.

Table of Contents

"It is no measure of health to be well-adjusted in a profoundly sick society."

– Jiddu Krishnamurti

1   Going to the Mountains

August, 1989

I tended my fire, smoked a lot, and drank the Yukon sparingly. I kept my eyes on the darkening tree line until night fell. I was conscious of the fact that I was alone in the wilderness, but I wasn't as frightened as I'd thought I would be. Still, I took it easy on the booze. I watched the flickering flames and thought about the boar, the girls at the Electric Chalet, the night in jail, and being out in the mountains alone. I wondered what drove me to these things, and the only answer I could come up with was testosterone. *It's more than that, Johnny Rez. More than that.*

A few hours after nightfall, I could take the solitude no longer, so I decided to lie down. I had hoped to be able to see the stars through the clear walls of my simple shelter, but the plastic was too opaque to see anything. I was warm enough with my single blanket, but I felt very vulnerable with just a thin sheet of plastic open on both ends covering me. I put my big, sheathed butcher knife under my head and kept one hand on it. I closed my eyes and said a few heartfelt prayers. Sleep wouldn't come easily. I lay there for a long time, hearing every sound in the living forest around me. I recalled my first few nights in these mountains when I imagined the worst after every creak and rustle and night cry that I heard.

Sometime in the night—I may finally have been dozing—I heard a distinct sound very close to me. Instantly, I was alert, yet I remained completely still. I didn't even open my eyes. My hand closed slowly around the handle of the big knife under me. Then an electric shock of adrenaline went through me ten times greater than anything I had ever felt before. Something was sniffing my head! It was only inches away, whatever it was. Instinctively, I kept my eyes shut. I fought to control my breathing, but my heart pounded wildly. I knew I was awake because the ground was hard beneath me. This was nightmarish, but deadly real.

The sniffing was at the back of my head. I couldn't tell if the creature doing the sniffing was large or small, but I knew it was close. *Oh my God.* Even a raccoon could tear my head up before I got the knife out. A bear could tear my face clean off in a heartbeat. The creature had to know I was alive by the sound of my breathing and the warmth of my body. Even opening my eyes could be enough to cause it to attack. *Play dead. Play dead. Oh dear God. Just play dead.*

Time stood still as I lay there perfectly still, listening to the sniffing sounds behind me, fearing for my very life. Over the sound of my own blood roaring in my ears, I heard the brushing sounds of the creature moving and its slight footsteps. Several lifetimes passed before I heard the thing start to move away from me, but it didn't go far. It only went as far as the other end of the pup tent, where it started sniffing my feet.

I still didn't dare move my body or my head, but I slowly, slowly opened my eyes. I found that I couldn't see a damned thing. I was lying on my side, and the bulk of my body and the walls of my shelter prevented me from seeing anything. I could only see the dark shapes of trees out in front of me and the blankness of the plastic. This was living hell. *What do I do if it bites into me? Lie still, or fight? Have to fight at that point, Johnny.*

Eons of time passed while it sniffed at my feet. I was sweating and itching and my muscles were aching from staying so still, but I knew I might die if I moved. I stayed still as long as I could, even after I stopped hearing any sounds. I listened so hard that it got to the point where I couldn't tell if I was hearing sounds or just imagining them.

Finally, I slowly—oh so slowly—lifted my head enough to look up over my body. Another shot of adrenalin surged through me as I saw the silhouette of a bear about twenty yards away. I could see it through the opening at the far end of my shelter. It was moving away from me, and I watched it gradually disappear into the trees. *Thank you, dear God. Oh sweet Jesus, thank you, thank you, thank you.*

The adrenalin level in me dropped so quickly that I felt giddy. Suddenly, I wanted to laugh or scream or cry. I moved my legs and there was blessed relief in that, too. I crawled out of my covering with my big knife in my hand, watching the point in the trees where the bear had gone in. I scanned the tree line with my flashlight, expecting to see shiny eyes reflecting back at me, but I saw nothing. I had a smoke to steady my nerves. Then I had a long drink straight from the bottle. I couldn't believe it; I had been nose to nose with a bear, by God. My first close encounter with a bear, and it had been right on top of me. I broke down and sobbed a few times, expelling the raw fear.

I stirred up the embers and got a flame going. Then I threw on a few sticks and sat beside the fire. I kept my eyes on the tree line and had a couple of long drinks. My thoughts drifted back to how it all began one rainy night in May of 1977.

3

Dan Rafferty and I were drinking Stroh's beer and smoking crappy Mexican reefer in my Galaxy 500, a car I had christened *The 5:15* after The Who song that went "Outta my brain on the train." We called it partying, but it wasn't really much of a party. Mostly we just stared out the smoked-streaked windows and listened to kick-ass rock 'n roll.

"Hey man," I said between songs, "I got a week's vacation coming. They said I can go any time after this month." I had spent the previous year, my first year out of high school, working in a hospital supply warehouse.

Dan came out of his stupor and thumped the dashboard. "I got a week off too! We oughta go to the Smokies, Johnny! It'd be cool."

Dan was enthusiastic about almost everything. Restlessness lurked in his fierce German Shepard eyes. He was a monster, three inches taller than my six feet, and as wide-shouldered and well-built as I was. We had met on a sandlot football field. He had been playing center, snapping the ball to the quarterback, and I was the middle linebacker, lined up directly across from him. On the first play, Dan hiked the ball, fired out, and crashed into me hard. Just to make a point, he brought his knee up into my crotch. It hurt, but it wasn't a direct hit. I knew it had been on purpose. As Dan snapped the ball for the next play, I pounded my right fist into the back of his neck as hard as I could and drove his face down into the dirt. When I looked to see how badly I'd hurt him, all I saw was amusement in his crazy eyes. We had been friends ever since.

"Alright," I immediately agreed. I had never been to the mountains, but I knew somehow that I was meant to be a mountain man. By some tragic twist of fate, I had been born in the flatlands of Cleveland instead, and I had never even laid eyes on a real mountain. Growing up, I'd never hiked farther than the couple of miles from our house up to the Lake Erie

4

shore, and I'd never slept on the ground except in some neighborhood back yards. "I've been wanting to climb a mountain for a long time."

But I was only eighteen, and I had no idea what a long time was. The thirty years I would spend searching for a mountain—now that would be a long time. Back then, though, a long time was waiting until June for my first trip to the Smoky Mountains.

We were going to backpack, carrying everything we needed on our backs and hiking deep into the mountains. Dan had backpacked in the Smokies once before, and he told me I needed all kinds of special gear, so we went to an Army-Navy surplus store where they sold outdoor equipment and surplus (meaning defective) military supplies. Dan walked over to me with a pair of Army combat boots in his hands. "What do you think of these boots, Johnny? You're gonna need some heavy boots on the trail."

"I was just gonna wear my work shoes." I had some scuffed, old, rubber-soled work shoes that I wore in the warehouse.

Dan shook his head. "No, man, you need thick soles like these. And they come up high so you won't get bit by snakes. You know there's rattlesnakes in Tennessee, don't you?"

I didn't know any such thing, and maybe this was the moment when I experienced my first twinge of anxiety, but I was full of ignorance and testosterone, and I would rather have chewed my foot off at the ankle than to have shown any fear. As casually as possible, I studied the high-topped boots. They were made of heavy black leather and came up well over the ankles. The soles were made of thick, hard rubber and bore the stamp "Made in China." There was no inside lining whatsoever. "I don't know, man. These inside edges are going to tear up my feet, don't you think?"

Dan acted as if he were a shoe salesman for the store and needed the commission very badly. "Naw," he said, "don't worry about that. Those edges will flatten out, and you'll be wearing two or three pairs of socks anyway. These are good, heavy boots, Johnny! Just make sure they're big enough. You don't want them pinching your feet."

I bought the Chinese combat boots and a bunch of other paramilitary gear to add what Dan judged to be sufficient weight to my backpack. I needed a mess kit, a compass, a poncho, a flashlight, a first aid kit, a snake bite kit, a canteen, and a rope. The snake bite kit fascinated me. It included instructions on how to cut X's into the flesh of the victim as well as suction cups to draw the poison out of the X marks. Sucking the venom out the way the cowboys did was cool, but it wasn't as safe.

I needed many more things, including a good knife with a sheath, fire starters, and personal toiletry items like a stainless steel mirror that I was supposed to use for shaving and signaling airplanes. My favorite item was an Army-style web belt with lots of riveted holes in it on which I could hang my canteen and my knife. When they rang up the sale, I was glad I had at least saved money by buying the cheapest sleeping bag and backpack I could find.

At home, I threw all that gear in a pile and then threw some clothes and food on top. Needless to say, everything in the pile wouldn't fit into the pack. As I started tossing aside things that had seemed necessary just a few minutes before, I began to grasp the first permanent truth that backpacking teaches—most of the material things we consider essential are not really essential at all. I crammed as much stuff into my backpack as humanly possible, and then I tied my sleeping bag on the back of the pack. Finally, I attached a few items to my web belt next to my canteen and my knife, and I was ready. All that gear was heavy as hell as I stood there fully laden, but I wasn't too worried about the weight. I went and looked in the mirror. I looked like Daniel Boone. I looked like a bad mammy jamma. For the first time in my life, I felt like a mountain man.

Dan's brother, Craig, heard about our trip and wanted to come along. Craig was a year and a half older than we were, but I had hung around with him from time to time. From what I could tell, Craig was pretty quiet. He was even taller than Dan but thinner, more of a basketball player than a football player, but a tough guy nonetheless. His nose had been badly broken once by a well-aimed elbow, which made him look even meaner. Still, he was "cool," which meant that he liked to party as much as we did, so I had no problem with Craig joining us.

Craig had also been to the Smokies, so he and Dan were in charge of planning the route we would take once we got there. The day before we left, I found them poring over complicated-looking trail maps like generals planning a military campaign, judging distances and elevations. I knew nothing about any of that stuff, and I didn't bother trying to learn. I went out to the disco instead with another buddy of mine who called himself Eddie Love, and we asked girls wearing tube tops and camel-toe pants what their signs were. In general, we laid down the boogie like the funky white boys that we were.

We left the next evening after work in Craig's 1976 Chevy Laguna S-3, a beautiful red coupe with a white leather interior and swiveling bucket seats. We drove straight through the heart of the Appalachian Mountains. In the days before I-77 was completed, many sections of the road through the mountains were only one lane in each direction. When Craig came up behind some lumbering tractor-trailer on the long uphill grades, he would nose the S-3 out into the oncoming traffic, looking to see if anything was hurtling headlong down the mountain toward us. Whenever a vehicle did appear in the other lane, Craig would hit the brakes hard, let the truck he was trying to pass gain ground on us, and then tuck the S-3 back in behind the truck in our lane. Craig thought it was great fun, but Dan and I exchanged nervous glances several times. We smoked pot at regular intervals to steady our nerves.

When I finally got my first glimpse of the Great Smoky Mountains early the next morning, I was awestruck by their immensity. These were huge, purplish behemoths with powerfully slumped shoulders, wreathed in smoky vapors. They were honest-to-God mountains, and they struck some deep, reverberating chord in my heart, just as I had always known they would. It wasn't love at first sight—it was awe at first sight.

With the mountains looming closer and closer, it seemed to take forever to drive through the little towns of Sevierville, Pigeon Forge, and Gatlinburg, but eventually we arrived at the Sugarlands Visitor Center, which was the main entrance on the north side of the Great Smoky Mountain National Park. One night while packing for the trip, I had found an old, red-felt cowboy hat that I had won at a county fair. I decided to decorate the hat by writing "Mountain Man" across the front of it with a magic marker. When Craig parked the car, I fished that hat out of my gear and put it on there in the Sugarlands parking lot.

Craig took one look at the little hat perched on my big melon and said, "What the fuck's wrong with you, John?"

"I'm not sure," I said sheepishly, but I kept the hat on anyway. Craig shook his head sadly, and I wasn't sure if his disdain was exaggerated or real.

Prospective hikers had to meet face-to-face with a ranger to get a permit in those days, so we walked into a building that looked like an old log cabin and found a ranger sitting behind a counter, sipping coffee. The guy seemed ancient. He was graying and heavyset and his movements were slow. He even spoke slowly. "Mornin'," he said. "What can I do for you boys?"

Craig spoke for us. "We need a backcountry permit for four nights."

"Sorry, all the sites are full up for the week." Our faces fell, and the ranger laughed a corn-pone laugh. "Haw! Just havin' a little fun with y'all. What days and sites are you lookin' for?"

Dan unfolded our trail map and laid it on the counter to help Craig. The ranger lifted up the corner of our map and pointed to the trail map mounted under the glass surface of the countertop. "How 'bout if we use my map?" the ranger frowned.

Dan put away our map. Craig pointed to the four campsites we wanted to use, referring to the two-digit numbers that were used to identify the camps. The ranger jotted down the four numbers.

"Did you ever stay at any of those camps?" I asked.

The ranger looked at me as if I'd asked him if his daughter liked it hard and sloppy. "Son," he said in a very controlled voice, "I spent my whole life in these mountains. There ain't a trail or a campsite that I ain't been on."

I decided that I would be better off keeping my mouth shut.

The ranger started filling out a triplicate form titled "Backcountry Use Permit." He took down Craig's name and address. "So y'all are from Ohio, huh?" he asked when he came to the space for the state.

"How'd you know that?" Craig asked. "Did our accent give it away?

"No, just your license plate. It's what we call 'a clue' in law enforcement."

After he filled out the rest of the form, he looked up and eyed us with evident concern. "Y'all ever camped in the backcountry before? It's serious business, boys, and y'all could get hurt if you don't know what you're doin'."

9

"I was backpacking down here two years ago," Craig said proudly. "Up in the backcountry."

"I was here too," Dan volunteered.

The ranger looked at me expectantly, eyeing my mountain man hat, but I said nothing. I was afraid he was going to tell me I couldn't go, but he handed Craig two copies of the permit and said, "Put one on your dashboard and keep one on your pack. Y'all have a safe trip now."

After we left the ranger station, we did yet more driving over roads that got smaller and smaller and less and less paved. Craig and Dan consulted the map more frequently. I was starting to internalize the concept of "backcountry." I had seen lots of people at the visitor center—rangers, people in campers, families, and even a few other people with backpacks— but now we were very alone. Road signs and telephone poles quickly disappeared, and soon there was nothing but a rocky, one-lane dirt road and vast woods around us. Finally, after thirteen total hours in the car, we were at the trailhead that would be our starting point and our ending point. The location was marked by a tiny wooden sign mounted on a 4x4 wooden post. Except for the post, this spot looked the same to me as the rest of the immense wilderness surrounding us.

I was suddenly, harshly aware that I damned well better have everything I needed in my pack. I was overwhelmed with pangs of doubt. I wondered if two packets of oatmeal were going to be enough for a breakfast. I wondered if I should have brought extra batteries for my flashlight. And I wondered how big the bears really were. I heaved my pack onto my back and put my mountain man hat on my head. I felt tired and scared and my pack was impossibly heavy, but I was thrilled to finally be going into the mountains.

Singing the Bob Seger song "Katmandu," I stepped onto my first trail in the ancient Appalachians. The day was hot and sunny. After no more than thirty or forty steps, we came to a deadfall, which was the backpacking word for a fallen tree lying across the path. Craig was in the lead and stepped over the deadfall almost without altering his stride. Dan stepped over it easily as well. I went to step over the deadfall, lost my balance because of the unfamiliar, heavy pack on my back, and toppled over backwards. I was lying there looking up at the sky, arms and legs flailing like some giant cockroach that had flipped over while trying to climb out of the sink. My career as a mountain man had begun.

After they got me back on my feet, we started trudging through the deepest, darkest woods I had ever seen in my life. In minutes, my buoyant spirits sank. Even though the day in the outer world had been bright and cheerful, these woods were dank, musty, and primeval. Huge trees blocked out most of the daylight. Prehistoric-looking ferns and bushes crowded the thin trail, and the ground seethed with snails and occasional lizards. Dan told me the lizards were harmless salamanders, but I wasn't sure I believed him. All I knew was that I was working damned hard. The flat, narrow shoulder straps of my pack were digging into my shoulders like piano wires, and my fake Army canteen hanging from my fake Army web belt was already leaking. I was drenched with sweat, and my felt hat was losing its rakish cowboy shape.

I found no joy in this: none of the beautiful scenery, serenity, and camaraderie I had been promised. For one thing, my head was hanging down like a water buffalo working in a rice paddy. I couldn't have seen any beautiful scenery if there had been any there to see, which there wasn't. We were in a valley in a dense thicket of trees with ten-foot-high bushes to the left, the right, the front, and the back. When I straightened up and risked falling over backward again, all I could see was a narrow swath of blue sky directly overhead.

Buddha Palguta

As for camaraderie, my so-called comrades were a hundred yards out ahead of me, apparently ready to abandon me without so much as a backwards glance. They were both outstriding me, and I was alone in my misery. After an eternity of hard, sweaty walking, I caught up with Dan and Craig. I felt pretty good about catching them until I realized they had only paused to rest at a wooden signpost. "This is fuckin' bogus, man," I said without preamble. I had a lot of pent-up bitching to get out of my system.

Craig pointed at the sign. "We've only got 4.8 miles to go!" He was sweating himself, but he was clearly enjoying my discomfort.

I wasn't sure what to make of this news. It felt as if we had already walked ten miles, so four and a half more wasn't so bad. But I had a nasty feeling that we really hadn't walked anywhere near ten miles. I cautiously asked, "How far'd we go so far?"

"One point six miles." He grinned broadly and damn near laughed as he said it. Dan actually did laugh—his crazy, slightly high-pitched "hee-hee-hee" that made him sound like an old prospector who'd been alone with bad whiskey and a frisky burro for too long.

I did the math. "So we only went a fourth of the way?"

"That was all uphill. That was the worst part, mountain man," Craig said. I knew he had thrown in the mountain man part to make me feel better, but it didn't.

I said again, "This is fuckin' bogus!"

We resumed walking. With my head hanging down and my friends far ahead, I had ample opportunity to study the trail, which was a ribbon of beaten earth no more than a foot wide in most places. The trail was not at all like the paths going through the city parks in Cleveland. Here, rocks and big roots stuck up out of the ground at crazy angles, making it necessary for me to watch where I placed each footstep. As the day wore

12

on and my legs grew weary, I found it harder and harder to lift my feet over these obstacles.

I was lost in my misery when I stumbled into a clearing in the woods where another wooden signpost marked a location of some significance. The signpost showed the two-digit number marking this place as a backcountry campsite. Dan and Craig were already sitting on a big log, smoking cigarettes with their packs off. I started unbuckling my pack even before I stopped walking.

"Johnny Rez! Glad you could make it," Dan joked. My last name was Reznick, and they called me "Rez" sometimes.

"This is it," Craig said happily.

"This is *what?*" I asked. Looking around, my disappointment was complete. The barren patch of dirt marked by the signpost was not a photo opportunity kind of place. It looked more like an Agent Orange kind of place. Besides the scorched-looking earth, all I saw was two different circles of rocks where people had made fires in the recent past and a few blackened logs. Obviously, someone had tried to burn these massive logs and failed. A few lonely, living trees were scattered around the site, but all the low branches were gone. The upper branches of the trees made a thin canopy. I noticed several ropes hanging down from these high branches, which gave the place a gallows kind of feel. The most remarkable thing was the ground itself. I saw absolutely not one single twig or branch on the ground and barely any living grass coming up. The barren ground revealed the roots of the trees, which stood out like the veins on an old man's hands.

I shed my pack and plopped myself down on one of the logs. I had only been a backpacker for a few hours, but I was already pretty good at taking off my pack. It felt wonderful to free myself from the cursed pack for the rest of the day, but as I looked around I was pretty sure I wasn't in for a night at the Hilton. Backpackers in the Smokies were only permitted to spend the night at designated campsites. A few campsites had sturdily built shelters that offered backpackers a roof over their heads for the night, but the vast majority were totally unimproved and offered only dirt to lie on and a moving water source somewhere within a quarter mile of the site. These were called "primitive" campsites.

After the hard work of hauling our packs up and down mountains all day, we couldn't wait to get royally fucked up. Dan had mentioned sitting around a campfire out in the woods and partying with no one around as one of the major appeals of backpacking. We were all still living at home with our parents, so finding places where we could drink and get high was pretty much what we did in our free time. The main drawback of this place was that we couldn't haul in any beer. We got out our whiskey bottles and our pot pipes and put on a good buzz before we even thought about food or shelter. If any one of us had ever heard of Maslow's hierarchy of needs, in which the psychologist Maslow stated that the primary needs of food and shelter and warmth had to be met before attaining higher goals, we'd have called Maslow a puss. Maslow was definitely not a backpacker.

After relaxing for a while, Dan got busy pitching the tent while Craig started cooking up some food. I, being the newcomer, was assigned the less crucial task of gathering firewood. I wandered in aimless circles around the immediate area of the camp, vainly searching for anything combustible. Dimly, I understood why this campsite was so barren compared with the miles of woods we had walked through all day. Scores if not hundreds or people had already been at this campsite, doing exactly what I was doing, and had snatched up every last twig and pine needle. As I widened my search, I noticed the stumps of several saplings that had been hacked down or twisted and ripped apart while still green. Even I knew that green wood wouldn't burn.

Finding Mount Guyot

Warily, I ventured further into the woods. This was my first time in the real woods, and I was more than a little apprehensive about what might be lurking out in the lengthening shadows past the perimeter of the empty clearing. I didn't wander very far at all, only far enough to find a miserable little armful of wet or rotten sticks to stumble back into camp with. I set down the sticks next to the tiny fire on which Craig was cooking our supper. Then I sat down in the dirt. I was tired. Craig eyed the pile of sticks. "I guess you don't plan on staying up too long," he said.

"What do you mean?"

He snorted derisively. "That won't last us half an hour, John, if it'll burn at all."

He was right. I got up, grabbed my flashlight and the little knife that was my only weapon, and went back out to face the lions and tigers and bears that lurked in the woods. Backpacking was becoming a major pain in the ass.

After a miserable supper of some dehydrated stuff that looked like Alpo, we had more work to do. We went down to the rocky creek that ran past the campsite and washed dishes. "You *gotta* wash 'em, Johnny, or the bears will smell the food and come into camp," Dan explained. Then we washed our faces in the cold water and brushed our teeth. Finally, our packs had to be closed up and put away for the night. The reverse side of our Park Service trail map said that backpackers should always hang their food up in trees as far as possible from the trunks of the trees to keep the food out of the reach of bears.

The first step was to get one end of a rope over the branch of a tree at least fifteen feet up in the air and then get that same end of the rope back down to the ground. Dan wanted to show me how it was done. He securely tied the end of the rope to a baseball-sized rock and threw the rock up over a likely tree limb. His first try fell short.

15

"Puss," Craig muttered.

Dan threw the tethered rock again as hard as he could and it sailed high into the tree, crashed through a few branches, and stuck there. At that point, I realized that the ropes dangling down all around us were from people who had gotten their ropes stuck the same way. Dan yanked on the rope and whipped it to and fro, and it finally came free. We watched it come sailing back down and failed to see the rock also plummeting to earth. It missed Craig by only a few feet.

Craig picked up the rock and barked, "Gimme the rope." If he had added the word "knucklehead," he could have been Moe from the Three Stooges. He retied the rope and got off a really good throw. We watched the rock taking a nice arc that would send it well over the branch, but the rock suddenly snapped back toward us, and we had to jump out of the way. We looked down and saw that Dan had been standing on the loose end of the rope just to mess with his brother.

Finally, we got the rope up over a stout limb. We tied all three of our packs to the end of the rope. Much of the weight had been taken out of the packs, but their combined weight was still considerable. We tried to hoist the packs up, but it seemed that the limb would break before the packs would lift off the ground. Dan had the bright idea to help the packs along by lifting them up over his head, which put the bottoms of the packs maybe eight feet off the ground. Craig and I tied the free end of the rope to a nearby tree. As soon as Dan let go of the packs, the rope stretched until the packs were no more than three or four feet off the ground. Even a developmentally-challenged bear could have plundered these packs. We tried again, but the best we could do was to get the packs maybe six feet off the ground, which was an effective deterrent to any midget bears that might happen by in the night. For any normal-sized bears of average intelligence, our packs were a smorgasbord waiting to happen.

Finding Mount Guyot

The packs being hung, our labors for the day were finally complete, and we had time to sit around our tiny campfire and watch it grow completely dark. The night was a living presence deep in the mountains. We watched the darkness come creeping in from all sides at once, silently devouring objects that had been visible only moments before. I looked around our camp and realized that the night had enveloped our entire little forest world except for the small circle illuminated by the fire and our flashlights. Then it was just the three of us, and we were utterly alone in that little circle of flickering light, surrounded in every direction by literally miles of wilderness and the beasts that lived in that wilderness. No matter what happened, no one was going to come and help us, and we couldn't even leave to find any help until the morning. The woods and the night owned our asses, at least until the dawn. And if a man says that that doesn't frighten him at least a little, then I say that man is a liar or a fool.

We got out our whiskey and our pot again and talked our proud, drunken talk around the campfire. I talked the talk, but I didn't walk the walk. Despite the whiskey and the brashness of youth, I didn't venture too far away from the fire when I had to take a leak, but then neither did Craig or Dan.

Finally, the sleep-deprived night in the car and the long day of hiking and partying took their toll, and we crawled wearily into the cheap four-man tent that we had borrowed for the trip. We were large and drunk and working in the dark, so we had a hard time getting situated inside the tent. None of us had yet figured out that it made more sense to take our boots off outside the tent, so there were clods of dirt flying and grunts and the sounds of zippers unzipping and occasional curses—much like the end of prom night in Arkansas—but we eventually laid ourselves down on the ground to sleep.

But sleep wouldn't come. For me, a tenderfoot, the sounds of the woods at night grew louder and more ominous as the laughter and the crackle of the fire subsided, and I lay there imagining all sorts of wild beasts creeping closer and closer as our sheltering halo of light diminished through the translucent wall of the tent. To a person like me unaccustomed to the sounds of the woods, every rustling of the leaves, every falling branch, and every snapping twig was enough to cause an adrenaline rush of fear. The night-calls of the birds and the cries of the animals made the blood pound in my head, and I lay there trying to rationalize each noise. My overwrought imagination turned every sound into a ravenous 600-pound black bear or a 250-pound hillbilly with a penchant for buggery.

The gnarly, finger-sized roots that we were lying on started to create pressure points no matter which way we tossed or turned. The night dragged on interminably as I flipped from side to side. I would lie on one side or on my back for as long as I could stand it, hoping to fall asleep before the discomfort became too great. Then I would reach the point where I could no longer stand a rock or a root digging directly into a hip bone or a shoulder blade, and I would have to move and thus begin the process all over again.

At some point in that endless night, it began to rain. I heard the first tentative drops hit the tent. Of course, my fevered brain assumed it was a bear gently tapping at the door, politely asking for a midnight snack, but then the raindrops came more earnestly. I had never really slept out in the rain before. In the past, I had always just grabbed the Pepsi and the potato chips and Mom's blankets and headed straight toward the back door of the house. That was not an option on this night. We had no house, no camper, no car to get into, no campground bathroom to offer shelter, nothing except the cheap, borrowed tent that was already starting to bead up with drops on the inside walls. There was nothing for us to do but get wet, which is exactly what we did. As I lay there on those roots with my five-dollar sleeping bag slowly becoming waterlogged and with dripping wet nylon two inches above my head, I thought that I was in complete misery. Years later, on other trips when I was experiencing real misery, I would think back to this first night in the mountains and laugh.

Whereas night came rapidly in the woods, it took forever for it to become day again. The color of the walls of the tent began to lighten infinitesimally, and I heard the birds' first tentative calls. Yet dawn was still a long way off. The surrounding mountains sheltered us from the rising sun, so even though the sky directly overhead was lightening, hours passed before it was light enough to get up. We lay there in our wet bags, trying to salvage some rest for our weary bodies in those slow hours when night passed away.

Finally I had to pee so badly that I had to get up. There was a lot of jostling and grunting—like my own prom night—as I emerged from the tent. The sky was heavy with gray clouds and drops still fell with regularity from the overhead branches. Everything in the camp was sodden and muddy. Even the air was sodden and muddy. It was impossible to tell if it was raining or not. The canopy of trees sheltered us from most of the direct rain when it was actually raining, but when it wasn't raining, drops continued to fall from the leaves for many hours. The result was a diffuse type of precipitation that came down steadily for most of the day. I didn't know it, but we were inside one of the clouds that hung in the valleys: the namesake wreaths of "smoke" that I had seen when I first viewed the mountains. I looked at our backpacks, which were now heavy with water and hanging about two feet off the ground from the wet rope. The packs might actually have pinned the bear to the ground if a bear had messed with them.

The first order of business was coffee. We needed hot caffeine badly. Craig fired up his camp stove and started heating some water. The stove was nothing more than a burner about the size of a tea saucer. The butane fuel tank was a small canister about the size and shape of an automobile oil filter. The burner screwed onto the top of the fuel tank, and the flat bottom of the tank sat on the ground. Craig balanced a pot full of water gingerly on top of the burner.

"Why don't we just use the stove all the time?" I asked.

"'Cause we'd have to carry three or four of these fuel tanks, and that would make our packs heavier."

"Oh."

Dan and I got the backpacks down from the tree, which took about three seconds. All of us had packed our own food in our own packs, and all three of us had packed badly. We all had damp food less than one day into the trip. We made a breakfast of damp instant coffee that came out of the jar in tarry chunks and instant oatmeal that thankfully came packaged in waxy envelopes that were apparently impervious to dampness. I had daydreamed about my first magical morning in the Great Smoky Mountains, imagining myself on some pristine Appalachian peak enjoying a steaming cup of coffee while gazing on the sheer grandeur of an unspoiled mountain dawn. Instead, I sat in a sodden valley on a wet log eating my lumpy gruel, washing it down with industrial-strength instant coffee flavored with chunks of powdered creamer and other unidentified particles. We were wet and chilled, groggy from lack of sleep, and slightly hung over.

Dan sipped his coffee and smoked his smoke. "Hey Craig," he asked, "what are these black chunks in my coffee?"

"Those are flavor crystals."

"Oh! I thought maybe they were something bad."

The coffee and the exuberance of youth worked their magic, and the pulse of life slowly returned. Dan explained what had to be done to get ready for the day's hike. "I get it,"

I said impatiently. "All my shit has to go back in my pack, right?"

Once we had stowed away all our belongings, we heaved the packs back onto our backs. My shoulders were tender as hell where the straps went, and my whole back was knotted and sore. Dan saw me wince. "Feels good, doesn't it?" he grinned. "The thing is, your pack's probably heavier now than it was yesterday because of all the water in it." He laughed his mad prospector cackle.

As soon as we got back out on the trail and I started trying to step it out with a purposeful stride, I realized that my heels were definitely tender. I stopped and tightened up my boot laces, trying to reduce the slippage of the boots on my heels. As the day progressed, I stopped repeatedly to make adjustments to my footwear. My pace slowed as I tried to baby my feet. I thought the previous day's walk had been tough, but this second day was far worse. Craig and Dan kept ahead of me most of the time to minimize the bitching that they had to listen to.

At one stop, Dan and Craig waited long enough for me to catch up. I must have looked close to the edge of despair because Craig decided to encourage me. "You gotta look at the big picture, John," he advised. And it *was* damned hard to look at the larger scope of the trip when it required a major act of will just to climb each rise in the trail. Craig got out a map with lots of squiggly lines on it—a better map than the free one I had picked up at the ranger station. He traced a big, crooked finger along the map as he spoke. "Look. We went all uphill yesterday, climbing this mountain here, and then we camped on the other side."

"Oh!" I said, suddenly grasping the concept. "These circles show the peaks and the parallel lines are the valleys, right?"

"Yeah, you got it," Craig agreed. "Now we're headed down into another valley to camp by this creek." He read a name off

21

the map. "Panther Creek, which is probably only a mile or two away." He saw the dubious look on my face. I had only spent a day and a half in the woods, but I was already wise to the "one or two more miles" bit. "Really," he said, "we're not that far away. We can wash up in the creek and you can soak your heels." He clapped me on the back. "C'mon. We'll drink some whiskey and you'll forget all about your heels." I got up and shouldered my pack. Craig had given me enough reassurance to keep me going.

Our campsite for the evening was much more inviting than the first one. This camp sat beside a sweetly babbling creek strewn with mossy rocks. I could tell that this site was not as heavily used as the last one because the surrounding clearing hadn't been completely denuded of vegetation. This was much more like the mountains I had pictured in my mind. I immediately pulled off my boots and my three layers of damp socks. Craig and Dan sauntered over to have a look at my feet. Neither one said much, except to make vaguely sympathetic clucking noises. Then they got busy setting up camp, giving me time to nurse my wounded heels.

I had a good, nickel-sized blister on each heel. Both blisters had popped, and the ragged flaps of skin hung there, limply covering the red underlayers of skin that were never designed to see daylight. Luckily, I had nabbed a bunch of band-aids, sterile gauze, and surgical-quality adhesive tapes from work. I even had needles and suture. I was hoping for the opportunity to stitch somebody up, but I didn't want to start on myself. I squeezed a little alcohol from an alcohol wipe into one blister. To my surprise, it burned like the fires of hell, and I jumped around and swore like Rumplestiltskin when he found out that he couldn't weave straw into gold. I decided that the other blister didn't need to be sterilized. I covered up the blisters with gauze and taped the gauze in place. I walked around barefoot for the rest of the night whenever possible.

Craig and Dan pitched the tent so it could dry out and then went down to the water to wash up. I grabbed my soap and hobbled down to join them. Dan was whooping like a wild Injun as he waded naked into the stream. He saw me and yelled, "Come on in, Johnny!" but I didn't follow.

The water was only about three feet deep in the middle, and it looked really inviting. Dan lathered up with a bar of Irish Spring soap as if he were in the showers after football practice. He let out a great war whoop and submersed himself in one of the deepest pools. The soap suds floated downstream and disappeared. Craig took a more modest approach. He stripped down to the waist and washed his head and upper body and then splashed water up onto himself to rinse the soap off.

My bandaged heels saved me from having to make a choice about going in all the way. I knelt on rocks at the water's edge and imitated Craig. The water was surprisingly cold. Most of the water in the high Smoky Mountains came from springs, but the water felt as cold as snow melt on my body, especially after a long, sweaty day. Still, getting the biggest portion of the sweat and grime off was very refreshing. Such a simple thing as washing up, even using cold water and kneeling in the dirt, became a luxury in the mountains. I felt like a new man when I was done. We never gave a second thought to the soap suds we were putting into that pure mountain stream.

After washing up, we ate more crappy, dehydrated food and then set about getting seriously loaded. After a few shots and a few tokes, I could take it no more. "Gentlemen," I announced, "I have to take a shit."

I had put off this moment as long as possible because I had never gone in the woods before, but there could be no more delay. The darkness was silently encroaching once again, and I did not want to attempt this maneuver in the dark. I grabbed my roll of damp toilet paper and my knife and headed off toward the edges of the camp. The knife was for self-defense, but it occurred to me that the knife could serve another purpose as well. I remembered once seeing a 1950s Boy Scout book that had shown an illustration of a happy-looking boy using a small shovel to dig a trench in which he would defecate, presumably with the same wholesome smile on his face. I thought that I could use my knife to dig a trench of my own because I wanted to shit in a thoroughly woodsman-like manner. In a reasonably clear spot in the woods, I tried to dig out a nice rectangular hole just like the one I had seen in the book, but the damned roots and rocks kept getting in the way. I ended up scratching out a depression in the ground about an inch deep. Not enough to bury any self-respecting turd, but it would have to do. Nature was calling urgently.

I found a new appreciation for what girls went through when they copped a squat outdoors. I discovered that it was hard as hell to pull my pants down and then squat and deliver the load. For one thing, it was hard to keep my balance with my ass hanging out and my pants holding my feet close together. I couldn't get the good wide stance my football coaches had always preached. For another thing, I had a hard time keeping my pants and underwear out of the line of fire. I assumed the position and let go with a little urine only to find that I was wetting down my underwear and the back of my pants. This was especially disconcerting because I had to wear the same pants for two more days.

I discovered that it was far easier to have a tree or at least a log to lean against as I proceeded. I wanted to avoid falling backwards into my own crap at all costs. As I struggled, Dan and Craig shouted words of encouragement, such as the requisite "How's everything coming out?" and "Hey, Johnny, there's a bear! Look out," which they found highly amusing. Despite these trying circumstances, I managed to fulfill my mission. I remembered that I was supposed to bury the stuff at least six inches deep, as if the rangers were going to come around with rulers and measure. I used my foot to kick dirt over my trench. As I made my way back into camp, I received a standing ovation from the assembled crowd.

We sat around our campfire and partied it up. I found that I was amazingly content. I had a full belly, a nice buzz on, and empty bowels. Somehow, I wasn't worried about much of anything. I was about to crawl into a wet sleeping bag in a wet tent in the middle of the biggest woods I had ever seen, but I felt good. "Wouldn't it be cool to live out here?" I said. Then, as if I knew what I was talking about, I said, "If I had a woman with me, I could live out here."

Craig laughed, "You can't even get a girl to go to the drive-in with you!" That pissed me off because it was true, at least on most weekends. I was shy around girls, and I didn't understand yet that some of them kind of liked my looks. I was no movie star, but I had high Slavic cheekbones, pale green eyes, and a good smile.

I stole a line from *Rocky* and said, "Yo, I don't see no crowds around you neither." Craig was even less confident with girls than me. I continued in my own voice, "I'm just saying how relaxing it is, man. I love this! No clocks, no schedules, nobody breathing down your neck . . ."

Dan picked up on my idea. "Nobody telling you to sit down and shut up," he said, undoubtedly remembering his childhood. He bellowed a wild holler simply because he could, and it echoed through the valley.

"Yeah," I continued. "Nobody telling you what you can or can't do. That's the thing. You do whatever the hell you want to out here. The only thing you have to do is eat and sleep and hike." I thought for a moment, then quickly added, "And not get eaten by a bear. But that's it! It's just simpler out here."

"Well, after about a week out here, you'd trade all that in for a couple of good cheeseburgers," Craig said dryly.

"I was just *talking*, Craig. What the fuck, man? You think I don't know that I couldn't live out of a backpack forever?" I paused to calm myself down and ended up staring into the fire, imagining my future. "Maybe I could live down here someday," I finally said. "Get married and build a house and look out at these mountains every day. Maybe write books or something. Don't you guys ever think about that kind of stuff?"

Craig answered, "I don't waste my time thinking about shit that's never gonna happen, if that's what you mean."

Dan cut in and said, "Well, that could happen, Craig. It's not likely that Johnny'll ever find a girl, but it could happen." We laughed a little, and that defused the argument that was threatening. We were all exhausted, so we went to sleep not long after the stars came out. We slept right through the night. I was too tired to worry about scary things like bears or girls or being told what to do.

I was reminded of the fact that my feet were injured as soon as I woke up. They were sore as hell. I bandaged my heels with a heavy-duty tape job, but it didn't last long once we started walking. I applied new tape jobs several times that day, but no matter how I taped them, the tape would quickly loosen and bunch up and become a wad of sticky fabric rubbing against my raw heels. Every step was painful. I hoped against hope that the end of the day's hike was around each corner, and each time we rounded a bend I was disappointed.

We walked on. We didn't know it, but we walked though forest lands once owned by a man named William Walker, who settled in that remote valley in 1859 when he was twenty-one years old, not much older than I was as I walked through his valley. During his life, William Walker became a local legend for his sharpshooting skills and for the way he gathered honey from his bee hives without wearing any protection.

During the Civil War, he did chores and chopped wood for his less-fortunate neighbors. Perhaps his biggest claim to fame was that he had three wives at the same time, believing that the Bible sanctioned polygamy. Evidently, his wives didn't mind this arrangement because Walker ended up fathering twenty-six children. In the 1900s, he did his best to protect his family's land from the encroaching lumber companies. After he died in 1919, the loggers had their way with the virgin forest lands until the national park was created in 1934. We walked through the area ignorant of the history all around us.

I tried everything I could think of to make it through the day. Finally, I found the only thing that helped, which was whining and cursing. First I cursed Dan. Then I cursed Craig because he was related to Dan. I cursed their whole damned Scotch-Irish, bog-paddy, spud-eating, drunk-ass family. Then I started in on my Chinese boots. I cursed the whole rice-eating Oriental race. I even accused Dan of being a fucking Chinaman in disguise. For my finale, I cursed myself for listening to Dan and buying the damned boots.

Somehow I made it to our camp for the night without Craig and Dan just killing me outright and leaving my carcass in the woods for the animals and insects to devour. I knew there was no way in hell I could hike for two more days. Finally, I said what Craig and Dan had been expecting me to say all day. "You guys, I can't do this. My heels are bleeding. I'm gonna end up losing a foot or something. I can't do this."

Dan was an apprentice in a meat packing house, and he loved to show off his expertise with the big, razor-sharp knife he was carrying. "Why don't you just let me cut it off right now?"

"Man, I'm not kidding! I can't do two more days of this." They both saw my stubborn streak coming out, and they realized that I wasn't fooling around.

Craig shrugged. "You don't have a lot of options, John. Look at the map. Find a quicker way back to the car."

"Gimme your map."

After yet another pitiful supper, I showed Dan and Craig my plan. There was a trail junction less than a mile from where we were that led to an unpaved road only three miles away. That road led after many miles to the place where we had left the car. The only question was how far down that road Craig's car was.

"One of us can leave his pack and hike out the ten or so miles to the car. Then he can drive back and pick up the other two guys and all the stuff." I made it sound very simple.

"You mean me or Craig can hike out," Dan said. Craig took the map from me without saying anything. I started thinking that this wasn't going to be an easy sell.

"Well, yeah," I said. "I'm really not the most likely candidate to hike ten miles tomorrow." We all knew this, but they had to hear me admit it. It was a guy thing.

"It's probably a lot further than ten miles," Craig said absently as he studied the map. I thought it might be closer to twelve or thirteen miles, but ten sounded a whole lot better. Actually, it was hard to tell just how far it would be because the road curved back and forth a lot.

It was my turn to be the shoe salesman. "It's hard to tell exactly," I conceded. "You might be able to shave some steps off by shortcutting through the curves." This was a reach, and I knew it, but Craig took a different tack than the one I expected next.

"So I'm the one who's going," he said. It was somewhere between a question and a statement.

Dan happily said, "It's your car, Craig, so you can go get it," and the matter was decided that easily. Craig had volunteered to go.

The rest of the night was a party. I was relieved that I didn't have to do any more serious hiking, but all three of us loosened up, as if we were only then sure that we were going to make it out of the mountains in one piece. We built the fire high and drank and smoked and bragged. We brandished our knives and challenged the bears to come out and fight. We called ourselves mountain men. We showed how very young and foolish we were.

The next morning, Craig got ready to leave camp early, carrying just the essentials—a map, a canteen, a knife, and his smokes. Traveling alone in the mountains was no joke. In addition to the more glamorous dangers of the Smokies such as bears and snakes, even a mundane problem like a badly-sprained ankle or an allergic reaction to an insect bite could be life-threatening to a person hiking alone. We were all relative newcomers to the mountains, but we knew this was serious business. Craig was looking forward to the hike precisely because of the risk. He lit a smoke and took off down the trail to find the road and his Laguna, eating up the distance with his long stride.

Dan and I watched him go. We had to split up Craig's stuff between us to carry it out. I was jamming some of Craig's stuff into my pack when I noticed that he still had a fair amount of whiskey left. "Hey," I yelled to Dan, "I don't think I can fit all this whiskey in my pack."

"Well then, we just might have to lighten the load a little."

I smiled slyly. "We should probably get rid of Craig's since he's gonna be driving anyway."

Dan walked over and grabbed the half empty bottle of Black Velvet from Craig's pack and took a good slug. He grinned and said, "That one was for Craig." I took a good swig too and let out a little whoop befitting the first shot of booze in the morning. It probably wasn't even eight o'clock yet, but the real beauty of it was that we had no idea what time it was. We were in the mountains and we had whiskey—that was all we knew and all we needed to know.

The sky promised another rainy, dreary day, but suddenly it was a beautiful morning. We cheerfully finished packing up. I packed a few items of Craig's stuff into my pack, and Dan tied the rest of Craig's half-empty pack to the back of his own pack so he could carry both packs out. Dan and Craig were going out of their way to help me get out of the woods, and I was silently grateful.

We shouldered our packs and hiked out to the trailhead. When we got there, we dropped our burdens at the edge of the hard-packed gravel road. Dropping my pack for the final time was pure joy. I felt a sense of accomplishment in having made it out of the woods, but other feelings intruded. Something in me—some vestige of natural man like William Walker that had not yet been ground down—had absolutely no desire to go back to my civilized, regimented life in Cleveland.

A lone car, a Plymouth Fury, was parked at the trailhead, but we saw no sign that Craig had passed this spot. We hadn't noticed any blood stains or long, skinny body parts along the way, so we weren't too worried. We did a shot to celebrate having made it out of the woods. Then we looked around like two guys at a bus stop who didn't know when the next bus might be coming. It began to drizzle more earnestly than it had all morning, or maybe we just noticed it more.

We got out the sheet of plastic that we had been using as a ground cloth under our tent. We tied two corners of the plastic sheet to the door handles of the Fury and then used ropes to attach the other two corners to some small trees near the car. The resulting shelter allowed us to sit down out of the rain and lean our backs against the side of the car. We sat like two refugees. Everything we owned was wet, and we stank with several days' worth of sweat and the musty, piney, mildewed aroma of the Smokies. We settled down in our cozy shelter, absurdly proud of our very modest accomplishment. We had no idea how long it would take for Craig to get back to us, and we didn't much care. We had food and whiskey and shelter, so the bottom levels of Maslow's hierarchy were covered. We decided that another shot was in order, so we got out Craig's bottle and had another drink. This time we left the bottle out.

The drizzly morning wore on. We wondered occasionally where Craig might be, but neither Dan nor I had a watch, so we had no idea what time Craig had left or how much time had elapsed since then. We hadn't even considered a Plan B. We did what people did in the days before cell phones; we waited.

It occurred to us that we were hungry. We both had a fair amount of whiskey in our bellies, so we were either going to eat something or pass out. Dan fished around in his pack and found a tin of Vienna sausages. All the backpacking books said that you should never carry canned food into the woods because of the heaviness of the liquid and the weight of the can itself. Fortunately, Dan had never read those books. He believed in the Dinty Moore Beef Stew theory of packing food in the backcountry, which states that if you can carry it, it isn't too heavy. He held up the little can as if it were a trophy.

Vienna sausages were something new to me. They were little, whitish sausages about the size of cocktail weenies packed in a salty broth. Nothing but hog lips, steer penises, and chicken asses pulverized into a pulp and then stuffed into a casing. I tasted one, and it was quite mushy and bland. I decided mine needed some extra flavor, so I dipped a sausage into the cup of whiskey that had magically appeared in my hand.

"Hey Dan, you gotta try 'em in whiskey!" If I had said, "Hey Dan, you gotta rub 'em on your feet and snort the juice up your nose," he probably would have done so. But as it

31

happened, the taste of the sausages truly was improved by the whiskey, so we ate the rest of the sausages dipped in whiskey. Then Dan discovered that he had another tin of Vienna sausages in his pack, and we devoured the second can the same way.

The one minor problem with our new taste treat was that our whiskey cups now had greasy residue and bits of hog lip and steer penis floating on the surface. This was in addition to the normal chunks of dirt and leaves and oatmeal. We decided that the best solution was to down the polluted whiskey in one mighty, mountain-man swallow and then start over with fresh whiskey. As we were refilling our cups, Craig's Laguna came roaring around the curve of the road, slinging rocks and blaring Bob Seger's "Ramblin' Gamblin' Man" from the 8-track tape player. *"You can have your funky world. See ya 'round."*

Dan and I were rather surprised to see Craig. We had totally forgotten that we were in the middle of the mountains waiting to be rescued, but we were happy to see him once we remembered where we were. "Craig, man, you gotta try Vienna sausages in whiskey," I slurred. Never mind that we didn't have any sausages left.

Craig somehow sensed that Dan and I were drunk. He got out of the car, surveying us and our little makeshift camp. "So you guys been having a good time today? I hike my ass off for four hours, and you sit around getting drunk?" We basically agreed with his assessment. Then Craig filled us in on his long walk. "There weren't any fuckin' shortcuts, John! That's for sure."

"How far was it?"

"I checked the mileage coming back," Craig said. "Eleven point two miles. All uphill. Plus however many miles it was to get to here from the camp."

Finding Mount Guyot

"The Bataan Death March," I muttered, but Craig didn't catch the reference, which was just as well.

Then Dan said, "But you gotta try sausages in whiskey, Craig. They'll blow your mind, man."

We packed our gear into the trunk of the car and drove straight back to Cleveland. For the time being at least, I had to go back to my funky world, but I already knew I'd be coming back to the Smokies.

2   Going Higher

A long year passed. I worked in the warehouse by day and started going to night school at a community college. When summer finally rolled back around, Craig, Dan and I set out for the Smokies again. Equipped with better shoes and more dope, we headed to a place called Beech Gap. I figured anyplace called a "gap" had to be wild and rugged. Guys like Daniel Boone went through gaps.

I studied the map as we drove around the southeast corner of the park, realizing for the first time just how big the Smokies really were. The national park extended about fifty miles from east to west and about twenty-five miles from north to south, and I knew very well how far even one of those miles could be in the mountains.

My companions were literally loaded for bear. Dan had helped Craig get a meat-cutting job at a butcher shop, so I was now hiking with two butchers instead of one. Craig carried a butcher knife like Dan, but Craig was packing a machete as well. The machete had a twenty-inch, heavy steel blade honed to a razor edge. Craig tied the machete inside its sheath onto the back of his pack so that he could reach back over the top of his pack and whip out the blade quickly.

If Craig was ready for a bear, Dan was ready for a war. Dan had his butcher knife, but he was also carrying a genuine meat cleaver—a big, thick eight-pound slab of steel with a keen edge and a sturdy handle. "Watch this, Johnny," he said, and when he scraped the edge of the wicked blade along the skin of his forearm, the blade shaved the hair off his arm cleanly. He tried to fix the meat cleaver to the back of his pack the same way Craig had, but the cleaver was so heavy that it kept falling off.

Dan also had two of the breaking hooks that were used in the slaughterhouse to lift up sides of beef and pork. Each one was a pointed metal hook about eight inches long with a tee handle on the straight end. A man could grip the tee handle in his fist and jab the curved end into the flesh of a carcass deep enough to hook under a bone. This was how the slaughtermen and meat cutters got a good grip as they broke the bodies down into smaller parts. With his cleaver, his knife, and his hooks, Dan was carrying at least ten pounds of weaponry in his pack.

"I feel sorry for the bears," I said. I was only carrying a little woodsman's knife with a four-inch blade, which left me feeling very inadequate. I had a bad case of blade envy.

We marched off along the Beech Gap Trail headed northeast toward a place called Laurel Gap. *Another gap! How much of a mountain man was I?* After no more than a quarter mile, the trail crossed over a big creek called the Straight Fork. The water was high and running fast, and I swallowed hard because I didn't much like the idea of rock hopping across fast water.

Dan stepped out onto the first rock in the creek and looked upstream and downstream. "This is it," he announced. "There isn't gonna be any better place."

I decided to approach this crossing with a confidence I didn't really feel. As soon as Dan stepped back off the rock, I launched myself across the rocks with only a vague idea of which rocks I would use as stepping stones. My feet found their own way for the first four steps, but out in the middle of the creek, the stones were farther apart and my foot missed the fifth step.

I had time to say "Shit!" as I went in up to my crotch. The power of the water surprised me, unbalanced as I was, and knocked me over. I came up gasping, shocked by the cold water, and only avoided being swept downstream by grabbing onto the rock I had missed with my foot. I stood paralyzed for a second, clutching the rock for dear life.

Craig and Dan were yelling to me above the roar of the water. Craig said, "Get out! Keep going!" and I wondered what the hell he was talking about.

Dan yelled, "Your sleeping bag's getting wet!" and I realized that the sleeping bag strapped to the bottom of my backpack must be underwater.

That stirred me to action. I took a step toward the far side of the creek, and the water nearly blasted me off my feet again. It felt as if I were running the football and someone had crashed into me hard and low from the side, trying to take my legs out. I leaned hard into the oncoming water and managed to stay on my feet.

After a few more steps, the water started getting shallower, and I knew I was going to make it. I stepped onto long, flat rock near the other side of the creek, and one end of the rock tilted upward as I did so. Without warning, a huge, slimy-looking creature exploded out from under the rock, lunging past me at an angle toward the shore. The thing was about three feet long and looked like a cross between a catfish and a lizard. It scared the living shit out of me. I stepped backwards, lost my balance, and went down into the water again. All I knew was that I had to get out of the water before the creature—whatever it was—got a hold of me. I sprang up and fought through the knee-deep water as if the hounds of hell were behind me.

Once I had both feet on dry land again, I looked around wild-eyed, making sure the lizard thing was nowhere in sight. Only then did I look over to my friends on the far bank. "Mother *fucker*!" I yelled. "What was that?"

Dan yelled, "Was it a fish?"

"It was a fuckin' sea-monster, man! Didn't you see it? It had *legs*!"

After seeing the trouble I had and the thing coming up out of the water at me, Craig and Dan took their time preparing to cross the creek. They found themselves good, stout branches to use as walking sticks, and Dan got his meat cleaver out for protection.

Dan crossed next, watching the water carefully as he drew near my side of the creek, but nothing leapt out of the water at him. With the aid of the stick, he made it without falling in. As soon as he hit shore, he said, "What was that thing? We didn't see it."

"I don't know, man. I didn't see it real good either, but honest to God, it looked like some kind of swamp thing! Fish don't have legs, man. I know that."

Craig made over to our side, and he asked the same question. "What the fuck was that thing?"

Dan answered, "He says it had legs, Craig!"

Craig seemed amused by the whole thing. "Man, I thought you were headed right for that whirlpool down there when you fell!"

"What whirlpool?"

Craig and Dan both pointed ten yards downstream to a big funnel of white water crashing between two large rocks. I hadn't noticed it in my hurry to get across the creek.

"You could've drowned in that," Craig said flatly.

I shook my head disbelievingly. "I didn't know you could actually *die* out here, man!"

"Now you know."

I found out later that what I had seen was a "hellbender," a giant salamander that lived in large, fast-flowing streams with rocky bottoms. Hellbenders were only found in the eastern United States, mostly in remote, mountainous places like the Smokies. They dined primarily on crayfish. Their slimy skin secreted a mild poison, but they really weren't dangerous to humans. They would bite, however, if they were provoked. They were called by a variety of colorful names, including "mud-devil," "Allegheny alligator," and my favorite, "snot otter."

After I wrung out my socks and calmed down a little, we continued up the Beech Gap Trail. My boots squished with every step. Our first destination was the Laurel Gap shelter. I had never seen a shelter, nor had Craig or Dan, so we were all anxious to get up to the campsite to see what they were like. I envisioned a one-room log cabin with wooden bunk beds and maybe a primitive kitchen with a water pump and a big fireplace. Something like *The Rifleman's* house. It would be nice, I thought, to be deep in the mountains and still have a few basic comforts. I couldn't wait to put on some dry underwear.

As so often happens in life, reality did not match my expectations. When we arrived, we saw a three-sided stone cabin with a flat roof that slanted back away from the long, open side of the building. A chain-link fence with a heavy-duty gate covered the open front, which gave the shelter a nice, homey feel—if home was a jail cell. The floor was dirt. Not dirty, but dirt. A tiny stone fireplace built into the wall filled one of the front corners of the shelter. The only other feature of note was the sleeping area. In the rear section of the shelter, away from open front, a framework of horizontal logs built into the walls formed two long sleeping platforms that were stacked double-decker. The lower tier was only a foot off the ground, and the upper level was about four or five feet off the ground. The sleeping surfaces were sagging chicken wire stretched across the framework of logs. Seven people could sleep on each level of the chicken-wire bedding. All in all, it looked like a miserable hovel.

I entered the shelter and found a treasure trove of graffiti inside. These were mostly initials and dates and hometowns, recorded over the years by the hikers passing through. Some creative souls with sharp knives and too much time on their hands had left more elaborate messages carved into the shelter's beams.

The fenced face of the shelter, which was there to keep out the bears and other large animals, did nothing to dissipate the odors. The earthy smell was a combination of wet ashes, musty sleeping bags, and a Municipal Stadium men's room after a Browns' game. In fact, I could see bits of poorly-buried toilet paper sprouting out of the ground out behind the back wall. The Park Service had a rule that "toilet use" had to be at least 100 feet from a campsite or a water source, but this rule was obviously broken on a regular basis.

We called it home anyway. We spread out our sleeping bags on the upper platform to claim the best spots for ourselves in case somebody else showed up.

I looked around outside for a water pump and saw a sign that said Spring 500 Yds. It pointed to a little trail that led down the side of the mountain.

Dan saw it too and said, "I'll go fill up the canteens. I want to see what the spring looks like." Sometimes it was very useful to have an ADHD case around.

I called after Dan as he walked away, "Watch out for swamp creatures!"

Dan whipped out one of the meat hooks he had on his belt and yelled back, "They better watch out for me!"

After Dan walked away, I asked Craig, "You guys ever use those iodine pills in your water?" The iodine was supposed to kill any nasty bacteria lurking in the water, and the Park Service literature warned about always treating the backcountry water before drinking it.

"Yeah, we had some iodine pills the first time I was out here, but they made the water taste bad, so I quit using 'em. I think the water up this high is pretty pure anyway." He took a big drag off his cigarette. "Just drink plenty of whiskey. That'll kill any bugs in your belly."

No other hikers showed up at the shelter that night, so we had the place to ourselves. We drank as much of our precious whiskey as we would allow ourselves to and smoked plenty of pot. I wrote "RAFFERTY BROS & JOHNNY REZ '78 CLEVELAND ROCKS!" in an empty spot on one of the beams. I couldn't think of anything better.

I was anxious to try out my new sleeping pad, which was a two-foot-wide, six-foot-long piece of half-inch thick foam rubber that weighed almost nothing and could be rolled up to fit nicely on the back of a pack. At first, the combination of the yielding chicken wire and my new sleeping pad felt like a feather bed compared to the hard ground. Knowing that we had sturdy walls and steel fencing around us made it easier to relax as well. But after a while, the wires started digging into my flesh, and the thin foam pad might as well not been there for all the good it did. I began to toss and turn, trying in vain to find relief from the pressure of the thin metal wires. Pretty soon, all three of us were fidgeting and squirming on our chicken-wire beds of nails.

As soon as it was light enough to see inside the shelter the next morning, Craig reached into the plastic baggie that he kept right next to his sleeping bag. He fished out a black beauty and muttered, "I didn't sleep at all," as he carefully separated the two halves of the jet black capsule. He put one half up to his crooked nose and snorted hard. His head snapped back, and a small, guttural sound came out of his throat. "That was a home run," he said. Then he did the other half of the capsule up his other nostril. He shook his head vigorously side to side as if to settle his brain back into its normal resting place and said, "Whoa! Back-to-back homers!" All this happened while he was still in his sleeping bag.

Dan and I couldn't wait to try it. I watched Dan snort his first. He didn't make any guttural noises, but his head snapped back involuntarily each time that powder hit his sinuses. After the second snort, he looked as if his eyeballs were going to pop right out of his skull, which I took to mean that it was safe for me to do mine.

We had all dabbled some with cocaine, which is where Craig had gotten the idea to snort the speed in the first place, so mine were not virgin nostrils by any means, but when the white powder from that black beauty hit my nasal passages, it burned like sin. "Yow!" I yelled. "Hot damn!" I pounded my fist on the rafter above me. The burning in my sinus tissue alone was enough to get my adrenal system pumping. Then the speed buzz kicked in almost instantaneously, and it suddenly seemed like a fine day to go hiking.

We were up and moving in no time. We heated some water for coffee and oatmeal, but the speed had suppressed our appetites. Craig studied the map as he drank his coffee and smoked a cigarette. "Eat up, guys," he announced, "We're gonna need the energy today!"

Dan liked the sound of that. "Why? How far we do we have to go?"

"Looks like at least eleven miles. Up into the big, bad-ass mountains!"

The day's hike was going to take us west to the spine of the Appalachian Mountains and to a trail that ran right along the tops of the highest ridges in the Smokies. The trail was called the "Appalachian Trail," or simply the "AT." Craig and Dan had been very excited when they talked about hiking on the AT, but I had never heard of it. I was more concerned with the distance we planned to cover. I had never hiked eleven miles under any circumstances, much less up into some big, bad-ass mountains with a pack on my back. I forced myself to eat a spoonful of my cold, gluey oatmeal.

The skies were dreary as we left the Laurel Gap shelter. I was beginning to suspect that mornings were almost always dreary in the Smokies. The trail was easy at first, and we were buzzing from the black beauties, so our spirits were high. The morning air was cool, and I found that I liked hiking in the cool weather. Without breaking stride, I fired up a smoke. On the level sections and the downhills, we could smoke cigarettes while stepping it out at a good pace with forty pounds on our backs and not even get winded. Sometimes I'd even light up a smoke on the moderate uphills, but I was nineteen years old then and nothing ever hurt.

The smoking and joking soon ended because the Balsam Mountain Trail slanted steeply upward. We took a short break after the sweat started pouring, and I took the opportunity to study my map. We were headed toward a mountain called Luftee Knob and eventually toward another mountain called Tricorner Knob about five miles away. We would meet up with the Appalachian Trail at Tricorner Knob, and we had another five miles to go after that. I was wondering what I had been thinking when I agreed to this route. Apparently, I had succumbed to the dreaded peer pressure that my old man was always warning me about. *"Your asshole buddies are important to you now, Johnny,"* he would say, *"but you won't even know those guys twenty years from now."*

Finding Mount Guyot

My asshole buddies and I slogged up the trail, breathing hard and sweating out the booze from the night before. The speed buzz seemed to wear off too. This was the hard-work part of backpacking. There were no breathtaking views to enjoy. I had nothing to do but keep my eyes on the trail immediately in front of me and pick out a spot between the jagged rocks to plant each footstep. If I even bothered to look up, all I saw was someone's ass in my face and a wall of green on each side. Occasionally, I wiped the sweat off my brow and hitched up my hated shoulder straps, but even then I never broke stride. I kept planting one foot in front of the other. I ascended the mountain by gaining four inches of elevation at a time, and when I allowed myself to think at all, I thought about how much it sucked to climb mountains, so mostly I tried not to think. When I succeeded, my mind shut down, my body went on autopilot, and my feet moved by themselves. This was the state of being I tried to achieve on the long uphill climbs, but I didn't always succeed.

As we neared Tricorner Knob and the junction with the AT, the wind picked up, and spats of rain slapped our faces. Our bodies were still warm from the hard hiking, but everything else was cold and damp. We were up at 6,000 feet, well over a mile high. We soon came to a signpost that told us we had arrived at the Appalachian Trail. In fact, this signpost had several wooden slats attached to it, and each slat had a different place name and a distance engraved into the wood. This was a veritable catalogue of information compared to the five long miles of nothing we had just traversed. There were no signs whatsoever on the trails between the junction points. A hiker could walk for miles and miles through the mountains with nothing to follow except a narrow strip of rocky dirt.

The signpost at Tricorner Knob told us that the Laurel Gap shelter where we had stayed was 5.8 miles behind us. Our destination, the Pecks Corner shelter, was 5.3 miles off to the south on the AT. The next junction to the north on the AT was the Maddron Bald Trail, which was four miles away. The bottom slat on the sign post indicated that a place called "Mt Guyot" was 1.9 miles off to the north on the AT.

"What's Mount Guyot?" Craig pronounced it "goy-ott."

I had studied French in high school. "I think it would be 'gee-oh'. It looks French."

"Is that so?" Craig said in a prissy voice that mocked my unmanly display of learning.

"Yeah, I think it is," I said with some passion.

Dan interrupted our snappy war of words. Looking at his map, he said, "It's another one of the high points on the AT. One of them big, bad-ass mountains, Craig. On the map, it looks like the trail goes around it but not to the very top. And Johnny's right, Craig. It's probably 'gee-oh'." Dan had taken two years of French as well.

"If we didn't have so far to go today," I said, "I'd say we should go check it out."

"Seems like a waste of time to me," Craig said. "The weather's crappy, and we still have a long way to walk. Let's just go."

Dan voted with his feet. He turned and headed south on the Appalachian Trail, away from Mount Guyot. I didn't argue. Mount Guyot was the opposite of the way we were headed.

A few yards down the trail, we came to another sign that pointed us to the Tricorner Knob shelter, which was a few hundred yards off the main trail. We decided to go into the shelter to get out of the wind and eat something for lunch. Our bellies were on empty after hiking all morning on only a cup of oatmeal.

The Tricorner Knob shelter looked even more used and abused than the one we had stayed at the previous night. The only real difference was that this shelter was made of logs instead of stones. But what captured our attention immediately was the two occupants. A man about thirty years old and a skinny boy about ten years old huddled near the fireplace, both wet and obviously cold. The boy was damn near blue. He was shivering uncontrollably. The man was trying to light a propane stove. "I need to get some hot food in this kid," he explained.

We had never even heard of hypothermia, but we could see that the kid was in bad shape. I learned later that hypothermia was a drop in core body temperature that could occur even in relatively mild weather, especially when a person got wet. It caused disorientation, which led the victim to make stupid decisions, and a stupid decision made in the mountains usually killed the person before the low body temperature did.

What we *did* know was that whiskey could work wonders. I said, "We have some whiskey. Why don't you give him a little shot?"

Dan laughed nervously. It was awkward for us young guys to be suggesting such a thing to a guy who was older than us.

We could see the man teetering on the brink of a decision. Craig tipped the balance by saying "It's a good idea. You gotta warm him up, man."

The man reluctantly agreed, and we quickly put three bottles of whiskey in front of the kid's face. "Choose your flavor," Dan said. The boy managed to smile even though he was shivering. This was definitely a moment he'd be telling the kids in school about next fall. He studied the labels on the bottles for just a moment and then pointed at Dan's bottle of Jack Daniel's. "You have good taste, kid," Dan said. Somebody produced a cup, and Dan poured a shot of Tennessee Sippin' Whiskey into it. The kid drank it down without hesitation and coughed a little. Then Dan said, "I believe I could do with one of them myself," and he drank a little drink right from the bottle. That broke the ice, and everybody, including the older guy, soon had a couple shots of whiskey warming his belly. The kid stopped shivering and was grinning from ear to ear in no time.

We found out that the boy was not the man's son, but his nephew. They had hiked down from the north that morning, past Mount Guyot. It was raining and really windy up there, the man said. That was where they had gotten soaked. We told him we had thought about going up to Mount Guyot but had decided against it. Today was not the day for it, the man agreed.

"So you pronounce it 'goy-ott'?" I asked the man. That was how he was saying it.

"Well, that's how I've heard it said."

Craig seized on this opportunity. "See! It's not 'gee-oh', queer boys."

I wasn't quite as ready as Craig to accept one man's opinion as the final word on the subject, but I didn't want to say so right in front of the guy. On ensuing trips, we would ask the locals from time to time how to pronounce the name. Sometimes they would answer "goy-ott," but sometimes they would say "gee-oh." I always found it odd that people supposedly familiar with the mountain didn't even agree on its name. But the mountain stood, impervious to what it was called. It was what it was.

Everybody had a lunchtime snack after our cocktails, and I took the opportunity to look around at all the graffiti on the walls of this shelter. By far the best inscription I found was written in pen on a ceiling rafter directly over one of the sleeping spaces on the upper platform. It said, "AT THIS SITE ON MAY 21 1974 SCOTT BRYANT OF AIKEN SC SET WORLD RECORD BY LIGHTING 53 FARTS IN A ROW. HE SUFFERED 3RD DEGREE BURNS ON HIS ANUS BUT HIKED TO SAFETY."

Someone had put some scorch marks in the wood next to this inscription which added a nice touch of authenticity. I read it aloud, and the kid, who seemed fully restored to good health but was now totally ripped, fell down laughing. He had yet another story to tell on the playground. We left the Tricorner Knob shelter and went our separate ways after many thanks from the man and his drunken nephew.

Craig ranged out ahead, and Dan educated me about the AT as we hiked it. "The AT goes from Georgia all the way to Maine. I think it's like a couple thousand miles long. I read an article about people who hike the whole way. These white marks on the trees mark the trail, and they follow the white marks all the way." He pointed at a rectangular spot of white paint on a tree about six feet up on the trunk.

I looked at the white mark, which was known as a "blaze." Sure enough, I could spot a similar white blaze on another tree about twenty-five yards out ahead of us on the trail. I turned around and saw blazes on the opposite sides of the trees as well. The idea of a 2,000-mile trail was beyond my comprehension. "Two thousand miles of this?"

"Yeah. It takes them six months to do it! I don't know if they have shelters along the trail all the way, but I know they have shelters every so often along the AT here in the Smokies."

"Man, that would be cool! Just living out here and hiking every day. But how do they carry enough food?"

"They have to stop in little towns and either buy more or have packages of food mailed to them at post offices along the way. That's what the article said."

"So the AT goes through towns? It's not all woods?" I was slightly disappointed by this thought.

"I guess. But I think they're just little towns in the mountains. The AT doesn't go through big cities." We both liked saying "the AT."

I looked at the trail I was walking on with new interest. At first glance, it looked much like all the other trails in the

Smokies that I had walked on. Yet ahead of me this thin ribbon of trail went on for hundreds of miles all the way down to Georgia, running south by southwest. Behind me, this trail started over a thousand miles back up in Maine in the very corner of the country. All I could say was "Wow." My mind was blown.

"And get this! The AT is the dividing line between Tennessee and North Carolina here in the Smokies!" Dan did a little bunny hop to the right side of trail and said, "I'm in Tennessee!" Then he hopped over to the left side and said, "I'm in North Carolina!" He hopped back and forth a few more times just to make sure I got the idea.

"Really? Very cool." I stopped and straddled the AT. "I'm in two states!" I'd never done any traveling to speak of, so the idea of being in two states at once was a novelty to me.

We noticed that the foot path of the Appalachian Trail seemed a trifle flatter and wider than the other trails. "That's because we're up on a ridge," Dan explained. "The AT stays up along the highest ridges all the way. It doesn't go up and down like the other trails." At the time, I had no idea how funny that statement was.

We caught up with Craig, who had stopped and was drinking from his canteen. He pointed to a rough trail that branched off to the right. "You guys want to check this out? Maybe there's a view."

We climbed out a short distance to a rocky outcropping that gave us an unobstructed view to the north. I saw what I had hoped to see when I came to the mountains, and it took my breath away. A vast, green valley thick with hardwood trees spread out in front of us, dappled with patches of darker green where pines grew in large numbers. The hulks of huge mountains sprang up at the edges of the valley. Some of the mountaintops were obscured by the smoky clouds, but the seething clouds only made the view more sublime. On the farthest horizon, where we could see for countless miles, the rounded mountains spread out in undulating waves that faded to dull purple and then gray and merged with the sky. The wind was in our faces, and the air was sweet and pure. This was the most beautiful place I had ever been. We lingered and smoked a bowl in reverent silence. Our eyes remained fixed on the scene in front of us. No roads or electrical wires or signs spoiled the view. We saw nature as untouched as possible. Even at nineteen, I knew this moment was a gem to be treasured and stored away with the most precious things in life.

Reluctantly, we pulled ourselves away and resumed hiking. The Appalachian Trail stayed along the lofty ridge the rest of the way, so the hiking was relatively easy. We actually went downhill as much as we went up. But dramatic vistas weren't found everywhere on the AT, or even on every mountaintop. Most of the time, the trees and the bushes were so dense that the grand views were totally obstructed. Knowing that the breathtaking views were there just out of reach was maddening after sweating and straining for hours to get to the top. I stopped at every clearing we passed, absorbing as much of the splendor as I could. I was drawn to these views by a magnetism I didn't understand, and I didn't try to analyze it. I just drank it in.

Toward the end of the hike, I started singing an old Motown song, "Twenty-Five Miles to Go." The song was from the 1960s and slightly before our time, but it was cool. "Ah, ah. Ah, ah. I'm so tired! But I just can't lose my stride!" Dan joined in. Craig wasn't much into singing, but he was smiling as we sang.

By mid-afternoon, we arrived at Pecks Corner, another shelter along the AT. We were still a mile above sea level. It looked just like the other Smoky Mountain shelters we had seen, meaning it was another shit hole.

We were cooking and making preparations for the night when three men of Middle Eastern descent walked into camp. They were all apparently in their twenties, all dark-featured and slight of build. They were probably as disappointed to see us as we were to see them, but they greeted us pleasantly in heavily-accented English.

From the first hello, we failed to disguise our contempt very well. We weren't alone in our prejudices. Many Americans looked at Middle Eastern people with suspicion in those days. Oil embargoes and rumors of war were in the air. The Iranian hostage crisis would happen the following year. Sadly, little has changed in all the years since. We grudgingly exchanged the usual pleasantries: "Where'd you start from? How's the trail? Where are you going?" This conversation was probably repeated hundreds of times a day in the backcountry. Occasionally, some information of interest was passed along, but not very often. The fourth question was usually "Where are you from?" but we skipped that question this time. We knew where they were from—they were camel jockeys.

Fortunately, it wasn't raining, so we could be outside and keep a fair distance from them as we cooked and ate our supper. We stayed on our side of the clearing, and they stayed on theirs. The talk within both groups was subdued.

After supper, one of the Middle Eastern guys set to work with a ball of thread, trying to hang a bag full of food from the rafters inside the shelter. We couldn't understand why the guy was using thread. The thread wasn't strong enough to hold the weight of the bag, and the thread kept breaking. The web became increasingly elaborate as the guy used more and more thread to suspend the bag from the rafters. We watched from our side of the clearing and snickered a little louder every time a thread broke.

Dan grabbed a length of rope from his pack and went over to the Thread Jockey in the shelter. The guy knew we had been laughing at him and probably wondered what new indignity was about to be heaped upon him by these infidels. "Do you need some better rope?" Dan asked. He could barely get out the words without laughing. Craig and I, listening from our side of the clearing, cracked up.

"Thank you. No." The guy was clearly hoping Dan would take the hint and go away.

Dan was not to be so easily dissuaded. "Why are you using thread? Isn't that camel meat too heavy?" Craig and I lost it completely.

The Thread Jockey either didn't understand everything Dan was saying or was far more polite than I could ever hope to be. Maybe he was just scared. He explained, "The mouse come down with food on the wide rope. Yes? But he not come down thread."

Dan searched for a witty response and came up empty. "Well, that's an amazing knot you're working on there," was all he could think of.

The Thread Jockey wasn't giving Dan much to work with. He just said "Thank you," which made us all feel a little foolish and infidel-like.

We wanted some space, so we went down to the watering hole that served the shelter. We took our whiskey and our dope and our knives with us. A wide dirt path dropped steeply from the shelter and brought us to a shallow, fast-moving creek with a rocky bottom. A large tree that had fallen across the water provided a perfect place for us to sit with our feet dangling at the water's surface. We sat facing downstream, looking off into the shadowy valley where our creek disappeared into the shadows.

As I took off my boots, I said what we all were thinking. "It sucks that you can't even be alone out here."

"What really sucks is that we have to share a shelter with camel jockeys! It ain't even their country!" Dan took an angry slug of Jack Daniel's.

Craig watched his brother drink. "You're not gonna chase that with any water?" This from a guy who had started the day by snorting amphetamines up his nose.

Dan was pleased that someone had noticed. "I use air for wash. If you suck in air real hard after you do a shot, the air cools your mouth down." He demonstrated with another slug from the bottle, exaggerating the air sucking so that we could observe his technique clearly.

Of course, Craig and I both had to try it. Craig drank Black Velvet, which was an exceptionally smooth blended whiskey. He liked to get "velvetized," as he called it. He took a drink and then drew in some air very sharply. As soon as he could talk again, he said, "Smooth as velvet," but I could tell it hadn't gone down all that smoothly.

I didn't have one regular brand of whiskey. On this trip, I brought a bottle of a bourbon called Heaven Hill simply because it was ninety proof. I took a good drink of my high-powered booze and sucked air in as sharply as I could. Dan watched me closely, and when I was done he asked, "Well?"

I tried to talk normally, as if the whiskey hadn't hurt a bit. "Let me put it this way, Dan. The people who make ginger ale aren't going to go out of business."

"You're probably not doing it right."

We experimented some more with the finer points of using air for wash. After my fourth shot, I pronounced it "smooth as your mama's ass."

Dan said, "Craig, is Mom's ass smooth?"

"Not as smooth as Mrs. Reznick's."

Dan said, "That's what I thought, too."

The newness of that trick soon wore off, and Craig went back to washing down his shots with a splash of water.

Eventually I did too. Even Dan, who clung stubbornly to his air-for-wash idea, finally took a few drinks of water. "I'm thirsty, that's all. I don't *need* any wash!"

We found that we could dip our drinking cups directly into the running water below us without even getting up. This was yet another novelty to explore, so we drank several more shots and sipped fresh, cold water from the creek for wash. This, we concluded, was a fine way to enjoy the mountains.

We sat on our log and recalled our busy day. "We saved that kid's ass today," Craig reflected. "He would've been dead by the time that guy got any water boiling."

"I couldn't believe he had to think twice about it before he let the kid drink," Dan said.

Before we knew it, the woods around us were dark. Getting off of the log without falling into the creek was a huge challenge. Once all three of us were standing on the side of the creek closest to the path and the shelter, Craig took a few steps and realized that his boots were sitting by themselves on the other side of the creek. The water was less than a foot deep, and the creek was so small that a sober man could have jumped across it, but there were no sober men around.

Craig waded across the creek, swearing as his bare feet slipped on the mossy creek bottom. He tried to grab onto the brittle branches of the fallen tree to keep his balance, but they broke off in his hand. Craig ended up with two knees and one elbow in the water. Dan and I laughed uproariously. When Craig finally made it to the other side, he threw his boots at us to shut us up, but he missed badly each time, even though we were only twelve feet away.

Dan said, "Missed all four of us, didn't you?"

"Kiss my ass!"

Craig came back across the creek on all fours. His butt was sticking up in the air, so Dan yelled, "There's a bear coming, Craig! I think he's got the hots for you!"

"Keep your legs together, Craig!" I yelled. "Like your dates do."

The dirt path leading back up to the shelter had become almost impossible to climb. We didn't know it, but we had climbed up to some of the highest peaks on the entire eastern half of the continent that very morning. Yet climbing a hundred yards up a hill was now too much for us. Once I got my body going in a certain direction, I couldn't change that direction, or stop, or even slow down. In fact, my feet accelerated without me telling them to as they struggled valiantly to stay under my body. The result was that I ran headlong into the trees on the side of the path. I repeated this a few times, noting with satisfaction that my brain was still working well enough to protect my whiskey each time I fell. Craig was having difficulties of his own. He was lying in the dirt, yelling "Man down!" as if someone were going to come to the rescue. Dan was down as well, although it might have been from laughing so hard.

The Middle Easterners up at the shelter were probably wondering if someone was being mauled by a bear or if they had simply chosen the wrong shelter on the wrong night. They must have known the truth because they didn't come to our aid. If they had been smart, they would have launched some kind of jihad attack and wiped us out. They would have had a more peaceful night if they had. Instead, we met no resistance. Cursing and laughing and crawling on all fours, we made it back to the shelter.

The shelter was dark when we got there. "Damn, they go to bed early," I said.

Dan whispered, "Maybe it's a trap," and we burst out laughing, thus losing the element of surprise. We stumbled into the shelter, whispering and being loud at the same time, the way only drunken people can do. We fussed with our packs, our whiskey, and our boots for a while, bouncing off one another and banging our heads on the damned bags of food hanging from the rafters. We made enough noise to rouse the dead, but the camel jockeys didn't move an inch. Clearly, they were pretending to be asleep.

I said, "Nobody was stirring, not even a mouse," which started us laughing all over again.

The Middle Easterners were sleeping—or pretending to—on the right end of the lower tier of chicken wire while our sleeping bags were on the left end of the upper tier, so we didn't have to crawl directly over them to get into our sleeping bags. Still, we were a mere few feet away from them as we finally crawled into our bags.

Every night in the Smokies, some primal instinct compelled me to keep my weapon right next to me or under me when I went to sleep. My Slovak ancestors in the Carpathian Alps had probably done the same thing. I slept a little better knowing I had at least some means of defense near at hand. Dan and Craig did likewise. On this night, we all especially wanted to have our weapons ready. Dan took his big meat cleaver out of its cardboard sheath and buried it into the rafter above his head with a heavy THUNK. Then he issued a warning for all to hear. "No camel jockeys better fuck with me!" It was inspiring. He was like Patrick Henry or something.

Craig followed Dan's lead. He slipped his razor-sharp machete out of its leather sheath and buried the front part of the blade edge into the rafter above his sleeping spot. It made a solid THWAK sound, followed by a nice metallic ringing. "Better not fuck with me either!"

I had no choice but to follow suit. Unfortunately, the only weapon I had was my little four-inch knife. I stuck it tip-first into the log above my head. It sounded like a squirrel dropping an acorn on the roof. I said, "Yeah, motha fuckas!"

in my best, deep-pitched, black guy voice. It was all I could do.

After we issued our challenge and brandished our weapons, we fell quickly into peaceful, drunken sleep. Nobody stirred in the shelter, not even a mouse, and the chicken wire didn't bother us at all.

It was full light in the shelter when we awoke. I could tell I had slept a long time. Dan and Craig were stirring as well. Craig looked over at me and said, "You look like you slept on a waffle iron," referring to the chicken wire imprints.

I looked at Craig with the machete above him and said, "Young man, you look as if you have the sword of Damocles hanging over your head," which was a great line for the first thing on a hung-over morning. I was alluding to the Three Stooges scene in which Moe is staring aghast at a pie stuck to the ceiling about to fall on a high society lady. She delivers her Damocles line, and Moe responds, "Lady, you must be psychic." Craig didn't catch the allusion, but he was used to me saying nonsensical things, so he didn't even question it.

Dan, who had slept closest to the camel jockeys, looked over the lower sleeping tier to his right and saw empty chicken wire where the camel jockeys had been. "They're gone!" We got up and looked around and found that our shelter companions were long gone.

"Damn, they were quiet! Sneaky bastards," Dan said.

Craig wasn't so impressed. "They could've been chopping wood, Dan, and we wouldn't have heard a sound."

"I know I was out like a light," I said as opened up my bag of black beauties. "I'm just glad they're gone. I think we—no, I think *you* guys—scared the living shit out of 'em! They probably couldn't wait to get out of here."

Dan pried his cleaver out of the rafter. "You know, it was worth carrying this thing out here just to scare those fuckers.

Can you imagine what they were thinking when we came back last night?"

"They were probably thinking what assholes we were," I said. Even at nineteen years old, I knew we hadn't behaved well.

Craig took the black beauty I was handing him and started breaking it open. "Yeah, but would you want to fuck with us?" he said. Then he put half of a capsule up to his good nostril and snorted away.

After breakfast, Craig went down to the water, washed out our cups and spoons, and filled the canteens. Like so many other things in the mountains, backcountry dishwashing was a skill that had to be learned. If the meal was something that wasn't greasy—like coffee and oatmeal--soap wasn't even necessary. A scouring pad, or simply some gritty dirt, and then a good swish through the water was all that was needed.

We left the Pecks Corner shelter and headed south on the Hughes Ridge Trail. We were leaving the AT, so the trail slanted mostly downward. We had passed the half way point of the trip, and despite all the booze we had drunk the night before, we were feeling good. Our packs were lighter, our legs were used to the work, and, most importantly, we were young. We never stopped to consider the poundings our bodies were taking from the exertion, the altitude, the lack of rest, the lack of nutrition, the alcohol, the drugs, or even the bacteria.

Craig, who had been lagging behind on the trail, caught up to me as we walked. "You got a light?" he asked. I fished my lighter out of a pouch on my web belt and handed it to him.

Craig stopped walking just long enough to light his smoke. "How you feeling, John?" I was surprised that Craig wanted to make conversation so early in the morning.

I couldn't resist the wisecrack. "What are you? A doctor?" Then I answered truthfully, "Actually, I'm feeling surprisingly good considering how much I drank last night."

"It's because we were drinking the whiskey straight and using water for wash." Craig spoke confidentially, as if he were imparting a great secret. "It's the carbonation in the wash and the beer that makes you feel shitty the next day. Like when the old guys drink scotch and water, they don't get hung over. They know what they're doing."

I was wondering if I'd ever be as wise as those old scotch whiskey drinkers when we came across a wide, low spot in the trail. Furrows six inches deep had been torn into the muddy ground. "What the hell did this?" I asked.

"You know what this is?" Dan was suddenly animated. "I think these are from wild boars! I read about them. They dig these ruts up with their tusks, looking for food. Grubs and roots." He said "wild boars" with reverence, the same way he would have said, "I think these are from *Abe Lincoln*."

We had talked about wild boars on the ride down. They were always "wild boars," and never just "boars." Dan explained that wild boars were meaner than bears, but they didn't get all the publicity. They had foot-long, razor-sharp tusks like a saber-toothed tiger and thick-necked, muscular bodies covered with wiry hair. They weighed up to 500 pounds, ran faster than cheetahs, and shot deadly laser beams out of their nostrils. They could also shoot the laser beams out of their assholes if they were being chased. They were the perfect killing machines of the Smoky Mountains, and they had beady red eyes full of hatred for mankind because they were trapped in such hideous bodies. (The boars, not mankind.) I was glad there weren't any wild boars around when we stumbled onto their mud hole.

We continued our long descent and arrived at our destination, a place called Enloe Creek, early in the day. We had a seat on a log next to a campfire ring. We lit up some smokes and considered the situation. "I wouldn't mind walking some more," I said.

Craig was already deep in thought, studying his map. "Neither would I," he said distractedly. After a moment, he looked up from the map. "Here's what I'm thinking. I don't have a whole lot of Velvet left, so I really don't want to be out here two more nights."

"Me neither, Craig," Dan said. "I was kind of worried about that myself. I think that kid back at Tricorner Knob drank most of mine, the little lush."

I was low on whiskey too. We had each brought along a fifth of booze, which evidently wasn't enough for four nights. "What'd you have in mind, Craig?" I pitched my cigarette butt into the cold ashes inside the fire ring.

"Well, we could keep going to the next camp, spend the night there, and then hike out to the car a day early."

Dan said, "Hey, we can spend tomorrow night in Gatlinburg, if you guys want."

Gatlinburg held the sweet promise of cold beer, good food, a hot shower, a cushy bed, and maybe even some cute Southern girls. "You're pretty smart for an imbecile," I told Dan, and Craig agreed wholeheartedly. Dan grinned like a simpleton. We smoked a bowl and did some more black beauties and strapped our packs back on our backs.

Less than two hours later, we arrived at #44, a place called McGee Spring. McGee Spring sat all by itself in the center of the huge valley we had spent the last three days circling. The campsite was up on a minor ridge inside the valley, so we could look around us to the east and north and west and see the outlines of the mountaintops and ridges we had hiked over. I thought I could see Pecks Corner out to the northwest. I gazed out at the high ridges, feeling victorious, as if I owned those mountains because I had walked them.

I started throwing my little knife to see if I could stick it in a tree. I gripped the blade and flipped the knife end over end toward an unsuspecting tree. I had seen this done in the movies a thousand times, except that the target was usually a card sharp in a saloon, a pioneer defending his ranch, or a prison guard. Of course, the knife always struck the victim blade-first in the movies. In real life, I found it much harder to make the knife stick. Even when the knife hit blade-first, it usually didn't stick. It had to be an almost perfect throw, unless the target was a Vietnamese prison guard sitting up in a watch tower. For some reason, those guys were like magnets, and thrown knives always struck them perfectly in the chest.

Every once in a while, though, I was able to make the knife stick, so of course Dan and Craig had to try their skill as well. Soon we were throwing the butcher knives and then the machete and finally the cleaver. It became a knife-throwing party. After a knife bounced back and barely missed Craig, we had to institute a rule about not throwing anything until everyone was behind the throwing line.

Once the heavy weaponry came out, it was only a matter of time before someone chopped through a tree. Craig and Dan both used knives all day long in their jobs, and their wrists and forearms were strong from doing that type of work. Craig took aim at a sapling about an inch thick, reared back, and swept the machete through in a flashing horizontal arc. The blade sliced cleanly through the tree, and the top half slowly toppled. I could tell by Craig's face that he had surprised himself, but that look was quickly replaced by a look of triumph.

Dan naturally wondered if he could do the same thing with his cleaver. He went into a wind up and struck a fearsome blow at a sapling about as big as Craig's tree. The tree broke where Dan hit it, but more from blunt trauma than from a clean cut. The blade of the cleaver was too thick to pass through the tree without binding. Dan was disappointed. "Let me try the machete, Craig."

My right wrist was strong too, and I wanted to try slashing a tree as well. I grabbed Craig's machete before Dan could get to it. I took a Babe Ruth swing at a nearby sapling, and I nearly broke my wrist with the effort. I buried the machete more than half way through the tree, but my swing had been at an angle, and the blade had bound up in the wood before it could slice through.

Then Dan had his turn with the machete, and he had more luck with the machete than with the cleaver. Another tree was dead. General mayhem ensued. Craig had to try a thicker tree, and I had to try again, and so on and so forth. We deserved to get slashed ourselves, but somehow no one was injured. We thought we were very big men indeed, wired on the black beauties, rambling drunk through the forest God had made, destroying living things with long, wicked blades.

A Native American Koyukon tradition says that it is considered disrespectful to talk about the size or majesty of a mountain while looking at it. This was considered "talking big," disregarding the need to be humble before something as large as a mountain. A child would be told, "Don't talk; your mouth is small." On that afternoon in 1978, I was like that big-talking child. I had no idea how small I was. The mountains, and life, still had many lessons left to teach me. Of all the things I ever did in the Smokies, hacking down those trees was the thing I would regret most.

As we walked out of the campsite the next morning, we had to soberly confront the carnage of the saplings we had destroyed the night before. I said, "I kind of wish we hadn't done that. We killed a shit-load of trees."

"Yeah, it seems like a waste now," Craig agreed.

Dan seemed unmoved. "At least me and Craig killed them, Johnny. You just wounded them and left them to suffer."

Later that morning, while Dan was out of earshot, Craig told me, "That *was* stupid cutting those trees down. I won't do that again," and I was glad he said it.

When we got back to the car at the Beech Gap trailhead, Craig popped in an 8-track, and we were soon jamming to ZZ Top's "La Grange." I sat down in the soft leather seat of the Laguna and felt the seductive embrace of civilization.

We drove north on the Newfound Gap Road, the only road that went all the way through the Great Smoky Mountain National Park. About half way through, the road passed over the Newfound Gap. The Newfound Gap, at 5,046 feet, was the low point where the road crossed over the spine of the Smokies. This gap was found in 1872 by a Swiss geographer named Arnold Henry Guyot. Guyot was a Princeton professor who traveled through the Smokies measuring the heights of some of the highest peaks. Apparently, that was all it took to get a mountain named after you.

The northern half of the Newfound Gap Road dropped us 3,000 feet in elevation out of the high mountains and into the streets of Gatlinburg, Tennessee. In the Johnny Cash song, "A Boy Named Sue," the narrator fights his father in the streets of Gatlinburg—"in the mud and the blood and the beer"—thus proving that Gatlinburg, the northern gateway to the Smoky Mountains, was once a rough and ready mountain town. In the 1970s, there were still plenty of saloons in Gatlinburg where a man fresh out of the mountains could wet his whistle. Something about coming down out of the mountains makes a young buck feel all wild and rambunctious, like a cowboy coming into town after a cattle drive. We survived that night in Gatlinburg without any involvement from local law enforcement officials. The following year, we would not be so lucky.

3 Going to Town

During the winter of 1978, people heard how we had saved an entire Boy Scout troop from freezing to death and how we had tangled with a battalion of vicious camel jockeys in the Battle of Pecks Corner. Selected listeners, such as Craig and Dan's cousin Rick, heard about snorting black beauties for breakfast and using air to wash down whiskey. I didn't know much about Rick, but he couldn't wait to go backpacking with us, and that told me as much as I needed to know.

We had to split up to drive down to Tennessee, so Craig and Dan went in Craig's Laguna, and Rick and I rode together in my brand new Datsun B210, a lime-green, four-seater hatchback with a tiny little engine and tiny little wheels. There was barely enough headroom for me, and Rick, who was taller than me, had to push the passenger seat all the way back and recline the chair as well if he wanted to hold his head upright. We had no hope of keeping up with Dan and Craig, so we made plans to meet up with them at the Tremont ranger station inside the park.

Along the way, Rick and I had the chance to get to know each other better. "How'd you get stuck riding with me?" I asked.

He flashed a toothy grin. "Well, I guess they thought they'd just put the two college guys together." Rick was going to a real college to become an engineer. Taking some daytime classes at a two-year college apparently made me a college guy as well, although I didn't much feel like one. I had left the hospital supply warehouse, but I hadn't moved up much. During the week, I worked part-time loading trucks in the small hours of the night and went to school by day. On Saturdays, I worked in a butcher shop where Craig had gotten me a job. My main responsibilities there were grinding hamburger, scrubbing the mold off old hams, and fetching drinks from the bar across the street. Saturday was my favorite day of the week by far.

Rick ignored the fact that his knees were in his chest and would be for the next seven hours. "What're you going to school for?" he asked.

I sighed heavily. "I don't even know, man. I'm just taking classes to see what I like. Sometimes I feel like I'm wasting my money. Look at how much Craig and Dan are making cutting meat. It doesn't take a college degree to do that."

Rick grunted noncommittally. He looked nothing like his cousins, which made it easy to forget that they were related.

I continued, "Why're you going to school?"

"Well, I spent a summer working at the Ford plant, relieving the guys working the lines, and I knew right away I didn't want any part of that shit."

"That's good money, though."

"Yeah, but have you ever been in a factory? It's hot and dirty and noisy and boring. It sucks, man. It's the same shit day after day, standing on concrete for ten or twelve hours straight. I couldn't take it. After a summer of that, I decided I was going to get a job sitting in an air-conditioned office someday."

"How much farther do you have to go?"

"Many moons, grasshopper." He was quiet for a minute, but then he said, "See, Craig and Dan are making good money now, but they're never going to make a lot of money cutting meat. And they're still gonna be doing that same shit, standing in a meat cooler, when they're fifty years old."

Fifty years old! Would we ever be fifty years old? It seemed impossible, but Rick had given me some food for thought. I just said, "Yeah," and watched the road disappear under the Datsun's wheels.

In the wee hours of the morning, we found the Laguna in a dark corner of the parking lot at the Tremont ranger station. "Park as far away as you can from those guys," Rick said. "Let's sneak up on 'em." Rick had a ready smile and an easy laugh, so I had a hard time knowing if he was joking or serious.

This time, he was serious. On foot, we snuck up to Craig's car and peeked in. The Laguna S-3 had bucket seats in front that swiveled 180 degrees. We saw that Dan and Craig had swiveled their seats around so they were facing the back of the car, and their legs were resting on the back seat. They couldn't stretch their legs out straight, but they could stretch out some, and they looked almost comfortable. Apparently, they had gotten to Tremont well ahead of us because they were already sawing logs. Rick signaled to me to back away from the car.

Rick and I slid noiselessly back to my car. Rick could barely contain his glee. He whispered, "Let's get our flashlights and pretend we're cops. We'll roust 'em out!" We retrieved our flashlights with fresh batteries in them, and then we snuck up on their car again, staying low. Rick went to the driver's side, and I went to the other. Rick turned on his flashlight and stood up. He shined his light right into Craig's face. I did the same to Dan. Rick banged on the roof of the Laguna and yelled in a deep voice, "Open up in dere, you boys!" He was trying to sound like a good ol' boy cop, but he sounded more like Foghorn Leghorn, the big rooster from the Looney Toons cartoons.

Craig and Dan both jumped a foot. Their heads swiveled from side to side, trying to understand what was happening. They were squinting, trying to see past the flashlight beams. I wanted to get in on the act, so I tried using a deep, Southern voice and said, "Let's see some ID, y'all!" but I sounded more like a black guy from the east side of Cleveland than a Tennessee cop.

I was trying not to laugh, and I could see Rick smiling too. We both knew that this ruse wasn't going to last long. He said, "Hey, dis boy heah look like a camel jockey!"

Craig and Dan caught on and called us assholes, but they grudgingly admitted that it had been a pretty good prank. After everybody calmed down, we grabbed what sleep we could. Craig and Dan rested a lot better in the Laguna than Rick and I did in the B210. Maybe it was karma.

In the morning, we got our permit and loaded all four packs into my car. Then we jammed ourselves into the Datsun as well, like the clowns at the circus who come piling out of the little clown car by the dozen. We left the Laguna in a parking lot and drove southwest down through the paved roads of the Cades Cove area. Cades Cove was a big, flat river valley about four miles long and two miles wide surrounded by the mountains. The earliest white people in the Smokies settled in the cove in 1818, and they never stopped coming.

No one ever mentions the Cherokees who populated the valley long before the white settlers came along. In fact, the cove was named after the Cherokee Chief Kade. The Cherokees signed away their rights to the valley in an 1819 treaty, although they remained in the surrounding mountains for another twenty years, harassing the settlers who had legally stolen their land. Even so, the white settlers prospered in the fertile bottom land of Cades Cove, farming and distilling whiskey. By 1850, there were almost seven hundred people living in the cove and the nearby hills. In the 1920s when the national park was being created, the residents of Cades Cove fought hard to keep their land from being taken over by the federal government, but they lost. Maybe it was another example of karma.

We came upon a bunch of cars stopped in the middle of the road. The occupants had deserted their vehicles and were standing at the side of the road, looking up into the trees. Several people were snapping photos. "What the hell are they looking at?" I asked.

No one answered for a while, but then Dan pointed out the window and said, "It's a bear! Up in that tree. No, two bears!" I threw the car in park, and we all got out and gawked like the other tourists. The bears looked distinctly unhappy, surrounded as they were, and I felt sorry for them.

After Rick took a few pictures, I said, "C'mon. Let's leave 'em alone."

When we reached the Gregory Bald Trail trailhead, we saddled up and left my shiny little B210 on the side of the isolated dirt road. Our thinking was that no hillbillies would even want a Datsun. The Laguna sitting unguarded in the remote woods, on the other hand, would have been a hillbilly dream come true.

Rick was limping noticeably as we started out. A day or two before our trip, he had sprained his ankle pretty badly and wasn't sure he would even be able to go. At the last minute, Dan had volunteered to carry Rick's tent and a few other heavy items out of Rick's pack, and Rick decided he could make it if he only had to carry a lightened pack. This meant that Dan had to leave his beloved meat cleaver behind, but he was still heavily armed with his knife and meat hooks and canned goods.

Meanwhile, Craig and I were going ultra-light. Neither one of us was carrying a tent or even a sleeping bag. We had decided to go with only a sheet of plastic, two blankets, and two flimsy, nylon-mesh hammocks. I had spotted these hammocks on sale in my outfitter's shop, which was called "Sporting Goods in K-Mart," and it had given me an idea. My brainstorm was to sling the hammocks one above the other a few feet apart between two trees, run a rope above the hammocks, and drape the plastic sheet over the rope to create a waterproof shelter. The guy on the bottom would put a blanket under him, and the guy on top would put a blanket over him. This would trap the body heat and keep both guys warm. I had pitched the idea to Dan first, but he called me a sissy. I tried Craig next, and to my surprise, he had liked the idea right away.

So, as Rick limped down the trail on his bad ankle and Dan hauled a fifty-pound pack, Craig and I blithely ambled along with our ultra-light, twenty-five-pound packs. For us, the trail was easy. I felt as if I'd been hiking all my life. After four miles of steady uphill, we came to our campsite for the night, a place called Sheep Pen Gap, #13. We had intentionally planned a short hike for the first day, so the sun was still relatively high in the sky when we dropped our packs.

Rick sat himself down on a log as quickly as possible. He didn't have to say anything. His face showed that it had been a tough walk for him. I was impressed that he had made it.

A signpost near our campsite indicated that a peak called Gregory Bald was only half mile from where we were, and I knew we would be going the opposite way the next morning. "What's a bald?" I asked to no one in particular. Nobody said anything. Not even a smart ass was stirring. Clearly, none of us knew. We had been planning this trip for months, and we didn't even know what a bald was. I laughed at all of us. "Maybe we should go find out."

Rick said, "Hang on. Let me check my book," and he hobbled over to his pack and pulled out an old, leather-bound book about an inch thick. He thumbed through the book for a few seconds and found what he was looking for. He read, "Gregory Bald is one of the highest points in the western end of the Park and offers beautiful views. In early summer, the bald is aflame with blooming azalea."

"Doesn't really say. Just says it's a high point," I concluded.

"It said it had 'beautiful views', too," Craig added.

That was all Dan needed to hear. "Let's go!"

I didn't know such a book existed. "Where'd you get that book, Rick? I thought it was a bible or something when you first got it out."

"My father gave it to me. I don't know where he got it, but it has a little write-up about most of the trails out here."

Dan was impressed, too. "It's like the bible for the Smokies."

Craig brought us back to the matter at hand. "Well, I say we should take a look at this bald."

"I'm thinking I should stay here and rest this ankle," Rick said, and we all agreed. The four of us smoked a bowl, and then Craig, Dan, and I took off for Gregory Bald. We left Rick to guard our packs in camp. Walking without a pack on my back immediately after hauling a pack all day was almost like flying or walking on the surface of the moon. I felt as if I were going to break the bonds of gravity and bound up into the sky with each step forward. Being high enhanced the feeling. We bounded up to the top of Gregory Bald in no time.

We were curious to see what we might find, but all we saw was an open, grassy field on a mountaintop. Gregory Bald, at 4,950 feet high, was the highest peak in the southwest corner of the park. The only vegetation was knee-high grass and some stunted bushes that popped up here and there. This was far different from the eastern end of the park, where the views from most of the high points were obscured by trees and tall brush. The day was clear, and every way we turned was another beautiful view. Still, we were slightly disappointed that a bald wasn't something more exotic.

"Too late for the azalea," Dan said. I looked at his face to see if he was joking, but he wasn't. I didn't even know what an azalea looked like.

When we got back to the camp, the tantalizing aroma of the hot food filled the air. "You making dinner, Rick?" Craig asked unnecessarily.

"Yeah, I thought we'd better eat before you boys get all hopped up and lose your appetites," Rick said, as if he weren't going to get hopped up right along with us.

The word "hop" triggered an association in my brain, so I said, "You look like Hop Sing, Rick, hobbling around, trying to cook." I was referring to the TV show *Bonanza* that featured an Old West family named the Cartwrights. Strangely, there were only men in this family. They lived on a ranch and had a Chinese cook named Hop Sing, complete with his braided pigtail and silk slippers. (This was back when racial stereotypes were cool.) When he wasn't busy cooking, Hop Sing mostly spent his time jumping up and down and cussing people out in Chinese.

Rick caught my meaning right away. It was not easy to imitate a pissed-off Chinaman, especially on a bad ankle, but Rick gave it his best. He jumped up and down on one foot and waved his arms around, yelling "Din jo bing ping dibjo zow!" quite convincingly. Then he looked really angry and yelled "Mau! Mau! Mau!" a few times, imitating a scene from *The Deer Hunter*, which had just come out. (In that movie, a Vietnamese prison guard tries to force Christopher Walken to pull the trigger of a gun pointed at Walken's own head. The guard yells "Mau!" over and over. However, the Vietnamese prison guard had one of those magnetic chests, so the bullet ended up in him. He should have seen it coming.) We loved Rick's Hop Sing impersonation, so much so that Rick became our trusty trail cook, Hop Sing, from that day forward.

After a hearty Hop Sing meal during which we used the name Hop Sing at least sixty-three times, Craig and I had to set up our hammocks. Never in a million years did we think that finding two trees approximately ten feet apart would be a problem in the middle of a damned forest, but it was. We had to range a fair distance from the fire ring before we found a suitable pair of trees. Even then, we had to cut back a lot of brush between these two trees.

Rick and Dan watched us struggle and enjoyed it mightily. This was their time to get even after having trudged and limped up the mountain earlier in the day. Rick asked, "Why're you guys cutting those pongee sticks right under where you're gonna be sleeping? Is that to stop the bears?"

Dan liked that one. "Hey! You want us to piss on them sticks for you? That makes 'em more deadly."

We ignored them and kept working. We tied the two hammocks about three feet and six feet off the ground. I tried to sit down in the lower hammock, but my ass sank all the way down and flattened some of the pongee sticks. I was lucky I didn't skewer my balls. Rick and Dan exploded with laughter as Craig pulled me back to my feet. We re-tied the hammocks higher off the ground and pulled them as tight as we could get them. I said, "You try it this time."

Craig warily sat down in the lower hammock, and when he transferred all his weight onto the braided nylon netting, he nearly flipped onto the ground. I caught his arm as he pitched backwards and stopped him from going over. More laughter came from our audience. "I think you have to spread your weight out more as you get in," I said.

"You try it! This was your dumb-ass idea."

I spread out as much as possible before I transferred all my weight to the hammock. The hammock sagged considerably, but it held and I stayed in. I looked up at the sky with my butt a foot off the ground. For Rick and Dan's benefit, I said, "Oh man, this feels good!"

Craig decided to try to get into the upper hammock while I was still lying in the bottom one. I foresaw myself getting badly squished, so I said, "Wait a minute! Why do you get to be on top?"

It was an unfortunate choice of words. Dan immediately yelled, "What's the matter, Johnny? You tired of Craig being on top?"

Rick chimed in, "Who's the husband and who's the wife?"

I tried my own Oriental imitation and said, "Oh, varry funny boys! Big laughs! Ha ha!"

Craig ignored me and was preparing to flop himself into the top hammock anyway. "Wait a minute, Craig!" I yelled again. "Why do you automatically get the top?"

"Because I'm taller." This was Craig's answer to almost everything and a constant source of irritation to me. In this case, it pissed me off even more because he happened to be right.

"At least let me get out first." I struggled out of my hammock and watched Craig wrestle himself into his. It was a good thing he was tall. He made it, but his ass sagged down almost into the empty lower hammock I had just vacated.

Craig said, "Hey now! This feels pretty good in here, doesn't it? Gimme a smoke, would you?"

I handed Craig a Camel and then crawled into the lower hammock to see if I could do it. I managed, but it certainly wasn't easy. I was lying on my back with Craig's back only a foot or two above me.

Dan said, "If a bear comes, who's gonna get out first?" He laughed his crazy prospector laugh, clearly delighted. "You guys are screwed!"

Above me, Craig took a drag off his smoke and said, "It'll be fine, John."

But it wasn't fine. At bedtime, Craig had to squeeze under the plastic sheeting and clamber into the top hammock. Then I had to spread out my blanket on my hammock and get in without disturbing the blanket too much, which was not easy to do, being drunk and stoned and holding a flashlight between my teeth and having a large drunk suspended above me. I felt as if Craig were my personal sword of Damocles, ready to drop at any moment.

Eventually, I wrestled myself into a sleeping position with my blanket under me. As soon as I settled in, Craig said, "Good night, little buddy."

Of course he was referring to *Gilligan's Island*, which is where I probably got the hammock idea in the first place. As they went to bed in their stacked hammocks each night, Gilligan would always say, "Goodnight, Skipper," and the Skipper would always reply, "Goodnight, little buddy." There was nothing sexual about the Skipper and Gilligan's sleeping arrangement. *Nobody* had sex on *Gilligan's Island*, even though Ginger and Maryann were practically begging for it.

Rick and Dan had apparently never seen *Gilligan's Island* because they didn't understand that there was nothing gay about two men being in hammocks above and below each other. They kept making very vulgar remarks about the proximity of certain body parts. I could almost understand them having some laughs at my expense, but they accused their own kin of things that were illegal in many states, and certainly unmanly in any state in the Union. "Nice family," I said under my breath.

"They weren't raised right," he said, and he was serious when he said it.

After a while, things quieted down in camp, and I could really concentrate on how uncomfortable I was. I was warm enough, but the human spine was not designed to remain in an exaggerated curl for six or more hours without relief. I was pinned in an increasingly uncomfortable position. The night became hardship and misery, but sheer exhaustion took over, and I managed to sleep a little.

The night passed like kidney stones. At the first sign of dawn, we couldn't wait to get out of our hammocks. Craig and I quietly made some coffee and watched a clear summer morning dawn in the Smokies. It was mystical. The eastern sky lightened behind the mountains, and the birds started softly, like musicians tuning their instruments. Then the low-hanging mist in the forest slowly dissolved as the sun's rays flowed like honey between the leaves of the trees. Imperceptibly, the subtle drone of the insects rose. It felt as if we were observing the dawn of creation. Craig and I didn't say much. We simply witnessed it. It made the miserable night we had spent almost worth it.

We had a good hike ahead of us, so we broke camp quickly and got started. After we crested a mountain called Parson Bald, I stopped to drink from my canteen. Dan, who was just a few yards behind me on the trail despite his heavy pack, caught up with me. He sighed heavily and said, "Let's do some T."

"T" was short for THC, which was the active chemical in marijuana, but we didn't really believe that what we were taking was THC at all. The rumor was that it was some sort of horse tranquillizer, but that made no sense either because the stuff made people anything but tranquil. "T" came in a powdered form, called "crystal T," and in a tablet form, which we called "tab T." In fact, like Satan, its names were legion. It was also known as "angel dust" or "crank." The truth was that we didn't care what it was. It was a powerful, manic high, and that was all that mattered. My pack was light, and the day's walk promised to be easy, making it an excellent day to be stoned. I didn't hesitate at all; I just said yes to drugs.

Rick and Craig caught us red-handed with bags of dope in our hands and decided that they should do some drugs too. Before the trip, we had all loaded up on whatever dope we could lay our hands on. They got out their own goodie bags, and the pharmacy was open for business. Rick decided on some coke. "I need a boot in the ass," he explained.

Craig dropped some microdot acid. A microdot high was different for everyone who did it. It came in the form of tiny, cylindrical pills, or "dots." If you did more than a few dots at one time, you would have hallucinations, which was called "tripping," and the hallucinations could be anything from melting walls to streaks of light to imaginary people. I once talked to a guy tripping on microdot who thought he had a little man sitting on his leg. "A little fucker about yay high," the guy explained, holding his hands a foot apart. "You really don't see him?" This guy talked to the little man and laughed at the funny things the little man said. That experience convinced me to stay away from large doses of microdot, but I had done small doses a handful of times, and it made me electric in the way I felt both physically and mentally. Craig was in for an interesting hike.

Dan and I each did a couple of hits of T, and then we all resumed the long, downhill hike. The coke hit Rick right away, and he kept up with us for a while in spite of his bad ankle, even leading the way at first. The tab T took longer to hit, but after a while I slowly became aware that I was buzzed.

We had spread out into our marching order. I was in front with Dan right behind me. Craig, who normally liked to be up front, was a distant third. Rick, with his coke buzz already worn off, had dropped way back. We walked in silence for what seemed like a long time.

The cloud cover thickened and the forest became gloomy. The landscape grew unfamiliar. The bush along the side of the trail looked overgrown and rank. I noticed that the bush was full of poisonous berries. I tried to stay in the exact middle of the trail so that the poisonous weeds wouldn't touch my skin or my boots. Then I saw that there was a powdery fungus everywhere on the rocks and the trees, and I knew instinctively that it was not healthy to breathe it in. I closed my mouth and tried to breathe through my nose, but the straps from the pack—*whose pack?*—made it hard to breathe. *Why am I carrying this heavy pack?* I found that I couldn't breathe right, and the weight of the pack was dragging me down into the poison weeds. I put out my hand to steady myself on a big rock, but there were two flies on the rock. I watched the two flies closely. They were horrible. *Flies puke on their food before they eat it.* The sound of the big horse flies was so loud that I almost couldn't hear myself think. *What was I thinking? Oh yeah. Weeds. There's probably a bear in those weeds over there. It could be on me in a heartbeat! Six-inch claws and faster than a horse. Oh God, what am I doing here?*

I stopped dead in the middle of the trail and shook my head vigorously from side to side. Some part of my brain knew it was just the T making me crazy. I lit up a cigarette and tried to get a grip. *It's just the T. Be cool.* I heard something come up behind me, and I jumped a foot off the ground. I spun around, ready to swing at whatever it was. Then I saw that it was Dan.

He stared me right in the eye and said, "You're OK, Johnny. You have a mean buzz on, that's all. I do too."

"I'll come down," I said. It was more a plea than a statement.

Dan spoke confidently. "Sure. Let's just walk hard for a while, and we'll be fine."

I didn't want seem like a puss. "I'm OK. It's just the fuckin' T."

"Let's just jog a little bit. Follow me." Dan took off trotting down the trail, his pack bouncing up and down. I followed him, and we didn't stop for a long time. I concentrated on not getting too far behind Dan. I blocked out everything else and tried to keep Dan's pack about eight feet in front of my nose.

We didn't stop until we came to a marker on the trail. We were both sweating freely. I was still stoned, but I wasn't feeling so paranoid. I felt foolish instead. "Sorry I freaked out."

"Johnny, you were scaring me, man! I never saw you like that! Your eyes looked all crazy. I was feeling pretty freaky myself. I just wanted to run."

I looked back down the trail the way we had come. "Rick and Craig are probably three miles back."

"Rick is, for sure."

We followed Twentymile Trail and got to camp before too long. Campsite #93 was called Twentymile Creek, and it sat right on the banks of the big creek. It was a horse camp, meaning that people traveling by horse were allowed to stay there. Only certain trails in the Smokies were designated to be used by horses. These horse trails were a little wider and less rocky than the pure hiking trails, which were often so steep and narrow and treacherous that a horse couldn't make it. Hikers on foot were allowed on either type of trail, but horses had to stay on their own trails and in their own camps.

We assumed that Craig would be the next one into camp, but about an hour after Dan and I arrived, Rick came limping in. He dropped his pack and plopped himself down on a log with a heavy sigh. Dan handed Rick a canteen. "It's got cherry Kool-Aid in it."

Rick took a long drink and said, "Hard to believe how good warm Kool-Aid can be."

"Did you see Craig?" Dan asked. It was not a good sign that Rick, on a bad ankle, had beaten Craig to camp.

"Yeah, but it was a good ways back. What happened to you two?"

Dan couldn't wait to tell the story. "Johnny had a bad trip!"

I was equally anxious to tell the story my way. "I just got all freaked out for a minute, so we ran for a while to wear off the buzz."

"His eyes were bugging out, Rick. He looked at me like he didn't know who I was."

Rick shook his head. "That T's some wicked shit. That's why I didn't do any."

"Two hits is too much," I said, implying that one hit of horse tranquillizer would be just about right.

"So what happened to Craig?"

"He was just taking his time. We walked together for a while, but he was going too slow for me." As an afterthought, he said, "He seemed OK though." Rick's deep concern for his cousin was touching.

After another fifteen minutes or so, Craig came strolling into camp. Dan said, "It's about time!"

"I was eating blackberries! What a rush!" A "rush" was having one's mind blown or expanded by a sudden realization of beauty or truth, or simply by an enjoyable physical sensation. Many things could be a rush if you were in the proper frame of mind. A "head fuck" was different. A head fuck was messing with somebody's mind for the fun of it, especially if he or she was high.

Craig told us how he had been sauntering along picking berries, stoned on acid. "It was a blast," he said. He failed to consider that bears liked berries, too.

"While you were doing that," I said ruefully, "I was thinking the weeds on the side of the trail were poison and I couldn't touch 'em."

Dan didn't laugh. "You were fucked up, Johnny Rez."

Rick said, "Baaad mojo!" as if he were some voodoo priest who had seen a zombie.

We set up camp and ate another Hop Sing supper. Rick had a talent for making crappy backcountry meals almost palatable. As we ate, we discussed what lazy fat-asses horse riders were and decided that if the rangers were going to have any laws at all in the backcountry, they should make horse riders pack out all their horse shit. In other words, we made light, pleasant dinner conversation.

Craig and I faced the prospect of another miserable night in the torture hammocks. Between my drug-induced episodes of paranoia, I had been contemplating the hammock problem, and I had another idea. Craig went along with it, showing how truly desperate he was. We removed the nylon sacks from the metal frames of our backpacks and used the stripped-down frames to support our backs inside the hammocks. The metal frames weren't long enough to support our whole bodies, but they gave us some support under our spines.

At bedtime, we crawled on top of our pack frames, and I said. "Goodnight, Skipper."

Craig answered, "Goodnight, little buddy."

A minute later, I said, "Skipper?"

Craig played along. "What is it, little buddy?"

"Are you boffing Ginger?"

"Yes. Now go to sleep."

I waited another twenty seconds. Then I said again, "Skipper?"

"Yes?"

"What about Maryann?"

"Yes. Her too."

After another pause, I asked a third time, "Skipper?"

Craig made his voice sound more aggravated. "What is it *this time*, little buddy?"

"At the same time?"

It was like sleeping on the world's most uncomfortable hide-a-bed with the bed half-closed. After a while, we both got up and laid our extra clothing down on top of the frames to provide some padding, but it didn't help much. We suffered through another night and dozed as best we could.

Craig and I were up and drinking chunky coffee when we finally heard stirring in the tent. Dan yawned hugely. "Mornin', Rick! How'd you sleep?"

"Oh, like a baby! How 'bout you?"

"You know, I had a little pebble or something under my sleeping pad, and it bothered me for a while, but then I rolled over and it was fine. It's nice to be able to roll over, isn't it?"

"The princess and the pea," I said disgustedly.

Dan feigned surprise. "Oh, are you guys up early again?"

We had another long hike ahead of us, but we were going to see a fire tower and a big man-made lake along the way, so we were excited. Still, Rick faced a long day on his bad ankle, and that gave me an opening. I knew I couldn't face another night in the hammock. As we were breaking camp and loading up our packs, I said, "Hey Dan, you want me to carry that tent today?"

"Why? So you can sleep in it tonight?"

Rick overheard this exchange, and in his Hop Sing voice, he said, "Ohhh, you vary clever boy!"

Craig saw what was happening and didn't want to get left out. "Hey, Rick, I've got some room in my pack, too. You want me to carry anything?" To Craig's credit, he didn't even try to be subtle.

Dan said, "Give us your whiskey, and you can sleep in the tent."

Craig said, "Why don't you give me a nice big smooch on my ass?"

"I don't think they're negotiable on that point, Dan," Rick said.

The whiskey was definitely not negotiable, but we struck a deal anyway. I carried the tent and ground cloth, which lightened Dan's pack, and Craig carried the cooking stuff and some food out of Rick's pack. In return, Craig and I would sleep in the tent with Dan and Rick. The hammock idea was officially pronounced dead.

We headed east toward a junction with the Appalachian Trail, and the trail became very steep. Dan had apparently decided to stick with Rick, who was moving very slowly, so Craig and I outdistanced them. When Craig and I got to the AT, the sign told us that it was another four tenths of a mile out of our way to the fire tower, which was called the "Shuckstack" fire tower. We hadn't slept much in three days, and it was beginning to take its toll. Even though we had been looking forward to the view, we were tempted to bypass the fire tower and save the extra eight tenths of a mile. We also toyed with the idea of dropping our packs at the trail intersection where we were, hiking up to the tower, and then coming back to our packs, but it didn't seem wise to leave our packs where animals or people could easily get into them.

As we were wavering in our decision, I remembered a quote from Vince Lombardi, the hallowed Green Bay Packer football coach. I told Craig, "Vince Lombardi said, 'Fatigue makes cowards of us all.'"

Craig said, "What's that s'posed to mean? That we're cowards if we don't go?" I had no quick answer to that, so

Craig kept going. "You think Vince Lombardi ever hiked his fat ass up into the Smokies and spent two nights in a fucked-up hammock?"

"Probably not." How could I argue? The logic was irrefutable.

Craig seemed satisfied that I had agreed. "You're damn right he didn't." So, because Vince Lombardi had never hiked in the Smoky Mountains and slept in a hammock, we bypassed the fire tower and continued east toward the lake.

We followed the trail downhill until we came to an arm of Fontana Lake that extended northward into the park. When the Fontana Dam was built, the rising water flooded more than twenty miles of the Little Tennessee river valley and many tributary creek valleys as well, so there were lots of inlets, both big and little, all along the shores of the lake. Craig and I stood at the north end of one of the big inlets, where a large stream called Eagle Creek fed into Fontana Lake. We were at the Lost Cove campsite, #90, which was evidently used by a lot of boaters sailing over from the Fontana Marina on the south side of the lake. We saw lots of beer cans and bait containers as well as a dead fish being devoured—eyeballs first—by big, fat flies. The flies reminded me of my bad trip on the T.

Craig looked disgustedly at all the litter. "They could at least pick up their beer cans. It's not like they have to carry them."

"Yeah, this bums me out." I was proud that whatever rules we broke in the backcountry, at least we never left any trash behind. If we couldn't burn it, we carried it out. "It's like you have to go way into the backcountry just to get away from the pigs! All the sites that are easy to get to are trashed."

Craig nodded. "Glad we're not staying here." We turned away from the lake and headed back toward the high country.

We had spent about one minute at the lake and couldn't wait to get back into the mountains.

We had to skirt along some marshy ground at the north end of the cove first. We saw some beaver dams and even a few of the raised piles of branches that the beavers lived inside. Craig pointed to one. "Look. One of their nests, or whatever you call 'em."

"Don't they call them 'lodges'?"

"Maybe. 'Beaver nest' doesn't sound right, now that I think about it."

"We'll ask Rick. He probably learned that in college."

Craig smiled. "They teach you about beavers in college?"

"It depends on the school. I think at those four-year schools, you learn a lot about beavers."

Craig shook his head. "Man, I gotta go to college."

The Eagle Creek Trail rose steadily, and we had to cross the big creek and the tributary creeks feeding into Eagle Creek several times as we made our way along. We were both getting better at rock-hopping across the creeks.

We took a short break at a camp called Lower Ekaneetlee and had a seat on a smooth log. I wondered how far back Dan and Rick might be. "If they went up the fire tower, they could be a couple hours behind us."

"Especially with Rick's ankle," Craig agreed.

"I should leave them a note here!"

So I got out my pen and my paper, and I made up my own little sign. It said, "LARGE BEAVERS HAVE BEEN REPORTED IN THIS AREA! IF YOU SEE A BEAVER, REMAIN CALM. FACE THE BEAVER SQUARELY AND SHOW NO FEAR."

I showed the note to Craig, who suggested another line: "DON'T SHOOT THE BEAVER!"

It was perfect. We left the note on a wooden post where Rick and Dan would be sure to see it.

Buddha Palguta

We marched on toward campsite #96, which was another mile and a half up the trail. Since I had my pen and paper handy, I decided to leave more notes for Dan and Rick hanging from the trees along the way. The first note said, "DON'T STOP NOW!" I put up another one just a few yards later saying, "YOU'RE ALMOST THERE!" Then I got creative. The next one said, "GRANDPA'S CHEESE BARN NEXT EXIT!" This was followed by a series of signs like the ones sometimes posted along the highways for roadside stands: "FRESH CIDER!" "COLD BEER!" "HOME-MADE PIES!" "GRANDMA'S FAMOUS BEAVER BURGERS!"

Craig saw the last one and said, "You're sick," but he had no sense of humor sometimes.

Campsite #96 sat on a little island in the middle of Eagle Creek; hence the name, Eagle Creek Island. The "island" was formed by Eagle Creek running along one side of a strip of land and a man-made channel diverted from the main creek running along the other side. The land in the middle was technically an island, although we had no problem rock-hopping across either the creek or the man-made channel in order to get onto the island. I found out later that the man-made channel was called a "sluice," and the sluice had been dug by loggers before the Smokies became a national park. The island had once been called "logging camp 10."

The camp looked heavily used, but it was a pretty camp nonetheless with the soothing sound of the water in our ears. Clouds of gnats and mosquitoes swarmed around our heads, but they were the only drawback. Craig found the best spot on the island for our camp, and I got busy gathering wood for the fire while Craig set up the tent.

We had been in camp for well over an hour when we heard Rick and Dan finally approaching. Dan appeared first. I was expecting some funny remark about beaver pie or something,

84

but Dan was quiet. To prompt him, I asked, "Did you guys stop for lunch?"

"No, we had to stop and pick up all the papers some dickhead left on the trail." Clearly, Dan wasn't his usual happy self.

"What's wrong, Dan?"

He threw his hands up. "You guys just took off! I figured somebody should stay with Rick."

Rick walked up at that moment. He had some trouble hopping across the rocks to get onto the island. If he heard Dan speak, he chose to ignore what he had heard. In his Foghorn Leghorn voice, he said, "How 'bout a cold beer and one o' dem beaver burgers?" Then he added, "Where's Grandma? Git her ass out here!"

I said, "She ran when she saw you coming."

"Did she at least leave some pie?"

"We ate it," Craig said. "It was damn good."

Dan saw that a serious discussion would go nowhere, so he packed a bowl instead. The smoke held the bugs somewhat at bay. We passed it around, had a couple of shots, and traded stories. Rick and Dan had taken the time to go up the Shuckstack fire tower and said it had been worth the effort. I regretted not taking the time to go, but I didn't bother trying to explain the whole Vince Lombardi thing.

On my first two trips, I had only soaped up and splashed myself off, but the cool waters of Eagle Creek looked really inviting on this hot summer day, and I resolved to go in for my first true bath in the mountains. I grabbed my baggie full of toiletry articles and looked for a fairly private part of the island.

My list of toiletries was short. In addition to toilet paper, I had a comb, a toothbrush, a small bar of soap, and travel-sized containers of toothpaste, shampoo, and deodorant to keep the stink down. I also carried some Stridex astringent pads for my face. The medicated wipes were the next best thing to hot water. Finally, I still carried my stainless-steel mirror because it was a good surface for cutting lines. It didn't reflect anything, but that was OK because I didn't have anything to reflect on.

I walked the perimeter of the island. Smoky Mountain streams such as Eagle Creek were full of stones ranging in size from as big as a house to as small as a golf ball. The bigger rivers down in the valleys were relatively flat and wide because the big rocks had been broken down and worn away, but the highland creeks were wild tumbles of massive rocks, fallen trees, white water, and waterfalls. Those big boulders sometimes became little dams, creating pools of fairly calm water. I was looking for such a pool, but finding one wasn't easy.

The first problem was getting down to the water's edge. The big, rubbery rhododendrons and the other vegetation were so thick along the sides of the creek that it was nearly impossible to work my way down to the water. I found a relatively clear spot and climbed down between the huge, slippery boulders, one hand holding my bag of toiletries. I went carefully to avoid busting my ass.

When I got close, I could clearly see beneath the surface of the crystal-clear water, which wasn't necessarily a good thing. I saw the rocky, mossy bottom of a likely bathing hole, and my mind flashed back to those colorful vinyl non-slip stickers that my grandmother used to have attached to the bottom of her tub. I thought those things were stupid when I was a kid, but suddenly I understood how wise Grandma had been. Then I saw the living creatures waiting to share my bath with me. Hordes of water bugs skittered to and fro, supported on the surface of the water by their widely-spaced legs. They were fascinating to watch, but I couldn't help but wonder if they liked skittering into bodily orifices. Then I saw crayfish at the bottom, waiting with their lobster-like claws to latch onto any tender body parts that dangled or protruded. That made me think of the snot otter. The memory of that fearsome creature nearly drove me back, but I was committed to doing the full Monty, so I stripped down and perched on a fairly flat rock at the very edge of the pool.

Standing naked in the forest felt remarkably good. The sun shone and the gentle breeze blew on parts of my body that were not used to such sensations. I felt free and natural there in God's creation. In that moment, I was as far from the bonds and conventions of society as I had ever been. The primal part of me was unleashed after twenty years of being covered up and beaten down and trained to jump through other people's hoops. I was a natural animal in the middle of the wild, untamed mountains.

All that noble sentiment evaporated the second I edged into Eagle Creek. The water was damned cold, even in high summer. The parts of my body that could attempt to hide did so. Threatened on two fronts by the onslaught of cold water and the impending threat from the crayfish, my proud, purple-helmeted warrior retreated hastily and tried to take his two men-in-waiting with him. They lived to fight another day. The rest of my body cringed from what it knew was coming.

I stood knee-deep in the frigid water with rocks jabbing into the most vulnerable parts of my feet. I wanted it over as quickly as possible. I started yelling. Nothing articulate—just long, sustained vowel sounds welling up from the natural animal within me. The yelling gave me the courage to submerse my body completely. I ducked into the deepest part of the pool and came up still yelling; I understood now why I had seen Dan yelling like a wild Injun as he bathed.

I hobbled across the rocks to the shallower water and quickly soaped up. At that moment, I couldn't have cared less about the pristine waters I was polluting. I was more concerned with getting shoes back on my hurting feet. But the cold wasn't as bad now. After dunking myself, my body adapted somewhat, and I felt relatively comfortable. Now I felt like a mountain man, wet and naked in the mountain stream and not giving a shit. My manhood even recovered (somewhat). I whooped again, simply for the sheer joy of it, and dove back in to rinse off. This time, the crayfish were the ones who retreated.

I climbed gingerly out of my bathing hole, feeling triumphant, and found the flattest spot to stand on. I didn't even bother with a towel. I had carried a towel on my first two trips, but those towels had been dead, damp weight after the first use. I used a three-day-old pair of underwear to dry myself off as best I could, feeling clean and refreshed.

The final difficulty was getting dressed without getting dirty all over again. I ended up getting sandy grit from the bottom of my feet on the inside of my jockey shorts as I slid them on. I was not about to hike miles and miles with grit in my drawers. Not even Daniel Boone did that. I shook out the grit and started over. The second time, I laid down my old, dirty underwear and stood on that as I put on the new pair. Nothing—not even getting dressed—was simple in the mountains.

We enjoyed a big fire that night and got absolutely wasted, but nobody did any of the tab T—it was bad mojo. When the four of us crawled into the three-man tent, I said, "Why don't we sleep Stooges-style? Head to feet? That'd give us more shoulder room."

Dan was the only one who even deigned to respond. "I'm not sleeping with your smelly Slovak feet in my face."

"I don't care," Craig said. "This still beats the hammocks." Even though he had no sleeping pad, Craig sounded quite comfortable.

Dan was not as content, proving that comfort was a subjective thing. "I should've carried the tent again and let you guys sleep outside."

Rick was almost asleep. He murmured, "It's OK, Maryann."

We had to go about nine miles the next day to cross over the AT and head down to our last camp at Anthony Creek. I was happy. Nine miles didn't sound nearly as intimidating as it used to. My feet were OK, and I had enough whiskey left for one more night. Craig and I remembered Dan's words about somebody hanging around with Rick, so we all stuck together as we walked. We headed north on the Eagle Creek Trail, following the big creek and watching it get smaller as we climbed.

We passed by the stone block foundation from the still house of an old moonshiner named Quill Rose. Quill Rose was a wild character, living way back in the Smokies at the dawn of the twentieth century. A Smoky Mountain explorer and writer named Horace Kephart described Quill Rose after meeting him in 1908: "Quill and his part-Indian wife, 'Aunt Vice', have lived for twenty-five years in the Eagle Creek wilderness, and to this day there is no wagon road, nor even a sled road, within five miles of their home. Quill has some notches on his gun stock; but he has turned over a new leaf, and is a jolly, good-hearted fellow." A photograph of Quill Rose shows a gray-bearded, healthy-looking man with intelligent eyes sitting on the steps of an old shack with a fiddle and a bow in his hands. Kephart described Rose's still house as being "so remote from roads and horse trails that it often re-echoes to the thrum of banjos and the eldritch [strange or unearthly] cries of midnight revelers who fear no law of God or man," but old Quill didn't seem to me to be any worse for the wear.

The Eagle Creek Trail steepened past the still house, and we were glad when we saw Spence Field at the top of the mountain. Spence Field turned out to be a grass-covered bald just like Parsons Bald or Gregory Bald, but for some reason it was called a "field" instead. We took a smoke break there at the Spence Field mountain crest and enjoyed the view. We were idly standing around when I turned and saw Dan by himself out in the high grass, kneeling down on all fours with a big tuft of grass sticking out of his mouth. He was slowly chewing the grass and gazing off into the distance, not even looking at us. I pointed, and Craig asked, "What the hell are you doing, Dan?"

Dan took the grass out of his mouth, said "Grazin' in the grass," and then put the grass back in. He was quoting the Friends of Distinction song that went, "Grazin' in the grass is a gas, but can you dig it?" That was all the explanation Dan gave. There was no rhyme or reason to it. We were merely the next generation of revelers, born in a different time but sharing the same spirit. We could dig it, and Quill Rose would have dug it, too. Either that or he would have shot us dead.

Before we left, we smoked a bowl up on Spence Field, and while I had my pot out, I decided to get rid of all the useless stems and seeds that had accumulated in the bottom of the bag. I scattered the pot seeds across Spence Field in a wide arc. Dan, who had given up his bovine pursuits, loved planting things, and he said, "You know those seeds'll probably grow."

Rick looked across the open field. "They'll really be grazing in the grass then."

We were getting closer to Cade's Cove and civilization, and we started seeing other hikers. We were the first to arrive at the Anthony Creek camp, but a couple of older guys in their thirties came in later in the afternoon. They chose the tent spot farthest away from us, which was a good choice because we finished off all of our remaining whiskey that night, and the camp "re-echoed with the eldritch cries of midnight revelers."

We only had a three-mile hike the next morning down to Craig's waiting car. We were going to spend the night in Gatlinburg, so Dan and I couldn't wait to get there. We walked fast and got way out ahead of Rick and Craig.

Dan and I liked to imitate the Wild and Crazy Guy characters that Steve Martin and Dan Aykroyd made popular on *Saturday Night Live*. They were two Czechoslovakian immigrants who wore gold chains and tight plaid pants and liked to "swing" with the American "foxes." The cheesy European accents came easily to us. As we hurried along, Dan yelled to me over his shoulder, "There are sure to be many foxes with big American breasts in the hillbilly town!"

"Yes, and they will be waiting to give themselves to us most easily!" I answered.

"The American hillbilly girls will certainly be impressed by our manly bulges!"

"Hey! Why not stick potatoes down our pants? Then we will be sure to swing tonight!"

Dan almost lost it when I mentioned the potatoes, but he stayed in character. "No, Yorgi. It really bummed me up when my potatoes moved to the back of my pants on the dance floor!"

"Yes! You looked like you made the poopies in your tight American slacks!"

Dan turned the conversation to Craig and Rick. "I think the two Americans behind us might need the potatoes in *their* slacks tonight."

"They do not swing with the foxes so much as us."

"Not many do!"

"It is because their buttocks do not protrude like ours!"

"Hey! Perhaps we can tell the foxes that our friends are deaf-mutes!"

"Yes! They can be deaf-mutes from Albania! Albanians are well-known to have the flattest buttocks!"

We were walking down a trail with a lot of protruding roots—protruding like my Slovak buttocks in tight American slacks—and Dan tripped over one of those roots and went sprawling face-first onto the ground. He caught himself with his hands as he went down, but the weight of his pack drove him down hard, and he skidded along the rocky trail before he came to a stop. It looked like a nasty spill, so I ran over and helped him up. He had some ugly-looking abrasions on the heels of his hands, but he was otherwise in one piece. An older hiker might have needed to have some bones set after such a fall, but we were young and made of iron. Dan got up, made sure everything worked, and laughed it off.

I got out my home-made first aid kit and cleaned up his scrapes as best I could. As I wrapped some sterile gauze around Dan's hand, I went back into my Wild and Crazy Guy voice. "Hey! Now the foxes will want to nurse on you! You will certainly swing tonight!"

The Anthony Creek trail flattened out like an Albanian's butt. When we finally saw Craig's Laguna parked on the other side of a locked Park Service gate, we literally skipped down the last fifty yards. Our packs bounced up and down as we went.

Once Craig and Rick showed up, we didn't waste any time. We picked up my Datsun, and as we drove through Cades Cove, we honked and hollered every time we saw a half-way attractive young woman. Outside the park, we stopped at a little mom and pop grocery store and bought some cold beer. Everything was a little bit sweeter after five days in the woods. Girls were prettier. Beer was colder. Driving in a car—even a Datsun B210—was a magic carpet ride.

We rolled into Gatlinburg, sipping beers and looking for a cheap motel. Apparently, some guy named Dewey Ogle owned half the town. We pulled in at Dewey Ogle's Motor Inn. We stood in the office like four reincarnations of Quill Rose, each wild-eyed and a little bit drunk or high on something. The clerk was not inclined to offer us lodging. He diplomatically told us that Dewey Ogle's Budget Motel down the road had better rates, and we weren't offended in the least. We went there and got two adjoining rooms. They put us way down at the far end of the long two-story building.

Everybody got a shower and a shave. The dingy motel bathroom with mildewed grout on the tiled walls was pure luxury, and the hot water was a royal spa treatment. Then we paced like newly caged beasts in our rooms. Something in the human spirit longs for open space and distant horizons, and that desire had been whetted in us. Luckily, both of our rooms had balconies off the back of the building that overlooked a tiny creek and some nice trees. We naturally gravitated toward the balconies, clinging to the last traces of nature.

We ate at an overpriced steakhouse on Cherry Street, but then Dan and I could stand it no longer—we had foxes to hunt. "Let's go molest some women," I said.

Dan looked to his brother and cousin. "Yeah, you guys, let's go!"

Craig and Rick didn't have the same gleam in their eyes as Dan and I. Craig was rather shy around girls. I didn't know Rick as well, but he was proving to be more like Craig than Dan. "You two are gonna get in trouble," Craig warned.

But Rick looked at Craig and said, "We gotta let these dogs hunt."

By mutual consent, we broke up into two tactical units. Craig and Rick's mission was to find a liquor store, acquire more booze, and note the positions any female friendlies they encountered. Dan and I had a much more perilous task. We were to engage as many females as possible and lure them back toward our command post at Dewey Ogle's. We would rendezvous there at 2000 hours, which we were pretty sure was eight o'clock in the evening.

Dan and I patrolled the main drag, eyeing young women and trying to get the courage up to talk to them. We passed a drug store with a sign in the window that read "Copies 5¢," and the light bulb lit up in my brain. "Hey, let's make some flyers showing where our room is and pass them out to girls!"

Dan looked at me seriously for a long moment. I thought he was going to tell me what an idiot I was, but he said, "Good! We'll tell them we're having a party."

We commandeered a piece of paper and a pen from the lady working in the drug store. In big block letters, I wrote, "PARTY WITH REAL MOUNTAIN MEN! FREE BEER! GIRLS ONLY! AT DEWeY OGLE'S BUDGET MOTEL ROOM 232 8 PM TONIGHT"

Dan frowned. "They're gonna think we're just after a piece of ass."

"They know that already! Besides, you want a bunch of hilljack guys showing up at our room expecting free beer? We'll be overrun."

"That's true," Dan conceded, "but 'Dewey' has two E's in it."

We asked the lady behind the counter to make us twenty copies. She seemed highly amused. She might even have liked to come over herself, but she looked to be almost forty, so she was way over the hill.

We hit the streets armed with our flyers and approached the first young women who caught our eye. Dan smiled and said, "Hey, girls, it's a beautiful day in the Smokies, isn't it?"

I handed them a flyer and said, "We're having a party tonight. If you're not doing anything, why don't you come by?" We were rapping with the foxes most smoothly.

The girls looked at the flyer, laughed, and walked away. We approached some other girls, but after the third rejection, Dan smelled his armpit. "Do I still stink, Johnny? Tell the truth."

Eventually we got some nibbles. We gave a flyer to another set of girls, and they didn't run away immediately, which was a breakthrough. One of them asked, "So you guys are the mountain men?"

Dan said, "Yep. We just came out of the mountains today and shaved off our beards."

The other girl spoke up, "So you live in the mountains?" Clearly, she wasn't the brains of the operation, but she had her brown hair pulled up in a bun, which I liked.

I thought I'd better say something. "No, but we just spent five days way up in the backcountry." I pointed south toward the high mountains.

"Camping out?" the second girl asked.

I laughed and was about to answer when Dan cut in. "We were backpacking. It's different than camping. A lot harder. Come on over tonight and we'll tell you about it."

The first girl, who was blonde, suddenly got spooked. "Yeah, well maybe we'll see you guys later. Right now, we gotta go." She grabbed the brunette by the arm and pulled her away.

"Alright. Maybe we'll see you tonight!" I called after them. Then I turned to Dan. "Nice going!"

"What?"

"You gotta be a little bit subtle, man."

"We're standing on a corner passing out *flyers*, Johnny! How subtle can we be? And I thought you said they already knew what we were after!"

He had me there. "Yeah, but it's a fine line you have to walk."

We talked to a few more girls after that, trying to be subtle and suave while we passed out our decidedly un-subtle flyers, but chasing foxes was thirsty work, so we headed back to Dewey Ogle's for some liquid refreshment. When we got back to the motel, Craig and Rick were stoned and sitting in front of the TV with beers in their hands and blank expressions on their faces. Television is especially mesmerizing when you haven't seen it for several days. Couple that with the fact that they were stoned, and the poor bastards never stood a chance. They were finished the moment they turned on the set. But Dan and I were full of adrenalin and testosterone from the fox hunt and were not about to let them vegetate in front of the TV on our big night in Gatlinburg.

I handed flyers to Rick and Craig. "Slow down, boys! You don't wanna peak too early. We're having a party tonight!"

Rick read the flyer and a big grin slowly spread across his face. "Girls only?" he asked.

Dan was over by the bottle of Jack Daniels that Rick and Craig had bought. "Yeah, so you and Craig are allowed to come."

Craig roused himself from his stupor. When Craig vegetated, he went nearly catatonic, and it took him a while to come out of it, but his wheels were slowly starting to turn again. "How many girls are coming over?"

Dan used his Wild and Crazy Guy voice. "None for you, big boy!"

I was over by Dan, pouring myself a healthy drink of whiskey. "For some reason, they all seemed pretty noncommittal, Craig."

Craig smirked. "In other words, none."

Dan didn't like Craig's pessimism. "How many girls did you guys talk to?"

Rick deadpanned, "We didn't see any."

I was learning to appreciate Rick's dry sense of humor, so I wanted to egg him on. "You didn't see *any* girls?"

Before Rick could think of a smart-ass answer, something happened that changed all of us forever. Banjo music started blaring from the TV. We all involuntarily looked at the screen just in time to see an orange race car jumping over a pond and landing heavily on the other side. A voice off-screen yelled a hearty "Yee haa!" and we were instantly hooked. Then we saw a beautiful, dark-haired woman in the shortest pair of cut-off shorts we had ever seen, and her ass was perfect, and the TV had us all—hook, line, and sinker.

The woman was Daisy Duke. The car was the General Lee. The show was *The Dukes of Hazzard*. None of us had ever seen the show before, and we didn't know quite what to make of it. We thought that it might be a local program. We just knew it was unbelievably cool. All conversation in the room stopped as we watched the Dukes, who were former moonshiners and good ol' boys never meaning no harm, battle the greedy but stupid Boss Hogg and Sheriff Roscoe P. Coltrane. Mostly we waited for Daisy Duke to appear on screen in her shorts. We nearly lost our minds when she did. We whooped and roared and drank whiskey and swore that Tennessee was the greatest state in the Union for having programs like this one and women like Daisy Duke.

We were all drunk and stoned, totally engrossed in the program. Our big night in Gatlinburg was momentarily forgotten, and the minutes flew by. The show was almost over when we heard a knock at the door. We looked at each other and froze. When there are drugs in the room and somebody knocks on the door, your first instinct is to hide the stuff, but we were caught red-handed if indeed it was the cops. Pot smoke hung heavy in the air, and the bathroom mirror was laying on top of a dresser with traces of cocaine on it. We had other kinds of dope strewn around as well. If they brought in a drug-sniffing dog, the poor animal would keel over dead.

Dan cautiously approached the door and looked through the peephole. "It's the foxes!" He opened the door, and the two girls who had suddenly retreated from me and Dan earlier in the evening were standing there, holding a flyer. We had totally forgotten that we were supposed to be throwing a party and that women might possibly be knocking on our door. The odds were so infinitesimal that we had dismissed the possibility.

The girl who was apparently the leader stood closer to the door. Her long hair looked strawberry blonde in the twilight. She smiled nervously. "Are you guys still having a party?"

Dan covered his surprise as well as he could. "Sure! Would you like to come in?"

They stepped inside but stayed close to the door. The second girl, who wore her brown hair down now, said, "It smells like the party already started!"

We ignored that comment for the moment. I walked over to the girls, a big smile on my face. "We didn't think you guys would show up!"

The brunette smiled a coy smile. "Is it OK that we did?" *Maybe she isn't so dumb after all.*

Dan and I assured them that it was perfectly OK. Rick and Craig looked absolutely head-fucked, as if First Lady Rosalyn Carter had just walked in and asked them if they wanted a hit off a bong. They stood toward the back of the room and said nothing.

The blonde girl looked at Rick and Craig. "We didn't know there were four of you guys. Are you mountain men, too?"

Before either one of them could answer, I said, "They're deaf-mutes from Albania."

Dan cracked up. He managed to say, "And they have flat buttocks," and I lost it as well. Nobody else in the room

Finding Mount Guyot

laughed, but Dan and I damn near fell on the floor laughing.
Once again, we were rapping with the foxes most smoothly.

Craig recovered his wits somewhat. "Hey, you girls want a
beer or something? By the way, I'm Craig and this is my
cousin Rick. These guys are too rude to introduce us."

The blonde brightened. "Sure, Craig! I'll take a beer, but
that pot smells really good!"

"Well then, let's smoke a bowl!" Dan was happy to oblige.
Craig gave each of the girls a beer. The blonde was named
Donna, and the brunette's name was Joyce. Most guys would
have said Donna was better looking, but I liked Joyce's
slender, librarianish looks.

We made some nervous small talk while Dan loaded up a
bowl. The girls were from the Baltimore area and had come
down for a vacation. We admitted that we were actually from
Cleveland although we were rugged mountain men
nonetheless. We passed around the bowl, but when it came to
me I muttered, "I'm already stoned," and passed it on to Joyce,
who was standing next to me. She passed it on without taking
a toke either. I was messed up, and I needed to clear my head
if I was going to make a move. I said, "I'm gonna go have a
smoke," and headed out to the balcony. I lit up a Camel and
leaned over the railing. It had been a long day already, and my
head was spinning. I looked out at the trees and the quiet creek
beneath me, but nature seemed far, far away.

To my surprise, Joyce appeared next to me. "You don't like
to party?" she asked in a quiet voice.

"Oh, I like to party just fine. I just can't smoke as much
dope as those guys." I was barely aware of what I was saying.

"I don't get high that much either."

Neither of us knew what to say next. My muddled brain
was racing, but I couldn't think of anything that would make
the remotest bit of sense. I heard Craig say something about
Daisy Duke from inside the room. They all laughed.

Joyce rummaged through her little handbag until she found something. She handed it to me and said, "Somebody gave this to me once, and I want to give it to you."

She handed me a business card, a little worn around the edges. It said: "This card is good for one free kiss." I read the card, but I didn't know what to do with it. My brain wouldn't compute the information. I said, "Thanks," and read the card again. Then, for some inexplicable reason, I said, "I can use this sometime" and stuck the card in my pocket. It truly didn't occur to me that the slim girl standing there on the balcony with me in the Tennessee moonlight wanted me to kiss her. I was too messed up to get it. She looked crestfallen, but I didn't understand why. After a few seconds, she turned and went back into the motel room without saying anything. I stood there and finished my smoke, knowing I had missed something.

I would remember the moment with a tiny pang of regret for the rest of my life. We regret most the things in life we *don't* do—not the things we do. We live with the consequences of what we do and move on, but the opportunities that we don't seize are the memories that truly haunt us. Some chances are only there for an instant. If we fail to seize that moment, we live with the secret knowledge of that failure for all of our days, no matter how we try to rationalize it or hide it away. If I had kissed that girl, I probably would have forgotten her, but now I never would.

I went back inside and looked at Joyce, but she wouldn't make eye contact with me. She was studiously watching Rick, who was doing one-legged, deep knee squats like a drunken Cossack, demonstrating a skiing exercise. The whiskey had miraculously healed his ankle.

More tentative conversation and drunken nonsense ensued, but the jokes were forced and the girls seemed tense. The ratio of women to men was wrong, and we all felt it. No other girls showed up for our mountain man party. I saw Joyce discreetly nod toward the door when she caught Donna's eye. They left not much later, thanking us for the beers and the pot. I didn't know what to say to Joyce, so I simply said goodbye. Quill Rose would have grabbed her and kissed her hard on the mouth. As soon as the door closed, Craig asked me, "What happened on the porch, John?"

"Nothing. Why?" I didn't feel like talking about it.

"Bullshit. That girl followed you out there, and then you were both weird when you came back in." Craig was pretty perceptive sometimes.

I knew I was going to tell them sooner or later, so I pulled the card out of my pocket and handed it to Craig. "She gave me this."

Craig read it and raised an eyebrow but didn't say a word. He gave the card to Rick, who read it, smiled ruefully, and shook his head. Dan took the card from Rick, read it, and exploded, "And you didn't kiss her? Are you fucking kidding me?" He opened his mouth to say something else, but no words came out. He just sputtered and fumed.

"It wasn't like it was the most private setting in the world with you goons watching me." I thought it sounded plausible.

Dan wasn't buying it. "Still, Johnny Rez, come on!" I was as if I had failed him personally after all the work we had done.

Craig asked, "So what'd you do when she gave you the card?"

"I put it in my pocket and said, 'Thanks, I can use this sometime.'"

We laughed at my stupidity. Rick said, "What a fucking idiot!" and he was right.

That might have been the end of the night for normal people, but we weren't done by a long shot. We hung around the room and partied for a while until Dan and I decided we needed to go to a bar. We were drunk on whiskey, high on pot, wired on speeders, and buzzed on coke. We tried to convince Rick and Craig to come along, but they decided that they didn't belong on public streets, and once again they were right.

We left on foot and ended up in a Tennessee version of Studio 54, the famous New York City disco. This place was full of big belt buckles and big hair. There was wood on the walls and beer on the floor. Blondie's song, "Call Me," shook the rafters. We made our way over to the bar and ordered some whiskey. We spied two girls dancing together near the edge of the dance floor. I elbowed Dan and pointed them out, but he was way ahead of me. We sauntered over to them as the next song, Peaches and Herb's "Shake Your Groove Thing," started. I had no earthly idea what to say. Evidently, Dan didn't either because what came out of his mouth was, "You girls want to shake your groove things with us?" These foxes clearly didn't understand smooth rapping, because they turned and walked away.

I yelled in Dan's ear, "Maybe we need potatoes in our pants!" I thought that working one on one might be easier, so I yelled again, "Let's split up. I need to be a lone wolf."

Dan didn't object. He yelled back, "I'll look for you by the bar later," and moved off toward the other end of the room. There were at least two different bars in the place, but I wasn't worried about finding Dan later. I wasn't planning any more than two minutes into the future.

I went back to the bar and ordered another whiskey. I surveyed the room, lone-wolf style. Then I lit up a smoke, lone-wolf style. All the girls were starting to look like Daisy Duke. I asked one Daisy where Boss Hogg was, but she didn't get the joke. I asked another Daisy to dance, but she turned me down cold. I ordered another whiskey.

In the blink of an eye, it was two in the morning and I was standing by the bar again. The bartenders were giving the last call for alcohol, and the DJ was playing Donna Summers'

"Last Dance." The paired-off bodies swayed to and fro, blue jeans pressing hard against blue jeans, making the most of their last chance for love. I needed one more drink, so I reached into my pocket and pulled out a fistful of crumpled bills. Then I saw the free kiss card jammed in with my money. I had forgotten all about it.

I walked over to the first single girl I could find and handed her the card. I said, "Thish is good for a free kiss." Before she could even read it, I puckered up and leaned in toward her. She shrank back in horror and retreated toward the other end of the bar. I called after her, "Hey, gimme back my card!" but it was too late. The card was gone. Karma had gotten me good.

Then they started flashing the overhead lights and taking away people's drinks. Dan was nowhere to be found. I made my way out of the bar, and when I got outside I wasn't at all surprised to find Dan engaged in a lip lock with some sweet young thing. They were standing on the sidewalk, leaned up against the side of the building, oblivious to the crowd walking past. He didn't see me, and I had enough sense to not disturb them. I would have been violating one of the primary Man Laws if I had. I crossed the street and stood in an inconspicuous spot, waiting to see if Dan was going somewhere with this girl or if he was coming back to our room.

The crowd around the bar thinned out quickly. Dan and the girl were almost the last people left, and I was starting to feel rather voyeuristic. A police car appeared out of nowhere, the way police cars always do, and pulled up to the curb next to Dan. I saw a big-bellied cop get out of the driver's side and a skinny little cop get out of the other side. Finally, Dan became aware of his surroundings and broke his lip lock on the girl, but it was too late. The cops, eager to defend Southern womanhood, were right there, asking both Dan and the girl for

103

some identification. From what I could hear, the big cop sounded even more like Foghorn Leghorn than Rick did.

I was powerless to help Dan, so I melded into the shadows and slunk away. I went through an alley and down another block. Once I put a little distance between me and the cops, I stopped to see where I was, but nothing looked even vaguely familiar. I might have stood in the same exact spot earlier in the day, but I couldn't tell. I had been going full tilt for about 21 hours, most of that time high on something. I tried to retrace my steps back toward the bar, but I found that I couldn't even do that. I sat down drunkenly on a curb and tried to think. Nothing happened. It felt good to sit. Slowly I began to recollect that our motel was on the east end of town on the main road. If I could figure out which way was east, I could get out of this infernal city. I would use my mountain man skills and navigate by the stars! I started walking again, looking up at the sky. Purely by luck, I stumbled upon a sign that said Rt. 321 East. I followed this road, not knowing if it was the right one or not.

My body was on autopilot. No one was manning the controls. I was lurching back and forth from one side of the sidewalk to the other as I made my way up the road. I passed Dewey Ogle's Motor Inn, and that name rang a bell. I knew then that I was on the right track and almost back to our motel. Soon, I saw the sign for Dewey Ogle's Budget Motel, and I breathed a sigh of relief. Getting back to the motel after a night at the bar had been more challenging than going through the Smoky Mountains with a pack on my back.

Just then, a patrol car slowly drove by, going the same direction I was. *Damn! How many cops are there in this town?* I hadn't come this far to be picked up by the cops at the last second, so I dodged into a used-car lot that I happened to be passing and ducked down behind the lined-up cars. I stayed low and made my way across a long row of cars, still working toward the motel. I thought I saw a searchlight sweeping through the car lot, but I wasn't sure. *They turned around! They're looking for me. Shit!*

In my drunken mind, I was Starsky or Hutch or somebody cool like that. Maybe even Baretta. I ducked and dodged and crawled through a few more parking lots until I came to our motel. Finally, I made it to the parking spaces in front of our room. I poked my head out from behind a car, and I knew instantly that I had been beaten. The police car was stopped right in front of our door. I couldn't figure out how they had known where I was staying, but it didn't matter. Maybe they would let me go since I was already back at my room. I stood up and started walking toward the cruiser, ready to give myself up peacefully.

At that moment, the skinny cop got out and opened the back door of the car. Dan popped out, all smiles, and thanked the cop for the ride. *Total head fuck.* I couldn't believe it. Dan walked over to me and said, "Oh my God, Johnny, you had us laughing!"

"Who?"

"Me and the cops! They saw you the whole time! They asked me if you were with me and I said yeah, so they let you walk back here."

I looked inside the patrol car and saw the fat cop with a big shit-eating grin like Sheriff Roscoe P. Coltrane. Dan led me to the room and opened the door with his key. The big cop called out the window, "Make sure y'all leave in the mornin' now, y'here?" Once the cops saw that we were indeed going into the room, they rolled out of the parking lot and into the night.

The door between our adjoining rooms was still open, so Rick and Craig woke up when Dan and I came in. Dan excitedly told us how the cops had taken him down to the station and made him blow into the breathalyzer. Who would have guessed that it was a crime to be drunk on the streets of

Gatlinburg, Tennessee? The legal limit was .0100 percent blood alcohol. Dan said he had blown a .0098 percent, so they had been obliged to let him go. Still, they thought it might be safer to drive him back to the motel, which is why they ended up at the door to my room before I got there. Dan had mentioned that we were leaving for Ohio in the morning, which is why the cops had encouraged us to leave town promptly.

I couldn't believe Dan had been sober when he left the bar. "Well, Johnny," he explained, "I met a nice girl from Georgia, and we were dancing and talking, so I wasn't drinking a whole lot. I wasn't lone-wolfing it very much."

"A Georgia peach," Rick said admiringly.

"Oh, and she was, too! Wasn't she, Johnny?"

"I couldn't tell with you all over her face."

"Well, she was," Dan said. "Too bad I'll never see her again."

In the morning, as we packed up our cars, Craig said, "Let's get a good breakfast in us before we go."

I desperately needed food in my belly, but I remembered the big cop's warning. "Let's stop at the next exit down the highway, Craig."

Nobody disagreed with me. As we drove out of Gatlinburg, I heard the theme song from *The Dukes of Hazzard* playing in my head. "Someday the mountain might get 'em, but the law never will."

4   Going Off Trail

Way led on to way, and several years passed before I made it back to the Smokies. During that time, I had hitchhiked across the country, lived in the Sierra Nevada panning gold with Rick Rafferty, gotten married (not to Rick), and then served in the Army, stationed in Germany. By 1987, all that was done. I was back in college again, determined to finish my English degree, but also working as an apprentice meat cutter. Dan Rafferty had gotten me the job.

Dan had also gotten married, but unlike my marriage, his had stuck. He had the whole package—a wife, two kids, and a mortgage. I visited Dan's house one day, and with rug rats crawling between our feet and the cloying smell of diapers in the air, we sat at the kitchen table with two beers and a Smoky Mountain trail map spread out in front of us.

The map that we looked at was a cheap, black-and-white version that the Park Service distributed for free. The trails were black lines, and the rest of the map was white nothingness. No rivers or mountains could be seen. I had always been intrigued by those empty spaces on the map where nothing, not even a backcountry trail, was shown. I pointed at the biggest white space on the map and joked, "That's where we ought to go."

Dan knew as well as I did that the big empty space on the map represented miles and miles of absolute wilderness. In our previous journeys, we had never ventured more than a few yards off the trails. As thin and obscure as the foot paths sometimes were, they were the last form of contact with the outer world and the human race. If we left the trails, we would be complete unknowns with no direction home.

The area I was pointing at was an inverted triangle, ten miles wide at the top and six or seven miles deep. The AT formed the northern edge, and the only trail that entered this vast area was one short spur to the south that extended one mile north up into the triangle and then stopped cold. To me and Dan, that blank spot and that one tiny trail were an irresistible lure. Dan looked at the white space for half a second and said, "Yeah, let's go there."

The leather trail book, the "bible" that Rick had introduced us to, said the short spur was called the Bone Valley Trail, which made it even more enticing. We read that the trail led to a small log building formerly used by herders. The remnants of another building, a "social club," were also located there. The bible said that the trail ended there, although a fishing path extended further up the creek.

Other people might have been interested in the log building, the old herdsmen, or the people who would maintain a social club way back up in the mountains, but all we could focus on was the "fishing path." Dan's eyes got real wide and his ADHD kicked in. "Johnny, we should do that fishing trail!"

I looked into Dan's maniacal eyes and said, "I think you're right! All we have to do is follow that creek upstream 'til it ends and then keep going north 'til we hit the AT. I bet the last part is steep as hell." I was already looking forward to the challenge of clawing up the last few vertical yards out of the wilderness to the Appalachian Trail.

A toddler screamed, but Dan ignored the commotion. We stared at the map, imagining what it was really going to be like to go where there was no trail. Dan finally said, "I wonder how bad it's gonna be."

I looked at the valley again on the map. "Hell, it's only five miles. How hard could it be?" The kid screamed again, and Dan decided he'd better go look after him.

We parked my truck near the east end of Cades Cove and started by hiking three miles up the Anthony Creek Trail. Dan was sucking wind more than I was when we got to the top. While I had spent the previous few years being all I could be in the Army, Dan had been standing in a meat cooler every day and then polishing a bar stool with his ass a little too often. Not that my ass hadn't sat upon many German bar stools, because it certainly had, but I was still feeling fine when we arrived at the trail at the top of the ridge, which was called the Bote Mountain Road. I went into my pack and pulled out a pint of whiskey that was packaged in a plastic, shatterproof bottle.

Dan watched me get out the bottle. "You're gonna start drinking already?"

"This is just a 'traveler' for the trail. I have a quart for at night." I pointed to the label on the plastic bottle. "See? It says 'traveler'."

"You're a lush," he said, but I wasn't worried about it. I knew I could hike all day.

The Bote Mountain Road got its name in the 1830s when some entrepreneur tried to build a toll road that would run north and south through what would later become the western half of the park. He wasn't sure exactly where to put the road, so he asked his Cherokee workers which ridge he should build the road on. The Cherokees voted on it, and they selected the mountain ridge that Dan and I stood upon. However, there was no "V" sound in the Cherokee language, so "bote" became the name of the mountain. If that toll road had succeeded, the park might never have existed, but the southern half of the toll road was never finished, leaving the region more or less undeveloped.

We hiked another two miles uphill along the Bote Mountain Road, which was not really a road at all, catching glimpses of the bigger mountains out to the east. Even a peek at the big purplish hulks in the distance filled my soul with reverence. I had been away too long, and I had almost forgotten the feeling of the Smokies. In the intervening years, I had seen the Rockies, the Sierra Nevada, and the Alps, and they were undoubtedly awe-inspiring and majestic, but there was something sacred and mystical in the worn ridges of the Appalachians. These mountains were nearly half a billion years old, some of the oldest mountains on the planet. When the Smokies were young, they rose higher than the Himalayas. Now they were ancient, and they held the very secrets of time. They inspired a quiet, more spiritual feeling than jagged alpine peaks.

At the end of the Bote Mountain Road, we hit the AT. We had already gained 3,000 feet in elevation, which was a good days' work. We were at Spence Field, the high mountain bald where Dan had grazed in the grass eight years before. We looked around for pot plants that might have grown from the seeds that I had scattered that day, but they had either not grown or had been cut down. Dan, who now had petunias planted around his house, was disappointed that the seeds hadn't grown.

I stopped to retie my boots, which were suddenly showing signs of serious deterioration. Dan scouted around, and he stumbled upon a big cage about three feet wide, four feet long, and three feet high that was made from heavy metal bars. A door on one of the short sides slid up and down even though the metal bars were old and rusty. "You think it's a bear trap?" Dan asked me when I walked over.

"Bears or boars," I guessed. I had never seen anything like it. "What else out here is that big?"

Dan used his Wild and Crazy Guy voice to say, "You are, big boy! Get inside, and I will make a photo of you to impress the foxes!"

I fell into the voice too. "Hey! It will be like that swinging S & M bar in Prague!"

"Yes! They caged you like the beast you are. Many firm buttocks were spanked red that night!"

"You are telling me! And I still have great fear for clothes pins, too!" I didn't know a lot about sadomasochists, but I knew they liked clothes pins. We took turns being photographed in the old bear cage, and while the camera was out we took some "grazing in the grass" photos for old time's sake.

After a half mile or so on the AT, we hit the Jenkins Ridge Trail. We had already covered more than six miles, but we had ten more to go, and the sun was definitely in the west. We had to hurry along. Since we were going downhill, I stopped to get out my traveler bottle again. This time, I left the bottle out and carried it in my hand as we walked. Before too long, I was feeling no pain, and I spontaneously burst into song. I favored Dan with my favorite marching song from the Army:

He said the world was round-o! He said it could be found-o!

That hypothetical, masturbating son-of-a-bitch Columbo!

The Captain had a first mate, that dirty little nipper!

He packed his ass with broken glass and circumcised the Skipper!

He said the world was round-o! He said it could be found-o!

That hypothetical, masturbating son-of-a-bitch Columbo!

Dan would have done well in the Army because he joined right in on the song. We hiked the rest of the long trail occasionally singing out "He said it could be found-o!" apropos of nothing.

The afternoon wore on. The Jenkins Ridge Trail ended at a "T." We still had four more miles to go, but Dan said, "I gotta rest my feet a minute." He plopped himself down on a big log at the edge of the little clearing that marked the trail junction. I took a seat beside him and lit up a smoke. The sun was setting and time was short, but there was no point in reminding Dan of what he already knew.

Very near where we sat, a copper mine and a cabin once stood. The copper was discovered in the 1880s and a mine was started up, but it was shut down in 1901 over legal disputes, marking one of those rare occasions when lawyers did something worthwhile. A few years after the mine closed up, in 1904, a soul-weary, alcohol-wasted librarian named Horace Kephart crawled up to that cabin to escape from civilization.

Life in the metropolis of St. Louis had not suited Kephart. He described his decision to head into the mountains: "I took a topographic map and picked out on it, by means of the contour lines and the blank space showing no settlement, what seemed to the wildest part of this region; and there I went." Kephart loved camping and the outdoor life and had even written some magazine articles on the subject. He ended up living in that cabin near the abandoned copper mine for three years. During that time, he traveled through the Smokies and was befriended by locals such as Quill Rose. Like the librarian he was, Kephart took many notes and ended up writing a book called *Our Southern Highlanders* that described the Smokies and a vanishing way of life. The book became a classic.

Kephart fully recovered from what he called his "emotional exhaustion" and went on to champion the creation of a national park in the Smoky Mountains. Mount Kephart is named after him.

Dan and I sat quietly on the log, oblivious to the story of an old alchie named Horace Kephart and the history all around us. Almost every trace of human activity in the valley had been disintegrated by weather or overgrown by vegetation. All we saw in front of us in the twilight was a narrow dirt path and a seemingly impenetrable forest. We were focused simply on getting to the #84 campsite where we could rest. In the morning, we were headed deeper into that triangle of wilderness where there were no trails at all.

We got up and resumed walking. I was sobering up, and Dan was getting tired, and suddenly it wasn't fun anymore. The thirteenth and fourteenth miles were just hard work. We shuffled along on tired legs. The shoulder straps were digging in tighter, and the miles were getting longer. Somewhere along the way, Dan's sleeping bag worked its way loose and half of the bag was hanging down from the bottom of his backpack.

I sighed, "Dan, we gotta fix your sleeping bag."

"I don't care," he said wearily. "We're almost there, anyway."

We were hoping that we would find an open tent site at campsite #84 even though our reservation was for the #85 camp a mile and a half farther down the trail. When we planned the trip using the park's new phone reservation system, we had been sitting in Cleveland drinking beer, and the extra mile and a half between the two camps had seemed like no big deal. However, when we got to #84 and saw all the tent sites filled up, it was a very big deal. We cussed and moaned, but there was no room at the inn, and we had little choice but to keep walking.

113

We didn't even stop to fix Dan's sleeping bag until it fell off of his pack completely. I took the opportunity to get out my traveler again and finish it off. Dan just scooped up his sleeping bag and carried it in his arms the rest of the way. We walked the fifteenth and sixteenth miles in the dark, me with an empty whiskey bottle in my hand and Dan with a crumpled sleeping bag in his arms. When we finally saw the sign for campsite #85, I sang out, "He said it could be found-o!," and Dan responded, "That hypocritical, masturbator, mother-fucker Columbo."

We heard laughter from the far side of the campsite. It came from two guys trying to get a propane stove lit. They had already pitched a tent, but thankfully it was the only tent we saw. One guy called out with a heavy Southern accent, "Y'all had a long walk today?"

I said nothing. Dan, tired though he was, could not resist a conversation. He answered, "Oh yeah. Sixteen miles."

The guy who had spoken sidled toward us. "Hot damn, that's a long way with them big packs! Where'd y'all start?" Once he came closer, I saw that he was a big guy with an Atlanta Falcons baseball cap on his head and a pretty good gut. He looked to be about forty.

Dan met the guy half way. He shrugged off his pack and rolled his sore shoulders. "Up by Cades Cove. Right, Johnny?"

I was already untying the tent from the back of my pack, and I wasn't about to be drawn into the conversation. All I said was "Yep."

"So you come across the mountains today?" The guy sounded doubtful that we had come over the spine of the Smokies.

"Yeah," Dan said. "Why? Where'd you guys come from?"

They had gotten to the part of the conversation that the southern guy had wanted to get to all along. "Well, my name's Jack, by the way, and that there is Critter." He nodded toward his friend. "We come across the lake and landed the bass boat down by #86, but #86 was full, so we had to tote our beer up here. Three miles a-totin' a cooler! Boy howdy!" What the guy was saying was that they had used a boat to cross Fontana Lake and taken it all the way up one of the inlets as far as the boat would go. The campsite there, #86, had been full of people, so he and his buddy had carried their camping gear and their beer three more miles up the Hazel Creek Trail to this campsite. It was a Friday night in the middle of summer, and the park was as crowded as I'd ever seen it.

Dan was unimpressed by a measly three-mile hike, so he ignored the guy's story. He asked instead, "Where you from originally?"

"Dahlonega, Georgia. 'Bout forty mile north of Atlanta." He said it proudly. "Where y'all from?"

"Cleveland, Ohio. Land of the free, home of the Browns." Dan was just as proud.

Jack chuckled. "No good mountains closer to where you live?"

"Not as good as these."

"Where y'all headed tomorrow?" Jack asked. He slapped at his ear to kill a mosquito.

Now they were at the part of the conversation that Dan had been waiting for. Dan said, "Off trail. We're going to follow this creek back up to where it starts, up by the Appalachian Trail." Dan gestured toward Hazel Creek, which ran right next to the campsite, but he meant the Bone Valley Creek.

The man from Georgia looked Dan up and down and then looked over at me. "Up to where it starts?" he asked incredulously. "How long you reckon that's gonna take?"

Dan knew what the guy was thinking, but he kept a straight face and said, "One day."

Jack didn't laugh out loud, but he looked over to his friend, Critter, who was listening just as I was. Critter chuckled.

"One day, huh? Boy howdy! I reckon that deserves a beer. Y'all some crazy mothers, that's for sure. I wish you luck, that's all I can say." He went over to their cooler and grabbed a couple of cold beers. He handed one to Dan and walked over to hand one to me.

Being given a cold beer in the middle of the Smoky Mountains was like being given a crisp, new thousand-dollar bill. I thanked the guy profusely, but there was one thing on my mind. "I don't mean any offense, but I have to ask you. What the hell does 'boy howdy' mean?"

He looked at me as if he had suddenly realized that I had a learning disability. His eyes got very sad. "It's just an expression. Don't mean anything at all, really."

He turned back to Dan, and the smile returned to his face. "Well, y'all enjoy them beers. And be careful! That ain't easy country where you're goin'."

Dan came back over to help me finish putting up the tent. "Why'd you have to say that? The guy was being nice to us."

"I was just curious! I didn't mean to hurt his feelings!" I felt bad about it. I had learned in the Army that a Southern accent did not indicate stupidity, as most Northerners believed, and I really hadn't been trying to make fun of the guy. I was merely curious about that expression. "Maybe we could offer them some pot?" I suggested. "Roll 'em a joint or something."

Dan slapped his arm. The mosquitoes were fierce now that we had stopped moving. "OK. But you do it."

I had brought some pot along simply because I felt like I was supposed to have some in the Smokies, but Dan and I preferred whiskey by a wide margin. After we pitched our tent and ate a quick meal, I rolled up a joint and took it over to the other guys' camp. Dan went to the creek to wash dishes.

Jack saw me coming and said, "Boy howdy!" I knew he was just messing with me, and I deserved it, so I laughed.

Critter said, "We can't spare no more beers."

"No, I know. Those are like gold," I said. "We really appreciate the ones you gave us. I was just wondering if you guys might want a joint in return." I showed them the joint that I had cupped in my hand. I was nervous offering pot to strangers, but the rules were different in the mountains, and even if they were cops, there was really nothing they could do. We were basically outside the reach of the law.

Jack said, "Hoo wee! I believe I'd slap somebody for a couple a tokes right 'bout now!"

"Does that mean yes?"

"Hell yeah, son! Fire that mother up!"

When Dan came back from the creek with the dishes, he found me, Jack, and Critter passing around the joint. I said, "Hey, you-all Yankee! Come on ovah heah!" and the three of us giggled like schoolgirls. We sat around their campfire for a while, and they told me and Dan about hunting black bears in the mountains of northern Georgia. We ended the night as great friends, but I was thinking of bears as I went to sleep.

The next morning, we arrived at the Bone Valley Trail, the little spur that went north up into the very heart of the Bone Valley triangle. I studied the map, fixing in my mind where we were and where we were going, while Dan dug down into his pack for something. When he turned around, I saw that he had pulled some leggings up over his calves. "What the hell are those?"

"They're gaiters . . . for skiing." Dan smiled broadly, quite pleased with himself. The gaiters were waterproof sleeves with elastic that held them in place just below the knees. They stopped snow from getting into your ski boots. In the Smoky Mountains, they just made you look silly, especially when they were combined with baggy gym shorts, an oversized, ratty T-shirt, and a floppy sun hat. It was a stunning ensemble Dan was wearing.

117

Dan saw the look on my face. "What? When we're up in the bush and you have twigs in your boots and your legs are getting all scratched up, you'll wish you thought of this!"

"Maybe. But at least I won't look like a dork." Compared to Dan, I was a fashion plate. I wore an olive drab army undershirt and a pair of gray, polyester baseball pants. The pants were from a pony league baseball team, so they were a little too small for me and barely covered my knees, but they were comfortable as hell and didn't snag on the underbrush. I still wore the army-style web belt I had bought for my very first trip, too. I couldn't stand wearing hats, so I left my lengthening forehead exposed to the July sun. At twenty-eight, my hairline was in full retreat, and I hated it. All the men in my family went bald, and the grim specter of baldness beckoned to me like the Ghost of Christmas Future beckoned to Scrooge on Christmas Eve.

We were anxious to get up to the fishing path and into the bush, so we hurried north along the easy Bone Valley Trail as it hugged the south-flowing creek. Bone Valley itself was named for a herd of cattle that froze to death in a late spring snowstorm back in the 1800s. The bones of the unfortunate beasts sat bleaching in the sun for years and gave the valley its name, but those bones were long gone now. We passed the old herder's cabin as well as the foundation from the social club, but our minds were on the journey ahead, and we barely commented on the relics as we passed them. The ruins were just silent testament that not every place should be civilized. I wanted to go where no men had ever been, not where they had lived and worked and socialized.

At the end of the maintained trail, Dan stopped and dropped his pack. "I'm gonna have my last smoke," he announced.

"What!?" I had heard him perfectly. I just didn't believe what I had heard.

118

"I thought this would be a good time to quit smoking, so I only brought one pack." He pulled one lonely Marlboro out of a beat-up hard pack. "And this is the end of it."

"You're not getting any of mine!" Like the addict I was, I was only worried that I would have enough for me. There were no convenience stores where we were going.

"I know! Shut up and let me enjoy this last one."

"Hell," I said as I reached for my Camels, "I'll join you." I was thinking that Dan wouldn't last a day without a smoke.

We enjoyed our smokes in silence there at the absolute edge of civilization, looking north into the big, big wilderness in front of us. When Dan had finished his last smoke, we plunged into the woods without saying much at all. Never before had any of us attempted to go miles and miles through these wild, steep mountains without a trail or a sign post, and now Dan and I were finally, really doing it. Experts called what we were doing "bushwhacking," but we didn't even know that. We just called it going off trail.

The fisherman's trail started to peter out as soon as we were out of sight of the old cabin. We followed the creek as it curved slightly west. As soon as we were around the curve, we were in a thick growth of deciduous forest, and any semblance of a path disappeared. The trees were so thick that we couldn't take one full step without having to maneuver between saplings. Step by step, we fought deeper into the Smokies.

Soon we came to a big ravine where a tributary creek came in from the west and joined the Bone Valley Creek. We stopped because we had to make our first real decision. I went to grab for the pack of Camels in my Army web belt, but I thought better of it. I grabbed my canteen instead, and Dan grabbed his. I made a semi-circular motion toward the west with my hand. "We could loop around it."

"That could take a while. And it's more of a chance of getting lost."

"It's not like it's going to be easy going straight ahead, either," I pointed out.

"No, but at least we'll be going north."

I agreed, so we went straight down into the ravine with Dan in the lead. The rhododendrons seemed to encircle us deliberately. Within six or seven paces, we were surrounded by stout branches that clutched at us from a dozen places at once.

The rhododendrons are thick in the Smokies, especially in the lower elevations and around water, but big patches of rhododendrons can even be found up on some of the high peaks. In short, rhododendrons are everywhere in the park. They keep their big, rubbery leaves all year long and flower with big, spectacular blossoms for just a few weeks in April. Rhododendron plants can be twelve or fifteen feet tall, and some of the tough, woody branches are easily as thick as a man's arm. The branches grow in all directions, so there was no typical shape to a rhododendron, just a wild tangle of branches and leaves from the ground up. The truly devilish part is that when the branches heavy with leaves came into contact with the ground, they established more roots from that new position. Dan and I discovered that the places where the branches dipped underground were perfectly designed to trip human beings and even break legs. The branches higher up were good for catching the frame of a backpack or scraping your face. These dense patches of rhododendrons can extend for a mile or more and are known as rhododendron "hells."

Dan and I found ourselves entangled in a rhododendron hell. We cussed and struggled, fighting our way forward in the direction we thought was north, stepping over the branches low to the ground and stepping under and between the ones higher off the ground. At times, the only way to move forward was to get down on our bellies and slither through. Every part of our bodies got stuck on something at some point, and the added weight and girth of our packs made it even more difficult to work ourselves through the ensnaring limbs. After half an hour, we were fighting the urge to panic.

Dan had brought along Craig's machete, and he took it out of his pack as a last resort. He tried hacking through some of the worst tangles as he approached them, but he soon found that swinging the machete expended more effort than it was worth. In addition, there was the real risk of slicing himself wide open with the razor-sharp blade. We didn't talk about it, but we both knew that a really bad cut so far out in the backcountry could kill you.

After what seemed like forever, we finally made it to the bottom of the ravine. We were both drenched in sweat. We stopped to catch our breaths and sat down on two large rocks right in the middle of the tributary stream. I lit up a smoke, not thinking about Dan's attempt to quit. He watched me inhale a big lungful of premium Turkish and domestic tobacco smoke, but he didn't say anything about it. Instead he said, "Boy howdy!"

I exhaled my smoke and accidentally it blew into Dan's face. "So much for staying down by the water!" I said. Looking at the thickness of the hell surrounding the little creek, I knew that my plan of walking right up the Bone Valley Creek would never work. The branches and heavy leaves reached out from the two banks of the creek to gather every possible ray of sunlight.

"Let's just try it. We're already down here." Dan pointed at the north side of the ravine. It was a solid mass of rhododendrons angling up at forty-five degrees. We couldn't even see the top. "Going up this hill doesn't look like any bargain either."

Looking at the hell on the north side of the ravine convinced me to listen to Dan. We stayed down by the water and followed the tributary east back toward the Bone Valley Creek. We had to balance ourselves on the rocks and duck through the rhododendron branches hanging down around our heads and shoulders. We struggled along, not going any faster than we had when we came down into the ravine.

When we got back to the main creek, Dan acted as if we had accomplished something, but I wasn't as impressed. We had merely succeeded in crossing over one of what was sure to be many tributary streams joining into Bone Valley Creek. We had sweated and struggled mightily, but we really hadn't gone very far as the crow flies. Already, our legs were quivering from the cumulative effect of the previous day's walk and the stress of fighting through the hells. We dropped our packs on a huge, flat-topped boulder in the middle of the main creek, and I got out my map.

I pointed at the first tributary coming into Bone Valley Creek from the west. "We don't even know if that was this branch or if it's still ahead of us."

Dan looked at the map with me. "We're not making real good time, are we?" The elation had gone out of his voice.

"I don't know," I laughed. "And there's two reasons why. One, I don't know where we are, and two, I don't know what time it is." Our plan had been to go all the way through Bone Valley and up to the Appalachian Trail in one day. After that, it was just a few miles to get back over to Spence Field, the site of Grazing in the Grass. We had planned on sleeping there at the Spence Field shelter on the second night of the trip, but, as we sat on that big, flat boulder looking at the map, I had my first inkling that maybe we weren't going to get out of this valley in one day.

We stayed on the Bone Valley Creek and walked up the stream to avoid the thicker hells along the sides. Occasionally, we saw direct sunlight shining down onto the big pools. Everything else was completely covered by huge rhododendrons that seemed to have been growing there very nicely since the dawn of time. We were no longer in the woods; we were in the jungle.

Dan took the lead again, using his long stride, and the distances we jumped from rock to rock gradually grew from two feet to three feet to leaps of almost four feet. I pushed off of one wet rock and tried to land on another mossy rock no bigger than a dinner plate. My left foot hit the target rock but slid off, and I went down into the knee-deep water with both feet. The image of a hellbender flashed through my brain.

"Mother *fucker*!" I said slowly and with feeling. I felt the cold water seeping quickly all the way down to the toes of my boots. I had just been mentally congratulating myself on becoming very good at rock-hopping. I made my way over to a rock big enough to sit down on and went through the laborious process of taking off my pack and then my boots. I wrung out my socks as thoroughly as possible, knowing from experience that it wouldn't do much good. My boots would be wet for the rest of the day, if not for the rest of the trip.

When we resumed hiking, I stayed closer to the bank of the creek, finding it easier to fight through the heavy rhododendrons than to follow the rocks out in the middle. I tried to find paths where the rhododendrons weren't too heavy, but the snarls of two- and three-inch thick rhododendron branches were practically impassable. Dan and I were both big, strong, twenty-eight-year-old men, used to hard labor. If we had any natural advantage, it was bull strength, but the twisting branches were stronger than any man. The problem was that the branches were intricately woven, so you were never pushing against only one branch. I learned how to move the branch that had caught me out of the way rather than fight against it and hope it would give. Even so, it was incredibly slow going and damned hard work. Our progress slowed to a virtual crawl.

Rick's trail book—the bible—had cautioned us about the dangers of hiking off trail. It said that while most backpackers can cover about two miles an hour on a trail, even fit, seasoned hikers can find themselves advancing less than half a mile an hour when traveling off trail. In these situations, the bible warned, one's stamina and morale will quickly erode.

The July afternoon wore on like a feverish nightmare: a sweaty, impressionistic blur of thick leaves and heavy, tangled branches going on and on and on. Our equipment took a beating as well as our bodies. Dan ripped open one of the pouches on his pack, and my canteen got torn off my web belt, but we pressed on. For some reason, we never gave in to panic, and we never considered going back. As long as we followed the biggest branch of the creek northward, we knew we would eventually get out of Bone Valley.

We worked our way uphill toward the ridge on the west side of the creek, yet we had to stay within sight or at least earshot of the creek because we feared getting lost. We also needed drinking water. We were sweating profusely and guzzling water like crazy. We tried to stay close enough to refill our canteens, but far enough away so that the hells were thinner. We twisted and crawled and hacked and cussed our way along the shoulder of the ridge until we saw the sun dipping close to the western ridge.

Dan looked at the sun and said what we had both known for hours. "We're not getting out today."

"Nope."

"We should start looking for a place to camp."

"Yep."

Finding a place suitable for pitching a tent was easier said than done. Our standards of what would make an acceptable campsite quickly fell. Soon we were just looking for any spot that wasn't too steeply pitched and too heavily overgrown. We angled our way up the ridge, hoping the ground higher up would be better. It took a major effort to gain twenty yards. The first pangs of anxiety were gently starting to squeeze my guts, but at that moment we caught the only break we were going to get all day. Just as the sun was disappearing, we stumbled into something resembling a clearing. The place was still overgrown, but it wasn't covered with rhododendron. We spotted an old piece of rusty metal near the center of the clearing. As we got closer, we saw a few more pieces and parts. I saw what looked like the wheel from an ancient wheelbarrow lying amidst the debris.

"It's some kind of old camp," Dan said as he shrugged off his pack. "Probably loggers."

I felt a big wave of relief wash over me. "As long as it's not a bear den, I don't care. We're sleeping here."

I took off my pack too and lit up a Camel. Dan moved upwind of me to get away from the wafting smoke. He kept his attention on the rusty equipment scattered around us. He picked up an old pail with no bottom and sang out, "He said it could be found-o!"

Automatically, I replied, "That hypothetical, masturbating, son-of-a-bitch Columbo." Then I added, "Damn! This does call for a celebration!" and reached into my pack for my whiskey. I had a few sips, and so did Dan, but we had no time to waste.

Craig's machete came in handy as we cleared away enough foliage to make a rough camp. We tore out the brush where the tent would go, but it was still going to be a lumpy spot on which to sleep. We were both exhausted, but we pushed ourselves to get the rest of the camp ready before dark. Everything was more difficult because we had to fight through the vegetation to move around, even inside our camp. The hard-packed dirt clearings and the fire rings found at designated campsites were distant luxuries.

We wolfed down a pot full of ramen noodles with canned chicken breast mixed in and then started eating trail snacks because we were still hungry. With my mouth full of trail mix, I said, "You know we're not s'posed to camp here."

"Says who?"

"The rangers. The Park Service. Says so right on the map." I got my map and read from the back side of it with the aid of my flashlight. "Rule number one: 'Camping is allowed only at designated sites and shelters'."

Dan snorted contemptuously.

I continued, "Rule number five: 'Fires are allowed at designated campsites and shelters only'. 'Only' is in bold print."

Dan started to say something with his mouth full of cheese crackers, but I interrupted him. "'Maximum fine for each violation is $500 and/or six months in jail.'"

"And who's gonna come get us?"

I hadn't thought about it in those terms. We were at least one day from the reach of civilization. I loved that idea. "You're right. They couldn't come get us if they wanted to!"

"Johnny," Dan said dramatically, "they couldn't get in here with a *helicopter*!"

"That's true. They couldn't land the thing. Or see us under all this cover. But the down side is that they couldn't save us, either."

The look on Dan's face told me that he hadn't thought about *that*. "That's alright," he said. "You were in the Army. You know first aid, right?"

I chuckled. "Yeah, I know some first aid, but I couldn't drag your big ass out of here! And what if *I* get hurt? Knock on wood." I rapped three times on the log I was sitting on.

"I'm not worried about that."

I nodded my head resignedly and reached for an after-dinner smoke, which caused Dan to jump up as if his pants were on fire. "I'll go wash the dishes," he said. Clearly, Dan's strategy for getting through the night without a cigarette was to stay busy. I was glad he had volunteered to go. Night was closing in, and it was a long, treacherous walk through the rhododendron down to the creek.

"Make sure you fill up the canteens so we have water for breakfast," I called after him. I was going to skip washing up even though I was covered with grime and had sweated quarts all day. Under the circumstances, a Stridex pad and a little toothpaste were all the hygiene I needed.

One good thing about being off trail was that there was plenty of good firewood. Nobody had gathered wood where we were for decades. I lit our campfire and hung our food up in a tree. Somewhere along the way, I had discovered that it was a lot easier to hang up only the food rather than the entire backpack.

In addition to my long-gone traveler, I had brought along a quart of my new favorite, "Yukon Jack." Yukon Jack was a 100-proof blend of Canadian whisky and honey-based liqueur. The label featured a mountain man in a big fur coat and a borrowed passage from a Robert W. Service poem: "There's a race of men that don't fit in, a race that can't stay still; So they break the hearts of kith and kin, and they roam the world at will." After reading that, how could I not drink Yukon Jack?

I moved a flat rock next to the big log we had been sitting on and made myself a seat by the fire. I leaned back against the log with a drink by my side and fired up a smoke. I soaked in the feeling of absolute freedom that was the reward for all the sweat and struggle of the day.

After a while, I heard Dan come crashing back through the vegetation. He burst into the clearing. "I'm glad you got that fire going! I wouldn't have found my way back without it."

"Well, you could have yelled to me." I felt compelled to point out the obvious.

Dan was a whirling dervish. He decided that we needed a huge fire to keep the bears away. "This is where the bears live," he told me as threw another tree trunk on the fire. "Away from all the people and trails."

I held out my bottle of Yukon toward Dan. "Have a drink, man. Relax."

"Nah. I still have some left. It'll just make me want to smoke."

That was the first reference to smoking that Dan had made since morning. I was curious because I had never even tried to quit. "Is it bad?"

"It's not good. You look pretty happy there, Johnny."

I sang out, "He said it could be found-o!" to demonstrate how happy I was.

"That hypodermic, crazy dog-fucker Columbo," Dan answered. I wasn't sure if he was messing up the line on purpose or not, but it didn't matter. It was hilarious.

When I stopped laughing, I said, "You picked a hell of a time to quit, Dan."

"Well, with the kids and everything, I thought I should give it a try."

It floored me that Dan had kids but was still out in the bush risking injury or even death. It occurred to me in an abstract way that I was old enough to have kids myself. I said, "If things had turned out differently, I might have kids at home too."

"Be glad you don't."

"Why? You wish you didn't either?"

Dan suddenly stood up and yelled "Haa, bear!" at the top of his lungs.

It scared the shit out of me. "You see something?"

"I just wanna keep 'em away. Let 'em know we're here."

The fire was shooting flames eight feet into the air and lighting up the woods for fifty yards in any direction. "Trust me, Dan. They know we're here," I said. I let that be and tried to pick up the thread of the previous conversation. "It seems so strange to me that a whole life can change based on one random event." I had been with Dan the night he had met his wife. We had been on our way out of a bar as she walked in, and Dan turned around and gone back in.

Dan rearranged the burning logs for the twentieth time. My wet boots were steaming two feet away from the fire, but I was sober enough to keep an eye on them. I had seen boots get burned that way. Dan said, "Maybe it just seems random. Maybe God has it all planned out."

"I try to believe that, Dan. I really do. But sometimes it's hard to conclude that it isn't just pure chance—or blind luck."

Dan sighed, "I know."

We stayed up for another hour. I sat by the fire, drinking Yukon and smoking Camels, while Dan tended the fire continuously and built the finest fire I ever saw in the Smoky Mountains. The flames climbed high into the night. We discussed our plan for the next day, which boiled down to "go north," but we had to talk about it anyway. Every once in a while, Dan would look out into the night and yell "Haa, bear!" at nothing at all. So once again, I was thinking about black bears as I went to sleep.

The next day dawned clear and hot in Bone Valley. This day would require a serious effort, so we were all business as we broke down camp and packed up. We figured we were only a few miles from the AT, and we were hoping to get out of

Bone Valley and all the way back to my truck before night fell.

We made our way down to the creek and paused to do the breakfast dishes and wash up a little before we started sweating all over again. We also needed to fill up our canteens, so Dan set his round, cowboy-style canteen on the bank of the creek and then squatted down to dip my Army-style canteen under the surface of the fast-flowing water. We always tried to take our water from the fastest-flowing part of the stream so that we wouldn't get sick. As soon as he squatted down, his round canteen rolled down the bank, fell into the creek, and started floating away. Dan had to move fast to grab his canteen before it floated away forever. Luckily, he snagged the shoulder strap before it sailed out of reach. I was up on top of the bank watching, and I chuckled at the minor mishap.

Dan set his canteen down again. This time, he chose a spot that looked like it would hold the canteen more securely, but the spot he chose was a few feet farther downstream. Once again, as he squatted down, the round canteen rolled down into the creek and started floating away. This time, he really had to scramble to catch his canteen before it went too far, and he got one boot wet in the process.

Dan's face was grim as he walked back to his original spot on the creek. I was enjoying the show immensely and trying not to laugh too much. I did my Inspector Clouseau imitation and said, "Steu-pid canteen!"

Stubbornly, Dan set the round canteen down once again. He set it down as if it were the last card in a house of cards. He watched it for a second to make sure that it wasn't going to roll again. Incredibly, the moment he turned away from it, the canteen began to roll again. Dan was ready for the canteen this time. He wheeled back around and grabbed the rolling canteen before it hit the water. Then he wound up and hurled the canteen as hard as he could at my big, laughing head.

It was a good throw from close range. The flat side of the canteen hit me up around the temple with a loud, hollow THUNK. Dan was afraid that I was hurt. He ran up the bank to me. "I didn't think I'd hit you!" he said.

I felt around on my head where the canteen had struck me, but I didn't see any blood on my fingers. I was surprised, but not angry. It was too funny for me to be mad. I said, "Cato, you fool! You might have killed me!"

After that incident, I realized that Dan might be a little edgy, so we didn't talk much when we resumed our trek. Nothing needed to be said anyway. We were bruised and scraped and sore, but we knew what we had to do, and we resigned ourselves to more of the same hard work we had done the day before. We tried to stay in the sweet spot where the rhododendrons were thinner but we were not too far from the creek.

We fought our way north, crossing over several more tributaries feeding into the main creek. Each time we passed a tributary, the stream we followed became noticeably smaller. The rhododendrons finally thinned out as well, so we began to make better progress. By the time we reached the last few branches of Bone Valley Creek, it was impossible to tell which was the main creek and which was the tributary. We used a compass and followed the branch that ran truest north each time.

The July sun was blazing directly overhead when we saw Bone Valley Creek finally reduced to a muddy trickle. The air in the valley was still and heavy and full of biting horseflies, descendants of the flies that had eaten the last scraps of flesh from the dead cattle that had given Bone Valley its name. We were jubilant nonetheless, knowing that we weren't going to end up as two piles of bleaching bones in a rhododendron hell.

131

We were reinvigorated, and we wasted no time in attacking the last and steepest part of the valley. This was the moment I had been fantasizing about: climbing up a nearly vertical wall to finally stand on the very crest of the Smokies with my hands on my hips, surveying the valley I had conquered.

Thankfully, the climb wasn't vertical because we wouldn't have made it. We approached the crest straight on rather than being smart and taking the incline obliquely in a series of switchbacks. Gradually, the rise grew steeper and the undergrowth disappeared except for tufts of grass. We resorted to going on all fours, breathing in huge gasps as we hauled ourselves and our packs higher and higher. For some inexplicable reason, it became a mad scramble to the top. Our tortured legs were on fire, and we were grabbing handfuls of grass to keep from sliding back down the mountainside. Finally, the last few feet before the crest became nothing but rock, and it was easier to find hand holds and foot holds. We pulled ourselves up onto the narrow, flat ledge that was the Appalachian Trail and sat there in the dirt and the rocks for a while, breathing in great heaves.

Once I caught my breath, I looked at Dan with a big grin on my face and sang, "He said it could be found-o!"

Dan grinned back and sang, "That hippopotamus-masturbator, dago-boy Columbo!"

We stood up and looked south across the valley, and the view was magnificent. The mountain dropped away sharply in front of us. The trees and foliage were so thick in the valley that we couldn't even see Bone Valley Creek. Further out, the southern horizon was an endless series of purple ridges, obscured by the hazy heat. We stood there for a long time, not really seeing the valley, but savoring the sublime moment of accomplishment instead. And the feeling was every bit as triumphant as I had dreamed.

Finally I spoke and broke the spell. "It seems so small from here."

"No one would ever believe how hard it was to get through there," Dan agreed.

Dan opened his canteen—his primary weapon—and took a sip. I got out my canteen as well and swished it back and forth a little to see how full it was. It didn't have much in it. Suddenly I realized that we had made a big mistake. I kept my voice casual. "How much water do you have, Dan?"

He swished his canteen. I could tell from the sound that his was nearly empty too. Then his eyes got wide as he realized that we had both forgotten to fill our canteens. "Oh shit!"

"We fucked up."

"Yeah we did."

We were up on a high, rocky ridge, and we knew there wasn't going to be any water for quite a while. Going back down to the creek was out of the question. We got out a map and tried to figure out how far we had to go to get to water. All we knew was that we were somewhere on a rocky, six-and-a-half-mile stretch of the AT. A shelter called Derrick Knob was somewhere to the east, and the Grazing in the Grass shelter was somewhere to the west. We knew that there would be a water source near both shelters, but we had no earthly way of knowing which shelter was closer. Ultimately, we had to go west to get to my truck, so we headed toward Grazing in the Grass and hoped that it wasn't 6.4 miles away.

"It won't be so bad," Dan said. "We just have to conserve." I had the urge to throw my canteen at him just then, but I needed the water.

We found no shade and no relief from the fearsome heat. The Gatlinburg temperature was in the nineties that day, but we were on the south side of a long, rocky ridge, and the July sun had been baking those rocks all day long. To make matters worse, the section of the Appalachian Trail that we were on rose and fell steeply over and over again, like climbing up and down endless, rocky staircases. I thought that I had learned the ways of the mountains and that I was past foolishly expecting to see the end of the trail around every curve, but I wasn't. The top of every rise became a fresh disappointment.

Soon, our hope that the shelter was just a short distance away evaporated. We knew then that we had to pace ourselves. We took a break and drank a few precious sips of water. I lit up a smoke, and Dan asked, "How many you got left?"

"Lots." Cigarettes were light, so I always packed plenty.

"Gimme one."

I knew it was supposed to be my duty to persuade Dan to not smoke, but I couldn't think of any good reason why he should continue to make himself even more miserable. At that moment, I didn't care whether he smoked or not.

Dan saw me wavering. "Just gimme a smoke, Johnny."

I gave him a cigarette and a light. He took a big drag and exhaled slowly. Despite our circumstances, he looked blissful. I counted up the hours and said, "Twenty-eight or thirty hours."

"Til what?"

"No. That's how long you quit for."

"That's a long time," he said, and he smoked his cigarette with true enjoyment.

We pushed on after our smoke break, and the trail turned consistently uphill, and we suffered as we climbed. Each man had to endure as best he could. I tried not to think at all. I retreated into some inner sanctum of spirit and tuned out the external world that was presently the source of so much discomfort. I entered into a walking trance. My head hung down so that all I saw was the three or four feet of rocky trail in front of me. I saw sweat drops falling on the rocks, but it did not occur to me that the sweat was mine. I saw boots

134

landing on the trail in short, regular intervals, but they weren't attached to my body. Vaguely, I noticed that the sole of one boot was flopping free every time it struck the rocks, but it didn't matter in the least. Dan was forgotten as well. The only things that were real were the mountain, the sun, and the pack on my back. I walked like a mindless machine.

Eventually, I saw the figures of a man and a woman who stood looking out to the south, and I wondered if they were real or some kind of Native American spirit vision. It seemed strange to see other human beings after a day and a half of seeing no one. I realized that I had come to a clearing where the trail stopped rising. I used my voice and it sounded like a croaking frog. "Is there water here?" I asked

The man said, "No, we're on a mountain top." The woman smiled at this, and I didn't understand that they were having a laugh at my expense. I walked over to a huge boulder sticking out of the ground and sat down on it. My mind was struggling to rejoin the external world. I noticed a shiny, golden disk about three inches wide lying on top of the big boulder on which I sat. I reached out to pick it up, but the disk was attached to the living rock. The metal, which seemed to be brass, was hot as hell. I couldn't read all of the inscription on the disk, but I could make out these letters: UNDERHEAD TN. USGS 5530 T.

I got out my crappy black and white map, but it showed nothing between Derrick Knob and Grazing in the Grass. I waited for Dan to show up. I had played a game with myself, putting the water out of my mind until I got to the high point of the trail. Now I was evidently at the top, so I rewarded myself with a tiny sip. I tried to work the water around in my parched mouth before I swallowed. I gauged that I had two hot, plastic-tasting sips left.

Dan soon appeared at the point where the AT dropped off to the east. He looked like one of the survivors at the end of a horror movie, only not dressed as well. Incredibly, he tried to strike up a conversation with the man and the woman enjoying the view from the summit. I couldn't hear what was said, but the body language of the man and woman told me that they wanted nothing to do with a huge, stinking backpacker in tattered clothing.

Dan gave up his attempt at being neighborly and came over to collapse near me on the boulder. "I was following your sweat drops before," he said dully. "You know where we are?"

I pointed at the brass disk. "I'm not sure of the name. I think it might be Dunderhead, Tennessee."

Dan shielded his eyes against the glare and read the inscription on the brass disk. He laughed, but it was the sound of a lizard choking on a cockroach. "It says Thunderhead Mountain, elevation 5,530 feet."

That name made more sense. "How'd you read those letters?"

"Those people just told me the name."

Dan explained to me that the brass disk buried into the living rock was an elevation marker. The United States Geological Survey placed these markers on most of the notable high points inside the park, but the marker on Thunderhead Mountain was the first one I had ever seen. Dan told me that he had seen such a marker on Clingmans Dome, the highest peak in the Smokies. We got out the good map, which had been in Dan's pack, and indeed I saw a peak called Thunderhead Mountain on the AT a mile or two east of where we needed to go. "It looks like a about a mile and a half to Grazing in the Grass," I estimated.

Dan looked uncharacteristically discouraged. "Looks closer to two," he said. Then he added, "Gimme another smoke."

I handed him my open pack of Camels. "Keep it," I said, and he did.

I went into my backpack to get out another pack of smokes and remembered that I had a small spool of fishing line in my pack. I carried the fishing line and some hooks in my pack on the off chance that I might have to catch a fish in order to survive someday. I cut a length of the line and tied one end onto one of the bootlace eyelets on my bad boot. Then I wrapped the line under the sole of the boot and through an eyelet on the opposite side. I wove the fishing line back and forth a few times and tied off the loose end when I was done. I took a few tentative steps, and it seemed as if the line would hold the sole in place.

We decided to drink the last of our water. We touched our canteens together in a pathetic little toast and drank the last tepid drops. We had two miles to go in the blazing heat with no water at all, and we were already badly dehydrated. I had some Yukon left in my pack, but this was one of those rare situations in which booze was not going to help. The trail was downhill past Thunderhead Mountain, and we began to hope that maybe it was downhill all the way to Grazing in the Grass. Our spirits rose, and we talked as we hiked.

"Johnny," Dan said confidentially, "when we were going up Thunderhead, I picked up my foot to take a step, and it came down in the exact same place! My legs are dead."

"I know. Mine too. I was just wondering if that thing about sucking on pebbles is true."

"What? Like Indians?"

"Yeah."

"Try it," Dan encouraged me.

In the old-time Westerns, people out in the desert sucked on pebbles to keep their mouths moist. My mouth was so dry that I figured I had nothing to lose. I found a rounded, fairly-flat pebble about the size of a marble, brushed it off, and put it in my mouth. It tasted terrible.

"Don't swallow it!" Dan warned me.

"I bet you never said that before," I mumbled.

After a minute my mouth was still dry, and I spit the pebble out. I had something to lose after all because now I had the gritty taste of dirt in my mouth.

The conversation stopped abruptly when we saw the AT turn uphill again. Dan groaned. I tried to hypnotize myself back into my zombie state as I climbed, but I couldn't stop thinking about how thirsty I was. The thirst was a devil on my back, sitting on top of my backpack and making it heavier. The devil was whispering in my ear about ice cold mountain streams and frosty beers. It tormented me mightily.

We crested yet another summit, but we were beyond caring what the summit was called. There was no marker that we could see, and we didn't bother getting out the good map to look. We found out later that we were on maybe the most famous Smoky Mountain of all—Rocky Top. There was a famous country/blue grass song about Rocky Top. Ironically, Dan sometimes sang the song as we hiked, but Dan wasn't singing as we passed over the actual mountain. We didn't even know we were there.

Past Rocky Top, the AT went up and down steeply for a while, and we didn't talk at all. We just tried to survive. My fishing line shoe repair broke, so my right boot sole was flapping again. I didn't care. I was starting to feel weird inside, as if I were trembling internally. I had never felt that way before, and it scared me. I didn't know if I was about to pass out or go into convulsions or what. I had never been so desperate for water. I knew somewhere deep inside that I couldn't last much longer. I was at a point in my college career where I was questioning the existence of God, thinking I was marvelously sophisticated for doing so, but as we walked, I started begging God to give us some water. All the hubris was gone. As the saying goes, there are no atheists in foxholes.

Finally, blessedly, the AT turned consistently downhill again. We shambled on like refugees—staring blankly, seeing nothing. The vegetation along the sides of trail became gradually thicker. Dan croaked, "This better be it."

A few minutes later, we saw moisture on the slanting, rocky wall that formed the right side of the trail. My heart leapt at the sight. Throughout the Smokies, it's common to see water dripping from the rocks on the sides of the trails. The rainwater that lands on the mountains slowly works down through the fissures in the rock and comes out in little springs and seepages all along the sides of the mountain, especially when there has been a lot of rain. The spring in front of us was barely flowing on a dry summer day, but it was more beautiful than Niagara Falls. A muddy puddle filled the shallow ditch at the side of the hard-packed trail. It looked a lot like the mud hole at the top end of Bone Valley Creek that we had left behind that very morning. Ages had passed since then.

We saw a tiny patch of brown water that was maybe a foot wide and an inch deep in the center of the muddy ditch and I didn't hesitate at all. I got down on all fours and drank like a stray dog. The water was as sweet as life itself. It *was* life itself. Dan rasped, "Save me some!" so I pulled myself away. Dan took my place at the trough. He made loud slurping sounds as he drank. I laughed in relief.

We took a break there in the hope that the water in the ditch would replenish itself, and it gradually did. We used a cup to carefully skim as much water from the ditch as we could and poured it into Dan's canteen. As careful as we were, the brown fluid was still full of floating specks of debris and who knew how many bacteria and parasites. I took a sip from the canteen, and Dan said, "Don't drink too much. This isn't the best water in the world."

"Yes, it is."

"We'll get better water at the shelter, Johnny. It's gotta be close now."

We kept going, and less than half a mile down the AT, we saw the big open field of Grazing in the Grass. We dropped our packs there in the middle of the grassy field, not caring who or what might take them, and stumbled the last few hundred yards down to the water source for the Spence Field shelter. We drank until our bellies were bloated. Then we stripped to the waist and rinsed off our stinking bodies in the cool, clear water.

We sat in the shade for a little while and felt the life force seeping back into us. I lit a smoke and so did Dan. He couldn't smoke them fast enough now that he was back on the weed. I said, "I'm gonna drink about fifty beers tonight."

Dan quoted a song that was popular that summer. "Everybody wang chung tonight."

I knew the song, but I asked anyway, "What the hell does 'wang chung' mean?" It had been bothering me all summer. Like many questions in life, my question went unanswered. Perhaps there was no answer, just as there was no answer to why we put ourselves through such hardship.

We still had four miles to go to get back to my truck, so we saddled up and left Grazing in the Grass behind. We made sure we filled our canteens before we left. We retraced our path down the Bote Mountain Road and the Anthony Creek Trail toward my truck. We were exhausted and bedraggled and my boot sole flapped, but it felt marvelous simply to be in the shade of the forest. We had walked through the valley of death and survived, so our spirits were light.

Dan said he wanted to try off trail again. "But without packs. We'll just wear hunting vests with lots of pockets and maybe those little fanny packs. No tents, no sleeping bags, no stoves. We'll just go super, super light."

"What are we going to eat?"

"Just energy bars and stuff like that."

That triggered an association in my mind. In Stephen King's novel, *The Long Walk*, a national sporting event is held once a year in some not-so-futuristic America. One hundred eighteen-year-old men are selected to walk continuously until they drop. When they can no longer continue, they are executed on the spot, and The Long Walk goes on until only one man remains. The event is televised and people watch and wager on it like the Super Bowl. The contestants eat energy bars along the way, which is what made me think of it.

I told Dan about the book as we walked. It had a special poignancy after what we had just been through. "So what does the winner get?" he asked.

"It didn't really say," I answered. "At the end, only the one guy is left, and all it says is 'Suddenly he had the strength to run.'"

Dan didn't like that ending. "Why the hell would he run?"

It was another unanswerable question. But when we rounded a bend in the trail and my truck came into sight, we both had the strength to run to it.

Buddha Palguta

5   Going Alone

A couple of years later, in 1989, I was jonesing to get down to the Smokies again, but none of my buddies could find the time to go. Each had his own busy life occupied with getting and spending, and mine was no different. I had earned my degree and was now in grad school, taking classes as well as teaching freshman English to pay my tuition, and still working as a meat cutter four days a week. Even with all that going on, I somehow found the time to party prodigiously and work out regularly. I was a whirling dervish every day, and I was on my way to becoming a professor.

I managed to string together a few days off, so I decided to go backpacking by myself. I consulted Rick's bible, which tersely advised that no one should ever backpack alone. Even something as simple as a sprained ankle could create a dire scenario, and if the weather turned bad, you might find yourself fighting for your very life.

The true drawback of hiking by one's self, it seemed to me, was that there was nobody else to help carry all the stuff. I had to cut some weight out of my pack somewhere, so I ditched my tent and my sleeping bag and decided to go with only a

142

sheet of plastic and a light blanket. I figured these would be sufficient for the hot August nights.

During the drive down to Tennessee, I multi-tasked by steering with my knees and doing isometric exercises to keep my chest and arms pumped up. I was quite the player in those days, and as long I was on the loose from my girlfriend, I was going to try to shag some Daisy Duke if the opportunity presented itself.

I rolled into Gatlinburg early on a Sunday evening, driving the Volkswagen Rabbit that I had purchased as a tribute to my days in Germany. I didn't want to head directly into the mountains after the long drive, so I was planning on hanging around in town for the evening and sleeping in the fully-reclining seats of the Rabbit. First thing Monday morning, I would head into the backcountry for a two-night trip. I parked in a municipal lot and took a stroll along the strip. The streets were packed with tourists—especially women—of every variety. I considered passing out flyers, but I had learned some subtlety over the years, so the only advertising I did was to wear a black, Patrick Swayze, Dirty-Dancing tank-top shirt as I sauntered down the Parkway. I got my share of glances and even some squeals from a car full of girls, but no real girlie action.

I regrouped back at the Rabbit. I ate the rest of the boloney sandwiches in my cooler. Then I found a public restroom and cleaned up hobo-style as I had learned to do in my travels out west. With that and a fresh shirt, I was ready to hit the clubs.

I already had a few nips of Yukon in me when I walked into the lounge. The place was called the Electric Chalet, and stuffed deer heads adorned the walls. Strings of tiny lights wrapped around the antlers added a touch of 1980s chic. The bar, with a big mirror behind it, took up one wall of the room, and the opposite wall featured a huge mural of a snow-capped mountain with a jagged, rocky peak. It looked more like

143

Mount Everest than Mount Guyot, but nobody seemed to notice. A tiny dance floor with a single disco ball hanging down filled up one corner of the room, and the mullet-topped DJ was playing Billy Ocean's "Get Outta My Dreams, Get Into My Car." The DJ was indeed live, as the sign outside had promised, although his taste in music had sadly died.

I ordered a Yukon on the rocks and a draft beer from a bartender wearing a very skinny leather tie. The place was mostly empty except for a few single guys nursing beers at the bar. They looked like locals hoping to score with tourist chicks. We were all disappointed because there wasn't a single woman to be found. But it was Sunday night and most of the bars in town were closed, so I waited to see what developed.

Near the end of my third Yukon, my patience was rewarded. Three women walked in and took seats at a table near the dance floor. I eyed them through the mirror behind the bar. They looked to be thirtyish—all do-able, but not unapproachable. They were like the Three Bears; one was a little too heavy, one was a little too thin, and one was just right. I couldn't tell from that distance whether they had wedding rings on or not.

It took a special kind of nerve for one guy to approach three women, but whatever courage my heart lacked was made up for by the Yukon in my veins. *Worst they can say is no*, I thought, and I got up and took the long, lonely walk from the bar over to their table. That walk was harder than the long hike through Bone Valley. I felt every eye in the place watching me, especially the other guys', gauging my chance of success. Even in my own mind, the odds weren't good.

I approached their table, smiling my best smile. "Would you ladies mind if I joined you for a while? I'm alone in town tonight and I'm just looking for some company," which was exactly what all shaggers said.

I tried not to act surprised when they said yes. I went back to the bar and fetched my drink and joined them at their table. They told me their names—Kelly, Sabrina, and Jill—and I promptly forgot all three. They were from Louisville, Kentucky, "just on vacation in the mountains." I doubted that any of them would come within ten miles of a real mountain, but I didn't say so.

"I am a matador," I announced in a crappy Spanish accent. "Don Pablo Cerveza El Toro. I am in America recovering from a bull-fighting wound." Sometimes the stuff that came out of my mouth amazed me.

Kelly, the cute but chunky one, said, "Where were you wounded?"

"In Barcelona."

"No," she giggled. "What part of your body?"

I tried to look sad. "Alas, ladies, I shall never make the sexy again! It was—how do you say, like the bull—my mountainous oysters."

"Oh, what a shame!" the thin one, Jill, smiled.

"Unless," I added hastily, "I receive the kisses of three maidens. This is what the doctor he says."

The just-right bear, Sabrina, had a ring on her left ring finger. "I thought you were just looking for company."

Apparently, I had gone too far, at least for her, so I backed off. In my normal voice, I said, "I'm sorry. I'm only playing around," which again was exactly what all shaggers said.

Kelly chided her. "He's just having fun, Brina!"

We talked for a while about our homes and our lives. Sabrina managed to mention her husband as well as Jill's boyfriend several times. I studied their faces and thought I saw annoyance on Jill's when her boyfriend's name came up, but I wasn't sure. Kelly was apparently single. Surprisingly, my girlfriend's name didn't come up at all. We decided to do some shots, and the girls ordered various kinds of flavored schnapps. This gave me the opportunity to mention that I had lived in Germany, where, I told them, peach-flavored schnapps had been invented. They were duly impressed.

The DJ, still clinging to life, started playing "Wild, Wild West," which was the hot dance groove for white people that year. I said, "You guys wanna dance?"

"All of us?"

"Sure! That's how they do it in Germany. Everybody dances together!"

They agreed, so we hit the floor. Normally, being the only guy on the dance floor terrified me more than a pack of wild boars, but the Yukon, the beer, and the schnapps were working their magic. We stood around in a loose circle. I cut loose with some matador moves followed by some Patrick Swayze, Dirty-Dancing pelvic thrusts, and I think Kelly creamed her jeans right there on the dance floor. The guys sitting at the bar watched in disbelief, wondering why this flaming asshole was with three women while they sat at alone.

These Kentucky girls liked to dance and drink, and we had a ball for the next few hours. The drunker I got, the more outrageous I became, and the girls didn't seem to mind at all. Or, if they did, I didn't notice. When the DJ played "Love Train" by the O'Jays, I started a conga-line "love train" of my own. We wound our way around the room in a single-file line with each person's hands on the hips of the person in front of them. Some of the other patrons even joined in. We had a blast.

And then, suddenly, it was closing time. I was drunk off my ass, beyond caring, so I swung for the grand slam. "How 'bout if I go back to your room with you guys?" I tried my best smile again, which I'm sure was crooked at that point.

The two attached girls, Sabrina and Jill, got sour looks on their faces, as they were required to do by law. Kelly, on the other hand, giggled and said, "What about your mountainous oysters?"

"Kelly!" Sabrina hissed, "He's not coming back to the room!"

The thin one, Jill, said nothing, and in my drunken brain I thought I might have had a chance for at least a triple if Sabrina hadn't been there. I was beyond caring, so I simply said, "It's OK. I had to give it a shot."

Sabrina, followed by Jill, hurried out of the lounge. Kelly lingered for a moment, so I gave it one last try for a solid double. "You know, the seats in my car go back all the way."

She smiled, but Sabrina turned back and called sharply, "Kelly!" Kelly looked at me and said, "Goodbye, matador," and hurried off to join her friends.

I stood alone outside the Electric Chalet. *Damn!* After all the charm and wit and sexy, I had struck out. *At least you went down swinging, Johnny.* I started walking back to my Rabbit, but the sidewalk was not nearly as stable as it had been earlier in the evening. I had experienced shifting sidewalks in Gatlinburg before. I did my best, but I was unable to stay on the sidewalk with any consistency. I lurched from side to side, trying to get back to the parking lot without falling down.

Then Barney Fife arrived. He was about five foot seven and a buck twenty-five, but it didn't matter because he had a big badge. That badge filled up the sidewalk in front of me and stopped me in my drunken tracks. Barney and I exchanged a few pleasantries, but those ended when he asked me to walk heel-to-toe along an imaginary straight line in the street. I made like a tight-rope walker and attempted to comply, but I failed miserably. After I stumbled for a second time, I gave up the heel-to-toe bit, turned around, and started lurching back toward Barney. "I can't do it," I muttered.

Maybe Barney thought I said something else because he pulled out his pistol and pointed it directly at me. "Stop right there!" he squealed. I had done something unexpected and that had frightened him.

I stopped cold. I even sobered up a little, but not nearly enough. I was so drunk that not even a gun in my face could straighten me up. In the blink of an eye, several cops seemed truly to appear out of thin air. One much bigger than Barney cuffed my hands behind my back and helped me into the back seat of a police car. I didn't resist. Barney and his large friend drove me off toward the station.

I had never been handcuffed before, and it hurt like hell. I leaned toward the front seat. "Hey," I said in a reasonable voice, "these cuffs are way too tight. Can you guys loosen them up a little?"

Barney and his friend looked at each other and chuckled.

"Come on! Please! These things are killing me! I'm not gonna escape or anything!"

They laughed out loud at that one, so I gave up asking. Instead, I decided to metabolize as much alcohol as possible before they gave me the breathalyzer or drew blood. I started breathing in and out as deeply as I could, hoping to burn up some of the alcohol. At first, I tried to do it quietly, but then I decided that it didn't matter. I started exhaling huge clouds of Yukon-laced fumes toward the front seat of the car.

The bigger cop turned half way around. "Cut that shit out!" Boldly, like Martin Luther King or Mahatma Gandhi practicing civil disobedience, I kept breathing heavily—only I did it more quietly.

The whole metabolizing booze thing turned out to be wasted effort. When we got to the station, they gave me a breathalyzer test and I damn near broke the machine, blowing over twice the legal limit and shattering Dan's old score. They told me I was going into the drunk tank to sleep it off, and I was immediately afraid that I might run into players of a different sort inside the jail cell. I did not want to become a shag-ee in some Tennessee drunk tank. I stole a line from that lecherous friend of mine, Eddie Love, and told the cops, "I'm too fine to go to jail," but they weren't amused. They threw me into a locked room that turned out to be empty except for a foam rubber sleeping pad. I was relieved that I was alone. I lay down on the pad, trying to think of the words to Johnny Cash's "Folsom Prison Blues," and promptly fell deep asleep.

They woke me in the morning. I felt terrible, but better than I would have if I had slept in my car. I was charged with the dastardly crime of public drunkenness. If I pleaded no contest, I could go free that morning and send them a check for $128 after I got home. I did not want to spend one more minute than necessary in captivity. Besides, I needed a cigarette very badly, so I signed the papers, and the cops, showing true Southern hospitality, drove me back to my car. If they had sprung for breakfast, it would almost have been worth the fine.

On the way to my car, we passed Dewey Ogle's House of Pancakes, and I asked the cops if they could let me out there. The people in the restaurant strained to get a glimpse of the desperado coming out of the back seat of a police car. I went in and was seated at a table. The other patrons kept looking toward me surreptitiously, checking out the criminal. I defiantly returned their glances. *"Any of you motherfuckers touch my pancakes,"* I wanted to yell, *"and I'll kill ya!"* but I didn't say a word because I didn't want to go back to jail.

I felt a lot better after I ate breakfast and cleaned up. I drove out to the Sugarlands visitor center to get my backcountry permit and went into the little log cabin that served as the ranger station. I didn't have any particular trip in mind, so I asked the female ranger sitting behind the desk to suggest a nice two-night trip. When I told her I was a hiking party of one, she got up from her desk and came to stand behind the counter. "What nights are you going?"

149

"Tonight and tomorrow night. I'll come out of the woods on Wednesday."

"That's too bad," she said with an enticing pout.

"Why?" I said defensively. I was feeling victimized by The Establishment that morning, and I thought she was going to deny me my permit.

"If you were going to go tomorrow," she said, "I could go with you." She looked me right in the eye, like a good ranger should. I was dumbfounded, then flattered. *A shagger ranger-ette!* She appeared to be in her mid-twenties with sun-bleached hair and a nice body hidden beneath her ranger uniform. She wasn't gorgeous, but she was attractive in a wholesome, outdoorsy way.

I returned her gaze. "A personally-guided ranger tour?"

"Sure. I know some nice spots," she said, and I felt definite stirrings.

"I bet you do," I managed to say. After the night I'd had, I wasn't at my best, and I didn't know what to say or do. A hard-core womanizer like Eddie Love would have changed his plans in a heartbeat and found some way to bed this girl, but I had a girlfriend, and I also really wanted to go backpacking. A brief but furious battle raged in my soul, and to my surprise, the mountain man in me gained the upper hand. I heard the mountain man say, "I wish I didn't have to be back at work on Thursday, but I do." Then the ladies' man, not ready to concede defeat, scored a surprise reversal and said, "But maybe you could give me a personally-guided tour of the station here."

She smiled a mischievous smile. "Right now?"

I felt my pulse quicken. "Why not? I'm a tax-payer," I said nonsensically. I felt flushed and my breath was a little ragged.

Her green eyes were aflame. "Well, maybe you'd like to start the tour in the back room?"

"Absolutely."

She came from around the counter and went to the front door. "Let me just put my break sign in the window." I checked out her ass as she flipped over the sign and locked the door. She turned around and caught me looking. She said, "I can't believe I'm doing this."

"I can't either," I said. "You're not gonna get caught, are you?"

"No. The door's locked. Come on." She led me behind the counter and into some kind of supply room. She closed the door, pressed up against me, and said, "We've got about fifteen minutes." Her breathing was ragged too.

I kissed her, and the desires of the mountain man and the ladies' man were one and the same. I unbuckled her bulky ranger belt because it was between us, and then she unbuckled mine.

Twenty minutes later, I left the office with my permit in my hand. She smiled as I left and said, "Have a nice hike, Mister Taxpayer."

A twinge of guilt hit me as I drove away. I was disappointed with myself and stupid games of sexual conquest. Some guys (like Eddie Love) would have said that it was my patriotic duty to take advantage of such a golden opportunity. I rationalized that no matter which choice I had made, I would have had to live with regret. I wondered if mountain men troubled themselves with such things.

An hour later, I parked the Rabbit near Clingmans Dome and headed west on the AT. I intentionally avoided the observation deck at the top of Clingmans Dome because I knew I would appreciate the view much more after climbing up the mountain from the bottom, which is exactly what I intended to do.

Clingmans Dome, at 6,643 feet, is the highest peak in the Smokies and the third tallest peak in the eastern United States. The only higher peaks on the whole North American continent east of the Mississippi are Mount Mitchell and Mount Craig, both in the Black Mountains fifty miles to the east in North Carolina. So, on the eastern half of the continent, Mount Mitchell is first at 6,684 feet, Mount Craig is second at 6,647, and Clingmans Dome is a close third.

The second-highest peak in the Smokies, Mount Guyot, is the fourth-highest overall at 6,621 feet, but the hardest one of the four to get to. The top three peaks in the East are easily accessible to almost anyone. Mount Mitchell has a road going right up to the top, and a big, fat, concrete, wheelchair-accessible observation deck squatting on the exact top of the mountain. Mount Craig is an easy one-mile walk away from the Mount Mitchell parking lot along a maintained trail. Clingmans Dome is just like Mount Mitchell with a paved road leading up to a big observation deck on the very peak of the mountain.

Mount Guyot, on the other hand, is at least nine miles away from any road whatsoever. In fact, no trail goes up to the top of Mount Guyot at all. The Appalachian Trail passes around the shoulder of Mount Guyot but, of the big Eastern peaks, only Mount Guyot remains relatively untamed. It rests mostly undisturbed by the world around it.

I felt the sliminess of modern life slough off of me like an old snake skin as I left the pavement behind. The deeper I went into the mountains, the better I felt. For the next two days at least, all I had to think about was where I was going to sleep and what I was going to eat. All the cares of the world, even the necessities of interaction with other human beings, were blessedly removed. I was curious to see how it would feel to be totally by myself.

The trail was all downhill in the direction I was going, and the walking was easy. I only had a four-and-a-half-mile hike to my first camp, but that was alright since I had had a busy morning. Being all alone in the mountains suited me very well,

I thought. I hiked for a good while through the high evergreen forest. I recalled a speech from *Jeremiah Johnson*, a movie about a fur trapper living high in the Rockies in the 1830s. A crazy, bald-headed mountain man named Del Gue proclaims the glory of the Rockies and the mountain man life. I didn't remember all the words, but I did remember him saying that great mountains were "the marrow of the world" and that in the mountains there were no laws for brave men and no churches but the mountains themselves. I wasn't in the Rockies, but I was alone in the mountains, and by God, I felt like a mountain man.

About four miles west of Clingmans Dome, I reached Silers Bald. I stopped and took in the views. The third highest peak in the Smokies, Mount LeConte, was visible to the north. I recalled a story I had heard of a hotel that could only be reached on foot way up on the top of Mount LeConte. It seemed like a backpacker's myth to me, like Eldorado, the City of Gold that the Spaniards sought as they explored the New World. Later, I found out that this myth was true. In 1926, a few years before the Smokies became a national park, a Tennessee man named Jack Huff actually built a lodge up on top of Mount LeConte, and that lodge still existed. In my imagination, that lodge was a place where Daisy Duke served Yukon Jack to grizzled mountain men as they told their stories and watched the sun set out beyond the distant mountaintops. They slept in soft beds covered with bearskin rugs, and I would go there when I was old.

Old Jack Huff could have told a few stories himself. After he started building his lodge on Mount LeConte, his mother wanted to see the place, but she couldn't climb the mountain to get there. Jack strapped a chair to his back and then strapped Mother Huff in the chair, and he carried her all way to the 6,593-foot top of the mountain. It must have been one hell of a ride.

I hiked on to the Silers Bald shelter. As soon as I got there, I wondered why I had listened to the ranger-ette. The place was a shithole, as all shelters were inside the park. I thought about bypassing it and going on to a regular campsite, but that meant another six or seven miles of hiking. I told myself that I was tired, but the truth was that I was not that eager to face a night all alone. Feeling a little less mountain-mannish, I unrolled my sleeping pad and my blanket on the top bunk inside the shelter. It was summer and I was on the AT, so I knew I would end up having company.

I was sitting under a tree writing the story of Mein Kampf in Gatlinburg when I saw a skinny guy with a big pack come straggling into camp. He plopped his pack down on the ground next to the shelter and announced, "Man, this sucks!" He looked really young, no more than twenty, and he was very tall. He had long hair parted on the side and wore a Pink Floyd "The Wall" T-shirt. When I saw the low-top sneakers on his feet, I figured he had to be a stoner out on his first hike in the mountains.

I knew I was opening the floodgate of complaints, but I asked, "What do you mean?"

"How could anybody think this was fun? I just climbed twenty-seven miles up this friggin' mountain, man, and this pack *sucks*!" He kicked his pack to emphasize his point. "And it's hot!"

Two more young guys walked into camp. They appeared to be in worse shape than the tall kid. One kid, just as skinny as the first but much shorter, had shoulder-length hair parted down the middle and a "Disco Sucks" T-shirt. The shirt was sadly outdated. Disco had died of an overdose years before. The third kid was all in black—black T-shirt, black shorts, even black hair.

The short one said, "Thanks for leavin' us, Rog. I didn't think we were gonna make it!"

154

The tall one, whose name was apparently Roger, answered the short one. "I know! This is fuckin' bogus, man!" The kid in black said nothing. He simply sat down in the dirt.

"If you go about a half-mile further down the trail," I suggested, "there's a pretty good view up on Silers Bald."

Roger looked down the trail doubtfully. "No way I'm walkin' another half mile, man. If it's on our way out, we'll see it tomorrow." Then he turned to Disco Sucks and asked, "You got any water, Hogger?"

"Not much. Get your own."

I had to ask. I looked at the Disco Sucks kid. "Your name is Hogger?"

Hogger and Roger cracked up, and the black-haired kid even smiled. "No, man, my name is Holgar. H-O-L-G-A-R. It's German. My dad was in the Air Force and I was born there, so they gave me a German name."

"But 'Hogger' is way better," Roger said, and he started laughing all over again.

The black-haired kid softly said "Hogger" and went back to scribbling in a notebook. He creeped me out.

I was very happy to see that they took the lower bunks farthest away from me. I saw Hogger pull a couple cans of pork and beans out of his pack. *No wonder they're struggling.* After they got their stuff put away, they went down to the spring to get water. I automatically assumed that they were going to burn a doob while they were there.

While the stoner trio was gone, a man and a woman walked into camp. I wasn't happy to see more people arriving, but the guy had a broad grin on his face as he walked up to me and said, "Hey, Buck! Heh heh heh!" He laughed as if he had just told me an especially raunchy joke, but all he had done was say hello.

"Hey, how's it going?" I answered. "You spending the night?"

"Yeah, if there's room at the inn. Heh heh heh." The woman had stayed a few yards back, waiting to see if I was going to attack or if I was civilized. She nodded to me shyly. It had to be difficult to be a woman in the man's world of the mountains.

"There's room. I'm by myself, but there are three other guys already here, too. They're down by the water."

"Well, that's good. The Lord provides. Heh heh." Then he stuck out his hand and said, "Name's Chris, and this is my wife Stephanie. We're hiking all the way through the Smokies."

"Across the AT, Lord willing," Stephanie added.

"Really?" I was impressed. "I know the AT a little bit. That's a long way." In spite of this guy's strange laugh, I kind of liked being called "Buck," and I saw the twinkle of crazy intelligence in his eyes.

"Seventy miles, Buck. This ain't our first rodeo," Chris said.

I looked at him with new interest. He was a smaller guy with a good-sized belly, probably in his mid to late thirties, but he was wide in the shoulders and well put together. He had huge calves. Stephanie looked to be in decent shape too, but she was certainly no tri-athlete. "So you started at Fontana Dam?" I asked.

It was Chris's turn to look at me with new interest. "So you know the AT, huh, Buck? Heh heh heh."

"My name's John. I've hiked some good chunks of the AT in the park. I ran out of water down around Thunderhead Mountain a couple years ago. That was rough."

"Well, we'll have to swap stories later, Buck." He totally ignored my name, but I liked Buck better anyway. "Maybe you'll say a prayer with us before dinner?"

Surprised, I said, "Yeah, maybe." Like a lot of people, I was leery of born-again types. I had no real reason to be. My family had gone to church, although we hadn't been overly zealous about it. People who talked about God and church and prayer simply made me nervous. I didn't need anybody bludgeoning me with their beliefs. The mountains were my church.

The three parties staying at the shelter remained separated at suppertime. Food was too precious in the mountains to be shared. I ate under my tree at the edge of the shelter clearing, and to my relief, Chris didn't ask me to do any praying.

The trio of young guys scrounged up some firewood and managed to get a fire going in the fire pit outside the shelter. Chris and Stephanie threw a couple armfuls of sticks on the wood pile and joined the guys around the fire. I was sipping Yukon from my coffee cup and watching the proceedings. *Three stoners, two born-again Christians, and me. This is going to be good.* I wanted to join the fun, but I had to contribute some wood to the effort. I took my flashlight into the woods and found a downed tree about three inches in diameter. I dragged it over to the fire, grunting as I wrestled it into the clearing.

"Hey, Buck, you need a hand? Heh heh heh."

Holgar asked me, "Aren't you worried about poison ivy or poison oak?"

"I've never had it, Hogger. I think I'm immune to it." I was going to use the name "Hogger" at every opportunity. The black-haired kid snickered again when I said it.

"You backpack a lot, Buck?" Chris was loading up a green stick with marshmallows to toast over the fire.

"Not as much as I'd like to. What about you? You probably hike all the time."

"We want to hike the entire AT, but we're gonna have to do it in sections. We can't afford to take six months off to hike straight through to Maine."

Roger looked confused. "This trail goes all the way to *Maine*?"

157

I looked at Roger. "You guys didn't know that?" Then I turned back to Chris. "What kind of work do you two do?"

"I'm a contractor. Kitchens and baths, mostly. Lot of painting, too."

Stephanie quietly said, "I work for a lawyer." She laughed a joyless laugh. "Been there since high school."

"Wow." I didn't know how to respond to that at all. It struck me as sad. Chris's story interested me more. "So Chris, you work for yourself then? It must be nice not to answer to anybody. Not to punch a clock."

"Only way to live, Buck! Heh heh heh. But I still have to work if I want to eat. Right, honey?"

Stephanie answered Chris with a quote from Genesis. "'By the sweat of your face you shall eat bread.'"

Chris responded with a Genesis quote of his own. "And 'Your desire shall be for your husband.' Heh heh heh." Stephanie smiled and elbowed Chris in the ribs, causing his marshmallow to momentarily dip into the flames. These two were different from any other born-again types I had ever met. They seemed more like real people. I wondered if the young guys even realized that Chris and Stephanie were quoting the Bible.

Roger said, "So how does this trail go across the highways and stuff?" Chris explained that sometimes the AT crossed over bridges, and sometimes the hikers just had to walk across the roads.

I decided to continue my survey and find out what kind of work Roger and his friends did. "Where do you work, Roger?"

Roger answered without looking away from the flames. "In Zanesville," he said absent-mindedly, and then added, "I work part-time at a gas station. It sucks. But my uncle's trying to get me in at Kraftmaid."

"That pays well?"

"It's union," he said, as if that explained everything. "My uncle gets twelve dollars an hour plus benefits." He said it as if that were a great deal of money. I had a union meat-cutting job that paid that much and I couldn't wait to get the hell out.

"What about you, Hogger?"

Chris pulled a blackened marshmallow away from his mouth and asked. "Why do you keep calling him 'Hogger', Buck?"

I took a sip from my cup. "I don't know. Why do you keep calling me 'Buck'?"

"Heh heh heh," was Chris's answer.

Holgar said, "I'm working for a roofer." Then he looked at Chris. "He's a contractor like you."

"That's hard work, Buck." I was vaguely jealous that Chris had called someone else Buck.

"No shit it is! I'm thinking about maybe joining the Air Force."

Roger sneered, "And get your ass shot." I'd never heard of airmen getting killed in great bunches like soldiers and marines, but I let that one go.

To everyone's surprise, the black-haired kid spoke up. In a quiet but clear voice, he said, "That still might be better than spending forty years in a cabinet factory."

The fact that he had finally spoken stopped the conversation in its tracks. After thinking for a few seconds, Roger shot back at the black-haired kid, "So what's your big plan, Ryan? Drawing pictures?"

The black-haired kid, Ryan, didn't answer. The rest of us sat there staring at the fire, feeling uncomfortable. Finally, Ryan got up and stormed into the shelter. He left the chain-link gate on the front wall of the shelter open as he went through, so Chris called out, "Hey, Ryan, close that gate for us, would you please? Don't need no bears in there. Heh heh."

"I'll get it," I said. Since I was there, I walked inside and fumbled around for the bottle inside my pack. I was trying to be discreet with my drinking since there were civilized people in camp. We were all keeping our packs inside the shelter to keep them away from the bears, who were probably at the edge of the woods going, "Heh heh heh."

I saw the dim shape of Ryan lying on his sleeping bag on the lower tier of bunks. "It's tough dealing with idiots," I said.

"Is that why you drink?"

"Maybe it is. You should try it." On an impulse, I handed the kid the open bottle. He took a swig of the 100 proof liqueur and coughed a little after it went down. "So you want to be an artist or something like that?"

"Yeah." He said the word defensively.

"Nothing wrong with having dreams."

"'Cept everyone is always telling me to forget it. That I can't do it."

I poured some Yukon into my plastic coffee cup. "The dirty little secret is that if you succeed, you make them face their own failures. And they don't want to do that."

"Why the fuck can't they just let me be different?"

"I just told you," I said curtly. "Different is bad. It's human nature, I guess." I took a sip from the cup and went on. "It's hard as hell escaping from the life you were born into. Hell, I'm almost thirty and I'm still trying. There's like this gravitational force that keeps pulling you back. But people do make it out."

"Those two never will." Ryan's head nodded toward his friends outside.

"No, you're probably right," I agreed. "*Most* people never will. But that doesn't make them bad people. Somebody has to stay in one place."

"And do the crappy jobs?"

"I don't know about that." I wasn't sure if I had done the kid any good or just added fuel to his resentment.

I moved toward the door and the black-haired kid muttered, "Thanks."

"For what?" I chuckled. "I just came in here to get a drink, man. Those people are cramping my style."

I rejoined the group sitting around the fire. Chris was putting the big end of the tree I had dragged into camp across the fire. He looked up at me. "What about you, Buck? What do you do?"

"Lots of things. I cut meat. I go to school." I laughed. "I try to stay out of jail."

Chris's voice took a more serious tone. "You find that hard to do, do you?"

I laughed again. "Last night I did!" The imp of the perverse took hold of me, and I decided to find out just how Christian these two really were. "I was in jail last night for public drunkenness, and I was guilty as sin. They let me out this morning, and I headed up here. This is the marrow of the world right here."

Holgar seemed delighted. "What'd you do, man?"

"I was just walking down the street, Hogger, minding my own business. I *was* staggering a little, I admit, but I wasn't bothering anyone."

Chris sat back down between me and Stephanie. "So you were hanging around in town by yourself getting drunk?"

"Yeah, I guess I was. No, actually I was with three women."

"Damn," Roger said, obviously impressed. I could have run for mayor of Zanesville, Ohio at that moment and gotten at least two votes.

Chris and Stephanie looked disgusted. Not horrified, as I had perversely hoped, but I could tell they never expected a story like this to come out of my mouth. Still, Chris wasn't intimidated in the least. "So you got drunk and ended up in jail last night, and tonight you're getting drunk again?"

I raised my cup. "It's been one hell of a vacation so far." I chugged the Yukon and got up to go get more. The cat was out of the bag and there was no use being discreet.

As I walked away from the fire, Chris said, "You got a problem, Buck. We'll pray for you."

"The problem is that there are too many damn laws in the world," I said, feeling rather mountain-mannish again after telling my jail story. "But that's fine! Thank you for your prayers. God knows I need them."

I went back into the shelter and into my pack and took another swig from my bottle, thinking of clever things I could say to Chris, but the exhaustion was catching up with me, and I was right there by my bunk, so I climbed up to the top tier and was out like a light.

I was alone in the shelter when I woke up. The others had all packed up and left without me hearing a thing. *I must've been exhausted.* I went into my pack to get out my breakfast and found a drawing of Holgar in an airplane shooting a vaguely phallic missile toward Roger's ass. The caricatures were excellent. The caption said, "Roger Gets Hoggered." I laughed out loud. *Good for you, Ryan. Maybe you'll make it out.*

I ate my oatmeal and enjoyed the quiet. Even in the relative silence of the mountains, there were still sounds to be heard. I listened to the whispering wind and the occasional calls of the birds. Down in the valleys, one would hear a running stream and the hum of the insects, but those were the only sounds, and they were serene. In the world below, though, people were constantly bombarded by noise. No wonder people went through their days anxious and agitated. They never heard what their true selves were trying to say.

Finding Mount Guyot

I packed up and headed south at a leisurely pace. I had all day to go a little over eight miles to the CCC camp, #71. The shagger ranger-ette had said something about the Civilian Conservation Corps, which explained the "CCC." That encounter seemed as if it had happened a long time ago, but it had been less than twenty-four hours. *A day is a long time in the woods. Time goes too fast at home.*

I walked along Welch Ridge and enjoyed the sunshine. I admired a hawk riding the air currents high above me until it glided away. I turned east down into the Forney Creek valley. There I studied the dark forest around me in way I never had before. *I have no one to meet, and the ancient empty street's too dead for dreamin'.* I studied the structure of the individual strands of moss within a carpet of moss and examined the gill-like walls on the undersides of some big mushrooms. I had no idea what purpose these things served. *If design govern in a thing so small.* I had seen such plants hundreds of times before, but I had been too stoned or too busy making Wild and Crazy Guy jokes to truly observe them. Being sober and observant was a rush all its own.

I came upon a wide, muddy spot in the trail that looked as if it had recently been raked up. Boars—wild boars—had been looking for whatever it was that boars ate. I dropped my pack and was bending down to study the tracks that the boars had left in the mud when I heard the leaves rustle behind me. A thunderbolt of fear shot through me. I spun around, not sure if I would see a big boar coming at me, but there was nothing there.

I relaxed a fraction, listening intently for the next sound. My hand went to my right hip, and I unsheathed my new weapon, a Forschner Swiss Victorinox butcher's knife with a razor-sharp ten-inch blade made from highest-quality stainless steel. *I whip out my big ten inch.* I had lifted the knife from work and crafted a custom leather sheath reinforced with brass rivets to carry it. The knife had a hard nylon grip and a wide, sharply-pointed blade, perfect for stabbing or slashing. It hung from my web belt, and I was glad it was there.

Another bolt of fear jolted me. A low snuffling sound came from the other side of a slight rise in the ground. The sound came again, a cross between a grunt and a snort, and I was certain that there was a boar over there, not far away from me. I had walked quietly into the clearing and had probably surprised the boar while it was eating lunch. *Rambo killed a boar with just a knife.* Part of me knew it was madness, but another part of me didn't know that at all. The blood was thudding in my ears and I was scared out of my mind, but I took a few stealthy steps toward the top of the rise. I heard the bushes rustle again

I inched forward. The bushes were thick near the top of the rise, but I tried to pass through them as quietly as I could. *If it comes at you, stab it in the heart. Heart of darkness.* I had never killed anything bigger than a perch in Lake Erie, but the blood lust was in me. I edged up over the rise with my big knife poised to stab and saw nothing but more brush. Then I heard it again, going away from me. I stayed near the top of the rise and moved in the same direction.

I peered through the bush and caught a glimpse of the hairy, brown hindquarter of a boar. Actually seeing the animal was enough to stop me in my tracks. The boar was retreating from me, exhibiting more sense than I had. My fleeting impression was that it was bigger, leaner, and meaner than I had imagined. The ass on this animal was nothing like Porky Pig's chubby, pink ass cheeks. Luckily, it hadn't shot me with any laser beams from its anus.

I retreated to the muddy clearing and my backpack. My hands trembled slightly as I lit a cigarette. Rationality returned, and I knew I was lucky that I hadn't caught up with the boar. The problem with listening to your true self was that sometimes your true self was an idiot. I still thought I probably could have taken the boar, but it definitely would have done some damage. Besides, what had that boar ever done to me?

Once I calmed down, I resumed my hike. The trail turned south and started following Forney Creek. I stopped to eat a snack for lunch in a shady spot overlooking the big creek and watched the white water thunder between the huge boulders below me. I ate my cheddar cheese crackers slowly because I didn't want to get to camp too soon and spend the whole afternoon and evening sitting in the same spot. Judging by the sun, it was only noon. I dawdled as much as I could and then hiked the rest of the way down along the creek to the old CCC camp.

I needed to make myself a shelter from the sheet of plastic I was carrying. I had planned ahead for this, bringing along some snap-together plastic grommets that would reinforce the holes I made in the plastic. The eight-by-eight sheet of plastic became a simple pup tent open on both ends. I used a couple of fairly straight branches for my tent poles, and I cut eight smaller sticks to use as pegs. The resulting structure was eight feet long and almost three feet high in the center. I didn't know if it would survive a real storm, but it would keep me reasonably dry if some rain came in during the night. I laid my foam pad and my wool blanket inside my shelter, and, be it ever so humble, it was home.

I had time to kill. I did all my routine camp chores meticulously, trying to fill up the minutes of the day. I smoked many, many cigarettes. Still the hours dragged. I hadn't been able to score any dope for the trip, but I hadn't tried very hard either. Deep down, I was tired of the drugs. All I had were some pharmaceutical pills that I had raided from my girlfriend's medicine chest. If I had any cramping or bloating problems, I was all set. I left the pills alone, and I didn't want to start drinking too soon either.

165

I kept my big knife at my side and watched the edges of the clearing. I kept expecting somebody or something to walk into camp, but no one did. It dawned on me that I hadn't seen a living soul from the moment I had woken up. I hadn't even passed anyone on the trail, and that was definitely odd in high summer. *One is the loneliest number.*

I ate my solitary supper, feeling like a cowboy alone on the range. *Grandpa used to stick two spoons in an open can of pork and beans and tell us that was how the cowboys ate. We loved it.*

Night started closing in, and I realized that nobody would be coming. Nobody but me and my buddy Jack. I got out my bottle and had the first drink of the day. *When I drink alone, I prefer to be by myself.* Back in the world, I never drank until evening when all my work was done, so it hadn't been any hardship to wait until night. But now the Yukon was calling. The problem was that I also heard Chris's voice echoing in my head, "You got a problem, Buck."

You're the one with the problem, man, judging people you don't know. I got no fuckin' problems. I'm in great shape and working on my master's. I don't give a fuck, got a heater in my truck, and I'm off to the rodeo.

I tended my fire, smoked a lot, and drank the Yukon sparingly. I kept my eyes on the darkening tree line until night fell. I was conscious of the fact that I was alone in the wilderness, but I wasn't as frightened as I'd thought I would be. Still, I took it easy on the booze. I watched the flickering flames and thought about the boar, the girls at the Electric Chalet, the night in jail, and being out in the mountains alone. I wondered what drove me to these things, and the only answer I could come up with was testosterone. *It's more than that, Johnny Rez. More than that.*

A few hours after nightfall, I could take the solitude no longer, so I decided to lie down. I had hoped to be able to see

166

the stars through the clear walls of my simple shelter, but the plastic was too opaque to see anything. I was warm enough with my single blanket, but I felt very vulnerable with just a thin sheet of plastic open on both ends covering me. I put my big, sheathed butcher knife under my head and kept one hand on it. I closed my eyes and said a few heartfelt prayers. Sleep wouldn't come easily. I lay there for a long time, hearing every sound in the living forest around me. I recalled my first few nights in these mountains when I imagined the worst after every creak and rustle and night cry that I heard.

Sometime in the night—I may finally have been dozing—I heard a distinct sound very close to me. Instantly, I was alert, yet I remained completely still. I didn't even open my eyes. My hand closed slowly around the handle of the big knife under me. Then an electric shock of adrenaline went through me ten times greater than anything I had ever felt before. Something was sniffing my head! It was only inches away, whatever it was. Instinctively, I kept my eyes shut. I fought to control my breathing, but my heart pounded wildly. I knew I was awake because the ground was hard beneath me. This was nightmarish, but deadly real.

The sniffing was at the back of my head. I couldn't tell if the creature doing the sniffing was large or small, but I knew it was close. *Oh my God.* Even a raccoon could tear my head up before I got the knife out. A bear could tear my face clean off in a heartbeat. The creature had to know I was alive by the sound of my breathing and the warmth of my body. Even opening my eyes could be enough to cause it to attack. *Play dead. Play dead. Oh dear God. Just play dead.*

Time stood still as I lay there perfectly still, listening to the sniffing sounds behind me, fearing for my very life. Over the sound of my own blood roaring in my ears, I heard the brushing sounds of the creature moving and its slight footsteps. Several lifetimes passed before I heard the thing start to move away from me, but it didn't go far. It only went as far as the other end of the pup tent, where it started sniffing my feet.

I still didn't dare move my body or my head, but I slowly, slowly opened my eyes. I found that I couldn't see a damned thing. I was lying on my side, and the bulk of my body and the walls of my shelter prevented me from seeing anything. I could only see the dark shapes of trees out in front of me and the blankness of the plastic sheet. This was living hell. *What do I do if it bites into me? Lie still, or fight? Have to fight at that point, Johnny.*

Eons of time passed while it sniffed at my feet. I was sweating and itching and my muscles were aching from staying so still, but I knew I might die if I moved. I stayed still as long as I could, even after I stopped hearing any sounds. I listened so hard that it got to the point where I couldn't tell if I was hearing sounds or just imagining them.

Finally, I slowly—oh so slowly—lifted my head enough to look up over my body. Another shot of adrenalin surged through me as I saw the silhouette of a bear about twenty yards away. I could see it through the opening at the far end of my shelter. It was moving away from me, and I watched it gradually disappear into the trees. *Thank you, dear God. Oh sweet Jesus, thank you, thank you, thank you.*

The adrenalin level in me dropped so quickly that I felt giddy. Suddenly, I wanted to laugh or scream or cry. I moved my legs and there was blessed relief in that, too. I crawled out of my covering with my big knife in my hand, watching the point in the trees where the bear had gone in. I scanned the tree line with my flashlight, expecting to see shiny eyes reflecting back at me, but I saw nothing. I had a smoke to steady my nerves. Then I had a long drink straight from the bottle. I couldn't believe it; I had been nose to nose with a bear, by God. My first close encounter with a bear, and it had been right on top of me. I broke down and sobbed a few times, expelling the raw fear.

I stirred up the embers and got a flame going. Then I threw on a few sticks and sat beside the fire. I kept my eyes on the tree line and had a couple of long drinks.

I woke the next day exhausted, but it didn't matter because I felt fortunate to be alive. I looked for bear tracks and found a few prints near my dishes and cookware. I couldn't tell for sure how big the bear had been, but even a medium-sized bear could easily have killed me. I had seen bigger tracks in the mountains many times, but those bears hadn't been up close and personal.

I put my cook pot in the red-hot embers from the fire and heated some water. If I counted the time I spent asleep at the shelter the night before, I hadn't seen anyone for thirty hours or more. Being alone was starting to play tricks with my mind. I wondered if something had happened in the world that I didn't know about. But this was the day I was going to climb Clingmans Dome and go back to civilization. I would know when I got to the top if the world was still intact. I had about ten miles to cover, and I would gain a little over 4,500 feet of elevation, almost one vertical mile. Every step was going to be uphill. With that thought in mind, I opened one more packet of oatmeal and forced myself to eat it.

I had learned my lesson on Thunderhead Mountain. The map showed no water where I was going, so I filled all my water containers before I headed up the Springhouse Branch Trail. The sun was already blazing through the trees, and the day's hike was going to be one of those where I simply had to grab my shoulder straps and become a walking machine.

I soon discovered that being in jail one night and being panty-raided by a bear two nights later took some of the starch out of a man. I struggled on the steady uphill grade. I stopped to rest and got out the pharmaceutical pills I had with me. I trudged along for a while with the bottle of pills in my hand, wondering if I should take them. *Why are you doing this, you asshole? 'Cause everybody must get stoned. Smoked a cigarette through a rotten green pepper to get high once, but it didn't work, did it?* I took a few of the pills and sang, "Valium would've helped that bash." My voice sounded strange in my ears.

The trail wound relentlessly upwards. My thoughts were a million miles away, and I had to remind myself that I was climbing the biggest mountain in Tennessee and the Smokies. The day was getting really hot, and I was sweating and churning my way up the Dome. *You're a two-hundred-pound Slovak tank, kid. Use your legs. Women weaken legs. Buns of steel. Shake your booty. Plundering booty. The bloody parrot's dead. No, he's pining for the fjords. Henry Fjord, who was friends with Thomas Vulva Edison, Alvin, and the rest of the chipmunks. I haven't even seen a chipmunk. They're all dead. Bring out your dead chipmunks. Chipmunks roasting by an open fire.*

Not a drop of rain on this trip. Just a bear. And a boar. A bare boar. We're going boaring, Chauncy, but I can't bear bores, old boy. Life, friends, is boring, although we may not say so. Suicide. The coward's way out. A mortal sin. Earl Morral. Did Broadway Joe beat him, or Johnny U? Johnny Yuma . . . was a rebel. He wandered alone. That's me—Johnny Yuma. Panther quick and leather tough. Uh huh. The rebel, Johnny Reznick. After four miles of uphill struggle, and under constant attack by savage Apaches, Johnny Rez reaches the top of Forney Ridge.

I climbed one ridge and found the beginning of the Forney Ridge Trail, which led six miles north to the top of Clingmans Dome. I was on the last leg of my trip, and still I hadn't seen a soul since the night at the shelter. Time was losing its meaning without anyone to share it with. I just walked and listened to the thoughts in my head as if I had a radio stuck in scanning mode. I was feeling the buzz in my body from the pills. I couldn't tell if my thoughts were strange, or if my mind worked this way all the time and I had never listened.

Solitary man. I'd have a hard time in prison. I'm too fine to go to jail. Shaggers. How you like me now, shagger ranger-ette? Little too smelly for you? Guys in prison don't even smell this bad. Nothing but a hobo bath for . . . how many days? Seems like a month. Let's do the time warp again. Pasties and a G-string, beer and a shot. Well, my time went so quickly. On the border. My God, your thoughts are weird when you really listen. Stop, children, what's that sound? Can't you hear me talkin' to ya?

I dimly perceived that the forest around me was gradually changing. The trail was becoming rockier too, and I hoped that I was nearing the end. Mentally and physically, I was spent. As if in answer to my prayers, the forest thinned out in front of me and the trail led me to an open, grassy area. As usual, there was no wooden sign marking the place. For a moment, I thought I had reached Clingmans Dome, but then I remembered that there was an observation platform on top of Clingmans Dome. I checked my map and saw that I was on Andrews Bald, a couple of miles south of Clingmans. I shed my pack and looked around. I was up at 6,000 feet, and the views were magnificent to the south. I never tired of looking at the endless, ageless ridges that imperceptibly changed from vivid green to dull purple. The purple of old church robes.

The sun was bright and the bald offered no shade, so I didn't linger. I was anxious to finally see the highest peak in the Smokies. I ignored my tired body and pushed on with grim purpose. The trail became rocky and steep again, but I knew I was close. I kept looking for a tower up above the trees ahead of me, yet I saw nothing.

171

Then I heard the sound of cars and voices, and a few steps later I saw the parking lot and the round, concrete tower at the other end of the lot. It was Wednesday afternoon, and these were the first people I had laid eyes on since Monday evening at the shelter. I trudged across the parking lot, feeling like some separate race. A mother pointed me out to her two small children as I walked by, and the kids gawked. These sunglass- and Bermuda short-wearing tourists were not like me. I needed them, I now realized, but I wasn't part of them.

I trudged up the ramp to the tower to see the views from the top, more than a mile and quarter above sea level. The tower was crowded and loud, and the people seemed to swarm all over each other like bees in a hive. They had driven up from Gatlinburg or Cherokee in their cars and Winnebagos. Some of them wore T-shirts that showed pictures of cuddly black bears. All they had done to earn this view was push a little harder on the gas pedal. I knew it was wrong, but I couldn't help but feel superior. I turned around and left after spending no more than a few minutes there.

I thought of some lines from Horace Kephart, the wasted librarian who had been reborn in the wilderness. In his book, he said that to a "thoroughbred camper . . . houses . . . are little better than cages; fences and walls are his abomination . . . It is not the clearing but the unfenced wilderness that is the camper's real home." I looked at the pitiful mass of humanity around me and their concrete monument to the mountains, and I understood what Kephart meant when he said, "I love the unimproved works of God."

6   Going to Mount Guyot: First Attempt

In 1990, Craig was suffering through a lengthy and debilitating bout of sobriety, the sad result of several crashes and a few drunken driving convictions. Being stuck without wheels, he had plenty of time to think about things, and one thing that bothered him was the idea that Dan had gone off trail when he hadn't. He never came out and said it, but it was true nonetheless. For my part, a few whiskey dents here and there hadn't slowed me down at all. I was still living in the fast lane and still ready for the Smokies anytime, so Craig and I decided to go that October and do some off trailing.

Studying the map, Craig and I found a place in the northeast quadrant of the park called the Ramsey Cascades Trail. On paper, it looked like another trail that extended into a big, empty area and just dead-ended. We consulted the bible, which said that the Ramsey Cascades Trail terminated at an impressive set of waterfalls located in a hidden hollow and warned that climbing on the rocks around the cascades was dangerous. But, in its typically cryptic and tantalizing fashion, the bible also mentioned that there were rumors of an old pioneer trail and a campsite above Ramsey Cascades, but that they no longer existed.

"They probably just don't want people going up there," I said. "It'll be like Bone Valley. All we have to do is follow the stream up past the falls to its source, and it'll lead us to the AT up here," I tapped the spot where the stream started very close to the AT, "by this mountain. Mount Guyot."

Craig leaned back from the map. "Mount Guyot," he said, savoring the sound of the word. "That's where we'll go."

"Weren't we there once?"

"No. That's where that guy with that kid that we gave the whiskey to was coming from. Remember? That kid that was turning blue?"

"That's right!" I recalled. "We saved that kid's ass that day."

"Whatever. But you're right. We were close to Mount Guyot that day."

"You know what my old man says? 'Close only counts in horseshoes and hand grenades'."

Craig clapped me on the shoulder. "Well, this time we get there—the top of Mount Guyot. The hard way."

We chose early October because it was the driest time of year in the Smokies, and we wanted to be able to climb right up the creek. We jumped into my new Toyota truck one October evening after work and drove through the night, doing line after line along the way. We didn't do blow often, but when we did, we did lots. Craig used a single-edged razor blade to chop the lines on a mirror while I drove. Craig had given up alcohol, but he still liked to party. With his newly straightened nose, he claimed he could snort twice as much.

We were tired yet wired when we pulled into a rest area on I-81 in eastern Tennessee at four in the morning. Our plan was to get a few hours' sleep in the truck and then head straight into the backcountry. We leaned our heads against our side windows and tried to get some rest airplane-style, but the cab of the truck was cramped and uncomfortable. We dozed as best we could. When the sun came up, we got back on the road and stopped at a very homey diner on the north side of Sevierville. It was going to be the last good meal for a while, so we each ordered two big breakfast specials. The waitress opened her mouth to make some remark about our order, but she looked at my bloodshot eyes and then at Craig's and changed her mind.

Inside the park, we stopped at the Greenbrier ranger station and wrote some nonsense on a backcountry permit. There were no campsites anywhere near where we were going, so it was hard to make up a trip itinerary that was even remotely plausible. The system had changed, and hikers no longer had to talk to a ranger in person or by phone to get a permit. We stuck the bottom copy of the permit in a drop box for the rangers to pick up later and beat it before we had to deal with any actual people. We would be up in the mountains before anyone would realize that the campsites listed on our permit were gibberish. Our real goal was simply to go up over the Cascades, follow the stream for two miles up to the AT, and then summit Mount Guyot. Then we would turn around and come back down the same way. We planned on two nights in the woods.

We drove for a few miles alongside a beautiful mountain stream called the Middle Prong of the Little Pigeon River, which started up near the Appalachian crest and flowed north out of the park. The river was wide and shallow and decorated with boulders and occasional rills of white water. When we stopped to take a leak, we could clearly see the big trout in the shallow pools near the banks. I was fascinated. "Isn't it

175

amazing the way they keep their noses pointing into the current all the time?"

"Yeah. Wow." Craig didn't share my fascination.

"Seems like they're just fighting all their lives to stay in the same place."

Craig smirked. "Is that the kind of bullshit you talk about in grad school?"

"Hey, they *pay* me talk about that kind of bullshit."

We got back in the truck and soon came to a fork in the road where a tributary called the Ramsey Prong entered the Middle Prong. The Ramsey Prong began up near Mount Guyot, dropped over the Ramsey Cascades, and flowed west until it met the Middle Prong. From the confluence of the two rivers, Mount Guyot was only about eight miles to the east as the crow flies. The Ramsey Prong was going to be our life line, the same way that Bone Valley Creek had been the life line for me and Dan. We turned east at the fork in the road, crossing the bigger river on a series of rickety wooden bridges. We took the gravel road that followed the Ramsey Prong east for two miles until it dead-ended at a little parking lot that was already crowded with cars.

"Lots of day hikers," I said. I was always disappointed that I had to share the mountains with other people, especially the candy-assed day hikers, who hiked up into the mountains for the day with no packs on their backs and then retreated to their motel rooms or campgrounds by nightfall.

"Doesn't matter," Craig said. "They're not going where we are."

We were already tired as we started up the Ramsey Cascades Trail with our heavy packs. The signpost told us we had four miles to go to get to the falls. Four miles didn't faze me much, but Craig hadn't had a pack on his back since 1979, eleven long years before. He started bitching as soon as the trail turned steep and rocky. "I forgot about this part. This is like fucking work, man!"

"You're just getting old, Craig. It's no different than it was ten years ago."

"It's not the years, John, it's the mileage."

"'Pain is temporary. Pride is forever.' I saw that on a T-shirt somewhere."

A little while later, Craig stopped to give his bony collarbones a respite from the hated shoulder straps. I was surprised that he had stopped so soon. "C'mon, I can still see the parking lot!"

"I don't care," he growled. He was hurting, so I didn't press him too much.

As we took our break, two squat, middle-aged women with short hair and flannel shirts passed us. I nodded to them as they passed. As soon as they were out of earshot, I whispered, "Even the old lesbians are passing us, man! It's shameful. It really is."

We resumed walking, and we passed the same women, thus recovering our dignity. The trail climbed steadily into the Smoky highlands alongside the fast-flowing Ramsey Prong. The leaves were still on the trees, but they had started to turn. The sunlight had that mellow October feeling, the air was pleasantly cool, and it was a perfect autumn day to be out in the mountains.

The last mile or so was tough. As Craig struggled, he fixated on the day hikers that we occasionally saw on the trail. They seemed to flit and frolic around us as we plodded upward like burros. Craig gestured toward a young couple with little, lunchbox-sized packs on their backs. "That's the way to do it!"

I couldn't resist. I sang, "We got to move these refrigerators," but Craig wasn't amused.

We felt Ramsey Cascades well before we saw it. The air grew cooler and the sound of pounding white water deepened as we drew closer. When we finally saw the falls, it was taller and wider than I expected. Most backcountry waterfalls that I had seen in the East were spindly little splashes of water a few feet across. This waterfall, the biggest in the Smokies, was different. The ledge where the water first dropped off was thirty or forty feet wide, and the water fell in large plumes that plummeted a good distance before they crashed into the succeeding tiers of rock. The water cascaded over four or five of these tiers before it joined the tumble of white water sixty feet below the ledge. Even with the water level low as it was in October, Ramsey Cascades was an impressive sight. After a big rain, it would truly be magnificent.

Ramsey Cascades was evidently a popular destination for day hikers because there were eight of them at the bottom of the falls, and eight was a veritable crowd in the backcountry. Craig and I sat down and had a snack and tried to decide how we should handle the situation. Our first problem was a big sign warning us that "Climbing On The Rocks Or Above The Falls Is Prohibited." We weren't shy about breaking the rules, but we didn't like to have so many witnesses around when we did it. We waited half an hour for everyone to leave, but as soon as one group left, another group took their place. We couldn't wait forever, so we decided that we'd have to go up no matter who was there to see it.

Our other problem was how to get up on top of the Cascades. The trail had put us on the north bank at the bottom of the falls, and there was no chance of crossing to the other side because the water was too deep and wild. The escarpment on the south side of the falls was almost a vertical cliff anyway. Our only option was to climb the steep and heavily overgrown rocks on the north side of the falls. In full view of God and everyone, we strapped our packs on tight and headed up. We heard the excited murmur of voices behind us as the day hikers realized what we were about to do, but no one said anything to us, proving, in my mind at least, that they were indeed candy-asses.

"Wow," I said. "One time in Germany, I was standing on a corner with a bunch of Germans, waiting to cross the street. I was in a hurry because I was late, so I crossed before the light changed. I could hear the Germans whispering behind me, like those people back there," I laughed. "They were shocked that somebody could break the law like that." I shook my head, remembering how regimented the Germans could be. "They have this thing about mindless obedience to arbitrary rules. After that, I always felt like I understood how they could have followed Hitler."

"So you'd call stopping for traffic lights an 'arbitrary' rule?"

"You know what I mean." It was just like Craig to pick out the one tiny flaw in my argument that wouldn't bear scrutiny.

We headed up quickly, afraid that a ranger might come along at exactly the wrong moment and ruin our whole plan. We were soon doing some serious rock climbing with forty-pound packs on our backs. On some of the biggest boulders, I had to boost Craig up, and once he got on top of the rock he would reach a long arm down to help pull me up. Other times, we had to take our packs off to squeeze between the rocks. At one point, we had to get down on our bellies to snake through a tight chute under a massive boulder. Craig stopped complaining and lost himself in the challenge of getting to the top. It had taken him a while, but he was back in mountain-man mode.

When we got to the top, we were sweating and scraped up and dirty, but what we found made us forget all that. The Ramsey Prong flowed wide and shallow just a few yards to our right, so shallow that the bedrock of the creek bed stuck up above the water level in many spots. This exposed bedrock made it easy for us to walk out to the very middle of the stream. We were only a few feet back from the edge of the

Cascades, but we were safe on the dry rock. We looked down and saw the hikers at the bottom looking up at us. To them it must have appeared as if we were standing in the white water itself. They took pictures of us, and I waved back.

Craig wasn't waving. He was looking out to the west, straight out at the far horizon. I followed his gaze and realized that we could see a long, long way from where we were, all the way out to where the mountains ended and the Tennessee landscape flattened out. The October sun hung in the middle of the scene, already past its zenith. Craig spoke reverentially, "I almost forgot why we come here."

Standing on the very edge of the Cascades was a moment that few ever have the privilege to enjoy, but it scared me just the same, and I couldn't take it for too long. I headed back to the north bank of the creek and had a seat on a rock. After another minute, Craig followed me back to safer ground. I lit up a well-deserved Camel. "Well, we should try to get upstream a little and make a camp," I suggested.

Up to that point, all our attention had been focused downstream. Craig surveyed the ground upstream going toward Mount Guyot for the first time and whistled softly.

"Yeah," I said, knowing what we had ahead of us. "Not easy."

The ground around us was damn near impassible. We were smack in the middle of a river gorge. The slopes rose up on both sides of the creek so steeply that one would have to go on all fours to climb them. The creek bed had been washed away to bedrock at the edge of the escarpment, but that soon gave way to a wild jumble of huge boulders and gigantic splinters of dead trees farther upstream.

Everywhere except in the creek bed, five- to ten-foot-high bushes densely covered the ground. Some of them, we would soon find out, were thorny greenbrier—what we called "pricker bushes" as kids. But the majority of the brush was mountain laurel, which seemed pretty benign at first. Mountain laurel looked like an average, leafy shrub with small leaves and lots of thin branches. The laurel grew like crazy in the Smokies. And like the rhododendron, the laurel could grow so dense that it was damn near impossible to fight through.

The other noteworthy feature up on top of the Ramsey Cascades was an entire forest of towering dead trees. I had seen swaths of dead trees before in the Smokies, but never so closely. There were hundreds, or maybe thousands, of fully mature but stone-dead trees on both sides of the gorge. We didn't know what kinds of trees they were or if they had died from acid rain or from insects or disease, but they stood as silent testimony to how quickly a forest could be wiped out.

We scouted around on both banks for any sign of the pioneer trail that the bible hinted at, but we found nothing except mountain laurel and prickers. We were both woozy from a lack of decent rest, and we quickly grew discouraged. Craig said, "What was it Vince Lombardi said, John? 'Fatigue makes us all sissies'?"

I suppressed a laugh. "Yeah, something like that. Why?"

"'Cause I think we should just look for a spot to make camp here tonight and start fresh in the morning. We only have to go two miles there and two miles back tomorrow. It's not like we need to get half way there today." I readily agreed, although Vince Lombardi might not have.

The slope was so steep and the bush was so dense that neither of us could find a six-by-six area level enough to pitch a tent. I finally found a little spot on the south bank just ten feet back from the water and thirty or forty feet upstream from the edge of the falls. We cut away as much of the small brush as we could and pitched the tent there. The bedrock was so close beneath the surface that we couldn't put the tent pegs more than a few inches into the soil. We worked like zombies as we set up camp. Craig fell back into the rhythm of camp life without missing a beat even though he hadn't done any of these chores in over a decade.

A few times, we peeked over the edge of the Cascades and saw people below, but they were on a different plane of existence from the one we now inhabited. We were only separated from them by a sixty-foot waterfall, but we were outside the grasp of their society and its myriad regulations and conventions. We were in that mountain-man place where there were no laws for the brave ones. Until we climbed back down, the only laws we were subject to were the laws of nature and the laws of God.

We made ourselves some supper, and we took our plates out to the very edge of the falls and sat on the dry bedrock of the stream as we ate. The food and the service were lousy, but the view was magnificent. I noticed that the sun was about to dip below a long line of dark clouds on the western horizon. "Those look like rain clouds to you?" I asked.

Craig shielded his eyes and studied the horizon. "Looks like a big-ass storm to me," he concluded. A long, pregnant pause ensued as it seeped into both of our sleep-deprived brains that we were in a really bad place if it rained very much. "Not good," Craig deadpanned.

"No. Not good at all. And it's too late to go back down."

"We might get back down over the falls, but we'd never get back to your truck. We'd be stuck on that trail in the dark in the middle of the storm."

"That still might be better than being up here in the middle of a storm." I studied the clouds again and it seemed to me that they looked a tiny bit closer. "We should move our stuff up to higher ground right now."

Craig leisurely lit an after-dinner smoke as if he were an investment banker in a five-star restaurant. He exhaled a huge billow of smoke. "There's nowhere to go up there. And we're not even sure that the storm's gonna hit us. It could blow right over."

Being from the Great Lakes region, we knew that big summer storms sometimes passed overhead without a single drop of rain falling. But more often, storms like this dropped lots of drops. "And it could just as easily wash us right over the fucking falls," I replied.

Craig corrected me. "The *cascades*, you mean. It could wash us over the *cascades*."

"I need a drink." I got up and went over to my pack and got out a fresh bottle of Yukon. I showed it to Craig. "Let me introduce my date for the evening."

Craig was on the wagon, so he studiously ignored the bottle. "Let's keep an eye on it, and if it starts raining hard, we'll move up to higher ground." We were both tired, and Craig's idea meant we didn't have to move, so that is exactly what we did. We stayed put and watched the storm roll in from far away. Somewhere in football heaven, Vince Lombardi chuckled softly.

The sun setting through the storm clouds created a surreal sunset, and we had the best seat in the state of Tennessee to watch it. We did a few lines and I had a few drinks, but we had a huge sword of Damocles hanging over our heads, so we were mostly quiet. The constant crashing of the cascades provided a thunderous and ominous soundtrack. The storm front didn't dissipate, and it didn't change course. The clouds moved inexorably closer. Now we truly could see them looming closer minute by minute. As it grew darker behind us up on Mount Guyot, the wind started blowing harder. The dead trees above started swaying and creaking threateningly.

Craig and I wrapped everything we could in double and triple layers of plastic. The coke was encased in five or six waterproof layers and put away. We put the other essential things—flashlights, cigarettes, maps, and compasses—in ziplock bags right next to our sleeping bags. If we had to bail out and head for high ground in the middle of the night, at least we would have these basic survival tools. I used my spare bootlaces to tie the corners of the tent to some cut-off laurel roots.

After we'd done everything we could think of to prepare ourselves for the coming storm, I told Craig, "If I'm gonna die, I might as well have a few good drinks in me." I took a belt of Yukon and said, "What we need is a fire."

"Just what I was thinking," Craig said sarcastically. "What we really need is some sturdy shelter." Something in the tone of his voice made me look at him. Craig was stoic by nature, but I could easily see the worry on his face. He sat with his back up against a big dead tree, alternately watching the trees above us and the storm front bearing down on us.

I stacked a few dry twigs in a depression ringed by the roots of a tree and coaxed some flames to life. I fed my little fire and hit the Yukon hard. We both smoked a lot of cigarettes. The dead trees above us swayed like drunks on honky-tonk barstools.

"I don't know which is worse," I said, "waiting for a big tree to come down on my head or for a flash flood to sweep me over the falls. This is fucked up, Craig."

Craig sighed heavily. "I know. But there's nothing we can do right now. Just be ready to head uphill fast."

"And say your prayers," I added. I had been saying silent prayers ever since the wind kicked up, even though I was busy getting drunk. After the close calls I'd experienced on my last few backpacking trips, I was beginning to suspect that maybe there was Somebody up there watching over me after all.

The rain started coming down in big, sporadic drops. The wind kicked up another notch, and the dead trees above us creaked as if they were being torn apart. It seemed impossible that not one of them had fallen yet or lost a major limb. I was as afraid for my life as I'd ever been. When the bear sniffed my head on Clingmans Dome, it had happened suddenly and had been over relatively quickly. On this horrible night, the danger grew relentlessly hour by hour.

"I know this is going to sound stupid to you," I said, "but I don't care. If I don't make it and you do, tell Maria . . ."

Maria was my on-again/off-again girlfriend, and my conscience was weighing on me in this moment of duress. I hadn't treated as well as I might have. What could I possibly say to her?

"Tell her that I never meant to hurt her." I knew how silly and melodramatic it sounded to a guy like Craig, but I wanted to get it off my chest. Craig didn't say anything. Maybe he even fought back a laugh, but it didn't matter. Not in a forest of swaying dead trees on the edge of a big waterfall with a terrible storm about to hit. He could laugh all he wanted.

The rain started coming faster. A little rivulet of water trickled down the hillside and ran right through my fire pit. The fire died with a hiss, and we were left sitting in the dark. It was a sorry little camp we had as we climbed into the tent to weather the storm. At least I had the Yukon. One of the good things about booze is that it allows you to fall asleep in situations where you normally wouldn't sleep a wink. I laid my head down on my sleeping bag with the rain drumming madly against the tent and the dead trees shrieking like lost souls.

Sometime in the night, Craig shook my shoulder and woke me. "John! We gotta go!"

I was alert in a second in spite of the booze. Craig had his flashlight lit, and I saw that the tent was full of water. The same rivulet that had put out my fire was now flowing through the door of our tent. The water was collecting in the back end of the tent and was already three inches deep. We had both kept our boots on, so all we had to do was grab our emergency bags and our sleeping bags and scramble out.

The weather was fantastic. Constant lightning flashes illuminated the scene around us. To my amazement, I saw strobe-light images of Ramsey Prong seething only two feet from the back side of our tent where my head had been a minute before. The wind howled in frenzied gusts, and the rain came at us in sheets. We could hear the dead trees whipping to and fro overhead. Craig pointed straight uphill. "Let's go!" he yelled above the noise.

"Wait a minute!" I reached under the tent with my free hand and tried to tug the plastic ground cloth out. The weight of the water in the tent held the plastic in place, but Craig saw what I was doing and lent a hand. Together we managed to drag the plastic out. I balled up the muddy sheet and brought it with me while Craig carried both emergency bags. We left our sleeping bags with our packs. That stuff wasn't important. We were racing to avoid being swept over the falls.

We plowed uphill in a straight line, not caring what was in our way. We crashed through the prickers and laurels that had stopped us dead the previous afternoon. We stumbled upward in the darkness, falling over deadfalls and rocks, banging into trees and the ground itself with our knees and our shoulders. All we knew for sure was that we had to get away from the rising creek. We only made it thirty or forty feet up the hill, but we gained a good bit of elevation. We stopped on the steep hillside and looked downhill toward the sound of the roaring water. It was hard to see anything clearly, but Ramsey Prong didn't seem to be any immediate threat to us where we stood.

I yelled in Craig's ear, "Cut it a little close, didn't you?"

He yelled back, "I had no idea the water was that high!"

"Let's find somewhere to sit!"

The best place we could find was a fallen tree that had taken some smaller trees down with it as it fell. We had to wedge ourselves inside a tangle of limbs and small branches, but we found a big limb that we could rest our asses on. It was better than sitting on the wet ground, but not by much. We threw the ground cloth over us even though we were already soaked to the skin.

Craig tried to light a smoke with his wet Bic lighter. The cigarettes had been in his emergency bag but the lighter had not. "Think this whole valley could get washed out? Like a flash flood?" he asked. Craig had never been west of Chicago, which made me, by default, the expert on flash flooding.

I was hoping fervently that Craig would get the cigarette lit. "I think flash floods happen more out West, like in canyons."

"No shit! I'm trying to figure out if we're safe here for a while."

I laughed mirthlessly. "We're a long way from safe."

The cigarette between Craig's lips was already soggy, and the lighter wasn't sparking. He let the cigarette drop out of his mouth and fall between his legs. "You know what I mean," he said disgustedly.

We never considered going farther up the hillside. We settled down inside the deadfall and tried to survive the night. We discovered another big limb behind us that we could rest our backs against. Eventually, our butts slid off the bottom limb into a soggy little trench. We sat with our backs against one branch and our knees supported by the other, as if we were in some ass-soaking, swamp-style Lazy Boy.

Misery and fear filled the long night. We shivered uncontrollably. Craig and I fidgeted and shifted, trying futilely to get warmer and more comfortable. The whole time, I still expected to hear the sharp crack of wood breaking and then the sound of a huge limb hurtling down through the canopy of smaller branches to land squarely on my head. Either that or a massive wall of water broadsiding me and driving me over a sixty-foot waterfall in less than a second. Before long, we were huddled against each other, trying to keep from shivering. As bad as the night was, it would have been a hundred times worse alone.

For the second night in a row, we dozed as best we could. I only slept a few minutes at a time. Every time I shifted my weight, the cold water under me seeped into a part of my wet pants that had finally gotten warm. Each time I awoke, I opened my eyes to the gray nothingness of the plastic that enveloped us like a shroud. The thousandth time I opened my eyes, I imagined that the plastic looked a tiny bit lighter. For the next hour or more, I willed it to be dawn. I never wanted so badly for a night to end. When I was finally certain that the sky was lightening, I pulled the plastic away from my head to look up through the trees.

The sky was low and gray and ugly and still dark in the west, but it looked beautiful to me. I was truly happy to have survived the night. I was surprised to find myself hip to hip and shoulder to shoulder with Craig. He stirred, so I turned to look at him. Craig opened his eyes and saw my bleary face an inch from his. "Get the fuck off me," he said, but I could tell that he was relieved to see the dawn as well. We dragged ourselves out of the deadfall and stretched our tortured backs. Rain still fell lightly, but we didn't care. I went to work trying to get a cigarette lit with my white, wrinkled fingers. I had kept my emergency bag sealed all night, knowing we would need a lighter and cigarettes and a map in the morning.

Craig went part way down the hill to look at our tent and the creek. He yelled to me to come down and look. When I got to where I could see, I couldn't believe how big Ramsey Prong had gotten. It had become a raging white-water torrent, boiling madly through the boulders and broken trees. It seemed impossible that we had been sitting in the middle of that creek eating our supper just twelve hours before. Our tent was gone. The water had risen enough to sweep it over the falls.

"Rick's never gonna believe how we lost his tent, " I whispered in awe. We had been using Rick's ancient tent, the veteran of almost all our trips to the Smokies, but now it belonged to the ages, or to some hillbillies farther down river.

Craig was shocked at the size and the ferocity of the water too. "Who cares?" he said. "That could have been *us* going over the edge."

I looked at Craig's grim face. "You saved my ass, man. Thank you." I meant it sincerely.

"I didn't sleep a wink, John. I was just laying there listening to the water. When it started getting deep inside the tent, I knew we had to go."

"I might've gone over the edge with the tent if you hadn't woken me up."

Craig wanted to dismiss the whole thing. "*Might* have," was all he said. He was right. The rising water would probably have woken me up, but there was still that "probably" there.

We had more pressing concerns. I looked over at the far side of the creek. "How the hell are we going to get back across?"

Neither one of us had a good answer to that question. Ramsey Prong was now twenty or more feet wide and who knew how deep. But the speed of the rushing water was the real obstacle. Even without a sixty-foot waterfall a few yards downstream, the creek was still a killer. The Cascades only ensured that you would die more quickly if you tried it. Wading across was simply not possible. I knew from experience that the power of the water would blast any man off his feet in a heartbeat. And rock hopping across would be like playing Russian roulette. The rocks were slick with rain, and the few that were showing through the white water were spaced far apart. One slip would take you on the last ride of your life.

"Maybe there's a better place upstream," Craig suggested.

I looked upstream at the dense thicket of laurel and prickers. I had no heart for fighting through that stuff. I needed coffee, food, and warmth. And a smoke. Fatigue, exposure, and Yukon Jack were making a coward of me. "Maybe we should stay on this side and cross over somewhere down below," I said half-heartedly.

My idea was stupid. If we tried to go down around the south side of the falls, we'd be descending a sheer cliff, and if we got past that, there would be no trail at the bottom. Craig ignored me and said, "I'm gonna look for a better place to cross up there." He headed upstream, working his way through the wet undergrowth along the south side of the creek.

I stood there ashamed of my momentary weakness yet unable to rouse myself to action. I longed for a big cup of steaming coffee. That would get my mind right. Surely that was not too much to ask on this, which was likely to be the last day of my life. I looked around for our food bag containing the instant coffee, but it was nowhere to be found. Then I remembered hanging the bag in a tree—on the other side of the creek. I looked across the roiling white water and saw our food bag looking lonely and abandoned.

I was wringing out our soaked sleeping bags when Craig came back from doing some real scouting. He was excited. "There's a big, wide log across the river about fifty yards up!"

"Good," I said absently. "The coffee's on the other side."

It rained lightly as we packed up our drenched packs. Neither one of us had anything edible in our packs, so we went hungry. Our packs weighed about a thousand pounds when we put them on. As we left, I looked back and said a silent goodbye to the camp from hell. More hell awaited just around the bend.

We bulled our way along the bank and found the log Craig had seen. The log was huge, and it had fallen in just the right position for our purposes. The root system was on our side of the creek with the trunk angling slightly downhill all the way to the other bank. The trunk was probably three feet or more in diameter, easily big enough and solid enough to hold our weight. All the bark was gone off the big log, which meant that it had been lying over the creek for some time. I shrugged off my pack and climbed up on our end of the tree. The smooth, wet wood was slick even though the rain had momentarily stopped. I carefully bounced up and down a little to test how solid it was.

Craig said, "OK, MacGyver, how are we gonna do this?" I had acquired the MacGyver nickname one night when I fashioned some dice for a drinking game out of tin foil and masking tape.

The reality of crossing the killer torrent with a big waterfall less than a football field downstream got my nervous system working again. Crossing this log was going to be as serious as a heart attack. A major "hydraulic," a concentrated funnel of white water, was in the middle of the creek a few feet downstream from the log. The water on either side of the hydraulic was easily strong enough to sweep a man over the falls, but if you went into that hydraulic, the force of the water would pin you down, drive the breath out of you, and kill you within seconds.

Two days before, I had been a meat cutter and a grad student worried about getting my hours in and writing my term papers. Now I was fighting for my life in a primeval mountain forest, and the world beyond the creek disappeared. Life was ground down to its diamond-hard essence—live or die—and Craig and I were reduced to our diamond-hard essences as well. I studied the situation for a long moment.

When I spoke, I had the whole thing worked out in my head. "There's no way I want to walk across that log with my pack on. Not even with my pack *off*."

"Good." Craig was with me on that.

"So what we should do is send one guy across the log, crawling on his belly with a rope around his waist, and tie the other end of the rope to a tree on this side, so if he goes in, the other guy can pull him out."

"There's no way you're pulling me out if I go into that hydraulic. I don't care how strong you are."

I raised an eyebrow. "So you're going first?"

Craig smiled a gallows smile. "Yep."

"I knew you would. OK, listen. When you get to the other side, tie off your end of the rope real tight on a tree. Then, I'll slide the packs over to you. You'll be lower over there than I am over here, so the packs should slide alright. Once we get the packs across, I'll go."

Craig clapped me on the back. "MacGyver!"

I wasn't so sure. "Yeah, if the rope can hold the packs up out of the water."

Craig prepared to crawl across the log. He twisted his belt around so the buckle wasn't by his belly, and he tied one end of the rope around his waist with several stout knots. We had plenty of rope, but we had no idea if that rope was sturdy enough to hold a 200-pound man. I tied the other end of the rope securely to one of the big exposed roots of the tree. When I turned around, Craig had managed to get a cigarette lit. He sat on the log, looking grim as death. He said, "If I go in, this rope isn't gonna do anything except hold me under."

I suspected that he was right, but I didn't want to say so. I shrugged. "So take it off. Just hold onto it."

He took a long drag and exhaled very slowly. "It isn't gonna matter either way."

I wasn't sure what that meant, and I didn't ask. Craig flipped his cigarette into Ramsey Prong and watched it speed away toward the Cascades. He said, "OK," and he turned his body toward the water, hugged the tree tight, and started across. I played out the rope as he went, leaving as little slack as possible. If he went in, I was going to try my damnedest to pull him out.

Craig's long arms reached half way around the log. His body slanted downhill, which looked awkward. He inched along, pushing himself forward with his knees and keeping his arms in full contact with the log at all times. Craig's head was plastered to the top of the log, and I could tell that he couldn't see anything except the log itself and peripheral glimpses of the roaring water. The actual width of the creek was maybe twenty feet, but the distance he had to crawl was closer to forty.

I yelled, "You're still over the bank," to let him know where he was.

"Shut the fuck up, John," I heard him say quite distinctly. *Fitting last words if he goes in.*

With maddening slowness, Craig worked his way across the creek. A little past half way, he stopped and rested for a few seconds, but otherwise he kept moving. When I was sure that he was past the water and above the bank on the other side, I yelled again, "You're past the water now!" He dared to raise his head a little to see where he was. He crawled a few more feet and then sat up, straddling the log. He dropped his head and slumped forward as if to drain the pent-up tension out of his body. Then he climbed off the log gingerly and set foot back on terra firma. He cupped his hands and yelled, "Piece of cake!"

While Craig collected himself, I untied my end of the rope from the roots of the big tree and threaded the rope through the metal frame of Craig's pack. Then I re-tied my end of the rope as high up in a nearby tree as possible, about eight or nine feet off the ground.

Craig pulled his end of the rope as tight as he could and tied it off to a tree on his side. When he was ready, I let go of the pack. To my surprise, the pack actually slid along the rope for about ten feet, but then it stopped dead. The angle wasn't great enough, and the rope wasn't tight enough. The pack stopped a few feet out over the water on my side.

"Push it!" Craig yelled.

I found a fairly straight branch about eight feet long, and I went as close to the water's edge as I dared and pushed the pack out as far as I could. Now the pack was smack dab over the creek.

Craig found himself a long branch with a natural hook on the end of it and managed to snag the pack. Even with his reach, he barely made it. Once he hooked the pack, though, he was able to draw it in. Before we transferred the second pack, we re-tied the rope a little tighter, and then we repeated the whole laborious process.

Then it started raining again, making the smooth log even slicker. I turned my face up to the rain and smiled a little, knowing this was a moment I would remember as long as life lasted. I made the same preparations Craig had made, having a few last drags and trying to get my nerve up. I stalled, hoping the rain would stop, but Craig yelled, "You might as well go before it gets worse!"

That convinced me to move. I sat down on the log and made the sign of the cross. I was finding religion fast on this trip. I hugged the log and loved it more than any tree-hugger had ever loved a tree. I inched forward the same way Craig had. I was correct in that it felt very unnatural to be tilted downhill. My center of gravity was up by my shoulders instead of down by my hips, and if I leaned my torso just an inch too far to either side, I'd slide off the log. Still, I had done similar things on Army obstacle courses. But at Fort Jackson, the drill sergeants had placed nice safety nets underneath the obstacles for their snail-shit trainees. There was no safety net here. If I slid off now, I was going to drown.

A thought came unbidden into my head. *This is a good day to die.* Supposedly, this was Crazy Horse's war cry at the Battle of Little Big Horn, Custer's last stand. The first time I heard the quote, I instinctively knew what Crazy Horse had meant. Better to die on your feet under God's sky doing something you love—something that matters to you—than to slip away in some bed, old and decrepit, after having merely existed.

I felt the cold, wet smoothness of the log and kept my cheek pressed against it. I inched over a big, rough knot on the top of the log, and it could have ripped my nuts right off my body for all I cared. I kept right on hugging. The violent sound of the roaring white water was huge in my ears. I was only eight feet from the surface of the water, and the maelstrom was all around me. The sheer, unfeeling power of Nature was overwhelming. The challenge was as much mental as physical. I had to fight to keep my focus, not to be engulfed by the unstoppable, destructive force all around me. Was this *my* good day to die? Was that why I kept coming here? To go out in a blaze of glory?

No. I desperately wanted to live. I kept myself centered and inched along. Craig's voice sounded close, and I looked up to see that he was only six feet away. I crawled the last few yards quickly, and Craig helped me down. "Welcome back," he said.

"It's nice to be here."

We still had to crawl and shimmy down through the rocks on the north side of the Cascades to get back to the trail. We were covered with mud from head to toe after we got done with that, but it seemed easy in comparison to crossing the log over the furious white water. When we got back to the

"Climbing On The Rocks Or Above The Falls Is Prohibited" sign, we finally had a good view of the swollen Cascades. The falls were wider across now and the wall of water pounding down was ten times thicker than it had been the day before. The creek below the Cascade was a wicked cauldron of seething water.

Craig looked at Ramsey Cascades and stated the obvious. "We'd a been dead in a heartbeat!"

I took off my pack and dug out my bottle of Yukon. "This definitely calls for a drink." I raised the bottle toward the falls and said, "To Ramsey Cascades. You win." I took a good slug of the sweet whiskey—the taste borne of hoary nights. Without thinking, I offered the bottle to Craig.

He shook his head slightly. He got out his canteen instead and raised it to the falls. "To Mount Guyot. You haven't won yet," he said, and took a long drink.

As I was putting away my bottle, Craig said, "If there was ever a time to drink, this would have been it."

"I'm glad you didn't, man. I would've felt terrible." I regretted being so thoughtless. I was impressed by the strength it must have taken for Craig to say no, but I didn't tell him so.

We hiked the rest of the way out like dead men walking. With the adrenalin rush of danger gone, the toll of two sleepless nights caught up with us. We found a flea-bag motel just outside the park in Cosby, Tennessee. This room wasn't even up to Dewey Ogle's modest standards, but we didn't care. We threw our wet, muddy gear in the corners of the room, showered, and fell into exhausted sleep on our beds. I dreamed that I rode a horse on a barren plain under a big sky.

Around sunset, we woke up feeling much better. We went out and got a big, greasy meal at the only diner in town. We still had a bunch of blow back at the room, so after supper we went back and did some serious lines. I was sitting on my saggy bed, thumbing through Rick's bible and looking for a hike we could do the next day. Craig was half-watching *The Cosby Show*. We had checked, but *The Dukes of Hazzard* wasn't on.

I nearly shouted, "This is it, Craig!" and stabbed my finger at the paragraph I was reading. "This is what we have to do! Porters Creek. This says it's the most challenging and treacherous trail in the Smokies! It's only for strong, tested hikers, and even they shouldn't try to go down it. It gains two thousand vertical feet in the final mile! Oh, we're going!" I exclaimed.

Craig grabbed the book from me and started reading. I fixed myself another Yukon on the rocks. At least the motel's ice machine worked. Craig read little bits of information aloud. "Almost six miles each way, but the bottom four miles are easy. Then it goes up to the AT." He looked at me. "What's a 'cairn'? It says to look for a cairn."

As an English major, I was expected to know all words in the English language and to have read every book ever written. "I have no clue."

"Then how are we going to know what to look for?"

"We'll figure it out when we get there." Like Hitler with his generals, I would brook no defeatism. This was a way to salvage the trip, which had taken an unexpected and unacceptable turn toward the mundane.

Craig considered for a moment. He thought aloud, "We could do it without packs."

"Yeah. We could just carry my little food bag as a day pack."

Craig smiled when I said "day pack." I had found the magic word.

The next morning, we were breezing along the tame lower section of the Porters Creek Trail. "Now this is more like it!" Craig said. "To hell with carrying those big packs!" We were hiking in damp clothes and wet boots, but otherwise the going was easy. We were candy-assed day hikers now, and I felt a little humiliated. I had a girlie little knapsack on my back that contained only a map and compass, the bible, some snacks, ponchos, and emergency gear. I didn't even have any whiskey on me.

"We look like a couple of lightweights," I complained, but it wasn't really true. We were large and dirty and mean-looking, and we carried big knives on our hips. Our faces were unshaven, and we were hollow-eyed from all the coke and a rough couple of days. We looked more like prison escapees than day hikers. I wouldn't admit it to Craig, but it *was* pretty nice to walk along the gently rising trail with just a few ounces on my back instead of forty or more pounds. The weather was good too. The front that had nearly killed us had blown through, and the sun shone on another crisp October day.

For all practical purposes, Porters Creek Trail ended at campsite #31, Porters Flat. The flat was a wide, level area spreading out from both sides of the creek. One could easily imagine the original settlers coming to this place and deciding to start farming. The flat was now a forest of mature pine trees, but two centuries before, the flat had been a field planted with corn and potatoes. The Whaley brothers, William and Middleton, were the first white men to come to this area. They came over the Appalachians from the east and settled the area shortly after 1800. In the 1850s, another settler, Benjamin Parton, built a house a little further down the creek. A few years later, during the Civil War, Benjamin Parton suffered a gunshot wound to the head, but he survived and became the great-grandfather of Dolly Parton, the country singer.

When Craig and I arrived at Porters Flat, we saw one lonely tent pitched along the creek and three figures huddled around a smoky campfire. Wreathed in the smoke as they were, they almost looked like the ghosts of the old Whaleys and Partons.

We greeted the figures from a distance before we marched into their camp. When they turned around, we saw that there were two men and one woman, all dressed in heavy coats. The woman had a scarf over her head for warmth. All three were middle-aged, at least in their forties.

"Cold morning!" the one guy greeted us. As a demonstration, he exhaled heavily so we could see his breath frost up. His two companions grinned at his comedic talent. The woman revealed a smile a few teeth short of a load.

They seemed pleasant enough, so we moved closer to their fire. "Where y'all headed?" the second guy asked.

"We're going to follow a pioneer trail up to the Appalachian Trail," Craig said proudly. He pointed roughly south toward the high ridge.

The two guys gave each other sidelong glances. The woman looked off to the south as if she might see something there she had missed before. The comedian said, "We been here three days now and we ain't seen nobody go up or come down from there. Pioneers or not."

The other guy chimed in, "That's a fact."

The woman gave her opinion. "I don't think you're 'lowed to go up there."

I couldn't help myself. I said, "Who's gonna stop us?" They didn't know quite what to make of that. Craig looked at me as if he wasn't quite sure himself.

"Well," the second guy said, trying to be diplomatic, "we'd hate to see y'all get lost up there. Be careful."

Craig tried to be conciliatory as well. "Oh yeah. We will. We know what we're doing." Based on our experiences on Ramsey Cascades and on some of my previous trips, I had to wonder if that was really true. The one thing that was certain was that the autumn days were short. We said goodbye to the Porters Flat campers and headed up the creek.

The trail continued well enough for a little way through a forest of tall reeds, but then it fragmented into a maze of possible foot paths. We tried to follow the detailed instructions given in the bible, which told us to cross the stream five times, but we had no idea where any of the crossings were supposed to be in the swampy ground.

Craig, who was following me, called a halt. "Are you keeping track of how many times we cross?"

"No. Are you?"

"Why'd we even bring the book if you aren't going to use it?"

"I'm sure it'll be useful at some point," I said. "You can go first if you want, Craig."

"Naw, you're doing alright. Just don't forget what the book says."

And we did consult the bible often as we went because the terrain seemed to change in character every quarter mile or so. The maze of reeds and swampy ground ended, and for a little while it was easy to follow the creek. We were able to climb up the huge boulders of the creek bed itself and thereby avoid the heavy underbrush. Every so often, when we were sure we had finally lost the trail, we'd see faint traces of the path that let us know we were still on the right track.

Then, just as the bible predicted, the stream disappeared altogether. The geologic story was that a forest fire in 1925 scorched the soil on the mountain above us so badly that nothing could grow. Then, in 1929, heavy rainfall caused a major landslide of the denuded earth, sending tons of that soil and rock crashing down the mountain. The bedrock of the gigantic geologic formation that formed the mountain, the Anakeesta Formation, was now buried under many feet of dirt and loose rock that had skidded down during the landslide. The creek water now seeped down to that bedrock and flowed under the top layer of debris from the landslide.

Finding Mount Guyot

After a quarter mile of walking across loose rock, we saw the creek reappear on the surface, and our climb became exceedingly steep. We were able to follow the water again for a while, hauling ourselves up an endless series of big boulders that were swept clean year after year when the rains became heavy. Now that I had seen Ramsey Prong immediately after a storm, I could easily imagine a torrent of water ripping everything out of this channel except the biggest boulders.

For a time, we had to work through dense laurel patches. Then the dull black slate bedrock of the Anakeesta Formation turned closer to vertical, and we fought to find small clefts in the sheer rock that we could use for footholds and hand holds. One little slip on the wet rock face could easily have sent me or Craig sliding fifty or more yards down the smooth mountainside. This was more like rock climbing than hiking, and I thanked God that I didn't have a big pack on my back as we climbed.

As we went higher, the creek fractured into a thousand little springs seeping out of the bedrock. We drank the ice-cold water dripping off the rocks and filled our canteens. We were on the north side of the ridge, where sun still hadn't hit. The air was downright cold, and we started seeing ice formations on the rock. We were both meat cutters, used to having cold, wet hands, so our frozen paws were merely another day at the office.

The smooth rock face of the mountain made it absolutely impossible to tell where the trail might be. We found a ledge deep enough to sit on, so we took a break and got out the reference book. I lit a smoke and took in the sweeping view. The ridge behind us was the spine of Appalachians. The sun shone brightly over that ridge without hitting us, and the autumn sky was brilliant blue. We sat in the middle of the giant, black-rock face of the mountain looking north without any trees to interrupt the view. The whole lush, green Little

Pigeon river valley spread out in front of us, and the black rocks below us were shiny where they were wet. The very best views were always the hardest to get to, and this place was proof of that, even if we were only day hiking.

Craig's breath came out in frosty wisps as he read about the trail, "It says we have to veer off to the south by southwest at about 4,800 feet and look for a small rock cairn. We turn left there."

"How the fuck are we supposed to know what elevation we're at?" I asked. "And what the hell does a 'cairn' look like?"

"Well, it's small and it's made of rock. We know that."

"So's your head. We know that too."

Craig didn't laugh. "You're the one who said we'd figure it out."

"And we will," I said confidently. We got out the compass and found south by southwest. We saw something a couple hundred yards up in that direction that might be construed as a path, so we worked our way over.

"Look for something on the left," Craig reminded me unnecessarily. A minute later, we both saw a slender tower of stacked rocks about four feet high off to the left. We angled over to it. The rocks were all flat, and the ones at the bottom were over a foot wide. The rocks got smaller toward the top, obviously having been carefully deposited by the hikers who passed this way.

"A cairn!" Craig smiled with relief. "Never doubt the bible, John!"

"Pretty amazing," I said. I was surprised at how big the cairn was and that it was just where the bible said it would be. "I wonder if it lasts from year to year or if it gets knocked over by big storms."

"Hello! There was a big storm two nights ago, remember?"

"Oh yeah." I had almost forgotten about the storm that had nearly killed me. Craig shook his head sadly in mock disappointment at my stupidity, but I knew it did his heart good when I said stupid things. We put two flat rocks on top of the cairn as anonymous mementos of our passing.

We started up a rocky gulley that seemed to be almost straight up and down. The gulley was nothing more than a tight, steep-walled chute paved with flat pieces of broken slate that slid out from under us as we walked. But it led uphill and southwest, so we followed it.

We prayed that we still on the pioneer trail. We were working hard, crawling on all fours, once again searching for hand holds and foot holds in the black rock. We grabbed onto exposed roots to pull ourselves up. The angle of the mountain was so steep that standing up without holding on to something was not possible. Again I was thankful that I didn't have a backpack.

We could sense that we were near the top, and a fine madness took possession of our souls that wouldn't let us stop until we reached the crest. We weren't racing anyone, and we certainly weren't going to be the first to ever reach this nameless point on the map, yet we pushed ourselves and our tired bodies until we dragged ourselves up over the edge and finally stood upon the AT. There was nothing there—no brass marker, no wooden sign, not even a good view—but we felt the quiet satisfaction of accomplishing a difficult goal we had set for ourselves. After the failure at Ramsey Cascades, this little triumph was doubly sweet. We hadn't conquered anything, but we had met the challenge.

We looked down the steep cliff we had just climbed up. "The hardest trail in the Smokies," I said with satisfaction.

"Yeah, but we didn't do Mount Guyot."

"I think we should enjoy what we just did."

Craig nodded slightly, but he couldn't let it be. "I know what you're saying, but we both know we didn't do what we set out to do."

"Well, Mount Guyot's not going anywhere, that's for sure."

Climbing down proved to be every bit as hard as climbing up, if not harder, but we made it back down without incident. It took us hours, and it was late in the day when we finally got back to #31. The Porters Flat campers had disappeared, just like the Whaleys and the Partons before them.

The valley was empty when we left it, except for a fragile cairn up in the highlands with two more little rocks on it, but that wouldn't be there forever. In the end, even the mountains would crumble. Everything eventually succumbed to the rules.

7   Going to Graceland

Against my better judgment, I took Maria backpacking in the Smokies the following summer. We were in one of our "on again" phases, and she kept insisting that she wanted to go with me to see what I enjoyed so much about being in the mountains. What she failed to realize, and what I couldn't say, was that one of the things I liked about the mountains was that she wasn't there when I went. Not that I didn't care about her, but the mountains were the one place where I could be my primitive self and not have to apologize for it.

I was absolutely certain that Maria was not going to make it in the backcountry. She was fit enough, but she was a foo-foo girl at heart. Her idea of a vacation was lying on a beach and slathering baby oil on herself so she could fry in the sun. She was a full-blooded Italian, brown-haired and brown-eyed, and her dark skin browned up very nicely, but she liked her jewelry and frilly clothes and fancy hair-dos too much. I tried to explain to her what the backcountry was really going to be like, squatting in the woods and all, but she insisted that she wanted to try anyway.

Being the chivalrous sort, I told Maria all she had to carry was her clothes, her sleeping bag, and her personal things like toiletries, but she wasn't as impressed by my chivalry as I was. "That sounds like everything I need," she scoffed. "Except for food," she added hastily.

I looked at her in disbelief. "Yeah, and except for the tent, the stove, and the pots and pans, and the rope, and about a dozen other things I can't even think of right now. Plus all my own stuff. There's a lot of stuff we have to carry."

As was her way, Maria glossed over the larger point and focused on a detail instead. "What do we need rope for? We're not going to be hanging over cliffs like those mountain climbers do, are we? There's no way I'm doing that."

"You never know," I said with a straight face. "We might have to." A hint of danger was a good thing sometimes.

In reality, I wasn't planning anything crazy for Maria's first backpacking foray. On the first day, I thought we'd hike the easy 3.7 miles up to Porters Flat, #31, and camp there for the night.

On the ride in toward the Porters Flat trailhead, Maria took in the tranquil views as we drove along the Little Pigeon River. We passed a few groups of people swimming and playing in the big, crystal-clear pools on the hot July morning. We saw a family picnicking and a couple of good ol' boys fishing. "This doesn't look too bad," she said innocently. I didn't say anything in response. I felt like Snidely Whiplash about to tie a woman to the railroad tracks.

At the trailhead, I helped Maria put on her pack. She was using my old backpack, a 1977 vintage model with lightly-padded shoulder straps, but her filled pack only weighed fourteen pounds, so I didn't think the straps would bother her too much. Her pack felt ridiculously light to me as I helped her saddle up.

We started out, and Maria did alright for the first twenty minutes or so, although she wasn't setting any speed records. Then she stopped and asked, "You think we've gone a mile yet?"

I couldn't help but laugh a little. I thought back to my first hike with a pack on my back, recalling how miserable I'd been. "No. Maybe half a mile," I said as kindly as I could. I didn't want to discourage her, but the truth was the truth.

She seemed to crumple a little bit at the news. She didn't say anything, but when we resumed, she started fidgeting with her pack more and more, and her pace slowed to a crawl. After perhaps another ten minutes, she stopped again. "These straps are digging into my shoulders really bad!"

I showed her for the second time how to cinch her waist belt tight. "The tighter this is, the more the weight is on your hips and not on your shoulders." The second time, she listened.

After a mile or so, the wide, jeep-accessible part of the trail ended. The trail turned into a true foot path, and the incline steepened slightly. The trail was still an easy one by any Smoky Mountain standard, but Maria had no way of knowing that. To her, we were on our way up Mount Everest, and I had her loaded down like the red-headed step-child of a Sherpa. She started complaining bitterly. "I'm probably carrying more than I should for my size, don't you think? I know you think my pack's light, John, but you don't realize I only weigh 110 pounds! Fifteen pounds is a lot for me!"

In fact, I had given considerable thought to how much weight I was asking her to carry. The backpacking rule of thumb was never more than thirty percent of a person's weight, but that number must have been invented by some masochist on steroids because thirty percent was one hell of a load. I did the math in my head. "You're carrying less than fourteen percent of your body weight, Maria. Probably more like twelve. And they say people can carry up to thirty." I was trying to encourage her.

"But you weigh 200 pounds. What percent are you carrying?"

I had weighed our packs before we left. I was carrying forty-eight pounds, and I weighed 210. I did the math again. "A little less than twenty-five percent. Maybe twenty-three."

She quickly dismissed the whole number thing and pouted, "But you do this all the time. I don't!" She plopped herself down on a log that had been placed along the side of the trail for weary day hikers. Such trail amenities disappeared deeper into the backcountry. I suspected that Maria wanted me to carry her pack, but I wasn't going to offer. I wasn't going to carry sixty-two pounds up a mountain unless somebody's life depended on it, and even then it would depend on whose life it was.

"I told you this was going to be hard, didn't I?" I said. She had no answer to that one. She just sat there looking down at the ground. "C'mon," I laughed, "don't sit there like a bump on a log." She smiled a little at that, so I went on. "C'mon, Maria. This is the hardest part. After today, it'll be easier. When this is all over, you'll be glad you did this. You'll be telling all your girlfriends how you climbed up mountains."

"Like you do?" she asked pointedly.

I winced because I had opened the door to a delicate subject. "No," I said quietly, "that's not true at all."

Angrily, Maria rose to her feet and kept going, but getting her to hike the rest of the way up to #31 was like herding a cat. I had to guide her and cajole her and coax her every foot of the way. We even took a lunch break after walking barely two miles, which was simply ridiculous.

About half an hour after lunch, I looked back and saw Maria sitting down again. I ran out of patience. I walked back to where she was and barked, "Do you wanna go back? Really.

I'm not going to drag your ass up this mountain." She looked hurt, so I softened my tone slightly. "What's wrong? You walk farther than this every day at work." Maria was a hairdresser and spent all day on her feet. She had used this very argument to convince me that she could make it in the mountains.

She started crying bitter tears. "I hate this pack! I hate it! It's killing my shoulders."

I had never seen anyone cry in the mountains. Backpacking was like baseball—there was no crying allowed. I was amazed that Maria had fallen apart so easily. In some ways, she was a very tough woman, raising a child and paying the bills all by herself. But two and a half miles with a pack on her back had reduced her to tears.

I soothed her head and used the "it's only another mile" bit that Craig had used on me many years before. "C'mon now. We've got about one more mile of this uphill stuff with our packs on, and then you won't have to carry the pack uphill any more for the whole trip. We'll do a few little day hikes with no packs on, and then we'll carry our packs back down this same hill. And our packs will be a lot lighter then. You'll see. It'll be a lot easier."

She looked up at me with her soulful brown eyes, tears and mascara running down her cheeks. My heart melted. I heard myself say, "I can carry your pack for a while, OK?" Then I heard a little voice inside my head saying "*Sucker!*"

"OK," she sobbed. "Just for a little while so I can rest my shoulders. Thank you, honey. Thank you so much." She sobbed a little more for good measure. A cynical man might have suspected that those tears were intentional, but I wasn't a cynical man.

I carried her pack like a suitcase for a while, switching hands every few minutes. When my hands got tired, I balanced her pack on top of my pack the same way that African women carried things on top of their heads. That method was actually easier. *I better get some tonight*, I thought as I trudged along. The only upside of this trip for me was that I was finally going to get to have sex up in the backcountry.

To her credit, Maria did put her pack back on for the last quarter mile of the hike, and I was relieved when she took it back. She thought her work day was over when she finally dragged herself into the campsite at Porters Flat. She dropped her hated pack like a hot potato, sat down on a big log next to a fire ring, and fired up a Virginia Slim. She didn't look as if she planned on moving anytime soon, so I let her be. I didn't want to push her too her hard. She was already teetering on the brink of blaming me for all of her misery. I set up camp and let her rest.

When I was done, I asked, "You want to wash up?"

'Where?" Maria looked around hopefully as if a big cinderblock bath house might suddenly have appeared in the middle of the forest. She had seen such a bath house back at the Greenbrier campground near the park entrance.

I pointed at Porters Creek flowing thirty yards away. "Running water. What more could you ask for?"

"We're supposed to wash up in *cold* water? Cold water doesn't get the dirt off."

"If you're worried about dirt, you're in the wrong place. Let's just go wash up a little and get the big chunks off. You'll feel better."

First it was too rocky for her to find a good place to kneel. Then it was too cold for her to keep her hands in the water. Then she felt too exposed to take her shirt off. "Anybody could walk up here and see me!" she complained.

I lost my patience. "Are you kidding me? You walk around half naked on beaches all the time with guys leering at you, and you're totally cool with that, but you won't take your shirt off for two minutes way out in the woods to wash your pits! We're four miles from the nearest dirt road, Maria. How many people you think are gonna come through here? You know what? I don't care if you wash up or not. You can stink for the next three days for all I care." *Besides, you're as flat as a pancake. I hate to break it to you, but guys aren't going to be hiking up mountains to see that rack, baby.*

I stormed off a few yards and started washing up. At that moment, I didn't care if I got laid up in the mountains or not. The whole thing was becoming a giant pain in the ass. And then, just as I had a face full of soap suds, I heard Maria scream.

I gave my face one quick splash to clear away the suds and lunged for my big ten-inch knife, which sat on a rock two steps away from me. As I grabbed the sheathed knife, I turned and saw Maria standing a step back from the water, looking down into the water with horror. I didn't see a bear, so I was instantly relieved of my worst fear. My second thought was that she must be seeing a snot otter. I went over to Maria and unsheathed the knife, ready to protect her. I looked down into the water, but I didn't see anything. The soap was starting to get into my eyes, and I yelled frantically, "What? I can't see it!"

From behind me, Maria yelled, "Big bugs! Like lobsters!"

I dropped the knife to my side and shook my head in disbelief. I kept my voice calm. "Crawdads? You're screaming about *crawdads*?" Then I remembered that I had been leery of crawdads too the first time I had bathed in a mountain creek too. "They won't hurt you. Watch this!"

I stuck my head down in the shallow pool where the crawdads were just to show Maria that they wouldn't hurt me. I needed to get the soap out of my eyes anyway. Then, with my head in the water, I thought of a way to get even. I jumped back from the water suddenly, grabbing my face. "Ow! Ow! Ow! Get 'em off me! Ow!"

Maria screamed again but quickly realized I was kidding. She ended up moving to a different spot along the creek a few yards away from me and washing up a little with a washcloth made from a clean sock. She wasn't happy.

Back in camp, I set up the propane stove and then started nipping at my Yukon as Maria made our supper. She knew I was a drinker, so it was no big deal. She even drank with me when we went out to the clubs, but she was nowhere near the drinker that I was. Not many were.

When she started wiping her hands on her pants, I felt compelled to say something. "Maria, I know you're probably already sick of me telling you what to do, but you really want to try to keep the food smells off of you and your clothes."

She said, "I know," which didn't leave much room for discussion. I weighed my choices and decided that I'd rather face a prowling bear than piss Maria off any worse. I kept my mouth shut.

In the fading twilight, we were relaxing on a log, enjoying the peaceful part of the day when there were no camp chores to be done. It occurred to me that Maria hadn't gone to the bathroom all day. I grinned at her. "You know you're going to have to go to the bathroom out here sooner or later. You might as well do it while it's still light out."

"Where should I go?" she asked shyly.

"Wherever. Just make sure you don't brush your ass up against anything poisonous." I knew the question that was coming next, so I said, "Just don't brush up against anything at all."

She looked around the perimeter of the camp with her roll of toilet paper in her hand, not knowing at all what she was looking for. I watched her, and it hit home to me just how hard this day had been for her. My heart went out to her. "You want me to find you a spot?" I asked.

"Yes. And could you stay kind of close by me, too?"

"OK." I picked out a spot for her behind a tree that gave her a bit of privacy and waited close by while she went. It took very little to be a hero sometimes.

And then it was time for me to get drunk in earnest. I deserved it after the day I had suffered through. I tried to get Maria to drink with me, but she only took a few tiny sips. She was too afraid of all the night sounds in the forest to relax.

Later, Maria wrote about her first night in the Smokies in a journal she started but never finished:

We sat on some really hard rocks and leaned back against the big log by the fire with a sore butt and John acted like leaning against a stupid log was really cool or something but he was drunk so I tried to ignore the stupid stuff he was talking about. He acted like he was a twelve-year-old playing cowboy and telling me about running out of water like he was in the desert but there was lots of water in the Smokies as far as I could tell. You'd have to be pretty stupid to run out of water in the Smoky Mountains I thought. Then he started getting all lovey dovey with me because he was drunk but I didn't mind him getting close to me because it was pitch black in the woods and I kept hearing noises that sounded real close to us. He seemed like he didn't care about the noises at all. He smelled like whiskey and pirsperation but I knew I did too so I didn't say anything about it. It was still pretty early but I was tired from carrying my heavy pack all the way up to the flat place. He acted like carrying my pack for a few minutes was some big deal so I knew he was hoping we'd have sex in the tent but there was NO WAY I felt like doing it since we were both dirty and smelly and all the noises surrounded us like that. The ground inside my sleeping bag was hard and I knew there was no way I could sleep like that. It felt like bugs were crawling around my head and John kept moving around on his side of the tent and oh my god I knew he was going to snore so loud! Inspite of all this I was so tired that I was starting to fall

*asleep. I wanted to fall asleep before he did. Then he shook
me by the shoulder and said hey Maria look at this so I rolled
over and he was kneeling up and had the flashlight shining up
from underneath on his thing and it was hard! He laughed and
said watch out for the snot otter and it was stupid but it was
kind of funny too and I knew he wasn't going to leave me alone
unless we did it so we did it in the tent and I ended up on the
hard ground between our two mattress things. I just wanted
him to get it over with and get off of me cause the ground was
hurting me but he was drunk so it took him a little while. When
he was done he cuddled with me for about ten seconds and
then rolled over and he was snoring fast. It took me forever to
fall asleep with the sounds of the bears outside and him inside
the tent. It was the most horrible night of my life.*

I woke up the next morning feeling good. I congratulated
myself on thinking of the flashlight trick and also for lasting
so long. I couldn't believe that the flashlight thing had worked,
but who could figure out women? The strangest things turned
them on sometimes.

My original plan had been to spend two days doing day
hikes and using Porters Flat as a home base. I thought that on
the first day we would walk back down to the car, drive over
as close to Ramsey Cascades as possible, and then hike up
there to let Maria see the falls. The total round-trip walking
distance would be about fifteen miles, but without packs. That
had seemed doable in Cleveland, but it now seemed about as
likely as Daisy Duke wearing a pair of baggy overalls.

The second day, I had been thinking about taking Maria up
the same pioneer trail to the AT that Craig and I had taken, but
I knew now that I had been just plain stupid to even consider
that.

Still, we had to do something to pass the day, so during
breakfast I talked to Maria in glowing terms about the beauty

of the Ramsey Cascades. I emphasized that we would be driving a good portion of the way and that she wouldn't be wearing a pack at all. In reality, I gave poor Maria little choice other than to say yes. I loaded up a day pack for myself and we headed back down the Porters Flat Trail to the car. We left our tent pitched and our backpacks hanging in a tree. I was hoping that anybody who might come through would think the owners were still nearby. On the trail, Maria reluctantly conceded that hiking downhill without a pack was a lot easier, but she still didn't seem very happy to be hiking again.

After 3.7 miles, we got back to the trailhead and our car. I hated to diminish our wilderness experience by using the car, but it couldn't be helped. Simply sitting down on the upholstered seats of the car and turning on the stereo made me feel as if I were betraying the mountains. Maria, however, had evidently been waiting for this moment because the second I put the car in gear, she said, "Can we go into town for a minute? I think I'm going to need some film."

I chuckled, "You just want to sit in the car as long as you can."

She didn't even try to tell me I was wrong. "Come on, John. It won't take long. We can get something cold to drink, too."

I gave in easily. "OK, but we really can't waste too much time. We still have a long way to hike."

We drove past the Greenbrier campground and out of the park all the way back to Route 321. There was an ugly cinderblock building there at the crossroads with a sign that said Groceries. A really bad mural of a black bear with huge teeth was peeling off the outside wall of the building. Maria looked at me questioningly, but I shrugged indifferently and walked through the front door. Maria stayed close behind.

The interior of the store was in worse condition than the exterior. The wooden plank floor was creaky and unvarnished. We saw what might have been a bar or a grill at one time with a counter where brave souls might have sat and ate or drank, but the counter was now piled with several years' worth of old newspapers and other debris. The Yoo-Hoo clock on the wall had stopped at 5:15, but there was no telling on what day or in what year.

A voice startled us. We turned around and saw two living, breathing stereotypes standing behind us at an old-fashioned cash register. The register was next to the front door and we hadn't noticed it coming in. The person who spoke was a middle-aged man with a huge beer belly. He wore a white button-down shirt and saggy jeans. The seat of the jeans was somewhere just above the backs of his knees even though he wore a belt with a big shiny buckle. Most of the buckle was obscured by his belly, but I could see enough of it to read the word "ELVIS," which explained his pompadour hair style and his pork chop sideburns. The man was grinning pleasantly, his smile revealing a beautiful set of store-bought choppers.

But the woman standing next to him was even more remarkable. She too was on the wrong side of forty, maybe even fifty, but she was dressed to drive the men wild. She was extremely thin, and her sleeveless, tiger-striped top showed off her bony shoulders and accordion-like décolletage. Whatever breasts she had were the sad victims of Newton's Law. She wore lots and lots of jewelry, and I was surprised that the big hoop bracelets stayed on her thin wrists.

She had a great pile of bleached blonde hair on her head done in a poofy, Tammy Wynette style. Her face was thin and heavily made-up, but it was clear that she had been a looker in her day. She held a lit cigarette in the corner of her mouth, and she looked as if that cigarette stayed there day and night. I thought I saw a trace of a smile appear on her bright pink lips when saw me eyeing her up and down.

Her pants of course were made of spandex, revealing a bony, saggy ass that looked like the back end of a thawed-out

216

roasting chicken. I couldn't see her shoes, but I was sure she was wearing heels. All in all, she looked like she had just rolled in from a long night of driving the good ol' boys crazy at the local bar. Maria and I were in the presence of royalty. She was the consummate Honky Tonk Queen, and he was the King.

The King said, "Can I help you find somethin'?" The Honky Tonk Queen didn't speak.

I told him we were just looking. We wandered through the aisles and eyed the sparse selection of overpriced goods. We chose a Yoo-Hoo for me and a diet Coke for Maria from a tired old beverage cooler.

I put our two drinks on the counter next to the cash register. The owner and the Honky Tonk Queen were still standing there. I got the feeling that they stood there pretty much all the time. The Queen still didn't speak, and I found myself wondering what she sounded like. She picked up the bottle of Yoo-Hoo and started looking for a price tag.

In a quiet voice, the owner said, "Those are seventy-nine," and then flashed his unnaturally bright teeth at me. "Where y'all from?"

"Cleveland. In Ohio," I answered. The Honky Tonk Queen slowly and deliberately pecked a few keys on the register with a long, pink fingernail.

"Goin' to Gatlinburg?" he asked me. Then he quietly said, "Those are seventy-nine too, darlin'," as the Queen studied the can of Coke the same way she had studied the bottle of Yoo-Hoo. The pink fingernail pecked out a few more keys and then hit the "total" button.

Very slowly, the Honky Tonk Queen read the total shown on the register, "One fifty-eight." She had the Appalachian twang, but a lifetime of booze and cigarettes had rendered her voice about three octaves too low.

I handed her a five and said to the owner, "No, we're actually camping up in the backcountry. We spent last night up at Porters Flat."

"That's purdy up there," he said, but his eyes never left the cash register. "No, darlin'. You only owe him *three* dollars and forty-two cents." Apparently, the Queen had concentrated so much on getting the forty-two-cent part right that she had messed up the dollar bill part.

"Well, if she can't count, at least she's good-lookin'," the owner said to me.

I couldn't tell if he was being serious or not, so I didn't respond. I smiled at the Queen instead and said, "Well, that's an easy mistake to make."

She handed me my $3.42 without saying a word. The owner said, "I'd git that dollar back one way or the other, wouldn't I, darlin'?" The Honky Tonk Queen smiled at that one, revealing an impressive set of tobacco stains.

Maria and I tried to hold back our laughter until we were out of the store. Maria started snickering as we walked through the door, and we both exploded once we were inside the car. Maria said, "You want me to dress like that? With the big hair?"

"Hell yeah!" I grabbed at her and said, "I'm gonna git that seventy-nine cents out of you one way or another, darlin'!"

We drove back into the park, laughing all the way, and headed up the side road that led to the Ramsey Cascades trailhead. I parked the car in the same parking lot that Craig and I had used the year before.

Maria's good mood evaporated when she saw the trail sign that said it was four miles up to the Cascades. She caught me by the arm and turned me around. "Wait a minute. We have to walk four miles to get there, and then four miles to get back here, and then four *more* miles to get to the tent?" Her Italian temper exploded. "What's wrong with you? You think I'm

218

going to walk twenty fucking miles up and down these mountains just to see some half-assed waterfall?" Maria could cuss like a sailor, but her math skills weren't much better than the Honky Tonk Queen's. "I'm not walking up there! I don't care if looks like fucking Niagara Falls! I've already been to Niagara Falls." Then the anger dissolved into tears. "I'm not fucking doing this, John. I'm not. I'm tired! I'm sick of this!"

I wasn't falling for the tears again. I got mad too. I didn't yell, but my tone was cold and hard. "What'd you think this was gonna to be, Maria? A fucking walk around the block? They call them 'mountains' for a reason. They tend to go up and down a lot. I told you it was going to be hard, didn't I? I told you you were going to hate it, didn't I? But no, you had to come anyway. You're the tough Italian . . ."

"Shut up!" she screeched. "Just shut the fuck up! Don't you ever get tired of being right? You were right, OK? Is that what you want to hear? You feel better now?"

"What kind of stupid shit is that? No, it doesn't make me feel better. It makes me feel terrible because now we're both having a miserable vacation."

"And it's my fault." She made it somewhere between a question and a statement.

In my heart I thought that it was indeed her fault, but I knew better than to say so. "I don't care whose fault it is. I just don't want to fight like this every second we're out here."

"Let's do something else then."

I looked at her tear-streaked face. She looked a lot less sexy after a night in the mountains. In the end, we compromised. We would go back up to Porters Flat and spend one more night in the tent. We had to go back up there anyway to retrieve our gear. Then the next day I could go up and down the Porters Flat pioneer trail by myself in the morning, and we would hike out in the afternoon. We would be in a hotel room by tomorrow night and then we would do some other, more civilized type of vacationing for the remainder of the week.

With that settled, we drove back to the Porters Flat trailhead and hiked the 3.7 miles back up to our camp. Maria tried not to complain too much on the way up, and I tried to act more cheerful than I felt. In camp that night, we had a big fire and ate all of our good snacks, including my tin of sardines. I drank as much of my Yukon as I wanted, knowing I could get more the next day. I tried to sex up Maria again, telling her I wanted my seventy-nine cents' worth, but she wanted nothing to do with a sardine-breathed drunk.

When we woke up the next day, I knew Maria was counting the hours until we left this God-forsaken place in the wilderness. I felt great after a cup of coffee and some oatmeal. I was looking forward to the challenge of doing the toughest trail in the Smokies all by myself. Maria watched me as I packed my day pack with a few essentials. I knew she didn't want me to go, not because she was worried about me, but because she was afraid to be alone for a few hours. I tried to avoid her accusing brown eyes.

Before I left, I said, "It's only going to take me two or three hours. Keep your knife on you, and stay in the tent if you want. It's broad daylight. There's really nothing to worry about out here. I doubt you'll even see anybody." She didn't say a word, which of course made me feel even guiltier. "C'mon, Maria. I might never be here again. I just want to do this one more time. OK?"

She sighed. "Just go get it over with."

A line from an old poem popped into my head. "I could not love thee, dear, so much, loved I not honor more."

Maria wasn't impressed in the least, or maybe she didn't understand it. "Just go."

I went. I wanted to see how fast I could make it there and back for a few reasons. One was simply because I was me, and the other was because I knew I shouldn't be leaving a woman alone in a tent in the middle of the mountains. But I rationalized that I had a right to enjoy at least a few hours of this trip my way. I was at the peak of my physical prowess. I was thirty-two years old, and in spite of all my drinking and smoking, or maybe directly because of it, I was a work-out fiend. I could bench press 300 pounds and run four miles in twenty-eight minutes flat. I told myself that my bad habits wouldn't catch up with me as long as I took care of my body. It was a nonsensical life, but so far it was working.

I practically jogged through the lower section. I had been there only ten months before, and it all came back to me as I hurried through. I made one wrong turn in the laurel hell just above the dry river bed, but I quickly realized my mistake and got back on course.

I paused on the smooth black slate where all the springs came out of the mountainside to enjoy the view and have a smoke. Standing all alone on that mountain, the sense of freedom and mastery was absolutely overwhelming. I reveled in the sheer power of manhood I felt coursing through my body.

I found the cairn with no problem. I made a mental note to tell Craig that the top part of it had fallen down over the winter. Then I scrambled up the chute—the final vertical section of the trail. It was still a lung-buster, but I knew what to expect, so it was easier the second time.

I stood on the AT once again, feeling the quiet exultation of it. Then I got out my trail map to try to determine more precisely where I was on the AT. I couldn't tell my exact location, but I knew that I was somewhere between two mountains named Laurel Top and Charlies Bunion, the latter being the coolest mountain name ever invented. I was in the section of the AT that they called the "saw teeth." I was sorely tempted to go see Charlies Bunion, which was somewhere off to the west, but I figured it was probably a good mile down the trail, and I couldn't take the time. Maria was waiting.

So, after about a five-minute rest, I turned around and went right back down the way I had come. The first few hundred yards were the toughest since they were practically straight down. This was why the bible said that the Porters Flat pioneer trail was one-way-only. The only way to proceed was butt-down on all fours, using roots and jutting rocks to check your fall, and dragging your ass along the rocks when you had to. It would be nearly impossible to do with a full pack on your back. Even without a pack, it would have been absurdly easy to catch a boot or a hand in the roots and rocks and end up breaking something. I went slowly and deliberately through the top section, quite conscious of the fact that I was alone and that a broken leg would be serious trouble.

I went faster as I worked my way farther down the mountain, but I found that it was much easier to lose my way going downhill. I made a few wrong turns in the heavy laurel. Craig and I had had the same problem the year before. Being alone, though, the wrong turns seemed a little more frightening, and I had to fight to remain calm as I backtracked through the hells until I rediscovered the faint traces of the foot path. I was having a blast, but the sense of danger was lurking in the shadowy corners of my mind.

Once I made it to the main creek, I knew I was going to find my way back out, and I started moving really fast. I leapt from rock to rock as I followed the creek down. I got reckless, jumping down six- and seven-foot drops from one huge boulder to the next. Sometimes, the surface below me was not a boulder but a jumble of loose, broken slate. The tricky part was knowing whether these loose rocks were stable, or if they would shift or slide out from under me when I landed on them.

I had to select which rocks to land on and which to avoid. Amazingly, I didn't even twist an ankle.

I jumped six feet down onto a long, flat boulder and found to my surprise that it was slick. Both feet went out from under me, and I was suddenly flying through the air feet first. By the grace of God, I landed on the small of my back in a pool of water.

The pool of water was only a foot deep. I sat up with my ass and my feet in the creek, stunned for a just a moment. I checked to make sure nothing was broken, and found that I was still in perfect working condition. I laughed out loud, got up, and continued down the creek. Much later, I realized how easily I might have broken my back or bashed in the back of my head on that slick boulder.

I made it back to camp soon after, no worse for the wear except for some wet boots and a wet ass. I found Maria in the tent. She had spent the morning alternately crying and reading the highway map that she had brought up with her from the car the previous afternoon. She had decided that she wanted to go to Elvis's mansion, Graceland, over in Memphis, so that's where we headed. We hiked back down to the car and drove west through Tennessee, but I insisted that we swing down through Tupelo, Mississippi first to see where Elvis had been born. I always liked the lean, mean, young Elvis best.

8   Going to the Tower

A few months later, I met a golden-haired woman from a wealthy family. She was attractive, smart, arrogant, and a good outdoorswoman too. We were both working toward our PhDs, and I knew right away that I had finally met my match. Maria was history. I started going out with Meredith, and we went backpacking every chance we could. Before too long, we got married and spent our honeymoon backpacking in the Colorado Rockies.

Inevitably, though, my steps led me back to the Smokies. In the fall of 1994, Meredith and I took a trip to the eastern end of the park because I wanted to finally see a fire tower there. We were headed for the tower on top of Mount Sterling, a mountain that had gotten its name from a wide vein of silver metal than ran through its base. The prospectors originally thought that the metal they had discovered was sterling silver; hence the name. To their disappointment, they found out that it was plain old lead, but the name stuck.

On the drive down, as I was running through a mental checklist of my gear, I said, "Shit! I forgot my big knife. I can't go in without my blade."

Meredith's ice-blue eyes left her book for a moment. "Are you serious?"

"Yeah, I took it out to sharpen it, and I know I forgot to put it back in my pack. Damn!" I was still a meat cutter three or four days a week, and like all good meat cutters, I insisted on keeping my knives razor sharp.

"If it's that important, you'd think you'd remember to pack it," she said as she went back to her book.

"Well, I'm remembering it *now*." I refused to go into the mountains without some kind of weapon, so we stopped at an outfitter's shop in Sevierville where I bought a fishing knife with a four-inch blade. The knife had a keen edge on it, but it felt puny in my hand.

We parked at the Big Creek entrance on the east side of the park. The Big Creek area was a huge valley bounded on the north by the spine of the Appalachians. The spine curved south, and Mount Guyot formed the western edge of the valley. Then another ridge called the Mount Sterling Ridge walled off the south side of the valley. All the water in this valley ended up in the Big Creek, which flowed eastward through the center of the valley and out of the park.

We started up the Baxter Creek Trail, which would lead us to the Mount Sterling fire tower. The bible said that the Baxter Creek Trail was a difficult climb, but the views from the tower were worth it. The fire tower was at 5,842 feet, and we had to climb 4,100 feet to get there. Some of the big trees we passed along the way were a massive ten or twelve feet in diameter. Looking at those giants, I recalled something I had seen once in a documentary. Talking over my shoulder, I asked, "Did you know that the first trees on Earth evolved in the Appalachians?"

"I remember reading about that," Meredith said. "While the mountains were still part of Pangea, right? It's up in New York state now, I believe." Having stolen my little bit of thunder, she went on. "Did *you* know that there are more species of trees in the Smokies than on the whole European continent?"

I grunted noncommittally. It was easy to be well-read if you were thirty-five years old and had never had a job. Meredith could tell you about the super-continent of Pangea forming 550 million years ago and the five-mile-high Appalachian Mountains rising out of that continent, but she didn't know how to pay the fare on a city bus or punch a time clock. It made for some interesting conversations between us. I had naively believed that my family was middle class until I stepped into Meredith's world. That, along with being around affluent and educated people in grad school, had awakened me to my own socio-economic limitations. To those people, I finally realized, I was part of the great unwashed working class. I couldn't believe that I hadn't seen it sooner.

When I met Meredith, she had just divorced her orthodontist husband. She hadn't taken advantage of him financially when she left, which I took as a sign of good character. Now she was in my world, struggling to get through grad school without relying on her family, but the subtle reminders of our differences were always there. We were most in tune with each other in the mountains. Class distinctions and job histories were irrelevant in the backcountry, where the measure of a person's worth was how much physical endurance, resourcefulness, and mental toughness he or she possessed. In those respects at least, we were well matched.

After four miles of steep climbing, we came to a sunny spot on the Mount Sterling ridge, so I dropped my pack and fired up a Camel Wide. I had tried to quit smoking the year before and failed after one miserable month. Meredith watched me exhale a huge billow of smoke. "It astounds me that you can carry all that weight up a mountain and then smoke a cigarette."

"It astounds me that you can have a drag once in a while and not get hooked," I said. "I wish I could smoke like you."

"I think that once you're truly addicted, you have to give them up completely," she said, and I nodded in sad agreement.

The grade was a little easier on top of the ridge, and we hurried along. We were both anxious to see the tower. The trees hid it from our view until we were practically standing at its base. I shouted, "Thar she blows!" when I finally caught a glimpse of it.

The Mount Sterling fire tower, built by the CCC in the 1930s, was a steel skeleton that rose eighty feet up from the very top of the mountain. Big steel beams sunken into cylindrical concrete piers formed the four legs of the tower. I marveled at the men and beasts who had dragged the steel and concrete up the mountain. As the tower rose, the legs tapered in toward a square shack that sat atop the steel frame. Several flights of metal steps led up between the legs of the tower to the shack.

I shed my pack quickly and started up the steps. Meredith was right behind. Every twelve steps or so, there was a small landing where the stairs reversed direction. A handrail was mounted on the inside side of the stairs, but the diagonal support beams crisscrossing between the four vertical legs of the tower were the only things there to prevent a climber from falling outward from the steps. And those diagonal supports were spaced far apart—far enough apart that a large Slovak man could easily fall through. My fear of heights seized me, and I kept a tight grip on the thin steel handrail.

Meredith noticed the handrails too. "They weren't too safety-conscious back then, were they?"

The anticipation of the view spurred me on. The endless waves of ancient ridges surrounding us stretched out farther and farther as we rose. At the top landing, we had an uninterrupted 360-degree view of the very heart of the

227

Appalachians. I was awestruck by the Smokies all over again. In every direction, the green mountains turned to purple and then to gray and then dissolved into the limitless sky. It was too much beauty to grasp all at once.

I heaved myself through an unlocked trapdoor in the floor of the observation shack and then pulled Meredith up. She was as light as a feather. The walls of the shack were made of metal sheeting, but each wall contained a full panel of windows that went from corner to corner, so the panoramic vista was uninterrupted. Some of the windows were broken out, allowing a stiff breeze to whistle through the shack, which was roughly eight feet square.

The metal roof of the shack had another trap door built into it directly above the trap door in the floor. There was no ladder leading to the top trap door, but I knew that some foolhardy souls probably climbed through that top door anyway to stand on the roof of the shack. I was not going to be one of them. The tower swayed slightly with the wind, and I was scared and thrilled just standing inside it. The wooden floor also seemed a little soft in spots, so I was careful where I placed my weight.

I joined Meredith by the windows facing west. An engraved wooden board depicted the profile of the western skyline and showed the names of the major peaks. The huge mass of Mount Guyot loomed almost directly west of us, and two more mountains also well over 6,000 feet—Old Black and Mount Chapman—were standing on either side of Mount Guyot like grim brothers in arms.

I pointed at Mount Chapman. "I was on Mount Chapman with Craig and Dan the day we met the camel jockeys. I think it's the highest point on the AT."

"Camel jockeys?" Meredith asked. "You mean people hiking with llamas?" She had read about people using llamas as pack animals in the Smokies.

I chuckled softly. "Never mind. It was a long time ago." Some things were best left in the past, and I knew I shouldn't be using the term camel jockey, even though I could never understand why it was supposed to be so damned offensive.

"I'm sure it was charming if Dan and Craig were involved," she said dryly. Not surprisingly, Meredith didn't think much of my friends.

The ridges beyond the one in front of us were shown on the embossed board as well, and we could see Mount LeConte, where the mythical inn was located, and Clingmans Dome, where I had hiked alone with the boar and the bear. Those peaks were in the center of the park, almost twenty miles away from Mount Sterling, but we could see them distinctly and many more ridges beyond them.

From the windows on the north side of the tower, we could see the Big Creek valley directly below us and beyond that the continuation of the Appalachian crest trailing away to the northeast. Looking out to the east, we could see the Black Mountains forty miles into North Carolina. The two highest peaks in the East, Mt. Mitchell and Mt. Craig, stood there. So, from the fire tower on Mount Sterling, we could see the five highest peaks east of the Mississippi: Mount Mitchell, Mount Craig, Clingmans Dome, Mount Guyot, and Mount LeConte. There were countless others, the names of which I would never know.

As spectacular as the views looking west into the park were, the views to south and especially to the east kept drawing my gaze. It was a feast for a mountain man's eyes. The time-worn ridges went on to infinity. Geography and time became somehow intertwined here. Meredith sidled up in front of me, and I murmured, "Time out of mind." I put my arms around her, and we stood for a long time simply gazing at the mountains.

Eventually, we had to climb back down to earth and set up our camp in the clearing at the base of the fire tower. Well over one mile high, the Mount Sterling campsite was the highest campsite in the park without a shelter. This meant that we had to deal with high winds, and we had to walk a long way for water.

A side trail more than a quarter mile long led down to a spring in a secluded glade. The spring was a weak but steady flow of clear water that trickled out of a metal pipe hammered into the rocky side of the mountain. This was the only available water source, so we used it for drinking and cooking, for washing dishes, and for bathing. I was sweaty and grimy from the steep climb up, and since we had the campsite to ourselves, I stripped down to wash myself off as best I could. I splashed the icy cold water onto my naked body and then stepped back from the water to lather up. I struck a pose and said, "Fine figure of a man!"

I hadn't even noticed that the shock of the icy cold water on my crotch had caused the Slovak Hammer to be reduced to a mere fraction of its normal, robust size. Meredith eyed my diminished dimensions. With a disapproving look on her face, she said, "I don't see what you're so proud of," which made me feel distinctly unlike a mountain man.

This was before the *Seinfeld* show made "shrinkage" a household word. For a second I wondered if she knew about the effects of cold water on the male anatomy. "C'mon, Mere. It *is* pretty cold out here."

She turned away from me to close up the filled canteens and said, "Sure it is," but I couldn't see her face to be sure that she was kidding.

That evening after supper, we went back up to the top of the tower to watch the sun set. I wanted to show Meredith right there in the tower how wrong she had been, but she said it was too cold and windy for romance.

We built a fire, and the steady winds fanned the flames high. I got out my Yukon as additional protection against the chill. I thought that getting married would help me drink less, but it hadn't worked out that way. I drank almost every day. Meredith thought that I drank too much, but she came from a drinking family and enjoyed an occasional drink of whiskey herself, so she didn't bitch too much. She had a few stiff belts, and I had several.

We stared into the fire and talked loquaciously about the literature classes we were taking and the poems we had read. In order to illustrate a point, I mentioned the meat department where I worked. Meredith took the cup of Yukon from my hand and took a long sip. She said, "Do you realize what a curious amalgam of bronze and gold you are?"

"I'm not sure what you mean, but if it's a compliment, I'll take it."

She handed the cup back to me. "Didn't you ever have to read Plato's *Republic*?" Meredith's daddy had sent her to some big-time university in Paris, which was why she knew about Plato's *Republic*.

"No, we must've missed that one at Cuyahoga Community College," I said pointedly. I had in fact studied a little Plato in college, but I had no idea what she was referring to.

"Plato said that there were three kinds of people in the world: bronze, silver, and gold. The bronze people were the craftsmen, or the workers. They were mostly driven by self-interest and—how would you say it?—their physical appetites. The silver people were the soldiers, and they were driven by duty and honor. And the gold people were the philosophers. They thought about the greater good and were supposed to be selfless. They were the ones who became the kings who ruled over the others."

"He would make the philosophers the gold ones, wouldn't he? Since he was a philosopher himself."

231

She ignored my plebeian remark. "My point is that you're half craftsman and half philosopher. You're like this crazy mixture of base desires and higher understanding."

Instead of being offended, I was pleased. At least I was partly gold. "I was a soldier too, you know."

"I know, but that's not really who you are."

I already knew the answer, but I asked the question anyway. "And which are you?"

"I can't help where I was born, John, or the way I was raised."

"No. No, you can't," I agreed. But I noticed that she implicitly acknowledged that she thought of herself as gold.

The wind was blowing even harder the next morning, but the rising sun was shining brightly over the mountains. I put my coffee in my canteen and took it up to the top of the tower, but Meredith decided that she would be too cold up top. The wind was really whipping once I got up above the trees, and I had to hold on to the handrail for dear life with my free hand, but the view from inside the shack was worth it. I could see large banks of Smoky Mountain smoke clouds slowly roiling in the valleys. This was the pristine mountain morning that I had dreamed of so many years before. I even had the steaming cup of coffee in my hand. It had taken me seventeen years to find this place and this moment, and I cherished it. In some respects, I was still alone, but I pushed that thought aside. I closed my eyes and tried to burn the image into my memory forever. Reluctantly, I left the tower and climbed back down to camp.

Some of the chill was gone from the air by the time we were ready to go. We headed southwest along the Mount Sterling ridge for a few miles and then turned north onto the Swallow Fork Trail that led down to the valley and the Big Creek itself. Meredith and I were making our way through a heavily forested area when I rounded a corner and saw a file of horsemen coming up the trail from the opposite direction. Four people on horses appeared—three men and a woman. They were all in their forties, and all were dressed in wanna-be cowboy apparel. Even though the day was dry, three of them wore long, duster-style coats with the half-length cape attachments draping their shoulders. The guy on the last horse was apparently still saving up for his pretend cowboy coat.

The man in front was a grizzled, beer-bellied guy. He called out to me in jest, "Where's your horses?"

My first thought was "*Horses? We don't need no stinking horses!,*" but instead I pointed to my legs and said, "These are my horses right here!"

The guy didn't even crack a smile. "Ours'll get us up the mountain a lot easier."

I borrowed a line from *Jeremiah Johnson* and said, "You can't cheat the mountain, pilgrim."

Standing right behind me, Meredith hissed "Be nice!" under her breath. Then she stepped out and said, "Those are beautiful animals you have." The horsemen acknowledged the praise, and Meredith made the necessary small talk about where each party was going and where they had been. Then we stepped aside and let the horses pass.

After the horsemen had gone, Meredith said, "What's wrong with you?"

"I don't think they should allow horses out here, that's all. They tear up the trails, and then you have to walk through their shit. Those people should have to walk like everybody else."

"Oh, so you're jealous!"

"I'm certainly not jealous of that guy! That fat boy couldn't make it one mile up this trail without a horse! I feel sorry for the damn horse."

We resumed walking, and after a few minutes of reflection, it dawned on me that maybe there was a smidgeon of truth in what Meredith said. "Their coats were pretty cool," I admitted.

The bottom half of the Swallow Fork Trail was wide and relatively easy. This part of the trail had been a railroad line for the old logging companies, so the grade was easy enough for horsemen and other sissies who didn't like to walk. We made it to campsite #37 on the banks of Big Creek by the middle of the afternoon. The place was called Walnut Bottoms.

We enjoyed a leisurely snack and a couple sips of Yukon. The afternoon was so pleasant and quiet that we crawled into our tent and took a peaceful nap. When I awoke, the walls of the orange tent were a dull rust color. I jumped out and saw that the sun was just about to dip down below Mount Guyot at the western end of the valley. I gently shook Meredith. "Get up, Mere. It's getting dark!" Meredith roused herself, and we got busy with our camp chores. I gathered wood as she prepared supper. We hurried to get everything done before full dark.

As the last light was draining out of the sky, our supper of canned chicken and ramen noodles in mushroom sauce was bubbling in a pot over the fire. Meredith was stirring the food, and I was tying off our food bag up in a tree when I heard Meredith gasp. I looked at her, and she was pointing to the other side of the clearing. A gigantic jolt of fear shot through me. The dark shape of a big black bear had materialized out of the gloom no more than twelve feet away.

Twelve feet can be a long way if, for example, you are putting a golf ball. But twelve feet is a very short distance indeed if that is all that is separating you from a big, hungry bear. And this bear looked huge and ravenous. He was far bigger than me if I were on all fours, and much, much thicker. I assumed because of his size that he was a male, easily weighing over 300 pounds. For all I knew he might have been 400 pounds. He raised his nose into the air to get a better sniff of our savory chicken dinner.

The dim light made him seem even more ominous. He stood there, a deadly black shadow in a forest of shadows, silently watching us and sniffing the air. My mind flashed back to the night on Clingmans Dome when the bear had sniffed my head. The fact that I could see this bear didn't make me feel any better. I was petrified. I stood motionless, staring at the menacing black hulk. With two quick leaps, the bear could have been on top of either one of us. All the stuff that I had read about reacting to bear encounters went right out of my head.

Meredith reacted first. The fire was between her and the bear. She dropped the spoon, turned away from the fire and the bear, and ran to the nearest tree, which happened to have a few low limbs. She pulled herself up into the tree as best she could, but her feet were still only six feet off the ground. The bear could have reached up with his terrible claws and dragged her out of the tree effortlessly.

Acting purely on instinct, I moved to put the fire between me and the bear, which also put me between the bear and Meredith. I would never know whether my primary motivation had been to save myself or to save my wife. I reached for the butcher knife I always wore on my right hip, but when my hand touched the hilt of the knife, I remembered that my big ten inch was sitting at home. *Shit!* All I had to defend myself against this 400-pound savage beast with razor claws and crushing jaws was the curved, four-inch blade of a fishing knife. I pulled it out anyway and held it in front of me. The knife felt even punier than it had before.

Reflections of yellow flames danced in the bear's eyes, making the bear appear even more malevolent—some rough beast slouching toward me, its hour come round at last. The bear sized up his new opponent. Meredith had been sitting beside the fire, making her appear even smaller than she already was. I was standing, which made me a much bigger adversary. The bear stood impassively, wondering if the food that smelled so good was worth fighting me for.

Another impulse seized me, and I grabbed the unburned end of one of the biggest sticks in the fire and extended the burning end toward the bear. With a courage I didn't really feel, I waved the burning stick and said, "Ha, bear! Hey! Go on!" or something like that. I meant the words to come out forcefully in hopes of scaring off the bear, but I was so frightened that my words came out as a harsh whisper. Some part of my mind, maybe the rational part, was screaming, "*What the fuck are you doing? Run!!!*" The bear eyed me with evident contempt, as if he sensed my fear and would have smirked at my false bravado if bears could smirk.

The bear stood his ground, unimpressed by the weakly burning stick. My reserves of courage were evaporating like Smoky Mountain clouds on a sunny day. The voice in my head was screaming louder and louder, "*RUN!*" I slowly backed away from the fire and toward the tree that Meredith was standing in. I walked backwards and stepped carefully, afraid that the bear would charge me if I tripped and went down.

The bear sniffed the air a few more times, and to my amazement, it slowly turned and glided back into the woods. Meredith whispered, "It's leaving!" It dissolved like an apparition into the darkest gloom and was gone as silently as it had arrived.

I went back to the fire and rearranged the logs with the burning branch I still held in my hand. I wanted lots of flames. Meredith, still perched in the tree, warned me, "It might come back."

"No shit! That's why I want more light! He might try to come in from the other side of the fire, too."

Meredith looked over her shoulder into the darkness behind her. She jumped catlike out of the tree and came to stand beside me. I felt giddy with the momentary relief. I laughed, "I don't think you're supposed to run like that when you see a bear. I guess you never read that black bears are good climbers, huh?" I had to get my shots in when I could.

Meredith wasn't sharing my sense of relief. She looked at me with fear and fury in her icy blue eyes. "It was simple self-preservation, John! Which you evidently don't understand. Are you trying to make me a widow, or what?"

I was completely blindsided by her anger. I was just starting to formulate the idea that I had acted rather heroically, facing down a bear. Keeping my eyes on the tree line, I said, "You can bitch at me later, Mere, if you want. Right now, let's just deal with the fucking bear, OK?"

Meredith changed tactics. "You're right. Let's build up the fire." She started throwing sticks on the fire in big handfuls.

"If we build it up too much," I pointed out, "we're going to run out of wood, and I don't know about you, but I'm sure as hell not going out into the woods to look for more."

Her mind raced a few steps ahead. "So we're stuck. We're going to sit here in the dark tonight waiting for that bear to come back and get us." As an afterthought, she asked, "Was that a big one?"

"Yeah, I think that was a pretty big one." I had only seen a few live bears in the woods before and some stuffed ones in museums, but ours had been the biggest by far. "Let's build this fire up just a little and eat our food."

"Are you serious? How can you even think about eating?" Both of us were scanning the edges of the campsite constantly as we talked. It felt as if we were being watched.

"We have to get rid of the food somehow! That's what attracted him in the first place. We shouldn't have been cooking after dark. We need to eat it or throw it in the fire." I was making it up as I went, but Meredith didn't know that.

We threw some wood on the fire to keep the flames going and ate our meal sitting back to back. I watched my side of the clearing, and Meredith watched hers. I wolfed down my plateful quickly. Meredith could only eat a few bites, and then she handed the rest of her supper to me. I ate as much of hers as I could and threw the rest into the hottest part of the fire.

Neither of us wanted to leave the fire to go wash dishes. Instead, we rinsed the pot and the two plates clean with water from our canteens. We made sure that the rinse water went inside the fire ring where the flames would destroy the food smell. Then we set the cookware right next to the fire where the heat would hopefully burn away any remaining particles of food. Finally, we washed our hands and our faces and brushed our teeth to get rid of any lingering aroma of food. The whole time, we watched the darkness just beyond our circle of light. If the bear was still lurking, we didn't see him.

Meredith, more nervous than I'd ever seen her, tended the fire and shined her flashlight at every sound that came out of the woods. I had a couple after-dinner smokes and thought about my bottle of Yukon, but I knew I shouldn't touch it. I needed to stay alert, and I didn't want the syrupy, sweet smell on my breath. Most of all, though, I knew Meredith would be livid if I drank. But if ever there was a hoary night when a lonely man struggled to keep his fire lit, this was the night. I left the Yukon in my pack, at least for the time being.

I wandered off toward the edge of our circle of light to relieve myself. Before I was half way there, Meredith asked, "Where are you going?" with a trace of panic in her voice.

"I'm just going to take a leak. Relax."

She exploded, "Relax? How am I supposed to relax? For all we know, that bear could be out there in the trees, waiting to pounce on us. And it'll probably pick me because you're bigger."

"Mere, that bear is probably a mile away already." I wasn't at all certain of that, but I had to be calm enough for both of us.

She called my bluff. She always did. "You don't know that at all."

I had to concede that point. "Yeah, you're right. I'm not certain of that. But why would he hang around if the food is gone?"

Even on the edge of panic, she knew I was right, so she said nothing.

I tried to ease the tension. "You were up that tree pretty quick, weren't you? Just gonna leave me to the bear, huh?" I put my arm around her affectionately. "It's like that old joke about the bear and the tennis shoes."

"What joke?"

"These two guys see a bear, and the one guy starts putting on a pair of tennis shoes. The other guy says, 'What are you doing? You can't outrun a bear!' And the guy with the shoes says, "I don't have to outrun the bear. I only have to outrun you!'"

Meredith's face broke into a little smile, and I thought that she was recovering her composure. But not a minute later, she screamed, "There it is!" and pointed with her flashlight to a spot in the tree line not far from where the bear had first appeared. She dug the fingernails of her free hand into my arm.

I aimed my flashlight there, but I didn't see anything except undergrowth and the trunks of trees. Nothing moved. After studying the tree line carefully, I asked, "Are you sure?"

"No. I mean I don't know. How can I be sure? The woods are black, and the bear is black. I thought I saw something moving though." She sobbed a little, not for dramatic effect, but because she couldn't hold it back any more. "We should just walk out of here right now and go back to the truck. How far is it?"

"About six miles." In the daylight, we could have hiked out in two or three hours. But in the middle of the night, it would take us at least twice as long. "But I don't think that would be such a good idea."

"Why not?" Her voice made the question sound like a challenge.

I sighed heavily. I had spent far more time living in the woods than Meredith ever would, yet I always had to explain myself. "OK. First off, our flashlights won't last until we get back to the truck—especially after we use them to pack up in the dark—so we'll be stumbling down the trail in the dark. Second, we'll probably have to rock hop across this creek a few times. That won't be easy in the dark either. What else? Oh yeah. There's a big ass bear somewhere around here, and if I see him again, I'd rather be beside a fire than on a dark trail with our food on my back. The bears use the trails too, you know. That's why we always see bear crap when we're hiking."

Meredith didn't like to concede any point ever, so she said, "We could leave the food here. We could leave everything here and come back for it tomorrow."

I tried to speak calmly. "Mere, I think that bear is probably long gone by now, and I really think it would be more dangerous for us to try to travel at night than it would be for us to stay here. I know you're scared, and I am too, but it makes no sense to run off into the dark woods right now. It'd probably be three in the morning by the time we got back to the truck anyway, so we'd still be in these woods most of the night no matter what."

Either I convinced her or she simply realized that I wasn't going to co-operate, but she relented. "Then let's pile as much wood on the fire as we can and get inside the tent. Maybe if the bear comes back, it'll leave us alone."

That sounded like as good a plan as any, so we piled our remaining wood on the fire. I tried to arrange the logs so that the biggest pieces would roll in toward the center as the fire burned down, thus giving us flames for as long as possible.

Meredith retreated into the tent. I took the opportunity to sneak over to my pack and pound down a couple healthy belts of Yukon. No way was I going to be able to sleep without a little bit of a buzz on. I didn't put the bottle away until I felt the soothing warmth in my belly start spreading up into my head. Then I had a cigarette to kill the smell on my breath.

When I crawled into the tent, I found Meredith stuffing wads of toilet paper loosely into a brown paper bag. She already had two bags lined up by the door with the open ends of the bags twisted shut.

"What are those for?" I tried to breathe away from her face, but that was impossible inside the confined space of the tent.

"Are you drunk? I can't believe you'd drink at a time like this! What's wrong with you?"

"I only had a few sips! I'm nervous too, you know. I just wanted to take the edge off a little." I tried to change the subject. "So what are these bags for?"

"What do you care? Go have another drink, John!"

"C'mon, Mere. Don't be that way. I'm fine! Really! Are these little torches or something?"

"I thought I could light them and scare the bear away if it comes back. We could even throw them at the bear if we have to."

"That's an excellent idea!" I said, trying to walk the fine line between enthusiasm and inebriation. "Fire's our only means of defense right now." I wasn't too sure about the wisdom of antagonizing a bear by throwing flaming toilet paper at it, but at the moment I thought it best to keep my doubts to myself.

Meredith finished preparing her incendiary devices, and we lay down to sleep. I listened carefully to the sounds of the forest around us for a long, long time, but eventually I was able to drift off to sleep.

The bear never came back, or if he did, he didn't bother us. The next morning, Meredith looked as if she had spent a miserable, sleepless night. "Did you get any rest at all?" I asked.

"I dozed a little, but I didn't sleep like you did. I think you kept the bear away with your snoring! I was jealous."

The embers of our fire were still smoldering, so I put a covered pot of coffee water right down into the hot coals. In the light of day, it felt as if the encounter had happened to someone else. I turned to Meredith, who was tossing her toilet paper bombs into the fire. I joked, "If I'd have had my big knife, I'd have went after that bear."

"I'd have *gone* after that bear. You always say *went* instead of *gone*."

She was right. Embarrassed, I said, "I don't do that when I write though. It's just the contraction that messes me up when I'm talking."

"You wouldn't really have fought that bear, would you?"

"Honestly? No. Not unless I had no choice. I'd run if I could."

"What if it was coming after me?"

I considered my answer. "I guess I'd have to try. Hell, I kind of did that last night, didn't I? But with just a knife I don't think I'd be able to do much."

Meredith didn't respond, so I knew that she didn't like my answer. "Sometimes no one can save your ass, Mere, except maybe God."

We were quiet for the most part as we broke down camp. The sun shone through the trees, the creek babbled cheerfully, and the woods were peaceful again. Already, it was hard to remember how scary this little clearing had been a few hours before.

We left Walnut Bottoms and followed the Big Creek Trail east. As we hiked the easy downhill route toward my truck and civilization, I asked Meredith, "So, are you ever going backpacking again?"

"Not unless you buy a gun." Clearly, she had already considered the matter.

I turned to face her and saw that she wasn't kidding. I said, "Guns are illegal out here." That fact didn't bother me, but I thought it might bother her.

"I don't care. I don't want to feel that helpless ever again. I thought about it last night. We were completely at the mercy of that bear."

I tried another approach. "Guns weigh a lot. Have you ever picked one up? I mean they weigh like seven or eight pounds. You expect me to carry another seven or eight pounds in my pack?"

"I can carry a few pounds out of your pack if you want."

Thrust and parry. "That's not really even it," I said. "I don't know if a handgun would even kill a bear. I'd probably only wound it, and then it would die a slow death. Either that or I'd just piss it off and it would *really* come after me."

Meredith didn't say anything, so I continued. "If we had had a gun last night—did I say that right? —we'd have shot that bear, and either we or that bear would be dead or badly hurt right now. Or I'd be in jail. And it would all have been unnecessary. That bear was just trying to make a living. We're the ones in *his* house."

Meredith shot back, "We could've been killed last night, John! I'm not like you. I'm not going to stand up in front of a bear. And you didn't either for very long, I might add."

That one stung, but I kept my mouth shut.

She continued, "Yes, in that situation, I'd do absolutely anything I could to save myself. How can you even argue with that?" She stared at me, full of defiance and melodrama.

That one revealed her overwhelming sense of self-importance, her presumed exemption from the hard facts of life, so perfectly that I had to respond. "We're all going to die someday, Mere, including you."

For that, I got the silent treatment the rest of the way back to the truck. As we hiked the remaining miles, I thought about Plato's three kinds of people. Certainly, I had shown the bronze in me the night before by drinking, but I thought that I had shown a streak of something finer as well. On the other hand, Meredith had shown a wide streak in her that wasn't precious metal at all, just like the streak of lead in the base of Mount Sterling. I wondered if she saw that as clearly as she saw my faults. Nobody was selfless and golden all the time, it seemed to me, or any other kind of precious metal. Especially not me. Everybody had their imperfections, and sooner or later we all had to face our beasts.

9   Going to Mount Guyot: Second Attempt

Ever since we got washed out on top of Ramsey Cascades, Craig and I had talked about going back and finishing the same route we originally set out to do. In the summer of 1997, we were finally able to put together a trip. We were going to be joined by Craig's cousin, Rick, whom I hadn't hiked with since we had been out in the California gold country back in 1981. Rick had been busy raising a family and hadn't spent any time in the backcountry in all those intervening years.

Rick was bringing along a fourth guy, an acquaintance of his named Freddie. I first laid eyes on Freddie when he climbed into Rick's minivan and we headed for the Smokies. Freddie was half Cherokee, and he looked it with his prominent cheekbones and piercing, dark eyes. Rick said Freddie was "cool," and it was a good thing that he was, because we had a whole shitload of cocaine on board. We were all right around forty years old, but we still felt the call of the wild. For a few precious days, we were going to turn

back the clock to our misspent youths. High times awaited—
as well as possible heart attacks.

In the wee hours of the morning, I was riding shotgun as
Freddie drove through the mountains of West Virginia. Craig
and Rick were trying to sleep in the back of the van. I took the
opportunity to get to know Freddie. "Rick says you've done
some backpacking before."

Freddie's dark eyes didn't leave the road. "Oh, sure! When
I was stationed up in Washington state, we used to hike up in
the Cascades. Now *those* are some mountains. Way bigger
than these." He waved his arm toward the mountains outside.

"I hiked just east of here last year," I said as I rummaged
around on the console, looking for my smokes. "In
Monongahela. It wasn't that great, really. Nothing compares
to the Smokies, if you ask me. In the East anyway."

"If you don't mind a Camel, you can have one of mine."
Freddie pulled a pack of Camel Wide Lights out of his shirt
pocket and handed it to me. "Wides" were thicker cigarettes
that delivered more smoke per puff, but they were still
"lights," which meant that they killed you more slowly.

"Thanks. I think Craig's sitting on mine," I said. "What
branch of the service were you in? I was Army."

"I was Navy. Would you light me one, too?" We both had
a little coke in us, which made us want to smoke a lot. And
talk. Freddie continued, "Yeah, I joined the Navy in '72 right
after high school. Ended up in Nam."

"Really," I said, my voice flat. I had met Viet Nam vets in
the service, but they had all been older guys. Viet Nam had
ended in 1973, as I recalled, so it was barely possible that
Freddie had been there. I lit a smoke and handed it to Freddie.
"That would make you about forty-four."

Freddie took a drag. "I'm forty-three. Same as Rick."

"I'll be forty next year. I guess I'm the baby of the group."
In reality, I was not very baby-like. My hairline had finally

gone down the drain, and I had recently decided at Meredith's encouragement to buzz my remaining hair down to crew-cut length. I still lifted weights and ran, but I was starting to put some middle-aged pounds around the middle. Freddie and Rick were packing even more excess poundage, but Craig was still as long and lean as ever.

"What'd you do in the Navy?"

"I was a SEAL."

"Really," I said again with even more doubt in my voice. Freddie didn't strike me as a Navy SEAL kind of guy, but I had just met him, so I wasn't going to call him a liar.

Freddie heard my tone and backtracked quickly. "Well, I did the SEAL training. What I ended up being was an electronics tech on a ship."

Whether it was true or false, it was a story I could live with, so we left it at that. We talked for hours, swapping stories of the military and the mountains, and drove on through the humid August night.

We did the usual song and dance with the rangers in the morning. We wrote some highly unlikely itinerary on a backcountry permit and hightailed it out before any rangers showed up. At the Ramsey Cascades trailhead, Freddie was immediately impressed with the Smokies. "Oh, wow! These mountains are way bigger than I thought! This is gonna be great."

Rick was smiling from ear to ear too. He inhaled the fresh mountain air deeply. "Oh man! It's been way too long since I was here!"

We plodded stoically up the steady incline to Ramsey Cascades like men going to work. We had heavy packs and stiff legs. Day hikers flitted around us like bothersome gnats. I hung back intentionally to see how the troops were doing. Rick moved pretty well, his Hop Sing cook pot swaying back and forth on his pack in a steady rhythm. To me, that swinging pot was Rick's trademark. Freddie looked a little more uncomfortable, constantly adjusting his pack and his boots.

Rick and Freddie were surprised by the size of the Cascades when we got there. Rick looked at the sixty-foot wall of water and said, "We gotta climb that? You're shittin' me, right?"

I remembered the thundering white water the last time I had seen the Cascades. "Looks a lot different than the last time, doesn't it, Craig?"

Craig was all business. He pointed over to the rocks to our left. "We'll go up over there through those rocks, unless you guys can think of a better way." Freddie and Rick exchanged worried looks but didn't offer any suggestions.

The place was crawling with day hikers. Guessing what we had in mind, they eyed us and our big packs with either resentment or admiration, or maybe a mixture of both. Once again, we heard the oohs and ahhs as we headed up around the falls. Craig and I showed Rick and Freddie how to work through the tight spots between the rocks, but watching Freddie struggle raised serious doubts in my mind about the effectiveness of the Navy SEAL training program.

I was smacked by deja vu at the top of the falls. The incredible supper on the edge of the waterfall, the long night of fear, and the desperate climb across the wet log all came back to me with great clarity. Craig pointed to the location of that ill-fated camp on the other side of the river bank. "That's the last place we saw your tent, Rick."

Rick said, "I got laid in that tent once."

Craig said, "That was one of the three times, huh?"

I was anxious to get the main event under way. I gestured vaguely uphill. "Well, gentlemen—and I use that term very loosely—shall we?"

Rick, who had never been off trail, asked, "How are we supposed to get through?"

I answered, "We told you, man. There *is* no good way to get through."

"Oh, man! Hop Sing no like this shit!"

Craig unsheathed his twenty-inch machete and said, "Let's get up the ridge a little and get out of this thick stuff." He didn't stop to discuss it. He started hacking a path that led diagonally northeast. The Ramsey Prong creek flowed westward between two parallel ridges. Craig was leading us toward the ridge on the north side of the creek.

He took a few tentative swings, and once he realized that the machete would cut through the bush cleanly with a good, full swing, Craig decided to cut a nice, six-foot by three-foot opening all the way to Richmond. That idea lasted for about ten feet. When he stopped to catch his breath, I suggested, "Craig, just cut the big branches. We can push the little ones out of the way." Craig nodded in acknowledgment.

After we had gone fifty or sixty yards, Craig came to a standing dead pine. He rasped, "I have an idea." With that, he stuck the machete in the ground and started climbing the dead tree, using the limbs like the rungs of a ladder.

Freddie looked at me and asked, "What's he doing?"

"I have no fucking idea. He thinks he's Daniel Boone or something."

Craig climbed up about fifteen feet until the limbs became too small to hold his weight. He looked out to the east for a second and came back down. Rick asked in mock seriousness, "What'd you see, Dan'l?"

"Lots of trees."

Rick smiled. "What'd you *think* you were gonna see?"

I was reminded of an old Cheech and Chong comedy bit. I sang, "Gonna go downtown. Gonna see my gal . . ."

Rick knew the next line. "Gonna sing her a song. Gonna show her my ding dong."

I said, "Did you see your gal, Craig?"

Rick added, "Did you show her your ding dong? Be pretty hard to see it from way up there, though." Rick and I laughed, but Freddie looked as if he were second-guessing his decision to go off trail with a bunch of lunatics.

Craig and I took turns leading with the machete as we fought our way east along the shoulder of the ridge. It was hard to tell how much time elapsed. Hacking and fighting uphill through the bush was damned hard work, especially in the August heat with almost sixty pounds on my back. We were all drenched with sweat in no time.

Finally, we came to a spot where the laurel hells thinned out, and we saw an eight-foot by eight-foot patch of ground that was nearly level. A level spot on the steep mountainside was a rare thing, so we decided to pitch our tent there. We used the machete and our knives to clear away as much brush as possible. We only had one tent: my state-of-the-art, four-man Eureka. Big as it was, it was still going to be cramped quarters, but we knew that we would never have found enough clear ground to pitch two tents together while we were off trail.

Rick and Freddie discovered that everything was more difficult off trail. Rick, alias Hop Sing, found a tiny clear spot between two huge, mossy logs that would serve as his kitchen. He had four hungry men to feed, so he loaded up his cook pot to the brim with noodles and canned meat and secret Chinese ingredients. We were ravenous like wolves, and the tiny propane stove took forever to cook our meal. The three of us sat on the mossy logs, smoking cigarettes and watching Hop Sing cook, waiting anxiously for our well-deserved supper.

Catastrophe struck. The pot full of food balanced precariously on the top of the propane stove tipped over, and the entire meal was gone. No survivors. All hands lost. We were grief-stricken, bereft of hope. The mood in camp plummeted. Such a simple thing as a hot meal meant so much to the morale in a backcountry camp. It would be another long hour before we ate. Rick felt terrible, but it had been an innocent mistake that could have happened to anyone. Even so, somewhere in the dark, twisted folds of our psyches, we were thinking "*Din jo bing ping dibjo zow!*"

Rick built a more solid base of rocks for the propane stove and started over. The rest of us tried to salvage what we could. We ate any little chunks that weren't too dirty and threw the rest into what would be our fire pit. Our big worry was that the spilled food would attract bears, but moving the camp was out of the question.

While we waited for our second dinner, Freddie said. "Anybody wanna smoke another bowl?" Freddie had brought along plenty of pot and was trying to smoke it as quickly as possible. Apparently it was part of SEAL training.

Rick said, "Sure, Freddie, I'll smoke a bowl with you." Craig didn't smoke pot at all any more, and I only took a toke very rarely, but I took a couple tokes this time for the hell of it. Pretty soon I was high as a kite.

The name "Freddie" had been nagging at me ever since I met him, and smoking the pot jarred loose the obscure association my brain was looking for. In the song "Rapture," Blondie rapped about a man from Mars who ate up cars. One of the lines was "Fab Five Freddie told me everybody's high," so that is exactly what I looked at Freddie and said.

Freddie, of course, had no idea what the hell I was talking about. He was stoned too, which didn't help. He stared at me blankly for a moment, thoroughly convinced that I was insane. He laughed nervously and said, "Yep, I got a buzz on."

I clasped him around the shoulder and said, "You're alright, Fab Five Freddie, you're alright."

Buddha Palguta

After supper, we got a good fire going and had a backcountry hootenanny that Quill Rose and his midnight revelers would have been proud of. Everyone partook of his drug of choice. Craig was off the wagon and carrying some Black Velvet, but he drank it sparingly. He usually stuck strictly to beer. Rick liked his Scotch whiskey, and after he got drunk, he alternated between a bad Scottish accent and a Chinese accent that was even worse. Sometimes his brain jumbled both accents together, rendering his words unintelligible, but it didn't matter because we were all fucked up anyway. Freddie was drinking 100 proof cinnamon schnapps, which seemed like a wise choice, and I of course had my trusty 100 proof Yukon Jack. I had packed a quart and an extra pint for the four nights in the woods.

But the staple of the evening was cocaine—coke, blow, snow, nose candy—whatever you called it, we had lots of it. Coke had actually gotten cheaper over the years, so the money was no object. We set up a mirror inside the tent where we did our chopping and snorting. For a few hours, we took regular turns stumbling over to the tent to do line after line after line.

Eventually, Rick and Craig had enough. Craig simply went over to the tent one time and never came back. Rick was more sociable. He bid us *auld lang syne* and a happy Chinese new year and crawled into the tent not long after Craig.

Freddie and I were just getting started. I was a fiend for the whiskey, and Freddie was a fiend for the blow. We sat around the dancing flames and talked about getting to Mount Guyot, only two miles off to the east. We were studying the map with our flashlights when I saw movement out of the corner of my eye. I ducked and instinctively went for my big knife. Freddie jumped too. Then we saw that the movement was from big mice scurrying around, eating up the traces of our spilled supper. We laughed heartily at ourselves. Since I had the knife out, I threw it at one of the mice, but I missed badly. The knife ricocheted off a big log and almost hit the tent. I said, "Damn near got me a white man, Freddie."

Freddie said, "Good!"

All the same, I knew it was time for bed when I started throwing knives around camp in the dark. Freddie and I crawled all over Rick and Craig getting into the tent, but they didn't care.

The sun was already peeking over the mountains when I crawled out of the tent. My brain throbbed and threatened to explode as I put my boots on. Everybody else was already up and moving, although Freddie didn't look too chipper. Rick and Craig were enjoying my pain. "What's the matter, Johnny Rez? Stay up too late?"

"I think maybe it's just the altitude," I said, and then I remembered a line from Mark Twain: "I think it's the altitude what has caused my balditude, too."

Freddie was busy doing something with his cigarettes. I watched him carefully remove the first half inch of tobacco from a Camel Wide. He left the paper of the cigarette intact and caught the spilled tobacco in the cellophane wrapper from the pack. Then he painstakingly sprinkled a little cocaine down into the hollow end of the cigarette. Finally, he funneled the loose tobacco back in and tamped it down firmly.

I had never seen such a thing. "You gonna smoke that?"

Freddie looked at me with deadly seriousness. "Later on. When I need a little boot in the ass."

"Fab Five Freddie, you're hard core, man."

We packed up camp, taking a few extra minutes to scatter our remaining firewood and to brush over the imprint left by our tent. I had learned about zero-impact camping, and I wanted to leave this remote place as pristine as possible. In a few months when the brush grew back, no one would ever be able to tell that we had been there.

Down at the creek, we paused to top off our canteens. I shed my pack for a minute and doused my throbbing head in the cold water. It helped, but not much. We started up the creek, led by Craig. Rick was next, then me, then Freddie. Although I wasn't thrilled with the idea, we had decided to climb straight up the creek. Craig had no problem hopping four or five feet from stone to stone. Rick, at six three, was able to follow Craig without too much trouble, but I and especially Freddie were struggling to make it from one rock to the next.

We worked our way up Ramsey Prong for a few hundred yards. I made a leap for a rock and came up short, and I got one wet boot for my trouble. "Shit!" I yelled up to Craig. "I wish I'd a knifed you last night, you daddy-long-leg mother fucker!"

A few minutes after I doused my foot, I heard Freddie let out a yelp behind me. I turned and saw him ass-deep in a little vortex of white water. His eyes were wide with fear. He had both hands on a boulder and was trying to pull himself out, but the weight of his body and his pack and the pull of the water were too much for him. If his pack started taking on water, he was done.

I jumped back onto the boulder that Freddie was clinging to. I grabbed the horizontal top bar on the frame of his pack and hauled him up like a sack of potatoes. "I slipped," he explained.

"I know," I said. "This is bullshit. We didn't come out here to fucking drown."

"Thanks, John. I thought I was going in."

Rick and Craig stopped to make sure Freddie was OK, but then they turned right around and continued up the rocks. The combination of a hangover, a wet foot, Freddie almost drowning, and Craig ruthlessly continuing up the creek pissed me off. I yelled above the roar of the water, "Wait a minute! This isn't fucking working!"

The two cousins stopped on a big boulder in the middle of the creek and waited for us to catch up. When Freddie and I got there, Craig acted impatient. "Let's go! We're making good time."

I couldn't believe what I heard. "What, you got a fucking date or something? We won't be making such good time if somebody drowns, will we?"

"He's got a point," Rick said.

Ever since we had stepped out of the van, Craig had been acting as if he had a vendetta to settle. I wanted to get the top of Mount Guyot too, but obviously it meant something different to him than it did to me. "Look," I said, "Freddie and I can't keep up with you guys on these rocks. If we try to, somebody's gonna get hurt, and then we're all screwed."

They nodded in general assent, so I went on. "I'm going to stay right along the edge of the creek where there's more rocks. If you guys want to stay in the middle of the creek, at least stay within sight of us in case something happens." I just assumed that Freddie would stay with me. We would have to fight through a little more vegetation, but it beat the hell out of drowning.

Craig shrugged and said, "Then do it," and headed upriver. Freddie and I worked our way over toward the south bank of the creek, where the vegetation didn't look quite as bad.

Before too long, we were surprised to find another big waterfall barring our way. This cascade was not as big as the main one, but, at thirty or forty feet high, it was still a major hurdle. We barely took the time to notice its beauty. Rick and Craig joined me and Freddie on the south bank, and we flanked the waterfall. The slope was steep and the laurel was incredibly thick, so the going was extremely slow. We spent nearly an hour getting around that single obstacle.

At the top of the second waterfall, Craig and Rick went right back to working their way up the center of the creek. Freddie and I stuck to the banks. The sun was near its zenith, and we suffered in the August heat. The only consolation was that we had all the water we wanted.

Freddie and I caught up with Craig and Rick after a while and found them kneeling on a boulder, peering down into the water. "What'd you lose?" Freddie asked.

"My machete," Craig said gravely.

"Oh shit."

"Yeah," Craig agreed, "we're screwed without it."

Craig had been jumping rock to rock when the weapon slid out of its sheath and fell into the three- or four-foot-deep water. He knew approximately where the machete had gone in, but the shiny silver blade was invisible under the sparkling surface of the creek.

Several times, Craig stuck his long arm in up to his shoulder, feeling around blindly amongst the rocks for his blade. He was in so deep that he had to turn his head to keep his nose above water. "Be careful you don't slice your hand, Craig," I warned. A hand opened to the bone would be just as devastating as losing the machete.

After several minutes of fruitless looking, I was ready to pronounce the blade lost. "You're not going to find it, man," I said. "We'll just have to make do with my knife." The blade of my big ten inch was only half as long as the machete and made of much thinner steel. It really wasn't an adequate substitute at all.

Craig said, "One more try," and reached back down to the bottom of the creek again. He fished around for a long time, and then his face slowly broke into a grin. He pulled the machete out of the water, holding it by the sharpened end.

"No shit," Rick said. "I wouldn't have believed it if I hadn't seen it."

256

With the machete back in our possession, we pressed on relentlessly. All day long, we kept looking toward the eastern skyline, expecting to see the summit of Mount Guyot rising somewhere ahead of us, but time after time all we saw was more trees.

Soon we saw a third waterfall, about the same size as the previous one, blocking our path. Once again, we decided to go around the southern flank. As we started into the bush, we noticed strips of faded red cloth about an inch wide tied to some of the trees. A series of trees marked with these pink ribbons extended up toward the south ridge as far as we could see. None of us had ever seen anything like it in the Smokies.

"Looks like some kind of surveyor's mark," Rick guessed.

"Maybe it's a trail," I said hopefully. I was tired of hopping rocks.

Freddie was the voice of common sense. "Well, it's *something*. Somebody went there, right? And we have to get around these falls anyway. Let's try it and see where it goes."

We followed the pink ribbons deeper into the mountains. For a few minutes, it seemed as if we had indeed discovered a pioneer trail or at least a path used by the animals. The going was relatively easy, at least by off-trail standards. We moved past the shoulder of the third waterfall, but instead of curling left back toward the water, we kept heading southeast toward the top of the south ridge. Soon, the vegetation closed in, and the animal path petered out. I took the machete and hacked a path up to the top of the ridge where we found the last pink ribbon tied to a dead pine tree. We looked in vain for another ribbon.

The brush was so dense that I had to cut back a space so the four of us could face each other. We had a choice to make—follow the ridge eastward to Mount Guyot or work back down to the water and follow the creek eastward. Craig and I studied the map and checked the compass. We still couldn't see the peak of Mount Guyot anywhere in front of us.

Freddie took the opportunity to fire up one of his cocaine-laced cigarettes. When the hot part of the ash reached the cocaine, he took a big drag and held the smoke in his lungs as long as he could. Then he exhaled, caught a breath of fresh air, and took another drag.

Despite our predicament, I was curious. "Did it work?" I asked.

He exhaled heavily again. "Oh yeah," he smiled, "I got a nice little buzz off that. I'll let you try next time."

I rapped, "Fab Five Freddie says everybody's high," but nobody knew what I was talking about. They were used to ignoring my more bizarre statements.

Rick brought us back to the matter at hand. "So how far away is this fucking mountain anyway?"

Craig looked up from the map. "It's hard to say, Rick. According to this, it's a little over two miles from the first waterfall—the big one—up to the top of Mount Guyot. And we should hit the AT before that. The real question is how far do we think we've already gone."

Rick rolled his eyes and whistled softly. "I don't know, man. It feels like we've gone more than two miles through this shit already."

Freddie said, "We had to go at least a mile. Don't you think?"

Craig agreed. "That sounds about right, Freddie, especially since we covered some ground yesterday before we made camp."

A mile sounded about right to me too. "Which means the AT is a mile or less up this ridge," I said. It didn't sound so bad when I said it that way. "To me, it doesn't make any sense to go back down and lose all the elevation we just gained. Let's just follow this ridge all the way up."

That next mile turned out to be the hardest mile any of us ever traveled in our lives. We were up on that God-forsaken ridge, exposed to the full August sun, and it beat down on us mercilessly. But the greatest adversary was the undergrowth. The laurel and the prickers were thicker than in any hell I had ever encountered in any forest anywhere. Several times, I threw my fully loaded weight of 280 pounds at the wall of vegetation and simply bounced back. The bush became a living enemy. It grabbed at us, clawed us, and tried to break us. It tried to pin us there on that ridge until we died of exposure and our rotted flesh became part of the soil of Mount Guyot. We fought back, cussing and bleeding, hacking forward inch by inch, climbing uphill with every step, crawling over and sometimes under downed trees, and working around the tangled deadfalls.

Craig and I took turns leading with the machete. We wouldn't have been able to move forward at all without it. Craig and I were both meat cutters, used to handling knives and used to hard labor, but we could only lead for a few minutes at a time. We would hack with the machete and stomp down branches and bull our way forward like barbarians at the gates of a palace, driving forward as long as we could. Then, dripping with sweat and gasping for air, we would hand the machete off, and the other guy would attack the laurels and the prickers the same way. For each turn we took, we might gain ten or twelve feet—that was all.

This vegetation was different from the rhododendron hells that Dan and I had fought through in Bone Valley. That had entailed more stepping over and crawling under the entangling branches. On Mount Guyot, the laurels and the prickers seemed to fill every square inch of space from the ground all the way up to over our heads. These bushes had to be cut down or beaten down before a person could pass through them. The second guy had only a slightly easier time that the lead guy.

259

By the time Rick came through in the third position, he was able to break back or stomp down some of the most troublesome branches or plants, but he was getting badly clawed up too. Freddie brought up the rear. He was hurting, probably because he was smoking cocaine, but he kept up, and he didn't complain.

We were well into the afternoon, and we had been sweating and working like mules in the ninety plus heat all day. We had to take frequent breaks to catch our breaths and drink water. Before too long, we were swishing our canteens to see how much water we had left. The peak of Mount Guyot was nowhere in sight, and things were getting desperate. We were deep, deep, deep in the bush and running out of water.

To our surprise, the ridge in front of us suddenly turned downhill. We didn't know what to make of it, but it offered us the first long-distance view we had seen all day. We were on a slight prominence, looking east, and the ridge dropped away into a shallow saddle. We could see where the ridge rose back up in front of us a quarter mile out and resumed running east. Beyond that, we could just barely see the tip of a rounded peak rising above the tops of the furthest trees, but that high point looked to be several miles away. "That's gotta be it," I said wearily. "Guyot."

"No," Craig protested, "it can't be that far!"

"Then what do you think that is?"

The maps and the compasses came out, and we debated where in the hell we were. I felt certain that we were still on the long east-west ridge that ran up to Mount Guyot. I remembered how long it had taken me and Dan to get through the bush in Bone Valley, but Craig, Rick and Freddie refused to accept the idea that we had worked and sweated and bled all day and had still gone less than a mile. Freddie fired up another special cigarette to help him wrap his mind around this new concept.

"Well, one thing is for sure," Craig said. "We have to get more water, so we have to head downhill." We continued due east into the saddle. As we neared the bottom, we heard the musical sound of water trickling, which sounded like angels singing our names and calling us to join them. But the sound wasn't coming from our left, so what we were hearing wasn't the Prong we had been following. This sweet, tinkling sound was coming from our right, farther down the sloping south side of the saddle.

We knew south was the wrong way to go, but we didn't care. Like wild-eyed horses in a flaming barn, we broke and ran headlong, every man for himself, down the south slope toward the maddening sound of the water. The ground became spongy under our feet, and we started to see moisture oozing up through the soil. The whole area under us was a large, seeping spring. As we ran farther down the hill, thousands of tree roots protruded from the saturated ground. We ran across this wild tangle of roots that could easily have broken someone's leg, but miraculously, no one even fell. Maybe there really were angels there. When we saw steady streamlets of water dripping from the roots and rocks, we stopped and gathered the cold water in our bloodied, filthy hands and drank our fill. Only then did we notice that it was blessedly cool in the shade away from the hated ridge. This would be our camp for the night.

We searched for any place close to the water that would be dry enough and flat enough to pitch the tent. The best spot we could find was a six-by-six patch of sloping ground on the uphill side of a huge tree. We couldn't even spread the tent out fully, but it was the best site available. It was like camping on the gently-pitched roof of a house.

After supper, we took care of our individual chores and squared away the camp as best we could. We stunk ferociously, but bathing was out of the question because the volume of water was too small. I saw Freddie sitting near the dripping rocks with his boots off, tending his feet, so I went over and sat beside him. He was looking at a broken blister the size of a quarter on his heel. The red flesh underneath looked raw and painful.

"Damn, Freddie! That's not good." Now I understood why he had been lagging behind all day.

Freddie tried to laugh it off. "The one on my other foot is worse."

"I feel your pain, dude. I had blisters like that the first time I came out here."

Craig caught the end of what I was saying. He looked at Freddie's heel and winced. "Don't let John kid you, Freddie. The blisters he had were half that size. And he was crying like a baby, too! I had to hike fifteen miles out to get the car for him 'cause he was crying so much!" I laughed at the memory as Craig spoke.

"I can't imagine John crying like a baby," Freddie said.

I was touched by the compliment, but I had to fess up. "Thanks, Freddie, but Craig's not too far from the truth. Except he didn't walk anywhere near fifteen miles. More like seven or eight. All downhill."

Craig shook his head and smiled. "You lying son of a bitch!"

I turned serious. "Anyway, I have some good tape and some Mole-Skin in my pack. The Mole-Skin might help. You gotta try to take care of those heels, Freddie. We still have a long way to go." Mole-Skin was an adhesive pad designed specifically for protecting tender spots on feet.

"Yeah," Craig added, "that doesn't look good, Freddie. At least you're taking it like a man, unlike some others I know."

"I just need to stay fucked up," Freddie said earnestly, "and I'll be fine."

After all the evening chores were done, the whiskey bottles and the mirrors and the pipes appeared. It was time for a heap-big powwow. The only semi-flat place where we could all sit around a map was inside the tent, so we jammed in there to figure out our next course of action.

I stuck with what I had said earlier. I was sure we were on the long ridge leading east to the peak of Mount Guyot. "This saddle we're in might look big to us, but it's probably so small that it's not even on the map."

Craig pointed on the map to the next creek south of Ramsey Prong, which also ran from east to west. "Maybe we crossed over the ridge, and we're down in here somewhere."

"Either way," I said, "all we have to do is keep heading east and we'll hit the AT."

Rick was, as the saying goes, not a happy camper. He looked at me and then at Craig. "So you're telling me we're out here in the middle of fucking nowhere, and you're not even sure which creek we're by? This is fucked up. I'm thinking I should just ditch my pack and follow this water downstream until I walk the fuck out of here."

Freddie was looking for the quickest way out too. "That's not a bad idea, if you ask me."

To me, it was about the dumbest idea I had ever heard. If we went the wrong way, we could easily end up fighting our way deeper and deeper into the trackless woods. We were on the verge of being lost in the Great Smoky Mountains, and *that* was serious business. "Look, you guys can go any damn direction you want tomorrow, but in the morning I'm loading up every ounce of water I can carry, and I'm heading back up the ridge. I think that was Mount Guyot that we saw the top of."

Craig sounded alarmed. "Splitting up now would be really stupid."

I could see the first signs of panic in the ranks. I said, "I read one time that the number one reason people get lost in the woods is because they refuse to believe their compasses. We know the AT is east of us. All we have to do is keep heading east and we'll find it."

For a moment, the powwow was silent. Then Freddie broke the silence by saying to Rick, "Hey, if you ditch your pack, can I have your blow?" That concluded the useful portion of the meeting. We tried to drink and carry on for a while, but we were just too exhausted.

We awoke the next morning jammed against the big tree. We had been packed together inside the tent like sardines to begin with, and now our knees were in our chests and our feet were literally shoved up against the tree. Except for the midget clowns that came piling out of the little car at the circus, heterosexual men have never been packed so tightly together.

We faced another brutal day. A heady feeling, the mingled anticipation of adventure and the sense of inherent danger, filled the camp. We were savoring a tiny taste of what the great American pioneers must have felt when they crossed mountain ranges and deserts. We carried ourselves with pride and purpose. Freddie taped up his heels as best he could. We bloated our bellies with water until they were about to burst, and we filled every water container we had to the brim. We were staking everything on finding the AT and then coming to water at the nearest shelter. If we didn't find the AT, we were going to have to turn around and come back down the mountain until we found water again. If that happened, there were certain to be defections in the ranks.

We started angling east by northeast, over to the where the evil ridge resumed. The mere act of heading back uphill was demoralizing. Eventually, we climbed out of the saddle and resumed making our way up the long ridge toward Mount

Guyot. Craig and I took turns leading, and we made slow, painful progress.

After an hour or so of working our way up the death ridge, Rick decided that he was going to take the lead. He grabbed the machete from Craig and moved to the front of our little column. I stayed in the second position, and Craig moved in behind me. Freddie, struggling with his blisters, wasn't budging from the fourth position. Rick hefted the machete in his right hand and measured up his first target. He took a nice, arcing, overhand swing and sliced cleanly through a thick laurel branch. As he followed through, the machete flew out of his sweaty hand and landed point-first in the earth directly between my feet. The razor-sharp blade thudded into the dirt, quivered for a second, and stopped.

Everyone was silent. If the machete had sailed another few inches to either side, or another foot higher, I would have been grievously wounded. My chances of survival deep off trail with such a wound, especially with the Doobie Brothers serving as my paramedics, would have been slim. I could just imagine Freddie putting a tourniquet around my neck and Craig telling him to make it tighter. Rick looked at me, waiting to see how I was going to react. I knew that it had been purely an accident, and I knew he already felt terrible about it. I pulled the machete out of the ground and shouldered past him up to the front of the column. All I said was, "I'll go first." There would be time to bust his balls later.

We continued, always hoping to catch another glimpse of Mount Guyot up ahead, but we couldn't see the mountain for the trees. After an entire morning of fighting up the ridge, the laurels and the prickers started to thin out, and we could feel that we were nearing the end. Finally, the woods opened up, the laurels disappeared, and the ground was carpeted with moist, gentle ferns. The ferns caressed our bruised and bloodied legs as we walked the final few hundred yards. Then we saw the thin ribbon of beaten earth threading through the woods and found a white slash painted on a tree and knew that we had found the AT. We high-fived all around and congratulated ourselves, but to me it felt more like survival than victory.

We decided that we needed to celebrate our deliverance from the evil ridge. The packs came off, and the liquor bottles came out. Rick raised his bottle of Scotch. "Here's to Mount Guyot."

We all drank to the mountain, and only after we drank did I point out the truth. "You guys do realize that we're not on top yet, don't you?"

Rick's voice sounded pained, as if I had just accused him of something unjustly. "What do you mean, we're not on Mount Guyot? Why do you fuckers keep changing the rules?"

Freddie interrupted and said, "I'm gonna do a line real quick." He pulled his mirror and his little kit out of his pack.

I rapped, "Fab Five Freddie says everybody's high."

"Forget that shit," Rick said. "What do you mean we're not on top of Guyot?"

Craig grabbed his cocaine kit out of his pack as well. "He's right, Rick. The top of the mountain is up there." Craig pointed to the steep mountainside that still rose to the east past the trail. Then Craig added, "I'm gonna do a line too."

"Mother fucker!" Rick laughed incredulously. "Here I'm thinking I climbed the damn mountain, and you guys are telling me I haven't."

Craig and Freddie were already spilling little white mounds onto their mirrors. "We're back in the world now," I reminded them. "Somebody could walk by here any minute." We were still deep in the mountains, but on the AT, it was entirely possible that someone could come by.

"Let's post guards," Freddie suggested. "John and Rick, you guys go watch the two ends of the trail and tell us if

someone's coming. Craig and I'll cut some lines for you."
Freddie was a regular genius when it came to doing blow.

I walked twenty yards south along the AT until I came to a
curve where I could see even further down the trail yet still
see Freddie and Craig. Rick did the same on the north end of
our position. Craig and Freddie got busy chopping some lines.
"Cut 'em some big ones, Craig," Freddie urged.

I heard what Freddie said and yelled, "You tell him,
Freddie! I want a line that'll cave in the back of my head."

No more than a minute later, Rick hissed, "Hey! Here they
come!" from his northern look-out. Craig and Freddie quickly
but carefully slid the mirrors under their backpacks. Just as
they finished putting away the goods, a troop of six or seven
boy scouts and their two adult leaders appeared from around
the corner where Rick stood.

Rick looked at the kids and forced a smile. "Hey, how you
guys doing?"

The Boy Scout group walked up to the spot where our
packs were piled on the trail and stopped. The older leader, a
fit man in his late thirties with thinning hair and a tan boy scout
shirt on, greeted us with a slight edge of wariness in his voice,
"Y'all alright?"

Craig laughed heartily and said, "Yeah, we're fine! We just
came up from down there." Craig pointed down into the huge
valley that spread out to the west. I noticed for the first time
since we had come out just how vast that valley looked.

The scouts and their two leaders eyed us as if they had
discovered mangled bodies lying on the trail. The boys'
mouths were agape. They saw four fortyish men in tattered,
filthy rags. Our legs were completely covered from ankle to
thigh with bloody scrapes and welts, and our arms were even
worse if that was possible. Our heads were badly sunburnt,
and we all had three- or four-day's growth of beard.

The older leader, the kind of guy I might have been except for a few twists of fate and some questionable choices, said, "Looks like y'all had a rough time of it." The younger leader, a small, clean-cut guy in his twenties, looked more frightened than his scouts. He didn't say anything at all.

I thought, *Hit the road, Jack. No merit badges to be had here*, but I said, "No, we're just regrouping for a minute."

The boy scouts left us and continued south. We had to re-post our guards before we could bring the mirrors back out and do our jumbo lines. We had been back in civilization for five minutes, and already it sucked.

Thus fortified, we headed south on the AT toward the Tricorner Knob shelter where Craig and Dan and I had given a freezing boy whiskey twenty years before. We had gone less than a quarter mile when we came to a wooden signpost that read Mt. Guyot 800 Yds. A barely discernable foot path branched off the AT and led up the steep mountainside. This side trail wasn't marked on any of the maps, so it took us by surprise. We had spent parts of three days sweating and cussing and bleeding to get to this point. Now, like a gift from above, the final half mile was evidently a clear path through the woods, as if God wanted to make it as easy as possible for us to get to the top of Mount Guyot.

"There it is, Craig," I said, "half a mile away. You going?"

Vince Lombardi had been so right. Fatigue does indeed make cowards of us all. Our legs were beyond dead, and going to the top would have meant another hard mile of hiking. At that moment, none of us had an extra mile left in the tank.

"Next time," Craig said as he walked past the side trail that led to Mount Guyot. "We'll go to the top next time." Rick and Freddie followed him.

I had my doubts. I knew how way led on to way and how some opportunities never came back around. I *knew* that, and still I didn't go up to Mount Guyot. Going downhill was so much easier. Somewhere, Vince Lombardi was laughing his big dago ass off.

Ten minutes down the trail, we had forgotten all about not climbing up to Mount Guyot. We smoked cigarettes and joked as we ambled along. Compared to where we had been, the remaining few miles on the AT heading downhill to Tricorner Knob were like walking from the living room to the kitchen for a snack. Only Freddie wasn't enjoying the moment. He was silent and limping badly, obviously in pain.

We were a day behind the phony trip itinerary written on our backcountry permit, so we weren't authorized to be staying at the Tricorner Knob shelter that night. It didn't really matter though, as long as the shelter wasn't full that night. But, as luck would have it, the place was packed with the same boy scouts that had interrupted our coke party, and they had valid permits. "These little shits are starting to be a pain in the ass," Rick muttered.

We talked with the two Boy Scout leaders and explained that Freddie was hurting, and if there was any room at all, we would appreciate it if Freddie could have a bunk in the shelter so he could get some good rest. Like the troopers they were, they agreed to help. Freddie could have a bunk, but there wasn't enough room for four, so Craig and Rick and I would have to sleep in our tent outside the shelter.

The younger troop leader finally spoke up. "Of course, you know you'll be breaking rule number seven." He read from the back of one of the standard-issue trail maps given out by the Park Service, "'Use of tents at shelters is prohibited.'"

The four of us looked at each other and tried not to laugh in the guy's face. I wondered which of those rules we hadn't broken over the years. I looked at the earnest young troop leader and said, "Well, we've bent the rules out here once or twice before."

269

The earnest troop leader didn't want to let it go. "Understood," he said, "but they have that rule for a reason. The bears like to come around these shelters because people leave food out sometimes. You'll be in danger out here in a tent."

I had a .357 Ruger Blackhawk revolver in my pack, so I wasn't too worried about a bear, although I still didn't think I could shoot one. I had given in to Meredith and bought the cowboy-style six-shooter, and now I was used to carrying the extra eight pounds. I liked the added sense of security it gave me in the mountains. The gun and the booze I was carrying were two of the reasons why my pack weighed sixty pounds. I intended to keep myself drunk and well-armed, like any good American.

I looked the guy in the eye and said, "Danger is my business."

Craig took an intimidating step closer to him and said, "We'll be fine."

The young troop leader decided to stop arguing. We pitched our tent in the clearing as far away from the shelter as possible. We cleaned up our wounded limbs and ate supper and marveled at how a simple dirt clearing could be so homey and nice. We tried to stay away from the boy scouts as much as possible because, in the immortal words of Doc Holliday, we had not yet begun to defile ourselves.

Fab Five Freddie was hurtin' for certain. He took a nap before supper and then retreated back to his bunk immediately afterward. We came to visit Freddie in the shelter while the boy scouts were down by the water. "How you feeling, Freddie?"

He said, "I'm reading all this graffiti in here." Then he realized why we were there, so he said, "Look at my heels." He spun around in his bunk so that his feet were facing out and then rolled over onto his belly. "I'm letting 'em air out."

Each heel had a blister easily bigger than a quarter. A few shreds of white skin still clung to the edges of the wounds, but most of that outer skin was torn away. The reddish layers underneath were plainly visible, and those layers had split wide open and bled. It looked painful as hell. Craig and I exchanged glances. We shrugged and shook our heads sadly, as if we were consulting doctors and the case was hopeless. *Close him up, nurse, there's nothing we can do for him.* Craig tried to say something encouraging. "Well, they don't look infected."

I was more pragmatic. "You were right, Freddie. You need to stay fucked up."

Freddie spun back around so he was facing us again. He took me seriously. "That's what I thought, John, but now I'm thinking I need to rest tonight. I'll stay fucked up tomorrow while we're walking."

"Unfortunately," Craig said, "there's no quick way to get you out of here."

Freddie knitted his brow. "What're you talking about? I'm not quitting. I just need to rest tonight."

I shook my head again, this time in admiration. "Freddie," I said, "you are one tough Injun."

Freddie smiled at the compliment. "It's a SEAL thing, John. You gotta be one with the pain."

"Whatever works, man." I didn't care if he was bullshitting about the SEAL training or not. He was proving that he had heart, and that was the most important quality of all in the mountains—or maybe anywhere.

Freddie assured us that he was cool with staying in the shelter, so we didn't feel like we were abandoning him when we left him with the boy scouts and went back to our tent. I got my loaded six-shooter out of my pack and placed it carefully under my sleeping bag. Craig and Rick didn't mind that I had the firearm. We were vulnerable where we were,

271

and if a bear came sniffing around the shelter for a free meal, at least we had some means of defense. I figured that firing the gun in the air would be enough to scare the bear off, but I hoped I didn't have to find out.

At first we were careful to keep the noise down. We assumed that everybody knew what the *tick-tick-tick* of a razor against a mirror indicated.

"Hey Rick," I whispered, "good thing you're better with that razor blade than you are with a machete!"

"See, and I thought you were gonna take the high road on that."

"You should've known better."

"Another foot higher," Craig laughed, "and you'd a split his dick long ways like a kielbasa!"

"The man with two dicks," I said, and that image brought back a memory. "I had a dream once that I had five dicks."

"That's probably because you associate your dick so closely with your hand," Rick guessed.

"I know I do," Craig admitted.

If the ticking of the razor on the mirror didn't give us away, the vacuum cleaner sucking sounds of us snorting our lines did. But after an hour of drinking and doing lines, we didn't much care. The forest was fully dark, and everyone inside the shelter had apparently gone to sleep. We sat outside our tent and had the clearing at Tricorner Knob to ourselves. We watched the stars appear.

"You think Freddie's going to make it?" I wondered out loud.

Rick sniffed hard to clear his nasal passages. "Oh, yeah," he said, "that hit the spot! Does he have a choice?"

"Not really," Craig answered, "but I'll tell you what, being in that kind of pain all day really wears you out. It just drains you."

"I know," I said seriously, "I've been through it."

Finding Mount Guyot

"John," Craig sounded exasperated, "your blisters were about half as big as his. Maybe."

"They still hurt, Craig," I started to say something else, but I let it go because it was, after all, twenty years in the past.

Rick changed the subject. "That guy was really something with his 'rule number seven,' wasn't he?"

"Rules!" I spat the word as if it were poison on my lips.

Craig rolled his eyes. "Oh, shit! Here we go."

"No," I held up my hand to stop their laughter, "There have to be *some* rules out here or else there'd be no woods left." I wanted to stop right there, but I couldn't. "It's just that some people absolutely *thrive* on rules. They fucking love 'em! Like that wormy little fucker in there." I waved toward the shelter. "He's probably a lawyer or something. He couldn't fucking wait to quote a rule."

Rick, with whom I had spent more nights in the mountains than anybody on Earth, leaned back and looked at me as if he had never truly understood me until now. "You've got problems with authority, don't you?"

I rubbed my hand over my eyes. "Maybe I do. Maybe that's why I do this." But it wasn't clear, even to me, what "this" referred to.

We drank well into the night. Craig lay on his back and looked up into the heavens. "I've never seen so many stars in my life," he said, and he wasn't exaggerating in the least. The night was clear, and the hazy cloud of the Milky Way could be seen running north and south.

"I read this one idea in school," I said quietly, "about the Natural Supernatural, or the Supernatural Natural. One or the other." I was very drunk but still lucid. "It was by an American writer—Emerson, Ralph Waldo Emerson."

"Ah, Emerson," Rick said drunkenly, as if he had any idea at all what Emerson was about.

273

I ignored Rick. "His idea was that if the stars only came out once every thousand years, everybody would say it was a miracle, but because we see the stars all the time, we don't think it's a miracle at all."

Craig said, "And . . ." He clearly wasn't impressed with Emerson yet.

"And that's why I'm not a teacher any more, 'cause my students were assholes like you guys."

Craig laughed, "No, go on, John. Please."

"Well, the point is that there are miracles—supernatural things, proofs of God, whatever you want to call them—around us all the time in the natural world, but we see them every day so we take them for granted, like these stars."

Rick asked, "Like when I planted that machete between your feet? Was that supernatural too?"

I pretended to be disgusted, but I knew they both got the idea. We drank until the exhaustion and the alcohol overcame the cocaine, and then we crawled into the tent to sleep. We hadn't mentioned Mount Guyot once all night.

Freddie was all bright-eyed the next morning because he had stayed sober and gotten a decent night's sleep. We asked him if he had heard us from inside the shelter. "No. The fucking boy scouts were lighting farts in there! There was some graffiti on the ceiling about setting the world's record."

"No shit!" Craig said. "We saw that one before. Long time ago. Remember, John?"

"You don't forget a classic like that."

Freddie said, "I told them I was the guy who set the record."

Craig asked, "How's your heels?"

"Fucked up. Good thing I got lots of dope."

We were all hoping Freddie's dope did the trick because we had a tough hike ahead of us. Our plan was to hike eleven miles south on the AT to the jump off that led down to Porters Flat and then hike down that supposedly uphill-only pioneer trail to make our last camp at #31, Porters Flat. The eleven-mile stretch was the jagged "sawtooth" section of the AT, the absolute highest and one of the most rugged sections on the whole two-thousand-mile trail. Freddie was going to do it with those horrible blisters on his feet. Sometimes, drugs were a useful thing. I didn't see how Freddie was going to make it otherwise.

Freddie carefully applied tape and Mole-Skin to his heels. He also loaded up more of his coke-laced cigarettes and rolled a couple of regular joints. All in a day's work for a SEAL. I decided to keep Freddie company on the trail to try to keep his mind off the pain. The first part of the AT out of Tricorner Knob was actually downhill, and Craig and Rick quickly outdistanced us. Freddie was taking it slow and steady, trying to make the tape job on his heels last as long as possible.

Inevitably, the trail turned uphill. Near Mt. Chapman, we reached 6,220 feet, the highest point on the Appalachian Trail. Several peaks in the park were higher, but as we had learned at Mount Guyot, the AT didn't actually cross over the very tops of the highest mountains. As the trail turned downhill again, I caught my breath and asked Freddie, "How's it feel now?"

"I'm one with the pain."

"You're a bad mammy jamma, Freddie."

"Let's talk about something else."

"OK. What?"

"There was one thing I was wondering." Freddie hesitated but went on. "Rick was telling me you used to teach at college and you quit. Why?"

"That's a long story."

"I've got all day."

"Well, I was a graduate student, OK? What they call a teaching fellow."

"Is that like a jolly good fellow?"

I laughed and reached into my belt pouch for my Camels. "It means I was still taking classes—working on my doctorate—and teaching classes too. It was just freshman English and shit like that, so it wasn't like I was a big-time professor or anything."

"But that's what you were going for?"

"Yeah. All I had to do was write my dissertation, which is basically a book that nobody ever reads. But, see, I finally realized that I didn't fit with those people . . . at all." I sighed and wiped my filthy bandana across my sweaty brow. I found it almost impossible to explain my reasons for quitting to someone who had never been in the ivory tower. I decided to take a different tack. "If you look in the want ads for professors, Freddie, every single ad says, 'Women and minorities especially encouraged to apply.' I was going to be on the bottom of every hiring list simply because I'm a white male."

"That sucks! Too bad you're not Cherokee."

"Yeah, that would've been perfect. But it was more than that." Now that I had gotten started, I wanted to get it all off my chest. "See, I thought grad school was still about getting good grades, but it wasn't." I smiled ruefully. "It's about schmoozing the right people and making connections. They're all these rich, upper-class people, and I wasn't one of them. They knew it the whole time, but I was a dumbass, and it took me a while to figure it out." I laughed bitterly. "I was going along, getting my A's and bragging about being a meat cutter, and they were looking down their noses at me the whole time."

"Couldn't you just finish up and teach at a two-year college or something?"

"I guess I could, but those people don't make any money. Maybe that's what I'll end up doing anyway. To tell you the truth, Freddie, I kind of lost my heart for it."

"But your wife is still going for her doctorate?" Freddie didn't realize it, but he was sticking red hot pokers up under sore fingernails with every question he asked.

"Yeah. I'm cutting meat and paying the bills while she finishes her dissertation."

Freddie knew that couldn't be good. "Ohhh," was all he could say.

The next mountain in our path was Mt. Sequoyah, named after the man who spent twelve years of his life devising the written Cherokee alphabet. The southern Cherokees burned down his cabin because they thought he was practicing bad medicine, but he persisted and eventually succeeded.

Freddie persisted as well, and we stayed together for the first five miles until we came to a trail junction and found Rick and Craig waiting for us, resting against their packs in the scant shade of a big rock. The sign post told us that the Pecks Corner shelter and a spring were a half mile down the adjoining trail.

It was another blistering day and there was no shade on the AT. I took a small sip from my canteen and noticed that it was pretty low. "Did you guys go get water?" I asked hopefully.

Rick said, "Siesta time, senor. No mas la agua."

"OK, Pedro," I said, "but you're gonna be crying the blues when you run out of water this afternoon." I remembered all too well the time Dan and I had run out of water. Lapping water from a muddy puddle like a dog left a lasting impression on one's mind.

Craig spoke up. "So do *you* want to walk the extra mile there and back?"

I looked around and pointed a finger at my own chest. "You talkin' to me?" I swished my canteen around and gauged that

277

it was about a third full. "I think I can make it to the jump off with what I've got." I didn't have to look at the map to know the deal. From where we were, it was about six more miles to the top of the Porters Flat pioneer trail. If we found it and went downhill there, we'd come to the spring water seeping out of the black rocks less than a quarter of a mile down. If we missed that unmarked turn-off, it was another 1.7 miles along the AT to the Icewater Spring shelter. We would definitely find water there. I knew from bitter experience that there wouldn't be any water on the AT before that. I was betting that I could walk six or eight more miles with the water I had left.

Everybody else was making the same mental calculations and weighing their thirst against going the extra mile. Somewhere, Vince Lombardi was watching. One by one, each man solemnly announced that he had enough water to see him through to the next watering hole. Nobody wanted to walk an extra mile, even without a pack. Somewhere, Ol' Vince started snickering once again.

Rick and Craig started off fast, as if they could get where they were going before their thirst caught up with them. They soon disappeared. After a few minutes, I turned to Freddie and said, "Freddie, I feel like I'm abandoning you, but it's killing me to walk this slow, man."

Freddie understood. "It's OK, John. Just don't head off down to Porters Flat without me. I don't know where that turn-off is."

I stretched out my stride and slowly left Freddie behind. I walked along for a mile or more without seeing anyone. I knew how ugly the next few hours were going to be, so I paced myself. I sipped my water sparingly. I tried to breathe through my nose instead of my mouth because I had read that you lose moisture breathing through your mouth. I didn't ever want to feel again like I had on Thunderhead Mountain when I got all shaky and weird inside.

278

Eventually, I saw Rick by himself up ahead on the trail. He was moving a lot slower now. I caught up with him and asked him how he felt. He croaked, "Agua, por favor."

He wasn't really in bad shape yet because he was still joking. I said, "No mas la agua, Pedro. Where's your cousin?"

Rick pointed west without saying anything and let his arm drop wearily to his side. His face became serious. "I'm hurtin', Johnny."

I didn't know if he was talking specifically about the lack of water or about his condition in general, but it didn't matter either way. The best I could do for him was give him some philosophical advice. I said, "Remember, Rick, 'That which does not kill me makes me stronger.' Nietzsche said that. He was a German philosopher who went nuts."

Rick repeated the words, "That which does not kill me makes me stronger." He rolled the idea around for a moment, and the slightest trace of a smile appeared on his cracked lips. He recited the saying a few times. I turned around and started up the trail, knowing Rick was retreating deep within himself, and behind me I could hear him chanting the mantra over and over again. He was still chanting when I pulled out of ear-shot.

I walked a long time by myself. We all walked alone on that stretch of the AT, enduring the fatigue, the heat, and the lack of water as best we could. I still had an inch of hot water left in my canteen, and I was determined to hang on to at least a few sips in case things got really bad. We passed some spectacular views, especially looking out to the south, but I doubt that any of us enjoyed them. We were back in survival mode.

The skies started darkening, and I hoped it would rain to cool things off. I was wondering how I might be able to capture some rainwater when I found Craig sitting against a rock at a high point along the trail. Craig briefly glanced toward me and then went back to staring into space. "I realized those guys don't know where the jump off is," he said.

"Yeah, we need to start watching for it," I muttered. I dropped my pack and plopped down next to Craig. "How you doing on water?"

"I'm OK," he said defensively.

"No, I'm OK too."

The two of us sat there for a long while, staring vacantly, not feeling any necessity to talk. A few drops fell reluctantly from the sky, and I carefully arranged my cheap plastic poncho on a rhododendron so that any water that fell on it would run off into my drinking cup. Craig didn't bother getting up. He just sat there with his head tilted backward and his mouth open.

While I watched a few pitiful droplets gather on the green plastic, we heard Rick approaching. When he got close enough, we heard him saying, "That which does not kill me makes me stronger. That which does not kill me makes me stronger." Once he reached us, he shirked his pack and sat down in the dirt.

Craig was amused that we had caught Rick talking to himself. "What were you talking about, Rick?"

"It's Nietzsche, Craig. German philosophy."

Craig said, "I thought he played linebacker for the Packers," and left it at that. I wondered if Rick had been repeating his mantra the whole time, but I was too tired to ask.

Rick saw what I had done with my poncho and spread his own out the same way. He was rewarded because it began to spit rain a little harder. We each collected a quarter inch of water in the bottoms of our cups and made a big fuss about drinking it down.

Freddie came trudging along, the pain showing on his face. Craig tried to muster up some enthusiasm and genially asked, "How's it going, Freddie?"

Finding Mount Guyot

"I'm one with the pain," he said wearily. We were all becoming philosophers.

Freddie saw what Rick and I were up to, and he did us one better. He started licking the wet rhododendron leaves, saying, "You just gotta make sure they don't have any bird shit on 'em."

Still terribly parched, we continued along the sawteeth. We told Freddie and Rick what we were looking for—a steep chute that dropped almost straight down off the right side of the trail. "Well, that narrows it down," Rick wise-cracked. But against the odds, we found the jump off with no trouble. A small cairn only three stones high marked the spot.

We parted the weeds on the side of the trail and peered down the chute. It was indeed almost straight down. Rick tossed one of the rocks from the cairn over the edge, and a long time passed before we heard the rock hit. A *very* long time. "No shit!" Rick said. "That's a steep mother fucker." Rick and Freddie were willing to go down the pioneer trail anyway. Freddie in particular was absolutely enchanted with the idea of going over the edge, but Craig and I, knowing just how difficult the path was, tried to temper their enthusiasm. Spirits were willing, but flesh was weak.

"Look," I said, "we're all on really tired legs. Plus, going down this thing would be twice as hard with a full pack on. I think we're asking for trouble if we go down right now. One of us could break a leg in no time."

Craig agreed. "Why don't we keep on going, sleep at the shelter tonight, and then come back here and go down in the morning?"

"What's the name of that next place?" Rick asked. "Icewater Springs? That sounds pretty damn good!" That decided it. We bypassed the Porters Flat jump off and headed for the luscious-sounding Icewater Springs. Freddie was the

281

only one that seemed truly disappointed, yet he was the one who would have had the most trouble.

Craig and I stayed together and stepped it out for the last mile and a half. I wanted to be sitting in the shade with my pack off, drinking cold water. Rick and Freddie fell behind, but everybody knew what the next stop was, so it was every man for himself. We passed a side trail going north to Charlies Bunion, the mountain with the intriguing name. Craig and I decided that we could check out Charlies Bunion—whatever it was—in the morning. We stayed on the main trail and kept heading west. I knew we couldn't have much more than a mile left, so I drank my last sip of hot, plastic-tasting water. I told Craig, "I'm hell-bound for water now, buddy. I'm not stopping 'til I get to that spring."

That was when the AT turned sharply uphill. That last mile was like climbing the long, steep staircase out of hell. My thigh muscles, which had been traumatized by three days of fighting through the bush up to Mount Guyot, screamed every time I lifted a leg to take another step. But we didn't stop. *You don't stop. You keep on eating cars. And then you're* in *the man from Mars.*

Finally we heard the musical sound of falling water. Soon we saw silvery ribbons of pure water dancing in the sunlight and cascading gently from the rocks on the right side of the trail. I stuck my head under the water and it was cold, cold, cold and better than sex. I drank some of the water dripping off the rocks and it was sweeter than life itself. Icewater Springs was aptly named. I drank until my belly was full. Craig did the same. Then we sat in the cool shade beside the water and waited for the stragglers to arrive.

Friedrich Nietzsche showed up next, still chanting his mantra, but it was the older Nietzsche, because he was now stark, raving mad. He dropped his pack, and he lie down in the shallow puddles of clear water beneath the springs and let the falling water drench him completely. He giggled and then snorted like a horse when the water hit his face. This was a man with a wife and three children and a desk job back in the world. Or, rather, the shell of that man.

When he had calmed down a little, I asked, "Did you see Freddie?"

"Ja wohl," Friedrich managed to cackle, "I heard somebody back there yelling 'Help!' and I figured it was him."

"You didn't go back to see if he needed help?" Craig was incredulous.

"Nein," Friedrich said casually, "what was I going to do for him?"

Craig filled his canteen with cold water and started back east the AT. He intended to rescue Freddie, but he had no idea how far back he was going to have to walk. Mad Friedrich Nietzsche and I stayed by the springs and discussed German philosophy.

Half an hour later, Craig returned with Freddie, who fell down worshipping the cold spring water. While Freddie wallowed in the water, Craig came over to stand by Rick and me and whispered, "Now I've got a friend for life."

We were all relieved that the thirteen-mile death march across the sawteeth was over. We walked the last hundred yards over to the Icewater Spring shelter only to be greeted by a big sign hanging across the chain-link gate of the shelter that read, "Shelter Closed Due to Vermin Infestation – National Park Service."

"What's a vermin?" Freddie asked.

"Maybe we can eat 'em," Rick said.

The shelter looked and smelled vile. This shelter was less than three miles from the junction of the AT and the Newfound Gap Road, so it was accessible to day hikers and other human vermin who trashed the place and apparently used it as a urinal. Nevertheless, we had little choice but to stay in the condemned structure. Hiking out to the Newfound Gap Road wouldn't have helped us at all because we had no transportation there, and we were too beat to go anywhere else. We considered pitching the tent outside the shelter, but we weren't sure if the vermin mentioned by the sign included large animals like bears.

"C'mon, John," Craig teased. "You don't know what 'vermin' means? What kind of half-assed colleges did you go to?"

"We didn't allow vermin to attend, so I'm not sure what one is," I said. "I don't *think* it means bears, but I wouldn't stake my life on it."

"Well," Rick announced, "I'm sleeping in the shelter. I don't give a shit about mice. I'd rather deal with mice than bears."

We set up camp and kept our food as far away from the shelter as possible. It was our last night in the woods, so Hop Sing cooked up whatever good food we had left in our packs, and we devoured our meal in the twilight. I asked Freddie, "So was it you that Rick heard calling for help back on the trail today?"

Freddie shot a glance at his betrayer. Rick smiled broadly back at Freddie and said, "Yeah, Freddie, what was that about? Was that some kind of SEAL thing?"

Freddie saw no way out, so he admitted it was he who had yelled. "I was just trying to see if there was anybody around." We all laughed heartily, and that encouraged Freddie to continue. "I yelled a couple of times. One time, I saw some people and they asked me if I was OK."

"They heard you yelling?"

"They must have. A guy and a girl. I was too embarrassed to ask them for any water though."

Finding Mount Guyot

I almost couldn't talk because I was laughing so hard. "So you were walking down the AT in the middle of the afternoon screaming 'Help! Help! Help!'?"

"Sometimes I yelled 'Water!'"

I fell off my rock. Freddie continued, "I was never so happy in my life as when I saw Craig coming with that canteen."

We partied hearty that night in the condemned shelter. Everybody had booze and blow left, although Freddie had gone through an astonishing amount of his stash. He showed me what he had left and I said, "What have you been doing, Freddie, pouring the stuff straight onto your heels?"

He stiffened. "I'm just dealing with the pain, John. That's all." I felt bad for saying anything because, after all, I had gone through an astonishing amount of whiskey in the same length of time. Who was I to say anything? I had my own problems.

We got out the maps and looked at the next day's hike. To get back to Rick's van at the Ramsey Cascades trailhead, we had to walk 1.7 miles back along the AT to the jump off, climb the rugged two miles down the pioneer trail, and then go four miles down the maintained section of the Porters Flat Trail. That was just to get to the road. Then we had to walk four more miles of gravel road to get to the mini-van at the Ramsey Cascades parking lot.

"Do you have another twelve miles left in you, Freddie?" Craig asked seriously. Freddie's heels resembled raw meat. The fact that he had walked thirteen miles on those heels up and down mountains amazed all of us. Freddie's words said he could do one more hike, but his face said otherwise.

"Or how about this?" I said. "One of us takes a day pack and hikes back to the van, and the other three take that guy's backpack, and they hike out to Newfound Gap. Then the one guy drives back around through Gatlinburg," I traced my finger along the twenty-five-mile route, "up to Newfound Gap and picks up the other three."

285

"So the other guys only have to hike, what, three miles?" Rick said. He raised his Scotch to me. "Aye, that's a good plan, laddie."

"So who's going to go get the van?" Craig asked. Then he glanced over toward a dark corner of the candle-lit shelter and shuddered. "Fucking mice in here."

"I'll go." I was tired of hearing about how Craig had saved my ass on my first trip. It was time to settle that old debt once and for all. Besides, I had already been up and down the pioneer trail twice, so I was the logical choice.

Craig saw what I was doing. "That's dangerous by yourself, John," he argued. "If you fall and break your leg, you could be there a long-ass time."

"Yeah," I said, "but if two of us go, the other two guys are each carrying two packs."

"John'll be alright, Craig," Freddie said, not understanding all the issues at play.

"Alright. If you don't come out, we can always tell the rangers where to look for you."

With that settled, we got down to real business and got trashed yet again. When we had all had enough, we laid out our sleeping bags on the upper bunk, thinking that the vermin would be more heavily concentrated on the lower bunk. Big Rick, with a full load of Scotch in him, had a hell of a time hauling himself up into the top bunk. "That's it, laddies, hoist away," he said as we tried to give him a hand. Apparently, Scotsmen talked very much like pirates.

The bunk platforms in the shelter were made of wood, not the chicken wire that they used in the old days. Craig got out his bug spray and emptied the contents of the entire can in a big circle on the wood surrounding his sleeping bag. I looked at him quizzically and he explained, "Mice freak me out."

"Are you kidding me?" I was astounded that something so little could bother someone so big.

A few minutes after we turned off the last flashlight and stopped talking, we could hear the pitter patter of tiny feet all around us on the upper bunk. Soon we felt the little creatures scurrying over our bodies. Craig tossed and turned and cussed, but the rest of us fell fast asleep.

In the morning, I put a few survival things in my day pack in case I did indeed get hurt, and the guys divvied up the rest of my gear. Rick strapped my tent and sleeping bag onto his backpack, and Freddie gallantly insisted on putting a few token things from my pack into his own. "That's my blow, Freddie. Take care of it," I said. Craig took my backpack and the remaining stuff inside and tied it to the back of his pack, and then we were ready to go our separate ways.

Craig looked at me seriously. He was the only one who really knew what I had ahead of me. "You make sure you go real slow on that top part. Take your time. We'd rather have you get there an hour later than not get there at all."

"Yeah, John, be careful," Freddie added.

"And don't wreck my van," Rick said. "My wife'd kill me."

I was touched by their concern, but I still couldn't stop grinning. This little mission felt like redemption to me, and I couldn't wait to get started. I said, "It'll probably take me at least three or four hours to get back to the van, then another hour to drive through town. So don't even look for me for four or five hours." I put on my day pack and said, "Man, this feels like a feather."

My steps were quick and light as the AT ran mostly downhill all the way back to the side trail that led to Charlies Bunion. I was there before I knew it. The responsibility I had for three other people was on my mind. My obligation was to get back to the van safely and to not mess around. But I thought again about how way led on to way in life, and before

I knew it, my feet were moving up the side trail toward Charlies Bunion.

After fifty yards, I could see that the north face of the mountain dropped away sharply in front of me. The side trail I stood on narrowed to a rocky ledge no more than two feet wide, and it curved out toward the extreme edge of the mountain. The inside of the trail hugged a vertical wall of black slate, the same black slate as the pioneer trail. There was nothing but thin air beyond the outside edge of the trail. I was afraid to even stick my head out over that ledge to look down. The fear of falling felt like a weight crushing my chest, and I had to fight against that weight in order to inch forward along the curving ledge. I kept my ass plastered to the black wall and inched along until I was standing on the northernmost point of the side trail. There, an outcropping of jagged, black rock stood between the outside edge of the trail and the precipice beyond, offering at least a tiny shred of safety. The absolute pinnacle of the mountain was behind my back, maybe thirty feet higher than where I stood. I stopped there, perched between the jagged outcropping of rock and the mountain's pinnacle, and beheld the view.

The outcropping in front of me was itself the "bunion," named after a man with sore feet, Charlie Connor. He was a local guide who had helped the old librarian Horace Kephart climb up to inspect the damage to the mountain after the big landslide of 1929. They found the whole north side of the mountain stripped away to reveal the sheer black bedrock and the outcropping on which I now stood. Charlie Connor was rubbing his sore feet after the climb, and Horace Kephart decided to make those feet famous. Charlie Connor, the man with the bunion, was in the right place at the right time.

The bible calls the panorama looking north from Charlies Bunion the best view in the Smokies. The cliff drops down a full one thousand feet, as big as the drop from the top of the

Empire State Building. A beautiful view of Mount LeConte and the whole Porters Creek valley opens up to the north, and it is indeed unforgettable. To stand on that outcropping and look out at God's creation was awe-inspiring in the truest sense of the word—an emotion of mingled reverence, dread, and wonder.

I didn't stay there long. I was on a mission from God. I continued inching along the ledge past the "bunion," finding the other half of the semi-circular side trail just as precarious as the first half. But the perilous part of the side trail was short, and I soon rejoined the safety of the AT.

I quickly found the jump off that led to Porters Flat and dropped down over the edge without hesitation. I felt very confident with the type of climbing I had to do now. I was fine as long as I had rocks and roots to grab onto. Still, I took the top section slowly, knowing people were depending on me to be smart. As I descended the near-vertical gulley, I knew we had made the right choice by not trying to go down the day before. Someone would almost certainly have gotten hurt.

My mind had never connected the Porters Flat pioneer trail with Charlies Bunion, but now I understood that they were parts of the same mountain. Once I got down to the springs seeping out of the rock, I could see that the trail was nothing more than the eastern edge of the huge, steep cliff that culminated with the outcropping of Charlies Bunion.

I had no watch, so I had no idea exactly how long it took, but I moved fast, and I gauged that it was still before noon when I made it to the campsite at Porters Flat, #31. I didn't even break stride when I got there. In fact, I kicked it into a higher gear once I hit the maintained trail. When I arrived at the gravel road that led to Rick's minivan, I put it in overdrive—*ElectraGlide*, I thought for no reason—and I ate up the remaining miles fast and easy like a big old Harley. When I sat down in the driver's seat of Rick's van, the muscles in my legs were jumping and quivering, but I felt good. I had covered the twelve miles about as quickly as they could be done.

As I drove back through Gatlinburg, I decided I could spare five minutes, so I stopped at a pay phone and called Meredith. I told her about the hell we'd been through, and the hike I'd just done to rescue my friends, but she didn't seem to understand what I was so proud of.

After I hung up, I stared blankly through the phone booth glass, unable to hide from the truth that my marriage was a hollow shell. It had started going downhill the moment I quit grad school. Maybe it had been doomed from the start. Something in my soul cringed at the thought of going home to face that. I bought some ice-cold beers to take to the boys. They, at least, would appreciate me. I drank two beers myself before I went any further.

I drove south into the park until I got to the huge look-out platform at Newfound Gap. The big parking lot there was jammed with tourists. The stonework built by the CCC workers was impressive, and the views of the mountains from the observation deck were beautiful, but my senses were too overwhelmed by the people and the noises and the fumes to enjoy the beauty.

I parked the van in one of the last open spots and walked around the edges of the lot looking for my friends. I saw a small group of people gathered around something, excitedly snapping pictures. I thought that maybe they were looking at a bear, but then I heard Freddie's laugh. I circled around the side of the crowd and saw my three buddies standing there with their packs on, posing for photos. Freddie was barefoot. He looked like Craig and Rick's Sherpa guide. I heard one lady standing next to me tell her friend, "They hiked all the way down from Maine!"

I couldn't believe it. I had power-hiked twelve miles, including the most dangerous trail in the park, but *they* were the rock stars. Craig saw me and yelled my name, and the guys came over and greeted me. "John! You made it!" Freddie was wild-eyed and amazed that I was alive.

"What the hell? Did you think I wouldn't? After all the shit we went through?" Some of the "fans" started to drift away, but a few others decided they should get my photo too. It was ridiculous. "What's with these people?" I asked.

"We're gonna be on the cover of the Rolling Stone, man!" Rick looked stoned himself.

"We just called the rangers on you!" Freddie said. "We were starting to get worried."

"I told you guys it was going to take a while," I said, trying to hide my disappointment. I felt as if they hadn't had any faith in me despite how hard I had tried. I was surprised at how keen the hurt was. "What'd they tell you?"

Craig said, "They said if the van was still over by Ramseys in the morning, they'd go look for you."

I considered that for a moment and said, "It makes sense, really. How long you guys been here?"

Craig rolled his eyes. "Hours. It was an easy hike out. We were here in no time. These two have been sneaking into the woods and smoking bowls all afternoon. Then Freddie told some people we were hiking the whole AT, so they started taking pictures of us."

The photo shoot ended abruptly when I told the guys that there was cold beer in the van. Five rugged days in the mountains were done, but more rugged days were ahead for me. Days that I couldn't hack my way through with a machete.

Buddha Palguta

10   Going Downhill

I wandered for four long years in the dark valleys of my soul. Most of the things I had once counted as certainties—marriage, kids, teaching, success—were gone. I was a hack writer, sitting at a desk every day grinding out instruction booklets that nobody, including me and the people that read them, cared about. All I had left, it seemed, was my friends, and my best friend of all was Yukon Jack. Yukon was how I coped. I fell asleep drunk every night and hid that fact from the world as best I could.

In the summer of 2001, Dan, Rick, Freddie and I planned a four-day trip in the easier west end of the Smokies, going back to the Gregory Bald area we had last visited in 1979. We were all into our forties and, if we measured them honestly, so were our waistlines. The trip we planned was a far cry from the times when we covered the whole eastern end of the park in five days. We intended to cover a modest five or six miles a day, but we were still going to venture off trail a little just to prove that we could.

292

We started in from the Parson Branch Road at the extreme west end of the park. The overcast sky held the humidity in the valley, and we quickly wilted in the July heat. About half way up the Gregory Bald Trail, we paused to rest. "This trail is steeper," I managed to say between heaving breaths, "than I remember."

Rick said, "Weren't you and Craig just carrying hammocks and blankets the last time we came up here?" He was wearing a T-shirt that had dozens of inspirational sayings on it, one of which was That Which Does Not Kill Me Makes Me Stronger.

"That's right," I brightened. "I wasn't carrying a tent last time. That must be it."

Dan was quick to burst my bubble. "Oh yeah, Johnny, I'm sure that's it." He was sober now and had been for several years, so he was the fittest of the group even though he still smoked.

"If you ask me, none of us are doing real good," Freddie chimed in. Freddie had become a member of our posse in the intervening years. He was wearing a Gold's Gym T-shirt that barely covered his belly and a black baseball cap that said SHERIFF in big, yellow letters. The hat was as ridiculous as the shirt when you considered how much dope he was carrying in his pack. At least he had well broken-in boots on his feet.

"We're just getting warmed up, Freddie, that's all," Dan said.

When we straggled into our first camp at #13, Sheep Pen Gap, Dan unwrapped a wide elastic wrap from around his middle that he wore to support his lower back. "I only need it when I have my pack on," he explained. "It keeps the muscles from spasming."

Rick told Freddie the story of how Craig and I had once slept in the Gilligan's Island hammocks at this campsite. I tried to find the exact trees Craig and I had used, but it was impossible to tell twenty years later. "We'd have to find some sturdier trees now," I admitted. I was up to about 240. A lot of it was still muscle, but too much of it wasn't.

Rick heard the regret in my voice. "Ah, it's natural for men to fill out, Johnny," he said. "You're just *robust*. We're all more robust than we were." Even so, none of us were ready to retire to our La-Z-Boys. We still felt the call of the wild.

Rick went to work preparing a seafood dish consisting of canned crab meat and canned baby shrimp cooked up in a cheese sauce and served over rice. It promised to be the crowning gastronomic achievement of his illustrious career. He preferred to be called "The Iron Chef," but old habits die hard, and mostly we stuck with calling him Hop Sing.

The rest of us had to range far up into the surrounding mountainside to find any decent fire wood, but Freddie and I teamed up and carried the trunk from a fairly large tree back into camp. We shrugged it off our shoulders and dropped it on the ground near Rick's kitchen area, and the shock wave was enough to topple the cook pot off the stove. Once again, our supper lay on the ground, soaking into the dirt.

Rick swore vehemently, and it wasn't in Chinese. "Shit! You stupid mother fuckers!"

"Hey, hey, hey!" Dan said. "There's no need to talk like that. Your kids aren't here."

"My seafood surprise, fucking wasted."

Freddie and I stood there like scolded children. I stooped and started picking the tiny shrimps out of the dirt and putting them in my dish. "Let's just rinse them off and use them again," I said. "If you guys won't eat 'em, I will." Soon we were all squatting on our haunches around the spilled food and picking little pieces of flesh out of the dirt, eating the cleanest morsels right there on the spot. Supper that night was a little gritty.

After supper, we put a buzz on and experimented with a new-fangled cable system for hanging food that we found installed at the campsite. A thick, braided steel cable was strung twenty feet in the air between two big trees. Four pulleys hung down from the horizontal cable, and a loop of thinner gauge steel cable passed through each pulley. These loops of thinner cable were long enough to almost reach the ground. Each loop of thin cable had two big S-hooks attached to it, spaced far apart.

At first, we didn't know what to make of the elaborate system of cables and hooks. "Maybe it's for stretching out your tent if you need more room in it," Freddie joked. "You put one guy on each corner and pull."

Rick tried to top Freddie. "No! It's for skinning vermins! You hang 'em up so you can peel their hides off easier."

I spoke in a professorial tone. "Both capital suggestions, gentlemen, that would no doubt work egregiously. However, these cables are obviously designed primarily as bear-proof sleeping habitats." I kept throwing out words. "For humanity. Emitting nocturnally, of course."

"Of course!" Rick thumped his temple with the heel of his hand.

I went on. "Mere child's play, Fester. You hang your sleeping bag on a hook and then get inside and hoist yourself up. You sleep comfortably above the bear's ursuline reach."

"How do you tie yourself off once you're up there?" Rick asked.

"Wait a minute," Dan said before I could think of an answer for Rick. "Aren't 'ursulines' nuns?"

"They can be," I said off-handedly. "Why? Would you prefer to have nuns attacking you as you slept?"

Dan shrugged, "Depends on what they look like."

"Good answer, Lurch!" I said. "The right type of nun can cause nocturnal emissions just as easily as a bear! Never forget that, gentlemen!"

"I still remember that from Catholic grade school," Dan said. "Seriously. In eighth grade."

We figured out that you were supposed to attach your bag of food to one S-hook, hoist the bag up, and then secure the other S-hook to an eye-bolt screwed into the base of one of the big trees. That would put your food bag twenty feet up in the air.

"Will this be on the final exam?" Freddie asked.

"You never know," I replied, but we kept drinking late into the night, and the final exam was postponed indefinitely.

The next morning dawned gray and dreary. We stood around the smoldering embers from the previous night's fire and took our time drinking our coffee. We smoked cigarettes and stared vacantly at scraps of instant oatmeal packets as they burned down to wispy ashes.

The comfortable silence was broken by slow, steady footsteps on the trail coming from the same direction we had come the night before. Gradually, an old man walking with the aid of a long walking stick came into view. He checked for a second when he saw us, but then he smiled and continued toward us. "It's a good day to be in the mountains, isn't it, boys?" he said in a creaky voice. He was easily the oldest person I had ever seen in the backcountry. His hands were gnarly and the skin around his eyes and his mouth was creased and sagged in heavy folds. Yet he stood fairly straight and held his head high. He wore a straw farmer's hat that was broken in two places and long pants and a long-sleeved shirt that looked like they came from Dickies or Sears. The pants were pulled up high on his waist above a little protrusion of belly that was smaller than my own. The rest of him looked pretty wiry. He carried a small knap sack and two plastic jugs on his back.

We were shocked to see anyone at all, especially someone older than the dirt we had eaten for supper. Dan enthusiastically struck up a conversation with the old man. "Yes, sir, it is!" he answered. "Every day's a good day to be in the mountains."

The old man chuckled softly. He was close enough now that I could see the cataracts in his pale blue eyes. "You boys from around here?"

"No, sir," Dan said. "We're flatlanders here on a vacation."

"But we love the mountains," Freddie added.

"You ought to live in a place you love. Life's too short not to." The old man reached into his pocket and pulled out a handkerchief that was probably older than I was.

Normally, I didn't like to exchange meaningless pleasantries with people we met on the trail, but this old man intrigued me. "Does it still seem short to you?" I asked. "Life, I mean." I wondered because mine seemed to be dragging on interminably.

He locked eyes with me for a few seconds before he answered. "That's a funny thing. A strange thing. The weeks and the months go fast. Lord! Even a year goes by fast now. But when I think about all the things I've seen in my time, and all the people that have come and gone," he paused for an instant and I wondered who he was thinking of, "then, no, it doesn't seem short at all. It seems like I've been alive a long, long time." He chuckled again. "I reckon that's not a very good answer, is it?"

I shrugged, "The truth is always a good answer."

Dan asked, "How long *have* you been alive?"

"Since the day I was born. Hee hee! But I wasn't born in no horse pistol!" He paused to see if we would laugh at his jokes, but we were all too enchanted, and his jokes were too lame. "I was born in the house my pawpaw built. Up by Maryville. In '22. Things were hard here back then. We didn't have much. But we had some good times, too."

The old man put the handkerchief back in his pocket without having used it. "Now I see folks runnin' around like chickens with their heads cut off so they can buy the latest do-dads on the TV! And they don't seem any happier after they get them!"

I loved to hear the old man talk, so I asked another question. "Where are you going today?"

"Oh, I'm headed up to the Moore Spring to get some good water. You boys know where that is?" We said we didn't, so he told us. "It's a nice spring southeast of Gregory Bald. Called Moore's Spring. There's a side trail that leads there from the old main trail. There used to be a shelter there too. He paused and then said, "I took a girl there once—a long time ago." He smiled at the memory, but the smiled faded. "Yep. She's gone now, but I keep a-goin'."

"What a minute," Rick spoke to the old man for the first time. "Where'd you start from this morning?"

"From the road down there." The old man pointed back down the trail we had all come up. "I believe I parked next to your vehicle."

Rick shook his head. "So you're going to hike five miles in and five miles back out just for some spring water?"

The old man beamed with pride. "I have to go somewhere, don't I? I might as well go somewhere I like."

I got out my trail map and asked the old man to show us where the Moore Spring was. He looked at the map for a few seconds but quickly gave up. "I don't see as well as I used to, boys, and I left my spectacles in the truck. I'm sorry." We told him there was no need to apologize.

"You don't need a map. Stay on this same trail," he advised, "and the side trail'll be on your right on the other side of the bald. You can follow me there if you want."

"Thank you, sir," Dan said, "but we still have to pack up camp. Some of these guys like to sleep in in the morning."

"Corn liquor'll do that to a man, won't it?" The old man chuckled again and started walking out of camp. "You boys be careful now. Watch which trail you take." And then the old man was gone.

"Oh man, he was awesome!" Freddie said. "I wanna be like that when I'm old."

Rick tilted his head cynically. "You believe he walked all that way?"

"And how'd he know we were drinking whiskey last night?" I wondered.

"Are you kidding me?" Dan said. "You guys smell like a distillery. And where the hell do you think he came from, Rick, if he didn't come from the road?"

We broke camp and hiked up over Gregory Bald, the bald famous for its azaleas, but once again we missed the flowers in bloom. On the far side of the bald, we walked along looking for the side trail the old man had mentioned, but we saw no wooden marker nor any other sign of a side trail. When we came to the intersection of the Long Hungry Ridge Trail, I suspected that we had somehow missed the old man's spring. "How in the hell could we miss the trail?" I said. "I was watching the right side the whole time."

"He told us to watch close. Remember?" Freddie said. "He probably knew it would be hard to spot." We wondered and hypothesized about the old man all day, but we didn't see him again, which made him seem even more mystical.

We started south on the Long Hungry Ridge Trail. Our next camp was only four miles down the trail, and after we topped a small ridge, the whole way was downhill. Dan and I outpaced Rick and Freddie, who had stopped to smoke a bowl. I finally had the chance to bring up something that had been on my mind for a long time. I summoned up my courage and blurted it out. "Was it hard to quit drinking, Dan?"

299

The question surprised him. We never talked about the fact that Dan had quit. I felt like a hypocrite even bringing up the subject. He considered his answer before he spoke, and he finally said, "No, not really. Not once I decided that I really needed to."

I wasn't sure what that meant, but having gone thus far, I pressed on. "Did you have to go to meetings or anything like that?" I had this irrational dread of having to go to meetings to stay sober.

Dan smiled a private smile that could have meant anything. "I've been to some meetings, but that's not how I quit."

Dan's whole demeanor told me that he didn't want to talk about it, but I didn't want to let it go until I got something I could use. "I'm just tired of it, you know? Feeling shitty every morning. Wasting the life God gave me." I felt like a complete fool, admitting my weaknesses.

Dan walked along, saying nothing. I talked to him over his shoulder as we entered into a big valley. "I've been thinking lately that I haven't gone a single day without putting chemicals in my body since I was probably sixteen years old." I barked a harsh laugh that was more despair than humor. "Not a single day for like twenty-six years! I don't even know who I am anymore without all the booze and the other crap. I'd like to go just one day without putting any booze or any other chemicals in my body. That's my goal."

Dan finally spoke. "I'll tell you this much. I wouldn't try quitting everything at once. *That* would really be hard. Try taking one thing at a time."

I considered which of my bad habits I could kick first. I only did the coke very rarely, once or twice a year, so I knew I could quit that, but drinking and smoking were another thing altogether.

I thought the subject was closed, but Dan spoke again. "See, Johnny, when you get to the point where you really want to quit, when you *hate* it, then it's not as hard. But until then, it's like me with these cigarettes. It's hard to quit if you still like doing it, even if you know it's bad for you."

"Uh huh," was all I could say. I didn't find Dan's ideas very reassuring. Almost every good time I'd ever had was associated with booze. How could I hate that?

Dan and I made it down to campsite #92, a horse camp called Upper Flats where two creeks joined near the bottom of the valley. When Rick and Freddie found their way into camp half an hour later, Rick was limping noticeably.

Freddie announced, "He rolled his ankle on the trail back there."

"I wasn't paying attention, and a flat rock tipped on me." Rick shed his pack and sat down heavily on a big log. "Fellas, we may have to have a substitute chef tonight."

We waited to see if a few belts of Scotch were enough to heal Rick's bad ankle, but the Iron Chef was down. I offered to make the evening meal. I spit on my hands and rubbed them together, saying, "Spread out! I'll show you chowder heads some cookin' what is cookin'!"

"I hope you wash your hands first," Rick said.

"You just saw me spit on my hands, didn't you, Freddie?"

"Sure!" Freddie agreed. "Just pass 'em over the flames now, John. That's the Indian way."

"Fab Five Freddie!" I said. "I learn so much from you, man."

The other guys whined and moaned about germs like little sissies, so I washed my hands in the creek, as if that would make any difference. Then I threw together a big pot of dried beef, ramen noodles, and beefy mushroom gravy mix. Everybody bitched about how salty it was, but they ate it just the same.

"Not like my grandma's, I'll tell you that," Dan said between spoonfuls.

"Not like my grandma's either," Rick said.

I said, "Speaking of grandmas . . ."

Dan interrupted me. "Don't even talk about our sweet grandma with that filthy pie hole."

"I wasn't going to. So fuck you . . . and your grandma. I was going to say that Craig and I were thinking about going on a seniors' cruise and snagging some rich, old broads. Some blue-hairs."

Rick didn't miss a beat. He said, "You have to make sure they're true blue-hairs."

"How's he gonna do that?" Freddie asked.

"Think about it, Freddie," Rick said. "How do you know when a girl's a true blonde?"

"Oh!"

"I'm glad to see you and Craig thinking about your futures like that." Dan said. "Sounds like a really solid plan."

"Yeah. We figure we can pretend like we booked the old-timer cruise by mistake and then tell them we're just making the best of it. We'd have our pick of any broad on the boat."

"What makes you so sure about that?" Rick asked.

Later in the evening, the subject came up again. Dan said, "Maybe I need to go on that cruise with you guys, Johnny, and find a rich old lady. The child support is killing me." After sixteen years and four kids, Dan had recently gone through a divorce. Even quitting drinking hadn't saved his marriage. In fact, all four of us sitting around the camp fire had been married and divorced. Wiser men might have perceived a pattern in that, but we didn't.

"Tell me about it," Rick commiserated. "I got twelve years before I'm a free man."

"At least I'm done with that," Freddie said as he poked the fire. He had a daughter—probably Vietnamese—that was full grown.

Dan was sober but a little coked up, so he wanted to talk. "Would you guys really get married again?"

I said, "I can't see being alone the rest of my life. But I'd have to be really sure this time."

"You were really sure the last two times."

"No. No, I wasn't. Not last time. And the first time, I was just young and dumb." I shook myself out of that train of thought because it led nowhere. "But I could still see myself married and living in a place up in the mountains somewhere. Hell, I'm a writer now, right? Maybe I could write a book or something."

"You've been saying that for a long time, Johnny," Dan reminded me, but not unkindly.

"I know. But it could still happen. It's not too late." I tossed a stick into the fire and watched it ignite almost instantly.

"What would you write about?" Freddie asked.

Rick said, "If you write about our gold-panning trip, I want half."

Freddie seemed intrigued with the idea of somebody he knew writing a book. "You could write about this— backpacking in the Smokies."

"Yeah, like anybody would want to read that."

The next day was off-trail day. We planned to leave #92 and follow the eastern branch of the Twentymile Creek that we were camped next to all the way to its source on the side of a mountain called Doe Knob. At 4,500 feet, Doe Knob wasn't nearly as tall as the big mountains in the eastern part of the park, but it was one of the higher peaks on the western side. The distance we had to cover off trail measured about two miles, but we were fairly certain that the terrain would be easier and the bush would be less dense than it had been over around Mount Guyot. We would camp off trail, and the following morning we would finish the climb and run into the

AT, which passed right across the top of the mountain. From there, we only had to go seven miles to get back to the car. Doe Knob was a pretty modest challenge.

Rick tested his sore ankle and resolutely declared that he would give it a go. He wrapped his ankle tightly with an ace bandage and announced, "The Iron Chef is ready."

We headed north along the east bank of the south-flowing creek. The going was fairly easy at first, as it always seemed to be. Dan, who was all gung ho to be back in the mountains after a fourteen-year absence, led the way. Fab Five Freddie, who was anxious to show what he was capable of doing when his feet weren't bleeding, followed right behind Dan. I was content to go third. Behind me, Rick limped bravely along.

The bush became more dense, but not impenetrable, as we followed the creek higher into the mountains. The bush was mostly trees and saplings, not the dreaded laurels or the hated rhododendrons. We were doing more ducking and squeezing through the bush than hacking and pushing. Dan carried Craig's machete, but he barely had to use it. For a time, we followed a deer or a bear path that was relatively easy going, but we saw that we were curving far away from the creek, so we paused inside a tiny clearing.

"What do you think, Johnny?" Dan asked. I forced my way around Freddie, scraping my pack against the trees and brush, until I stood next to Dan. He had his compass out, and he was looking northwest, back toward the creek we had just climbed away from.

"I think it's gonna rain; that's what I think." The morning clouds had sunken lower and thickened considerably.

Dan ignored my weather report. "This little deer path seems like easy going, but I'm afraid we're heading too far east."

"Well," I said, "we know we can't get too far from the water." Everyone agreed heartily with that. "So I'd say we need to follow more true north on the compass and stay by the creek, even if it's harder work."

We crashed back into the thicker bush, angling northwest so that we could rejoin the creek gradually and not lose all of the elevation we had just gained. We fought through the thickest bush we had seen all day.

Without warning, Dan stopped dead in his tracks in front of me and yelled in alarm. I couldn't see around him at first, but I heard something thrashing in the thicket immediately in front of Dan, and it sounded like something big. Dan leaned back, machete in hand, and I leaned sideways to see around Dan. A full-grown, white-tail deer buck, trapped by the heavy limbs all around us, stood no more than eight feet in front of Dan. The buck was wild-eyed with fear. He thrashed about with his front hooves and his antlers. The buck looked uninjured and strong. In fact, he looked downright dangerous. Neither of us had any idea what the big animal might do. Dan and I scrambled backwards as quickly as we could, giving the frantic animal some space so he wouldn't attack us. As we backed away, the buck managed to force himself through the bush and away from us, heading downhill. The buck quickly disappeared into the wilderness, snapping branches as he went.

"Oh man! I thought I was gonna have to cut that thing," Dan said.

"How the hell did we sneak up on it?" I asked.

Freddie, who had done some deer hunting, explained, "They bed down during the day, and that one must have been sleeping when you came up on him, Dan."

Rick was incredulous. "What the fuck? Was that thing deaf? We're making enough noise here."

We pressed on through the bush for another hour. Freddie and I both took turns leading when Dan got tired. We stayed on the steep hillside but within sight of the creek. Rick managed to keep up, but walking across the steeply pitched terrain was hard on his bad ankle.

The temperature dropped suddenly, and the wind picked up. We didn't need a weatherman to know which way the wind blew. We stopped in a relatively clear space to put on our rain gear. We all dropped our packs and propped them up against the uphill sides of trees to prevent the packs from sliding down the mountain. Freddie dug into his pack and pulled out a brand-new, Gore-Tex rain suit complete with pants and a hooded jacket. He donned his rain suit, and then he put a water-proof pack cover over his backpack to keep that dry too. Freddie had some nice gear, and I was mildly jealous. I put on a hooded Gore-Tex windbreaker about eight years old that had slowly lost any trace of water repellency. I didn't have anything at all to cover my legs or my pack, but I was in better shape than the Raffertys.

Dan and Rick pulled big, green garbage bags out of their packs. I thought maybe they were going to use the bags to cover their packs the way we sometimes did, but when they hurriedly cut round holes in the bottoms of the bags I knew that the garbage bags were going to be their ponchos. On our earliest backpacking trips, we had all carried garbage bags for rain gear, but some of us had matured a little in the intervening twenty-four years.

Dan slid the open end of a garbage bag over Rick's head and pulled it down over Rick's torso until Rick's head popped through the hole they had cut. Rick stood there with his arms pinned to his side, grinning like a moron. Then Dan pulled another bag over his own head and wriggled and shimmied until his arms and body were covered the same way. They stood on the mountainside that way, looking quite pleased with themselves. When they realized they couldn't do anything at all except stand there, they worked the bottoms of their bags up around their elbows so they could at least use their hands. Freddie and I helped them light cigarettes, and all four of us stood on the steep mountainside in the middle of nowhere, listening to the big drops start striking the canopy of trees above us.

In a matter of seconds, the drops became a torrential downpour. Dan and Rick dropped their smokes and tugged their bags back down, as if that would make a difference. They stood there looking like some kind of low-budget commercial for Irish condoms. I laughed, "Oh, wouldn't your sweet grandma be proud of her boys now!"

Freddie and I were laughing so hard that Rick and Dan started laughing at themselves. The steeply pitched ground we were standing on had become slippery with the rain, and Rick's feet went out from under him, and he slammed to the ground like a big green sack of potatoes. He squirmed on the ground, unable to get up. We convulsed with laughter, and Dan went down next, splitting his garbage bag wide open as he hit the ground. Freddie and I were hanging onto trees to keep ourselves from falling down as well.

The rain lasted longer than the laughs did, and we had no choice but to stand there and get wet. Rick and Dan were completely drenched before they ever hit the ground. In a few minutes more I was soaked as well, and the rain eventually even seeped into Freddie's Gore-Tex suit.

We were relieved when the rain stopped after half an hour. A half an hour was a long time to stand in a downpour, but we knew that it could just as well have kept raining all day and into the night. The skies remained dark and threatened to open up again at any moment. The rain had dampened more than our clothing; our spirits had been dampened as well. We picked our way north for a little while, but none of us demonstrated much zest for continuing to fight through the wet undergrowth.

Rick said what we all were thinking, "This is bullshit."

"We're losing our motivation," I said. We were somewhere near half way to Doe Knob, and it was still early in the afternoon. Despite the rain, we would probably make it to our destination if we kept going.

"We should call Craig," Freddie joked. "He'd motivate us."

"Why don't you?" Dan asked. "You got your cell phone, right?" Freddie had insisted on bringing along his cell phone. I had argued against it, but the world in general and our society in particular were moving in the opposite direction. Even my Cherokee spirit guide, Fab Five Freddie, was going high tech on me.

"I don't know if I can get a signal here. I doubt it," Freddie said, but he dropped his pack and got out his phone anyway. I didn't even own a cell phone, so I had no idea what Freddie meant by a "signal." I stepped aside and lit up a smoke and watched the proceedings.

Freddie powered up the cell phone and held it out away from himself as if the thing were full of cooties. He spun in a slow circle, eyes fixed on the cell phone at all times, offering an electronic sacrifice to the great spirits of the north, south, east, and west. "There!" he said with satisfaction as he faced roughly east. "I got a bar for a second!"

"Try it," Dan urged.

Freddie punched in Craig's number, but evidently nothing happened. "Searching," he said disappointedly. "Still searching."

I turned my back to the group and covered my mouth with my hand. "Hello," I said, "this is Craig. What the fuck you want?"

"Craig!" Rick said excitedly. Rick was always up for a gag.

I stayed turned around to maintain the feeble illusion. "Hey," I growled, "whaddya want? I'm busy makin' sausage here."

Dan joined in the silliness. "*That's* why all the girls like you!" All meat cutters believed as an article of faith that women got turned on by watching sausage being made.

"I need more sawdust and ice," I yelled. Adding sawdust or ice to sausage were two ways for unscrupulous meat cutters to add weight to the product and thereby make more money.

"Craig," Rick yelled as if he had a bad phone connection, "we're off trail and we don't know what to do!"

"Have you climbed a tree yet?" I asked. "You should climb a tree and show 'em your ding dong."

"How will that help?" Rick chuckled.

"It won't," I said, "but you'll feel like King Salami when you're done."

"Can you come pick us up, Craig?" Freddie asked.

"I can't be saving your ass every time, Freddie!" I buried my mouth even deeper in my hand and make some static noises. "Sorry. You're breaking up."

The mock conversation with Craig failed to motivate us. We studied the map and determined that the AT was probably no more than half a mile to the east, up on top of the ridge we had been shouldering for hours. "Let's bail out and head for the ridge," Rick suggested. "I can't walk on the side of the mountain like this anymore." It was enough of an excuse for all of us to gladly give up. Vince Lombardi was laughing at us once more, but this time it was middle age, not fatigue, that had made cowards of us.

We turned right and headed straight up to the ridge. We had to go on all fours at times, but the bush thinned out quickly, and before too long we could see the top. We were sucking wind when we got there, but we made it to the crest far more quickly than we thought we would. It turned out that we had been no more than a quarter mile away from the AT for most of the day. We saw the familiar white blazes of the AT and suddenly it seemed that civilization was not so far away.

Once we gave in just a little, full surrender became inevitable. We studied our maps, looking for the shortest path back to the car. Dan was the only one who was for extending the trip by heading south on the AT toward campsite #113, Birch Spring Gap, but that meant unnecessary steps and an unnecessary night in the woods. The rest us decided it would be better to start heading north on the AT and back toward the car.

The AT rose steadily for a mile or more as we climbed up to Doe Knob. We rested at the top, and Freddie tried his cell phone again. "Fab Five Freddie, calling the mother ship," I said like a radio man. Then I asked, "Are you getting a signal now, Freddie?"

"Nothing. But it's one o'clock. Took us five hours to get here." I was surprised that the phone told him what time it was, but I didn't reveal my ignorance by saying so.

"Five hours to go two miles," Dan said. "That's not very good time."

"That's nothing, Dan," Rick bragged. "It took us two *days* to go two miles over by Mount Guyot."

Dan was already tired of hearing about the trip up and over Ramsey Cascades that he had missed. "Yeah, I know," he said. "Me and Johnny did the same thing in Bone Valley before you guys ever *thought* about going off trail."

We were all wet and chilled, so we didn't stop for long on Doe Knob. We left the AT and turned west onto the Gregory Bald Trail, the far end of the same trail on which we had started our journey. Rick's car was only seven miles away. We didn't know it at the time, but the trail we were walking had been part of the original Appalachian Trail back in the 1930s. When the Fontana Dam was built during World War Two, the AT was routed to the south so that it passed over the top of the new dam. The Moore Spring and the shelter that the old man had mentioned were part of that original section of the Appalachian Trail.

Within an hour, we were back in the vicinity of the Moore Spring on the old Appalachian Trail. The side trail was easier to spot coming from the other direction. We found the hidden cove where the shelter once stood, but the structure itself was long gone, just like the young man and young woman from Maryville who snuck five miles back into the mountains for a lover's tryst sixty years in the past. The years were relentless, I reflected, and they were catching up with me and my friends too, just as they had caught that old man. We spent the night at the Moore Spring, drinking and snorting and trying to act like young bucks, but we were running against the wind.

We hiked the last five miles out the next morning, feeling appropriately shitty and subdued. For me at least, there was no joy in going back to my so-called life. As we drove down the Parson Branch Road headed out of the park, we passed a young couple setting out the things for a picnic. The young woman was spreading out a blanket, letting the blanket fall gently to the ground on a cushion of air. She had on a light sun dress, and the sun behind her shone through the dress to show off her figure and highlight her hair. It seemed to me in that moment that she was the prettiest, the sweetest, the most natural woman I had ever seen. It made me realize how terribly lonely I was. I wanted someone like her very badly. I wanted a lot of things I didn't have.

11 Going to Mount Guyot: Third Attempt

For the next few years, getting to somewhere I liked proved more difficult than I could have imagined. Then, in 2003, I met a pretty, petite woman named Lauren. She was gentle and smart and funny, and I fell madly, desperately in love. I shocked myself by quitting smoking because she couldn't stand it, but I couldn't put away the booze as easily. Lauren stopped seeing me when she discovered how much I drank. I couldn't blame her, but I was devastated nonetheless. Somehow, though, I stayed off the cigarettes even after she was gone. In doing so, I proved to myself that I had at least a few shreds of fortitude left.

Thus encouraged, I tried again to give up drinking, hoping I could win Lauren back, but ol' Yukon Jack put up one hell of a fight. He kicked and bit and scratched and threw dirt in my eyes. I'd hold him down for a while, fighting as hard as I could, but then he'd come back swinging like Apollo Creed and knock me on my ass all over again. When I went down, I stayed down for weeks at a time. Something inside me would break, and I would lose all restraint. During those times, I drank morning, noon, and night. I steeped by brain in booze. My guts ached and my hands shook. It was the final round, and I could feel myself going down for the count.

On New Year's Day in 2004, I threw one last, desperate punch. I was so sick from drinking the night before that I crawled home half dead, dragged myself inside, and got down on my knees and asked God to save my miserable, drunken ass. To my utter amazement, He did. I barricaded myself inside my house and didn't see anyone for weeks. I spent most of that winter alone, going for long walks in the bitter cold and the biting wind, and by the grace of God I made it through without a drink. The judges scored the bout a draw, but I knew I had been lucky to come out alive.

For a good while, being around people who still smoked and drank was difficult. By 2005, though, I was feeling stronger. One day in the early summer of that year I was sitting with Craig in his back yard, watching him smoke cigarettes and drink beer, which he did exceedingly well. Craig was bothered a lot more than I was that we had never gotten to the tippity top of Mount Guyot. Sometimes when he had a bellyful, Craig would rant as if he were Captain Ahab and Mount Guyot was the mighty white whale. "It's still there, John," he would rave, "and it's kicked our asses every time."

In my mind, we had climbed Mount Guyot the hard way and conquered the hardest part of the mountain when Craig and I had gone with Rick and Freddie. All that was left was a little 800-yard side trail to the top. Still, I had to admit that we hadn't finished what we set out to do, so I agreed to go one more time. Too many times, I had left things unfinished, and I didn't want to live with any more regrets than I already had.

I got in touch with the rest of the *Pequod's* whaling crew— Dan and Rick and Freddie—and everyone signed on. We were all pushing fifty or were past it, and we were going back to finally climb Mount Guyot. Nobody came out and said so, but it felt a lot like the last hurrah.

Freddie and I studied the map and looked for a route up to Mount Guyot that was different and challenging, yet not so challenging that we would fail. We decided on a non-loop route that would take us up to Mount Sterling first, then about twelve miles over maintained trails to Mount Guyot. From the top of Mount Guyot, we would take the off-trail route downhill to the top of Ramseys Cascade, and then down the Ramseys Cascade Trail to a waiting car. Freddie and I figured that it would be a lot easier fighting downhill through the bush.

We needed two vehicles, so we drove down in Dan's Explorer, a normal-sized SUV, and Freddie's new Ford Excursion, which was as big as Moby-Dick himself. It seated eight comfortably with room for cargo left over, and it was bigger than some of the places I'd lived. I dubbed it "the Condo."

Craig and I rode down with Freddie in the Condo. Dan and Rick followed in the Explorer. Sitting in the driver's seat, Freddie couldn't see where the corners of his vehicle were, so he drifted in and out of his lane and drove a stately fifty miles an hour. The Condo's GPS decided that we should go all the way down into North Carolina and then follow a backcountry road to the Tennessee side of the park.

I could see on my old-fashioned paper map that the route proposed by the GPS was stupid. The backcountry road we were supposed to use was a twisting dirt road through the mountains. I told Freddie that I knew a better way, but he was adamant that we would follow the GPS. "Relax, John," he said, "we'll get there."

Two hours later, we were deep in the pitch-black mountains on a gravel road that Freddie could barely squeeze the Condo through. With Freddie driving, we were in imminent danger of rolling down the side of the mountain.

314

Freddie slowed down to zero miles per hour. I was apoplectic because it was already two thirty in the morning, and people with regular-sized brains would have been where they were going an hour before.

By three thirty, we had been on the road for eleven hours. We were on Route 32 on the Tennessee side of the park, looking for the turnoff that led to Cosby campground, but we couldn't find it. A light fog had settled, making it hard to see road signs. Moreover, we had lost Rick and Dan somewhere in the endless turning-arounds-and-going-backs. We rounded a corner, going slow and trying to read the signs, and we almost ran smack-dab into Dan's Explorer, which was parked at a jaunty angle across both lanes of Route 32. Idiocy was running rampant.

Freddie stopped the Condo in the middle of the road, and I got out and walked over to talk to Dan and Rick. "Are you guys fucking nuts? What if some drunk comes flying around the corner?"

"We didn't want you guys to miss us," Rick deadpanned.

Dan said, "There's nobody on the road, Johnny. Relax."

"You're the second person tonight that's told me to relax."

Eventually, we made it to the Cosby campground, and we settled in to get a few hours' rest inside our vehicles. The Condo slept our family of three comfortably. We might still be idiots, but at least we had graduated from the days of sleeping sitting up in the cab of a pick-up truck.

In the morning, we left Dan's vehicle at the Ramseys Cascade trailhead and drove the Condo all the way back around the northeast corner of the park where we had started the night before. We followed that gravel road south to the trailhead of the Mount Sterling Trail, a new trail that hadn't existed when Meredith and I had gone to the fire tower years before. This new trail rose 2,000 feet in two miles. We saddled up like the veterans that we were and headed uphill, bound at long last for the top of Mount Guyot and glory.

As usual, the other guys were happy to let Dan and I haul the heaviest gear. Craig in particular was carrying next to nothing. He was worried about having any wind left in his leathery lungs, so he was hiking without extra clothes or even a bar of soap. He called it ultralight backpacking; I called it just plain nasty.

I had gotten rid of my six-shooter, so I wasn't hauling that weight, but I was toting a twelve-pack of O'Doul's non-alcoholic beer instead. I was nervous about how I would handle being sober in the mountains for the first time. Originally, I had allotted myself two O'Doul's per night so I could have something in my hands as we sat around the campfire, but at the last second, I panicked and threw the remaining six cans into my pack as well.

After a few steps we were huffing and puffing, and before too long we were pausing for breathing breaks with great frequency. After a mile, it was every man for himself. Dan and I, the two burros, hung together. We were the non-smokers, and we hiked out in front, setting the pace. To our surprise, Craig passed us to take the lead near the top of the trail. After Craig went by, Dan scoffed, "Yeah. He's carrying like fifteen pounds." Rick and Freddie, the two oldest guys, brought up the rear, engaged in a contest of their own.

We were drenched with sweat when we topped the ridge. A sign indicated that the campsite and the fire tower were still a third of a mile farther up, so we dropped our packs and took a break in the September sunshine. Craig smoked while Dan and I sipped from our canteens. Freddie and Rick arrived a little while later.

Dan looked around the ridge and said, "I'm starting to think that I've been here before."

Finding Mount Guyot

"Yeah, me too," Freddie agreed, although he had only been backpacking in the Smokies twice, both times with us.

"If you'd ever been to Mount Sterling, you'd know it," I said. "It's the best view in the park. You can see for miles and miles."

"I can see for miles and miles," Dan repeated. "That's The Who, right?" He was pleased with himself because the only lyrics he usually knew were Ted Nugent's song "Wang Dang Sweet Poontang" and Glen Campbell's "Rhinestone Cowboy."

We finished off the hike, not seeing the fire tower until the last hundred yards. Craig and Freddie got there first, but they didn't run up the steps of the tower right away. When Dan and I joined them a few minutes later, they were sitting on a log, lighting up Camels.

"What are you waiting for?" Dan asked.

"We thought we'd all go up together," Craig said. "Let's wait for Rick."

Dan's ADHD kicked in, and he couldn't stand still. His restless German Shepard eyes danced around the campsite and lit on a sign that said Spring 500 Yds. "Let's go get water, Johnny. We're gonna need it anyway." Dan looked at Freddie and Craig, who sat silently like two old men killing time in front a barber shop. "You guys'll wait, right?" It was still early, but that was easily the dumbest question of the day. Freddie and Craig were content to wait.

When Dan and I got back, the other three were ready to climb the tower, cameras in hand. As we climbed the rickety flights of steps, the view expanded in all directions. While the rest of them took in the unfolding panorama, I noticed that the shack's plywood floor looked even more dilapidated than it had eleven years before. Clearly, nobody was maintaining the tower. I made a mental note not to stand in the middle of the floor, especially not with Rick or Dan, the two other heavyweights.

317

Buddha Palguta

Up in the shack, the astounding views held us all spellbound. The skies were perfectly clear, and the visibility was unlimited. We took scores of photos from the four sides of the tower. Even though I'd been there before, I was no less enraptured with the endless mountains encircling us. Freddie said, "You're right, John. You can't forget a place like this."

Craig kept returning to the west window, staring out at the crest of the Appalachians. I stood beside him and unnecessarily said, "The big one in front is Guyot."

"Mount Guyot," Craig said, enunciating each syllable distinctly. The very name had come to stand for more than just a mountain. He didn't have to say anything else; I knew what he meant.

Then I heard Rick call out in surprise, and I turned to see Dan's ass and legs dangling from the hatch that went up onto the roof of the shack. Dan pulled himself through, and soon we heard his footsteps a few inches above our heads. There was no safety railing up there. The four of us stood inside the shack shaking our heads. "He's not normal," Freddie said to no one in particular.

Craig, Dan's own brother, chose to answer. "No, he never was."

"Oh, man!" we could hear Dan say. "You guys gotta come up here!" Then Dan's grinning face appeared in the hatch upside down. "Johnny, you gotta see this!"

"Dan," I said, "I'm scared shitless *inside* this thing! There's no way in hell I'm going up on top of it." He looked me in the eye and saw that he had no chance of changing my mind.

Dan reached his arm down through the hatch toward Freddie. "Freddie, what about you? C'mon, I'll help you up." Freddie shrank away from Dan's extended hand. Dan laughed his crazy prospector laugh and forgot about trying to coax anybody up onto the roof. Craig and Rick had learned long ago not to go along with Dan's most demented schemes, and

318

Dan knew it. He went back to admiring the unobstructed view by himself.

That evening after supper, Hop Sing, alias the Iron Chef, produced five tin-foil pouches. He poured cool water into the pouches, and to our disbelief, a few minutes later we each had something very much resembling an ice cream sandwich. There were a few dry, cardboardy spots, but the taste was very good. Hop Sing received great acclaim for his latest culinary achievement. "I am," he reminded us, "the Iron Chef."

We all went back up the tower, and this time I took some nose candy with me. I had wrestled mightily with the decision on whether or not to go in with Freddie on a little bit of coke for the trip. I hadn't done any drugs or chemicals of any sort since I'd quit drinking, but I decided it would be too torturous for me to be out in the mountains with the boys and not do anything at all. Still, I felt guilty as hell when I snorted that first line up into my head.

The guilt went away almost too easily, and for a while I enjoyed being buzzed and watching the sun set through the gathering clouds from the top of the fire tower. But as beautiful a place as it was, I still felt an insatiable hollowness inside. The coke only seemed to make it worse. The guys there were my best friends in the world, but I couldn't express my emptiness even to them. Watching the sunset from the fire tower was as good as my life could be by myself, and it wasn't anywhere near good enough.

As we sat around the fire that night, the wind rose steadily and the clouds rolled in to partially obscure the magnificent array of stars. Dan drank water, I drank O'Doul's, and the others drank their chosen drinks. Craig looked miserable taking his little nips of whiskey, and I could tell he was missing his usual quota of beers. Fab Five Freddie and Rick were sipping their booze and feeling no pain.

Craig and Rick and I were all wearing new boots purchased specifically for the trip, and we were inspecting our bare feet for any damage. Rick said, "I've got one starting on my heel here." Dan shined his flashlight on Rick's heel, and we could make out a whitish bump maybe the size of a dime.

Craig said, "You call that a blister? That ain't shit, is it, Freddie?" Freddie didn't want to embarrass Rick, but he was forced to agree.

Somehow, I had failed to notice Rick's boots on the hike up, and now I couldn't believe what I was seeing. He had a pair of clunky winter boots with rubberized soles and uppers, and the thick linings that went inside the boots were made from heavy, half-inch-thick felt. "Are you wearing fucking *snowmobile* boots?" I choked. "Are you kidding me? You know better than that!"

Rick, feeling besieged, tried to defend his choice. "I wore them for a few weeks at work and they felt good, so I went with them."

"But you don't walk around at work," I said. "You sit at a desk!"

We were laughing, but the style of boots we called snowmobile boots were not designed for long-distance walking over rough terrain on hot days. His feet would get hot, the felt lining would bunch up, and he would inevitably get blisters. Rick looked wounded by the laughter, but he knew we were right.

We went to bed not long after, and the rising wind on top of Mount Sterling whipped the walls of our tents wickedly as we settled in. Even so, I had no problem falling asleep sober in the Smokies for the first time in my life.

The remnants of an Atlantic hurricane blew in sometime during the night, and the day was raw and cold when we awoke. Mount Sterling was enveloped in a storm cloud. We couldn't even see the top of the fire tower, but we heard it creaking above us. The cold rain, driven by the gusting wind, blew in every direction. Breakfast was out of the question. We had to get off the mountaintop as quickly as we could. We hunched our shoulders and turned away from the buffeting winds. Our sleeping gear got soaked as we broke down camp and stowed our things away.

I looked into the grim faces of my friends as they packed wet equipment into soggy packs. Freddie was wearing his nice rain-suit and looked as if he were coping pretty well. Dan wasn't his usual smiling self, but he didn't look completely miserable either. Rick, never one to hide his discomfort, scowled and grumbled relentlessly. Craig looked to be in the worst shape. He didn't have any rain gear or warm clothes, and he was suffering now for having packed so lightly. He said nothing, but his lips were drawn tight and appeared slightly bluish. He looked like a badly embalmed corpse.

Mount Sterling had been witness to many grim faces and at least a few corpses over the centuries. During the Civil War, deserters from both armies hid out in the remote mountain valleys around Mount Sterling. Raiders and bushwhackers—guerilla fighters from both sides—also roamed through the area. Once a Confederate unit swept through and arrested three local men suspected of being Union sympathizers. They hauled those three men up to the top of Mount Sterling, where they forced the one man, a fiddle player, to play a tune. Legend has it that the man played a song called "Napoleon's Retreat." It was the last song the man ever played. When he was finished playing, they hanged all three men right there on top of the mountain. The Civil War was especially brutal in the Smoky Mountains because loyalties were always in doubt.

I tried to rally the grim troops around me with something I remembered from basic training. "Remember, boys, it doesn't rain in the Army. It rains *on* the Army."

Rick was the only one who bothered to respond. "That's a stupid fucking saying."

"Well, maybe you had to be there," I said mildly. "It seemed clever at the time." If I had been an officer, I would have been shot in the back at that point.

We retreated to the trail junction. The wind diminished greatly and the rain let up slightly as soon as we came down off the peak. We paused beside the wooden sign where the two trails diverged. Everybody knew the route by heart. We had to head west to begin the eleven-mile hike over to the Tricorner Knob shelter, which would put us within a mile or two of Mount Guyot. The other trail led back down to the gravel road and Freddie's Condo.

Rick sidled over toward the short trail, and I saw what was coming. "I don't think I'm going," he announced without preamble.

"What?" Freddie was completely blindsided. He stared open-mouthed at Rick, unbelieving.

Craig, still looking hypothermic, took two steps toward Rick. "I'm not going either." It was my turn to be shocked.

Dan looked at his brother and then at his cousin. "You guys are kidding, right?"

Freddie took a few steps down the long trail and looked back with his dark eyes blazing. "Well, I'm fuckin' going." I had never seen Freddie so mad before. I had never really seen him mad at all. Dan and I sidled toward Freddie, and the lines of confrontation were set.

Rick faced the three of us standing on the other side and said, "Look, I already have a blister. I wish I didn't, but I do. It would be stupid for me to go hiking eleven more miles today and then go off trail after that."

We talked a little across the divide that separated us, but Rick and Craig refused to budge. Everyone was highly upset and not very cogent. Nobody screamed and nobody made accusations, but friendships were being put to the test.

In the end, it came down to blood. Abruptly, Dan went and stood with his kin, leaving Freddie and me speechless all over again. Dan looked at us apologetically. He shrugged, "I gotta stay with my family."

Freddie was beside himself. "It's not even fucking raining now!" It was true that the rain had momentarily stopped. Freddie stormed a few yards farther down the long trail, as if he were going to go alone.

I went and caught up with him. I spoke so that the others couldn't hear. "Freddie, we can't do it, man."

"What?" he asked belligerently.

"We can't hike all that way and then go off trail with just the two of us. What if one of us gets hurt? I can't carry you out by myself, man. Or vice versa." There was some truth in what I said, but the deeper truth was that I didn't feel confident enough in Freddie's ability to go down into the laurel hells with only him. At that moment, I didn't know if I trusted anyone enough.

Freddie seemed partially persuaded, but he was still furious. "This is bullshit! I should just take my keys and go. They can't take my truck without me."

I rolled my eyes. "Yeah, you could do that. But then they wouldn't give you *their* keys." Freddie didn't say anything for a while, so I continued, "Look, you're right. This is bullshit. I'm just as pissed as you are, but we can't go without them. Let's go back down, and maybe we can do some day hikes or something like that for the rest of the week. Maybe those guys'll just fucking go home."

Freddie blustered and stormed for a while longer, but once I made it clear that I wasn't continuing with only the two of us, he gradually acquiesced. We were a silent, dispirited bunch of old warriors as we made our soggy way back down

Mount Sterling. "Napoleon's Retreat" would have been appropriate accompaniment.

When we got down off the mountain, we piled back into the Condo and headed north toward Cosby. The only bit of civilization we passed on that gravel road was a backcountry tavern located near the point where the AT exited the eastern end of the park. They sold hot food, hot showers, and basic supplies to hikers passing through. It served as the nexus between the outer world and the mountains, but to call this place "civilization" was a stretch. The unpainted wooden building was a ramshackle one-story structure, obviously added onto many times over the years, sitting in the middle of the deep mountains. The gravel road that passed in front of the building simply widened out to form the parking lot. The outside of the building was adorned with the antlers and animal skulls in the style of the American West. Above the front door, sticks and branches nailed to the store front spelled out the name Mountain Mama's. Freddie parked the Condo in the rutted parking lot, and we all got out.

Craig and Rick went inside. I told Freddie and Dan, "This is fucked. I came here to be out in the woods, not to sit in a restaurant." They both murmured in agreement.

Craig stuck his head out the front door and yelled, "Hey! They got burgers and beer in here. C'mon in," and disappeared back into the building. A wooden door with a ripped screen slammed behind him.

None of us in the parking lot moved immediately. Then Dan said, "You're right, Johnny. I can sit in a restaurant anytime. I'm not going in."

Freddie, performing one of the most sudden changes of heart I had ever witnessed, simply said, "I am," and walked into the building.

Dan and I stood in the gravel lot, surrounded by puddles, and looked at each other. "What we need now, my friend," I said, "is Vienna sausages."

Dan grinned. "Yeah. In whiskey."

We walked over to a collection of old machinery that was piled at one edge of the clearing and sat down next to a rusted tractor. "That's bullshit the way they ordered a meal without even asking us," I complained.

"Did you really expect them to be considerate? After what they did up there on the mountain?"

"I truly couldn't believe what I was hearing."

"I didn't know what to do," Dan blurted out. "I was standing there looking at them, and I thought, 'Man, that's my brother and my cousin there. I can't just leave 'em.'"

"Yeah, you were in a tough spot, I guess." I wasn't sure yet exactly what I thought, but I knew that Dan was the one sitting outside with me now. The rest of them might as well have been sitting in a beer joint in Cleveland. "They pussed out big time," I concluded. Dan didn't respond, but I knew he agreed, blood or no blood.

We spent a little time examining a big homemade billboard on the other side of the parking lot. License plates from almost every state in the Union and most of the Canadian provinces were nailed up there. Some of the oldest plates were covered with rust. "Look," Dan pointed at one rust-pitted old plate from Kansas. "The year we graduated—'76!"

Then we checked out the only other vehicle parked in front of the building that looked as if it might still run. It was a battered, four-wheel-drive Toyota pick-up with a sign in the back window that said "HOGGIN." We could see a rifle and a shotgun propped up against the window. Cautiously, we approached the truck and saw the carcass of a boar laid out in the bed of the truck. Even in its presently deceased condition, it was a fearsome beast: lean and mean and hairy with huge, curved tusks. I wondered how I could ever have been so stupid as to stalk such a creature with only a knife.

Freddie came out. As he admired the dead boar, he said, "Why don't you guys come in and get something to eat?"

Dan decided to be surly. "Which beer are they on? Their second or third?"

Freddie, who had probably just finished his own second beer, said, "You're here, so you might as well grab a burger."

I was damned hungry after missing breakfast and then hiking down a mountain, but it was a point of honor now not to go inside. "I'll grab some food out of my pack," I growled. Freddie went back in to report that Dan and I were being assholes.

It started drizzling again, but only enough to piss us off. Dan and I were sitting near the license plate billboard finishing off a small bag of trail mix when the Burger Boys came out. They were all smiles until they saw us sitting there in the drizzle, looking grim. Craig tried to act as if everything was fine. "So what do you guys want to do?" he asked with forced cheerfulness.

"Oh, I don't know. We were thinking about maybe going backpacking . . . if you guys are up for it." I said.

Dan was even more sarcastic. "Maybe you shouldn't sit in the car. You might get blisters on your asses."

Rick stormed away and went to stand over by the Condo. The rest of us tried to hash out a plan for the next three days. Dan and I suggested that we do the four-mile hike up to Porters Flat and camp there at #31, and then maybe day hike up the pioneer trail to Charlies Bunion the following day. Freddie liked the idea, but Craig balked. "The TV inside said showers all day today and most of tomorrow," he argued.

"It rains sometimes in the Smokies, Craig," I said, barely controlling my temper.

The only thing that was certain was that we had to go back to the Ramseys Cascade trailhead to retrieve Dan's Explorer, so we drove back to that parking lot. No one said much of anything when we arrived. Dan and I tersely announced that we were driving over to the Porters Creek trailhead, the jumping-off point for going up to #31 and Charlies Bunion, and then took off. We didn't give anybody time to argue. Freddie, unwillingly stuck in the middle, didn't know what to do other than follow us with the Condo.

The minute we arrived at the trailhead, Dan and I started preparing to head into the backcountry. We were going to camp up at #31 no matter what anybody else did. Freddie followed suit and started squaring away his pack, leaving Rick and Craig to sit inside the Condo staring out into the gray drizzle. Clearly, they didn't want to go, but just as clearly, the rest of us were going. The tension was thick, and no one said a word.

When Dan and Freddie started up the trail, Rick and Craig were still sitting sullenly inside the Excursion, making no move to get ready. I decided that somebody had to say something. I walked back to the Condo with my pack on my back and opened one of the doors. "What's wrong with you guys? I can't believe you're gonna let a little rain scare you away." Afraid that I might get punched for my trouble, I didn't wait around for a reply. I stalked off after Freddie and Dan. I did manage to sneak a quick look back before I lost sight of the parking lot, and I saw that Rick and Craig were at last getting their packs ready.

I tramped the familiar path comfortably until I caught up with Dan and Freddie. "Are they coming?" Freddie asked worriedly.

"Yeah, I think so. But I don't know if they'll be talking to me."

"They just better lock up my truck, that's all."

Buddha Palguta

The four-mile hike up to #31 seemed twice that distance. About half way up, Dan, Freddie and I paused to rest. We were all sucking wind. This was the place, I recalled, where I had begged and pleaded with Maria to take just a few more steps and had ended up carrying her pack. These were different times. Now I had all I could handle to make it up to the campsite myself. Freddie gradually outpaced me, but Dan considerately stayed with me. I could feel the last reserves of energy draining out of my body. I had eaten only a handful of trail mix all day, and my body was simply out of gas. I paused and put my hands on my knees and told Dan, "I think my blood sugar's dropping. If we don't get there pretty soon, I'm gonna have to stop and eat something."

At that very moment, Craig, fueled by burgers and beer and carrying his light pack, caught up and strode past us without uttering a word. I knew he was feeling smug and even vindicated, and it pissed me off royally. "Son of a bitch," I snarled. I straightened up and pushed myself onward, struggling to at least keep Craig within sight, but I couldn't do it. He outdistanced me. I was on the ragged edge of my endurance, and I had to stop a few more times before Dan and I finally saw the sign that marked campsite #31.

Craig and Freddie were peaceably sitting on a log smoking cigarettes. Craig watched me without expression. I looked back at him and, in spite of myself, broke into a grin. "You think you got me, don't you?" I asked.

Craig didn't smile, but I saw the pleasure in his eyes. "And yesterday too," he said laconically. I thought for a brief second about listing all the mitigating circumstances, but I let it go, knowing we would have time to argue the point in future days and years. Rick came into camp a minute later, hobbling slightly in his crappy footwear. We were all together and in the backcountry once again, so of course it began to rain.

We sat there in our ponchos and endured the rain. "What was that dumbass thing about not raining on the Army, Johnny?" Rick asked, and his gallows humor helped soften the tension. We were going to sleep in the wet, and there was no help for it. When the rain slackened, we set up camp in a steady drizzle. We hadn't had any opportunity to dry out our wet tents or our damp sleeping bags.

We managed to get a good, hot fire going after supper and partied as best we could, but it was a far cry from the old days. Quill Rose would have been ashamed. Before too long, we were forced to retreat into our tents to get out of the constant drizzle. My tent, the ancient K-Mart special, had lost any semblance of water-repellency, so Freddie and I laid ourselves down in puddles an inch or more deep. Our new-style, inflatable sleeping pads kept our asses up out of the water a little bit, but we were still in for a miserable night. The floor of the Rafferty's tent was a lot drier, although their sleeping gear was still damp.

After a while, I heard commotion from the other tent and then gales of laughter. Freddie and I poked our heads out and saw the thin, pale figure of Craig stalking through the trees. He was clad only in his tightie-whities and a pair of canary-yellow Crocs. The ultra-light, plastic camp shoes made Craig look like the world's tallest transvestite doing a runway show. I sang, "I'm too sexy for my shoes, too sexy for my shoes." Craig, who had gotten up to take a leak, laughed so hard that he couldn't pee.

The rain let up a little, so Craig and Rick got up again to sit by the fire, and Freddie soon joined them for a few more drinks. I stayed in my wet bag and tried to rest, and Dan stayed in his tent as well. I was drifting in and out of an uncomfortable doze when I heard my name being mentioned. Rick said, "He was picking food out of the pot while I was cooking. Like I want his dirty fingers in my fucking supper!"

I heard Craig grunt in apparent agreement. After a pause, he said, "He thinks he's all healthy because he quit drinking and smoking, but I still beat him up to the top both days."

I felt the flush of anger, but I stayed silent. I was just as guilty of talking about them sometimes, and if we couldn't bitch about each other after a day such as this, when could we? Still, as I lay there listening to the crackle of the fire and the muffled voices, I was reminded of how my new life had distanced me even from my closest friends. At that moment, the sober path seemed like a very lonely one.

The forest was still dripping in the morning, but the rain had stopped and the skies looked lighter. My tent looked like an overused kiddie pool with grass and other detritus floating around in the water. All that was missing was a Flintstones band-aid and maybe an escaped turd. "Good morning, Fab Five Freddie! We're lucky we didn't drown last night."

Freddie was pulling on his wet boots and had apparently woken in a surly mood. "Why the hell do you call me that anyway?"

I looked at him blankly for a second, and then it dawned on me what he meant. I laughed, "You mean I've been calling you that for what—five or six years—and you don't know what it means?"

"No!" Freddie laughed in spite of himself. "What the fuck are you talking about?"

I explained that it was a lyric from the Blondie song, "Rapture," and I rapped the line in question.

"Ohhh! I thought maybe it had something to do with the Beatles."

"No, man. Fab Five Freddie is way cooler than the Beatles ever were."

"Damn straight," Freddie said proudly, and he went back to pulling on his boots.

Over breakfast, I talked about going up the pioneer trail. "This time, we can go all the way up to Charlies Bunion. It's less than a mile away once you get to the top." I concentrated on persuading Craig, Rick, and Freddie, who were listening to me but looking rather dubious. Dan needed no persuasion; he was going. "It really is awesome, you guys," I said. "You should see it."

Craig said, "We were right there last time, and we didn't stop to check it out."

I was tired of the endless negotiations on this trip, so I finally shut up. Whoever went, went. In the end, Craig decided to come with me and Dan. Rick decided to rest his blister in camp, and Freddie, in yet another remarkable turn-around, opted to stay with Rick. I had to wonder how much fight Freddie would have had in him if we had headed off to Mount Guyot by ourselves.

We left camp carrying only our day packs, canteens, and weapons. The clouds were breaking up nicely, and it promised to be beautiful autumn day on which to do the toughest trail in the Smokies. Dan wanted to lead even though Craig and I had done the trail before, and he wound his way through the reeds on the confusing lower portion of the trail, hesitating a few times but finding his way very well. Then we scrambled over the huge boulders along the side of the creek until the creek went underground and temporarily disappeared. Dan marveled when he saw the creek reappear further upstream.

The way became very steep, and we picked our path through small laurel hells for a time. At one point, I thought I saw a better route than the one Dan had chosen. I tried to push through, but in no time, I was hopelessly tangled in the bush. Dan and Craig were moving away from me, unaware that I was struggling. The panic hit me like a punch in the chest. They were still within sight, so I yelled, "Hey, I'm stuck!" trying not to sound as panicked as I felt. They made some dismissive comment and kept going. I yelled again, "Don't leave me, you guys! I'm trapped in here!" and this time they must have heard the panic in my voice, for they stopped.

I heard Craig say, "Oh wow, he really is stuck," and they had to wait several minutes as I extricated myself from the hell and rejoined them. We continued up the mountain, but I was surprised at how quickly the panic had struck me, and I wondered why I felt so much less bold than I had on other trips.

When we approached the top and clambered up the almost-vertical gulley that led to the AT, I found myself in the lead purely by chance, and I didn't give it up. It was petty on my part to even care, I knew, but for some reason, it mattered to me. One by one, we pulled ourselves up onto the AT. As we stood on the crest savoring the accomplishment, I extended my hand toward Dan, and between ragged breaths I said, "Welcome to the club." Dan grinned from ear to ear.

We turned right to get to the Bunion, and within a mile we came to the side trail. I let Dan and Craig go first. I hugged the mountain like a long-lost friend as I made my way out to the point, which still scared the hell out of me. We followed the narrow shelf out to the place where the bunion outcropping looked north over the huge valley. The skies were blue, and the far-away summer haze was the only hindrance to the majestic view. It didn't matter in the least that I had been there before; I was awed all over again. Rick and Freddie were below us somewhere in the huge valley, but it felt more like the entire world was below us.

Right away, Dan had to scramble out onto the black rock outcropping that formed the extreme tip of the Bunion. Craig and I warned him to be careful, but we should have saved our breath. Careful people didn't climb out where Dan was. People had died falling from the Bunion, but Dan wasn't satisfied until he was as close to the edge of the precipice as possible.

Finding Mount Guyot

We took some photos and ate some snacks and then we had to go. Dan, who in an eccentricity of old age had taken to wearing a watch, informed us that it was already past two. As we re-entered the top of the chute, Craig warned his brother, "It's just a long, controlled fall, Dan. That's all it is." Dan might have been crazy, but he wasn't stupid. He took the top portion cautiously and stayed under control.

We paused to admire the view again as we worked our way down the smooth black face of the mountain where all the springs seeped out of the rock. "Remember when this was all ice the first time we came up here, John?" Craig reminisced. I noticed how the conditions that day had changed from occasional patches of ice to "all ice" over the course of the years, but I agreed with Craig just the same.

As we passed through the laurel hells on the way back down, Craig asked Dan, "Would you do this trail by yourself?", alluding to the fact that I had done so more than once.

Dan hesitated but finally nodded. "Yeah, I would."

"I don't know if I would," Craig admitted. "It'd be awful easy to get lost. Or hurt."

I didn't say anything, but I was thankful for Craig's implicit compliment. Already, the hard feelings from the previous day were softening. These guys were my oldest and dearest friends in the world, and I could no more walk away from them than I could my own family. We were stuck together for life now, despite the fact that we were becoming cantankerous old men.

The sun was westering in the soft September sky, and we had no time to waste. We moved quickly through what would have been an extremely treacherous trail for most people. In the fields of huge boulders farther down the mountain, we had to clamber down through the four- and five-foot drops between the massive rocks. Dan, enjoying himself as much as I had ever seen, was bounding from boulder to boulder, leaping six or eight feet at a time, landing flat-footed with a thud and then racing forward to the next big drop. For a little while the years melted away, and Dan forgot all about his touchy back and his child-support payments. I had attacked this trail the same way years before, but I wasn't in good enough shape to do much of that now. He ranged out ahead of us, and I told Craig, "Look at him! He's like a dog let off the leash."

Situations can change in a heartbeat in the backcountry. Dan leapt just a little too far and crumpled as he landed. He yelped with pain. Craig and I were by his side within seconds. He was lying on a flat boulder, holding his left thigh, and writhing in pain. I was certain his leg was broken because Dan never showed pain if he could help it. "What hurts, Dan?" I asked.

"Everything." His eyes were squinted shut.

"Care to be more specific?" Craig asked. Despite his flippancy, I could see that Craig was worried.

Dan felt gingerly along the big muscle in his left thigh and then reached down to touch his ankle. Only after that blind inspection did he open his eyes to look into our concerned faces. "I rolled my ankle when I landed and then I crashed into that big rock." He pointed at a big boulder with a sharp edge jutting out about thigh high.

"Good thing you didn't smack your balls into it." Craig could always see the bright side of things.

"Damn! I banged the shit out of my thigh though." Dan tried to stand, and we helped him to his feet. He was able to put weight on his left leg, which was an excellent sign. He dropped his pants and examined his wounded leg. Just above the midpoint of Dan's quadriceps, a big contusion was already turning reddish and purplish. A few drops of blood showed at the point of impact, testifying to the amount of force with which Dan's leg had struck.

Craig whistled softly. "That's going to hurt tomorrow."

"Kind of hurts right now," Dan said distractedly. He was putting weight onto his leg, shifting from side to side, gauging how bad the thigh and the ankle were injured.

"Well," I asked, "you gonna live?"

Dan took a few tentative steps and announced, "Yeah, I'm OK."

"Good," Craig said. "Then pull your pants up 'cause John's starting to look at you funny."

Dan slipped into his Wild and Crazy Guy voice as he pulled up his pants. "None for you, funny boy!"

Within five minutes Dan was walking pretty normally. The daylight was dwindling though, and the shadows were getting dangerously long as we descended to flatter ground. Craig hurried us along, worried about finding camp in the dark, but I had been down this trail enough to know where I was. When we caught the welcoming smell of campfire smoke wafting up the valley, we knew we were back to safety. We walked into camp feeling that we had salvaged something from a disastrous trip.

All the sleeping bags were hanging out to dry, and a cheerful little fire crackled in the fire pit. A nice mound of firewood sat piled next to the fire as well. Rick and Freddie seemed bored out of their skulls because they barraged us with inane questions. Rick asked, "So did you guys cheeseburger the summit?"

Craig thought he had heard wrong. "Did we *what*?"

"Eat a cheeseburger at the summit," Rick explained. "I saw people on the Internet eating cheeseburgers at the tops of mountains. It's a thing they do now."

Craig did a passable imitation of a Clint Eastwood glower. "Where the fuck were we gonna get a cheeseburger?"

"You take it with you when you go, dumbass," Rick said, sorry he had brought it up.

Craig shook his head. "And you guys wonder why I'm not wired on the Google, or whatever you call it."

I had just enough time to jump into Porters Creek and wash up. I still found nothing more liberating than standing naked in a stream in the middle of the mountains. In another life I might have been a nudist. I whooped for the freedom and joy of it. Dan decided to join me. We kept a good ten yards between us—a respectable heterosexual space—but we were close enough to each other to laugh and joke around.

When we got back to camp, the Iron Chef was dishing out supper, and the Burger Boys had to have their sport with us. Never mind that Dan had a bunch of kids and that I had been married at least twice that I could remember. We were now homos. "What," Craig started, "are you two in love?"

"Yeah, Craig," Rick yelled from over by the stove, "I think they're gonna elope."

"You guys could never understand," I said haughtily, "what it is we share."

"Butt buddies!" Freddie added cheerfully.

"Ignore them, Johnny," Dan said. "They're just jealous."

After supper, we sat around the fire, enjoying our last night in the woods. The night was cool and clear, and the stars were becoming visible in bunches in the open spaces between the branches above. As we sat hypnotized by the flames, Craig turned to Freddie and quietly asked, "How many smokes you got left?"

Freddie carefully counted the contents of his Camel Wides hard pack. "Seven," he said with a trace of desperation. "And I gotta have at least two for tomorrow."

"I've got eight," Craig said. "That should be just enough." Everybody heard the grim tally.

Dan and I, the two nonsmokers, were delighted. "Oh man!" I laughed. "That would suck to be up here drinking and not have any smokes, wouldn't it, Dan?"

Dan asked with feigned surprise, "You guys didn't buy any in town?" We hadn't exactly passed a town after leaving Mountain Mama's, but we had passed two general stores where they could have found cigarettes.

Rick, an occasional smoker who believed that he wouldn't get hooked if he didn't buy a pack, had been bumming smokes for two days. "I guess I should've bought some," he glumly admitted, knowing he wasn't going to be smoking any more cigarettes on this night.

"Ya think?" Dan grinned. It seemed to me that they all should have brought more cigarettes, but I kept that opinion to myself. Nobody was laughing except me and Dan.

The wood pile was running low, so Craig and I wandered far into the eerie woods looking for firewood. The thought of bears was far from our minds, maybe because there were so many of us in camp, or maybe because we were inured to the danger after so many years. We found the solid trunk of a dead hardwood, twelve feet long and at least eight inches thick, and we wrestled it back to the clearing. We knew it would burn well, but the problem was getting it onto the fire.

Dan said, "I'll show you how to break that thing," and he laboriously wedged one end of the log between two live trees a few feet apart. Then he lifted up the loose end of the log and put all his weight against it, trying to crack the log. He threw his body into the log several times, and each time the log recoiled and threw him back.

I said, "Hey, I'm stupid too," and I jumped in beside Dan to help. We put almost 500 pounds of beef into it, and the log cracked a little before throwing us back. Once we heard that first crack, we knew we could break it. We started using the recoil to our advantage, putting our shoulders into it again and again in rhythm. The log started cracking a little more each time, and I said, "Watch out. It's gonna snap all at once and send us flying," but we kept going anyway. Sure enough, the log broke with an echoing crack, and Dan and I went sprawling.

As I got up and dusted myself off, Craig told me, "I wanted to help you guys, but I can't afford to get hurt."

"Why not?"

"My pension. I'm about a year away from being able to collect, and they'd love to get rid of my ass now before they have to pay me for the rest of my life."

Rick overheard Craig's words and asked, "You get a pension after thirty years?"

"Yeah," Craig shrugged. "If I make it."

Rick was astounded. "Wait a minute. You mean some drop-out can stand in a meat cooler for thirty years and get a pension by the time he's forty-eight, but I went to college and I have to work 'til I'm sixty-five?"

"Well, it's not really enough to retire on. I'll still need the Social Security."

"It's still bullshit." Rick said.

"You try standing in a refrigerator and risking your fingers every day for thirty years," Craig shot back, "and see how much you like it."

I said, "You ever wonder why you have to spend the best years of your life busting your ass just so you can be comfortable when you're old?"

"That's how life is," Freddie said.

"No," I said, "you only do that because that's what you saw your parents do, so you think that's what you have to do too. Really, you don't think about it at all. You just do it."

I popped the top of my last O'Doul's and took a good drink. "Before you know it you're our age and it's all over. You don't have any options left. You hope you make it to retirement, and you take a few lame-ass vacations in tour buses with fat old ladies, and then you die. Big fuckin' whoop. Life well spent."

"People have to make a living, John," Craig countered. Craig believed fervently in his union, his pension, and the working-class American Dream. "If you work hard and play by the rules, you can retire early . . ."

"Why would you want to live your life by somebody else's rules?" I interrupted. "That never made any sense to me."

I shifted a log in the fire with my foot and sent sparks flying up into the night sky. "Even if you retire at sixty, Craig, are you gonna go out and tear it up like when you were thirty or forty? Are you really going to have *fun*? Yeah, you might get to Hawaii some day and go snorkeling for an hour, but you sure as hell aren't going to be walking barefoot in the sand at two in the morning with some little hottie, wondering if you can do her right there on the beach. More likely, you'll be sitting at a slot machine in a casino, hooked up to an oxygen tank, telling yourself how exciting and sexy it is."

"What if I *like* playing slot machines with fat ladies?" Rick asked.

I realized half way through my rant that I was setting myself up for some kind of sarcastic response, so I wasn't surprised when I got it. "Then God help you," I said. "There's nothing I can do for you."

"I liked him better when he drank," Craig pretended to whisper to Freddie, but he said it loud enough for us all to hear.

"No kidding!" Freddie said, and we all laughed.

I sat down and gazed into the fire, wondering how true I could remain to my own ideals as old age loomed closer and closer.

In the morning, Craig and Freddie smoked their last cigarettes as if they were receiving sacraments. I elbowed Dan and nodded toward the two of them. Dan looked and said, "Thank God I quit."

The hike back from #31 was a gentle, downhill glide along the banks of Porters Creek. We enjoyed the cool breeze, the soft sunshine, and the music of the water. The trail and the conditions were as kind as they could ever be in the Smokies. Freddie pulled up even with me as we ambled through a wide spot in the trail and said, "Man, I'm feeling really good today. I think I'm hiking pretty good."

I grunted noncommittally. My own legs were sore as hell from doing the pioneer trail the day before, but this was still an easy hike out. "Why didn't you go up to Charlies Bunion with us, Freddie?" I asked quietly. It was a can of worms that no one had wanted to open up the night before, but I was curious.

Freddie didn't look up as he spoke. "My legs were tired from the day before," he admitted. I suspected there was more to it. I wondered if he simply hadn't thought he could make it. Yet the day before he had been ready to go to Mount Guyot and tackle the off trail with me. I was glad that I hadn't marched off in a huff with Freddie that morning. I had a feeling it wouldn't have ended well.

Dan and Craig had sore legs too—especially Dan's left one—but neither was limping as badly as Rick. His heel had indeed sprouted a good-sized blister, but he had Mole-Skinned it, and he manfully toughed out the last four miles. Whether he would ever backpack again was another matter. It seemed to me that his hardcore backpacking days were behind him.

That left me with only two backpacking companions, and of those two, I had to wonder how much fire Craig really had left in his belly. Physically, he could still do it, but in spite of all of his brave Captain Ahab speeches about Mount Guyot, Craig had readily abandoned ship on Mount Sterling.

My thoughts were interrupted when we spotted a green-striped snake about two feet long sunning itself on the side of the trail. None of us was sure what kind of snake it was—we were all painfully ignorant that way—but it looked harmless enough. It certainly wasn't a rattler, and it didn't have the triangular head that the nature books always warned about. Freddie decided to mess with the snake, prodding it gingerly with the toe of his boot.

I was secretly hoping the snake would bite Freddie on his stupid ass. "Freddie," I said in a pained voice, "what did that snake ever do to you? Leave the poor thing alone." The threatened snake lifted up the front portion of its body and bared its fangs toward Freddie's boot, causing Freddie to chuckle like Beavis or Butthead, whichever one was dumber. Still, the snake was no threat to us whatsoever. It wasn't blocking the trail, and all we had to do was walk around it. "Let's go," I urged, and I tried to lead by example, walking down the trail past the snake. Rick and Craig followed me. I looked back in time to see Dan, who was standing a few yards behind Freddie, throw a pebble at the snake and hit it squarely.

The snake, evidently uninjured, stood its ground.

Rick got pissed. "Dan, what's wrong with you? That thing's got as much right to be here as we do!"

"Yeah, Dan, leave it alone," I muttered. I was glad that Rick was taking my side.

"I didn't think I'd hit it!" Dan yelled defensively. It *had* been a hell of a shot, I had to admit, but his excuse was no excuse at all. Dan's words hung in the air as Rick and Craig and I walked away.

We spread out and hiked the rest of the way in relative silence, each man lost in his own thoughts. When we got back to the trailhead, the normally quiet parking lot was buzzing with excited voices and laughter. The place was swarming with little kids who were piling out of a big, yellow school bus. The kids, who were perhaps first and second graders, surrounded us as we walked through the top end of the lot. The kids were fascinated by us, but we were just as fascinated

341

by them. We stopped to talk with them, and they peppered us with questions.

"How far did you walk today?" a tow-headed boy asked.

Freddie pointed at the highest visible summit. "You see that mountain there? We came from a mountain even bigger than that one, and twice as far away!"

"That's where we're going!" the boy said excitedly.

"Do you live up there?" a cute little girl asked Dan. I remembered another cute girl who had asked Dan the same question twenty-five years earlier.

Dan knelt down on one knee to answer her. "We lived up there for a little while, but no, honey, we don't live up there all the time. I have a house and a little girl who's just about your age."

"What's her name?" she asked, as if she might know Dan's daughter.

"Do you ever have to take a bath?" one boy asked me.

"Well, I do," I said. "But that big guy there," I pointed at Craig, "he *never* takes a bath!" One of the teachers laughed at that one. The teacher was pretty cute herself, I noticed.

A chubby girl asked, "Do you know my Daddy? He goes up in the hills too."

Rick responded to that one. "I don't think we met your Daddy, honey. Not this time."

"Where's your pillows?" another boy wanted to know.

"We use our dirty underwear for our pillows," Rick answered with a playful snarl, and all the little girls cringed.

"Do you have guns? I want a gun!" one boy asked. He might become a mountain man, I thought, or maybe a convict.

"We don't need any guns," Craig said. "We just make the bears look at that bald guy," he pointed at me, "and they all run away." I made the most horrible face I could, and the kids squealed in delight.

"What do you eat?"

Freddie looked at Rick and said, "Chinese food," and we all laughed, but of course none of the kids got that one.

"When are you going back up there?"

All five of us were quiet for a long moment, and finally Dan answered, "Pretty soon." He looked at me. "Right, Johnny?"

I smiled and nodded, "Yeah. Pretty soon." It seemed there was only me and Dan left, yet sometimes I wondered what demons still danced behind Dan's restless eyes.

12   Going to Mount Guyot: Fourth Attempt

The failed trip left a bad taste in everyone's mouth. Fab Five Freddie dropped out of our little gang altogether and never told us why. Rick just stopped talking about backpacking. Craig would occasionally bluster about going back to Mount Guyot. "Straight up the creek, John! Jumping rock to rock! To hell with you and your short legs! This time we get to the fucking top!" Still, he never made the time to go. When I talked to Dan about it, we agreed that our backpacking careers could not end on such a sorry note, so in the fall of 2008, he and I decided to go once more unto the breach.

Dan had someone else he wanted to bring along—a dog he had found in the Smokies the year before. He and his sons had been camping up at the Mollies Ridge shelter when they saw a skinny, wild-looking, yellow dog eyeing them from the edges of the clearing. The poor thing's ribs were obscenely easy to see, and her paws were scraped bloody from the rocky terrain. They spoke kindly to her, and the unfortunate animal acted submissive, so the boys gave the dog what scraps of food they could for the next few days, and she followed them (forgive me) doggedly. They started calling her "Mollie."

They took Mollie home, and the vet said that Mollie was an approximately six-month-old Carolina Dog, which was a recognized, rare breed sometimes called the American Dingo. Carolina Dogs were feral dogs found in the forests and swamps of the Carolinas and Georgia ever since the colonization of America. They bore a striking genetic resemblance to the Australian Dingo, hence the second name. When Dan asked me if I minded if he brought Mollie, I told him I was happy to have her along. Dogs weren't allowed in the backcountry, but we'd broken so many rules that one more wouldn't matter.

When Dan came to pick me up at five in the morning, Mollie the American Dingo jumped out of the SUV with a joyful yelp and started sprinting around my yard. I had never seen Mollie before, but I loved dogs more than I loved most people. I called her, and she bounded over to me and gave me a quick nuzzle hello. I tossed my gear into Dan's SUV, and we hit the highway fast. Our plan was to get to the Smokies by two in the afternoon, hike three miles back up into the mountains, and then set up camp before dark. Once we were under way, Mollie wanted to make friends, and I got the full benefit of her powerful canine aroma. She had a bad case of doggie BO, but I hadn't seen Dan in a long time, and I didn't want to offend him right off the bat by complaining about how bad his dog stank. In a few days, I would smell worse than the dog.

The miles passed quickly as the morning unfolded, and I wondered why we hadn't left before dawn on our previous trips. I flatten the trail map out on the dashboard and said, "Let me show you how I think we should go. I'm not planning on going up Ramseys Prong."

Buddha Palguta

Dan wasn't interested. "I trust you, Johnny. We'll get there."

When we arrived, we weren't surprised in the least to see the skies darkening even though the forecast had called for clear weather. We were more worried about getting Mollie up into the backcountry without anyone stopping us. The rule was that no dogs were allowed in the backcountry, leashed or unleashed. Dogs were notorious for not burying their poop the regulation six inches deep.

We changed quickly into our hiking clothes and stuffed the last few items into our packs, and I felt the old excitement rising up inside me. Even after more than thirty years, it was still a thrill to launch out into the wild where there were no laws for the brave ones. Fools that we were, we debated who would carry the tent. "I don't think I've ever *not* carried the tent," I argued.

"Me either."

"So we'll take turns then."

"Alright, but I'm carrying it today," Dan said, stubborn to the end.

Dan strapped Mollie's saddlebag packed full of dog food on her back, and we were ready to go. The sign post at the Gabes Mountain trailhead told us that we actually had closer to five miles to go to get to campsite #34, so we started out at a good pace. I had been working out regularly for a while, and my legs were starting to feel some of their youthful vigor. Toward the end of the hike, the skies were threatening to bust wide open, and I was damn near jogging through the woods. Dan, carrying the heavier pack, trailed right behind. Mollie happily trotted along in the middle position.

Campsite #34, Sugar Cove, was an ugly, overused little camp with several tent sites strung together along one side of a creek. We saw one tent already pitched up on the highest ground when we got there, so we were walking downstream

346

scouting the remaining tent sites when we saw the people who belonged to the pitched tent. They were a young Indian couple—Asian Indians, not North American Indians. They smiled nervously as we approached.

Dan strode straight up to the man, who was a slim guy maybe twenty-five years old. Dan got up within eighteen inches of the guy's face and said, "Are you the keeper of the eternal magic knot?"

Dan didn't realize how physically intimidating he could be. The young guy was clearly scared to death. He was 5' 8" tops, alone out in the woods with his sweetheart, and here was this huge guy up in his face babbling incoherently. He stammered, "What?"

Dan repeated, "Are you the keeper of the eternal magic knot? You know, the knot that keeps the mice off your food."

The young guy had no way of knowing that Dan was usually harmless. The only thing he could think to do was offer us water. "We have been boiling water for three hours. Would you care for some?" he asked. This was apparently a peace offering, like giving beads and trinkets to savages.

I knew that Dan was having flashbacks of meeting the camel jockeys back in the days before political correctness. To let the couple know that one of us was not insane, I said, "No thanks, we'll get our own. We'll camp down here somewhere to give you guys some space." The young couple warily watched us work our way farther downstream.

The best spot we could find was a rocky patch between two big boulders. We couldn't open up our tent fully, but there was no better ground anywhere in this miserable camp. I glanced up the hill, and even though there was still some light in the sky, I saw no sign of life around the Indian couple's tent. They were probably huddled inside, hiding from the huge man who spoke nonsense.

A light drizzle became steady rain, so we decided not to mess with a fire. After supper, we crawled into the tent and prepared to go to sleep early. I noticed that Dan hadn't brought a sleeping pad. "What're you gonna do? Just sleep on the rocks?"

"Well, Johnny, when I was packing, I was thinking 'Go light.' But right now it seems like I made a bad choice."

"So basically, you haven't learned anything in thirty years." Dan didn't respond, so I continued, "Man, a sleeping pad's a *necessity*! Especially at our age. I almost brought two for myself. Damn, you're in for a miserable night."

Again, Dan was silent. He lay down on top of his sleeping bag and called Mollie over to him. Mollie was curled up on the foot of my inflatable sleeping pad, already having found the softest spot in the tent, so he had to call her a few times before she would go over to him. Dan wrapped his arms around Mollie and said a terse "Goodnight." Mollie groaned deeply, knowing she too was in for a rough night.

I lay down on my self-inflating Stearns sleeping pad, the same Stearns people who made those nice mattresses, and I had no problem falling asleep totally drug-free in the Smokies for the first time in my life.

We woke up to more drizzle. It had rained hard periodically through the night, and we found drops of water on the inside walls of Dan's battered, old tent and little puddles of water on the floor. "I guess the waterproofing didn't work all that great," Dan said with drops of water an inch from his nose.

"I guess not," I said gruffly. "How'd you sleep? I had this one rock right under my hip that I kept hitting no matter which way I turned."

That got his goat, as I knew it would. "You gotta be kidding me! I slept on the *ground*, Johnny, the fucking *ground*! And you're gonna cry about one rock?"

I rolled over toward him with a big smile on my face, and he changed his tone. "I slept fine," he said. "Right, Mollie? We slept just fine."

I had a few surprises in store for Dan. I had read somewhere that eggs didn't actually need to be refrigerated, so I had packed some along for a breakfast treat. Dan was boiling water on the stove for coffee, and as he hunched over the cooking pot, I dropped a few into the water. He acted as if I had just dropped in big, fat rubies. "You got eggs!"

I stole a line from my favorite horror movie, *The Hills Have Eyes*, and said, "You be a good dog, you git some!" *The Hills Have Eyes* was about a family of mutants who lived out in the Mojave Desert near the nuclear test ranges. They raided—and sometimes ate—the city people who passed through the desert. More importantly, they said cool shit to their victims like, "You fat! Baby fat! Fat and juicy!" and "I'll be back fer you later, girlie!" I used quotes from the movie on a regular basis, especially with the ladies.

I was impatient, so I scooped an egg out of the pot after what I judged to be three or four minutes. "Mm mmm! This is gonna be better than Hop Sing's cooking!" I peeled away the shell, but the center of the egg was still the consistency of snot. I ate it anyway and pronounced it delicious, but I let my other eggs cook longer. We tossed the egg shells into the fire pit, thinking we would pack them out later with our trash, but Mollie had other ideas. We caught her wolfing down the egg shells, all covered with dirt and gray ashes.

After we drank our coffee made from boiled egg water, it was time to unveil my other surprise. I had brought a kilt along, thinking it would be comfortable to walk with nothing rubbing between my legs. (Well, not *nothing*.) Technically, it wasn't a real kilt. Genuine kilts were outrageously expensive on the Internet. I had gone to a resale shop instead, where I received a few odd looks as I rifled through the plus-sized ladies' skirts. I had envisioned a little red plaid number, but I found that big ladies didn't wear red plaid skirts. That was more for private-school girls. The closest thing I could find was a gray, hounds-tooth-checked skirt from a husky lady's business suit. It was actually too big for me, so I had to take in the waist when I got home. The hem of the skirt hung down over the bottoms of my knees, which was good because I didn't want to look like a slutty schoolgirl.

I hadn't mentioned my kilt to Dan. I put it on while he was closing up his backpack. When he turned around to say something to me, his mouth opened to speak, but nothing came out for a few seconds. Then he started laughing in great whoops. He was standing on a steeply-pitched section of muddy hillside, and he literally fell down laughing. His feet went out from under him and he went down on his ass, but he never stopped laughing. Mollie ran for cover. His response was all I could have hoped for. Dan got up, still laughing, and pointed at my crotch. "What's that?" he gasped.

"This is my fuzzy squirrel," I said with great dignity. He started laughing some more and nearly fell over again. I explained, "You know how they hang those little purse things down over their crotches when they wear kilts? This was the best thing I could find."

"So this is a kilt?"

"Of course! What'd you think? I'm a Highlander, man."

"You're gonna hike like that?"

"Yeah." I explained how I had been hiking one day that summer with a girlfriend, and I had been complaining about my jeans chafing my thighs. She suggested a kilt, and I had liked the idea immediately. Using the squirrel-shaped cat toy as a sporran, which is what they call that little purse, had been a last-minute burst of inspiration.

We left camp #34 without seeing the young Indian couple again. I was disappointed because I wanted someone besides

Finding Mount Guyot

Dan to see me with my kilt on. We climbed toward Mount Guyot, gaining some serious elevation as we hiked up the Maddron Bald Trail. The conditions weren't very favorable, but we barely mentioned it. I trudged on like a Scottish warrior. I was having trouble climbing over the deadfalls without ripping the seams of my kilt, but I eventually figured out that I had to hitch it up around my waist in order to straddle the logs. Being a Highlander wasn't all glamour.

Toward the end of the hike, I was climbing a steep section of trail by myself, working my body hard and enjoying the exertion. I stopped for a moment to catch my breath and experienced an optical illusion. Instead of objects moving toward my eyes as they had been doing all morning, it seemed as if the trees, the mountain peaks, and even the clouds were expanding away from me in all directions at once. I felt an inexplicable sense that my soul was expanding outward too, becoming one with the world around me. I had never felt such oneness with God's creation.

When we finally made it to camp, it was raining steadily. Campsite #29, Otter Creek, was another rocky piece of ground without a single decent place to pitch a tent. I was heartily sick of being wet and sick of crappy campsites. My oneness with creation was gone. As we wandered through the deserted campsite in the rain vainly searching for a flat spot, I vented my frustration.

"You'd think they'd make sure there was at least one flat spot big enough to pitch a fucking tent before they called it a campsite, wouldn't you? What the hell good is a campsite if you can't site a tent? God forbid they should actually pick up a shovel and make a level spot! They'd rather build some interactive nature center bullshit with fucking computers for fat-assed kids who'll never set foot in the mountains!"

Dan was laughing, so I kept ranting. "And why the hell is it raining? This is supposed to be the driest month, and every time I come here in October I almost fucking drown!"

Dan knew I was exaggerating. When I was done, he said, "It'll all be worth it when we get to the top." We both knew that the harder and the more uncomfortable the trip was, the more we would cherish the hard-won moments of beauty, and the more we would recall this trip in the years to come. The hardship was part of the backpacking experience—the yin and the yang of wild beauty and physical discomfort—and you couldn't have one without the other. If we had simply driven up to the top of a mountain in an air-conditioned car and gotten out and climbed some nice, even steps to an observation platform, we wouldn't truly appreciate the majesty of the mountain. But when you suffer and sweat and approach a mountain on its own terms, you truly experience the mountain, and you remember it forever.

The rain was cold and the wind was blowing, and as soon as we cooled off from the hike we were pretty miserable. We made a meal and shoveled the food down our gullets as quickly as possible. It would have been nice to sit down and stay dry while we ate our supper, but we knew that no matter how bad the weather, we couldn't take the food smells inside our tent. We stood in the rain and ate as our plates filled with rain water.

Mollie was beside herself. She stood by the door of the tent and whined pitifully, so Dan put her in the tent, but then she wanted to come right back out. She started digging a hole in the rocky soil between two trees and balled herself up inside the depression. She'd lie there and shiver for a minute, and then get up and dig the hole a little deeper and lie back down again.

Like the night before, a fire was out of the question. It was still light out, but there was nothing else for us to do except retreat into our wet tent and try to stay warm. We found at least an inch of water puddled on the low side of the tent. We could see the rain dripping right through the seams. "Dan," I announced like a plumber who had been called in the middle of the night, "we need to cut a hole to let the water out."

Dan did not immediately share my vision. "No way you're cutting a fucking hole in my tent!" was the way he put it.

"But the bottom's holding the water in! Imagine how much water we're going to have in here by morning."

Dan saw the truth of what I was saying. "Give me your big knife," he said. He cut the hole and it drained out some but not all of the standing water.

Drain hole or no drain hole, Dan was in for one of the more miserable nights of his life. He was wet, his sleeping bag was wet, and he was going to sleep directly on the rocky ground again. I offered him what little help I could. "I'll take the low side since I have the sleeping pad. It'll keep me up out of the water."

We crawled into the tent, but it was only six o'clock, and we were too damned uncomfortable to sleep. We had been in unrelenting wetness for more than twenty-four hours straight.

I talked to pass the time. "It doesn't get easier as you get older, does it?"

"It does get easier, Johnny. You don't realize how much of this we take for granted now. Stuff that used to be hard, like lighting a fire or pitching a tent, we do it now without even thinking. And we hiked pretty good today for two fifty-year-old guys. That was not an easy hike we just did."

"Yeah, we did alright. It was a good eight miles uphill, and we have heavy packs. I felt really good today," I said, thinking of my epiphany on the mountainside. "Except I rubbed my thighs raw with that damned kilt."

"I've got the perfect stuff for your thighs! You ever try diaper rash ointment?"

"For what? Chip dip, or a dessert topping? What makes you think I would've ever used diaper rash ointment?"

"Yeah, I guess you wouldn't have. But I'm telling you the stuff is great. It'll heal you up overnight if you put it on a rash."

"So why're you telling me this? Are we gonna go to the store and get some?"

Dan had in fact brought along a tube of diaper rash ointment, the only first aid item he had bothered to bring, and it was exactly what I needed. I spread some on my raw thighs and felt instant relief. "I hope this stuff works. We have a long way to go tomorrow." Almost lost in our discomfort was the fact that we were going to find the Holy Grail, the top of Mount Guyot, the first thing in the morning.

I awoke in the night, jammed into the wall of the tent on the downhill side. The rain was seeping through the tent into my clothing, and my ass had slipped off my sleeping pad and was now sitting in standing water. I tried to shift myself back onto my mat, but Mollie was curled up quite comfortably there. She groaned a little because I had disturbed her slumber. My love for dogs was momentarily forgotten. I booted Mollie off and cussed at her as I tried to find a comfortable position on top of the pad.

It was always difficult to get the right amount of air into the new inflatable pads. Too much air made it like trying to sleep on a balloon, and too little air allowed the lumps in the ground to come right through. Soon after I rebalanced myself, Mollie furtively edged back onto my pad. Her extra weight made the sleeping mat balloon up, causing me to slide off again toward the downhill side. This worked right into Mollie's evil plan and gave her more space. I was engaged in a battle of wits with Mollie, and I was losing. For the rest of the night, I kept pushing her off my sleeping pad, but she was diabolical and relentless.

I woke up again later and noticed that the rain had stopped. I needed to pee, and I suddenly couldn't stand to be inside the fetid dog-stink for another second. I climbed over Dan and got out. There was still no sign of dawn, but the fresh air was wonderful after the overwhelming stench of the tent. Only a few wispy clouds were left after almost thirty-six hours of constant rain. Even more amazing was the sight of city lights out to the northwest. We were situated on the edge of a little gap that opened to the northwest, and I knew I was looking out at the lights of Pigeon Forge and Sevierville. I had never seen the lights of civilization from the Smokies at night. Looking down onto the cities was a novelty, but I hated the reminder that we really weren't very far from the world below.

Dan yelled from the tent, "Is that a flash flood coming through?"

I was feeling giddy, so I gave him a wake-up line I had learned in the Army, "Drop your cock and grab your socks!"

Dan made up one of his own. "Let go of your dick. You make me sick."

I was exhausted to the point of silliness, and that struck me as one of the funniest things I'd ever heard. I stood barefoot in the mud in the middle of the mountains at four in the morning, stone cold sober, laughing until it hurt. "Hey, sicko," I said when I recovered by breath, "you gotta come out here and see this! The stars are out! You can see the city!"

"No way, man. There's something wrong with anybody who laughs like that! And leave my dog alone, too."

I growled in my *Hills Have Eyes* voice, "Bring yer little dog out here! C'mere, girlie!" (The mutants ate dogs too.) "Hey, when're you gonna bring your daughters and their friends out here?"

"Which ones should I bring?"

"The fat and juicy ones!"

Buddha Palguta

When it was light out, Dan had a breakfast surprise of his own—a package of pre-cooked bacon. Anything other than oatmeal was a welcomed change. Mollie liked the bacon so much that she ate the waxed paper wrapping.

While I munched on my bacon, I packed a few essentials for the day's hike in my little daypack, the same knapsack I'd been carrying for twenty years. I dressed lightly, but I knew the misty morning could still turn cold and rainy, so I threw a high-tech sweatshirt into my day pack, as well as a poncho and a tin-foil "space blanket" in case worse came to worst. I also had a map, a compass, a first aid kit, two whistles, some paper and a pencil, my big knife, a full canteen, a camera, and some trail snacks for lunch. Finally, I threw in one of my O'Doul's to celebrate with when we reached the summit.

I looked at Dan, who was wearing a sleeveless T-shirt and walking shorts and carrying a canteen. He had no pack whatsoever. "Are you bringing *anything*?"

He patted his pants pockets. "Yeah. I got a camera and some snack bars."

I said, "You know it could turn cold up there."

He gave me a smirk, as if to say, *Yeah, like we're ascending Mount Everest.*

I fished a high-tech, long-sleeved undershirt out of my big pack and threw it into my daypack. "For you, 'cause I love ya, man," I said. And with that, we left to finally scale Mount Guyot.

It was a steep mile and a half on the Maddron Bald Trail up out of #29, but with pants on, it felt easy. The trail cut through a rhododendron hell with walls of rubbery leaves ten feet high on either side, but we barely noticed because we were so excited.

Lots of smoky clouds hung down into the valleys. It sprinkled on us once or twice in sudden cold bursts as we moved through those clouds, but the cold water felt good

356

because we were hiking fast. We reached the Maddron Bald itself, which was a rocky prominence overgrown with stunted laurel bushes. We followed a short side trail up to an observation point hollowed out in the center of the little hell. We could see a jagged line of high peaks just off to the south— the sawteeth of the Smokies. Serious gray rain clouds were scraping over those higher peaks. It was a raw autumn morning and a wild, rugged view.

"That one has to be Guyot." I pointed at the highest point on the ridge, no more than a few miles away as the crow flies. The main peak was completely obscured by rain clouds scudding across the top, making the silent mountain look even more daunting. We studied it without saying anything. We were face to face with Guyot.

The Maddron Bald Trail merged with the Snake Den Ridge Trail, which was named for all the rattlesnake dens on the mountain. We caught more glimpses of Mount Guyot as we approached it, and I yelled "Geeee ooohhhhh!!!" a few times, the same way Rocky yelled "Draayyy goohhhh!!!" in *Rocky IV* when he was training to fight the giant Russian boxer, Ivan Drago.

We quickly reached the AT, and it was like meeting an old friend. The sign post said it was only 1.9 more miles to Mount Guyot, which buoyed our spirits. We were standing once again on the very spine of the silent and ancient Appalachians, and I appreciated that fact much more than I had when I was young. I was feeling pretty blessed to be where I was. Not many people our age could make this journey. Despite of our misspent youths, we were still pretty healthy.

We raced south along the crest toward Mount Guyot. Out in the big valley to our right, Ramseys Cascade began its headlong run to the sea. We walked along the edge of that valley and came to a section that had relatively few trees and some pleasant-looking ferns growing. "See! It was just like this!" I told Dan. "Somewhere right along here is where we came out when we came up from Ramseys Cascade."

I looked out into that immense valley again. To my fifty-year-old eyes, the valley looked impassable. The trees closed in more thickly just a hundred yards down the side of the mountain, and I knew what impenetrable laurel hells lay beyond. I was struck by the steepness of the mountainside and the sheer size of the valley. I couldn't believe that I had hacked my way through that wilderness and made it out in one piece.

Dan had heard all the stories dozens of times, but he had never seen the place with his own eyes. "Craig's probably right," he said dismissively. "You'd have been better off following the creek up."

Farther up the ridge, I noticed a chunk of something metallic about ten yards off the trail. My first thought was that it was a junked car, but not even moonshine runners like Bo and Luke Duke could have gotten a car up where we were. I walked down and saw a long hinge on one side of the curved piece of thick aluminum. I couldn't believe what I was seeing. "Hey, Dan, it's an airplane!"

Dan and Mollie followed me down. We looked around and discovered lots of other pieces of metallic debris. "You're right. I wonder if it just happened," Dan said, but we soon realized that the wreckage had been there a while. Nothing was burnt on the hillside, and we could even see faint footprints showing that other people had walked down to where we stood. Dan went up and over to the other side of the trail and found more wreckage over there. He came back after a few minutes, and as we continued down the AT, Dan speculated on the cause of the wreck.

To me, it didn't matter why. They were dead, whoever they were, and probably had been for a long time. Mount Guyot got 'em. After some years passed, the woods would grow over those metal pieces, and no one would ever know it had happened. Mount Guyot would still be there, the same as it had been for hundreds of millions of years.

The AT rolled along, going gently but steadily uphill. I started looking for the side trail off to the left that would take us to the peak. Ten years earlier, there had been a wooden trail marker pointing the way to the top of Mount Guyot. I remembered stopping and doing some blow not far from that sign.

When the trail flattened out, we could tell we were at the top of the mountain and walking along its shoulder. The skies had cleared fairly well, and we could look up over our left shoulders and occasionally see bright daylight through the trees. Feeling jubilant, I yelled "Geeee ooohhhhh!!!" again. I was finally going to find Craig's white whale.

We continued south, walking fast but looking carefully for the side trail. At one point, we passed a small cairn, five stones high, on the left side of the trail, but there was no side trail there that we could see, so we kept going. We walked for perhaps another mile, but the trail had clearly peaked. "We're going downhill," I said. "This is definitely not right. We missed it somehow."

"You don't know that for sure."

I was disappointed and exasperated. "Yes I do! Look around. Do you see anything higher than where we just were?"

"You can't go by that," Dan argued. "There might be something behind that hill there." He pointed at a random mountain.

"Dan, we're looking for the second highest mountain in the Smokies. We'd see it if it was there."

"Johnny, I'm gonna get to the top of Mount Guyot today. You guys have been this far before and not gotten there. I *know* it's on this trail, and I'm not going to stop or turn around 'til I know for sure that I passed it."

Buddha Palguta

He had a point. We brought out the map. The next trail intersection to the south was the Balsam Mountain Trail, about two miles past Mount Guyot. Dan was suggesting we walk two miles there and two miles back just to make sure that the second-highest peak in the Smokies wasn't somehow still in front of us, even though everything in front of us was lower than where we had just been. To my surprise, I agreed with him. If we had been carrying full packs, I might have argued a little more, but my legs felt good, it was a nice day, and we weren't hauling any weight. More importantly, if I didn't succeed on this trip, I'd probably never get another chance to find Mount Guyot. So I said OK, and we walked the slightly downhill trail all the way to the next trail marker. When we saw the sign that said Balsam Mountain Trail, we knew for sure that we had missed the damned mountain. Dan was undaunted. He turned around and started walking back the way we had come.

I was mad at myself for having been so hasty. I said, "Let's take a good break, eat something, and look at the map." We had been foolish to keep hiking when we knew we were going the wrong direction, but Dan and I had a long-standing tradition of headlong foolhardiness. We had just walked seven miles at elevations over 6,000 feet—almost all uphill, all going fast—on tired, fifty-year-old legs. Despite that, I felt fine, and I could tell Dan did too. Still, it was smart to take a break. We had a lot of walking yet to do.

Munching a granola bar, I realized our mistake. I looked at Dan and said, "The cairn!"

His eyes got big. "Yes!" Then he let out a heartfelt "Damn!"

"Yeah. Shit! We were in too big a hurry. That had to be it! There was nothing else it could've been." The old wooden post marking the side trail was evidently gone. Maybe the trail was there, but so overgrown that we hadn't seen it. The only thing

360

we could do was retrace our steps back toward that cairn and look for any sign of a trail along the way.

We started walking back. It was uphill going this way, which was slightly discouraging no matter how mindlessly optimistic we tried to be. Still, the day was comfortable. This was by far the best weather of the trip, although the skies turned dark and threatening every now and then. We walked along at a good clip, and I surveyed every foot of the right side of the trail for even the slightest sign of a trail going to the top.

I laughed bitterly. "This makes the fourth time I've set out to get to the top of this damned mountain, and I haven't gotten there yet. Hard to believe."

"This day's not over yet, Johnny. We'll get there." Dan was confident, and he was right to be. The mountain was smack dab in front of us.

After hiking a mile or more back toward the summit, we met a young guy coming down the trail from the north, the same direction from which we had originally come. Mollie gave him a big greeting but lost interest when she determined that he wasn't handing out egg shells or bacon paper. This guy was alone and wearing a day pack. Dan, who never seemed to tire of these insipid conversations, asked the usual questions. I petted Mollie, resigned to letting their pointless conversation meander to its inevitable and merciful end.

But this AT meeting was noteworthy. This guy looked to be in his early twenties—tall and thin, acne-scarred, but well-spoken and obviously bright. His name was Tory, and he hailed from Sevierville, just a few miles north of Gatlinburg. "It's 'se-VERE-ville', not 'SEE-vur-ville'," he said when Dan pronounced the name of the town the Yankee way.

He said he was looking for the top of Mount Guyot too. Dan immediately said, "You passed it. Follow us." I would have stated our position a little more theoretically, but Dan was obviously still in headlong foolhardiness mode. I did cut

361

into the conversation enough to tell Tory where we had been and where we were going. I asked him if he had seen the cairn.

"Sure," he said, "I saw it. It looked like there might be a trail there, so I followed it up, but it didn't go anywhere. I saw some pink ribbons on a few trees, but they petered out."

"Pink ribbons?" I was suddenly curious.

"Strips of fabric somebody tied to the trees. They were probably red once, but now they're pink."

"I've seen ribbons like that when I was off trail. I think they're surveyor's marks or something. In fact," I added, "I've seen them right down here in this valley, up above Ramseys Cascade." I pointed down into the big valley that was now on our left. "And I *know* there's no trail down there."

Tory looked at me. "You've been up on top of the Cascades?"

"Yeah. A couple times. Why, have you?"

"No. But my friend told me about it. Said it was pretty flat but got steep at the end."

"It's tough all the way, trust me."

Dan was focused on Mount Guyot. "The cairn and those pink ribbons have to be it."

I told Tory about the wooden sign and the side trail to the summit of Guyot that had been there ten years before. We all agreed that the only thing to do was to retrace our steps toward the cairn. As we walked, Dan and Tory resumed their pointless, strangers-on-an-airplane conversation. Tory apparently enjoyed that type of talk as much as Dan because they found much to discuss.

I walked ahead and kept watch for the missing trail. I knew there was a trail there, and I was not going to miss it again. We walked through a huge curve in the trail, and we could clearly see the highest point on the high ridge in front of us. That point appeared to have living trees on it. A little further on to the north, or to our left as we viewed it, we could see that the ridge line was full of dead trees.

As it turned out, Tory had been born in Warren, Ohio, where Dan currently lived. Tory's family had moved away and settled in Sevierville, Tennessee. Sakes alive! What a small world! What were the odds? He even had family in Warren. In fact, his uncle had a tattoo shop in Warren, and Dan knew where it was! Would you believe it? Dan drove past that shop all the time! And not only that, but this uncle had been voted the best tattoo artist in the country or the world or something like that. From right there in Warren! And to top it all off, this uncle had been on TV! That just took the cake! Boy howdy!

In spite of myself, I listened to this vapid conversation with one ear. I wanted to ask them who voted for the best tattoo artist and what the criteria were, but I bit my lip. I thought the focus should be on finding the elusive trail, not on famous tattoo artists from Warren, Ohio. After a little more inane conversation, I could take no more. I wheeled around and said, "I thought we were supposed to be looking for the trail."

Dan, of course, had no idea that I found the conversation so annoying, so my tone of voice took him by surprise. But he was used to my sudden changes of mood and calmly replied, "We can talk and look for the trail at the same time, Johnny."

I felt foolish for losing my temper. I sat down dejectedly on a white rock and said, "I just don't want to miss it again. This has to be the peak here." Tory was probably wondering what kind of Abbot and Costello lunatics he had hooked up with and how he could get away.

We walked on, and the summit looked tantalizingly close. Again, we could see sunlight peeking between the trunks of the uppermost trees which meant there was no more mountain there. The peak looked to be no more than a few hundred yards away. The trees and undergrowth were especially dense for those few hundred yards, but I judged that it was doable. I'd been through worse, and so had Dan. We came to a trickle of water coming out of some unseen spring in the side of the mountain. "This might be the highest running water in the Smokies," I said. Mollie took a little drink and wagged her tail.

Near the water, I spied the vague semblance of an opening leading up toward the crest, perhaps a little less dense than the surrounding woods. This was certainly not the old trail, yet it looked like a good place to scramble up to the top. I said, "If we don't find the trail, I'm going up here." This chance might never come again, and I had come too far to be denied.

I was hoping at least one of them would agree with me, but neither one did. We continued north and the trail started to drop gradually again. Clearly, it seemed to me, we had walked past the summit of Guyot. Then we came to a slight rise in the trail, and it appeared as if the rise of ground we were standing on was every bit as high as the supposed peak we had just passed. It was becoming difficult to gauge the distances we'd travelled, and nothing was making sense.

All three of us were exasperated. I got out my map and so did Tory. His showed a lot more detail than mine. Dan didn't have a map at all, which must have made him feel kind of left out because he said, "I'm going to the cairn," and kept heading north on the trail. No discussions. No "I'll meet you at such and such." Just gone, and his little dog too.

Tory and I stood there and watched Dan and Mollie go. Splitting up in the mountains, especially when we had no plan and he had no map, was extremely foolish. I was pissed, but I knew it was pointless to call after him. His mind was made up. Tory was now thoroughly convinced that he had happened upon two lunatics wandering clueless through the mountains. I said, "Never hike with a stubborn Scotsman."

Tory stayed with me. I took off my day pack and sat down on a mossy log. I pulled out a bag of trail mix and offered him some. He accepted. He was intrigued that an old man like me had been up above Ramseys Cascade, and he asked me where I had gone from that point. I told him the stories of getting washed out the first time and then, the second time, making it up to the very trail on which we now sat. I could see the respect in his eyes, and it made me proud. I couldn't resist saying, "For a guy from up North, I've been through a fair part of the Smokies. I've done a good bit of off trail, too."

Tory told me about a few of his own off-trail adventures, scrambles up to mountaintops like the one he was attempting now. He got out his map and pointed to Mount Cammerer in the northeast corner of the park. He said, "Here's a pretty easy one you guys could do."

I ignored his condescension and said, "No offense, but right now I'm just worried about Mount Guyot." He had the good sense not to push it, which made me like the kid even more.

We studied his map for a while, a good map that showed contoured elevations and the names of some peaks not shown on most maps. He pointed to a peak just north of Mount Guyot called "Old Black" and said, "I think we're here." The map showed the elevation of Old Black as 6,370 feet, which was only 250 feet lower than Mount Guyot.

"You're probably right," I granted, "but that still doesn't tell us how to get to the top of Guyot."

Tory admitted that I had a point. Now that he knew my hiking resumé, he believed that there had indeed been a side trail and a sign post ten years ago. And now that I knew his resumé a little better, I quizzed him about the pink ribbons and the cairn. He repeated that that little trail had disappeared quickly, and I believed him.

"Well, I'm going to do something kind of stupid," I concluded. "Not a lot stupid. Just a little stupid. I'm gonna go back to where that water was and try to off trail it to the top. I'm just going to try it and see if it's fairly easy."

I pulled a stub of pencil and a sheet of paper out of my day pack and scribbled a little note for Dan. I gave it to Tory, saying, "Do me a favor. If you see my buddy on the trail, tell him I'm going back to the water to try to summit from there. It should only take half an hour, and then I'll catch up with him. Tell him to wait for me! If you don't see him, just stick this note between the rocks on the cairn or somewhere where he'll see it if he went up there." The note said basically the same thing I had just told Tory. I shook hands with the young man, and we wished each other well. He went north on the AT toward the cairn and Dan, and I went south back toward what I hoped was the peak of Mount Guyot.

It only took a few minutes to get to the highest-flowing water. I scouted around for the likeliest place to head for the top. The spot that had looked relatively easy an hour before didn't look that way anymore. The bush always looked pretty easy until you actually went in. I could see the sunlight between the trees on the ridge probably no more than three football fields away. The mountainside was very steep, and the woods were dense pine forest. But I was there and life was short, so I decided to try.

I took my walking stick, which had been a cross-country ski pole in a past life, and jammed it into the mossy turf to mark the point where I was going up. If I got lost up in the trees or broke a leg, the searchers would find the pole and at least know where to look. I was very conscious of the fact that Dan was ahead of me and not coming back. *No one* was coming behind me, and no one knew exactly where I was. That thought took a little of the starch out of my shorts.

I started straight up the mountain. The pitch was so steep that I found it necessary to grab onto saplings to pull myself up. The soil was six-inch-deep decayed leaves and pine needles covered by a carpet of moss. My feet broke through the moss and sank in deeply with each step. The damp, earthy smell of the Smokies hung in the air like incense. I had to climb over huge fallen trees, some so old and rotted that they collapsed when I put my weight on them. I couldn't follow a straight path, so I followed little folds and ridges, weaving back and forth along the "easier" ground but going uphill all the time.

I stopped to catch my breath. I had covered maybe seventy-five yards. Already, I couldn't tell exactly where I had come from. I told myself it didn't matter. All I had to do on the way down was follow my own tracks and I'd find the AT. I was definitely in primeval forest. The thought that no human may have ever set foot where I was standing thrilled me. Just me and Guyot all alone. Guyot had been here for time out of mind, literally hundreds of millions of years. I was only here on an October morning for a few minutes, but for those minutes I was part of Guyot, and I was awed by it. I remembered a quote from a Native American who said that when you considered a mountain to be a living entity, you gained a whole new respect for it.

I resumed climbing. The woods were lovely, dark, and deep. The thought came into my head unbidden; *this is where the bears live.* I started thinking about how easy it would be to break a leg and how long I would sit here before someone found me. *Did the people on that airplane die right away? Or did they sit there on the side of Guyot and suffer for days, waiting in vain for rescue?* I tried to shake off the negative thoughts. I could almost see the top of Guyot just a few hundred yards away. But the adrenaline rush was gone, and the cold grip of fear began to squeeze my guts. Something had spooked me, and I suddenly lost the will to push through to the top. I stood on the side of Mount Guyot for a few minutes, up to my ankles in pine needles, torn between my pride and determination on one side and cold fear on the other.

I tried to reason away the fear, but the whole endeavor was beyond reason. Reason didn't take a person to the top of a mountain. I was in a precarious situation. If I were with someone, or even if someone knew where I was, I would certainly have pushed on to the top. At least that's what I told myself as I turned around and climbed back down to the AT. *Damn Dan!*

I had to hike a long way to find my ski pole once I got back down. I had lost my own trail in just the short distance I had gone. Bitterly disappointed, I started back toward Dan. I was now retracing my steps on this part of the trail for the fourth time in one day. I had also been here at least once before in my life, and two other times I had failed to get even this far. *What was it with this mountain? Was I fated to never get to the top?* I headed toward the cairn, still watching the right side of the trail carefully for signs of the lost trail to the top.

I hadn't gone very far when I heard Dan yelling out to me from across a valley. I was facing roughly north, or at least what seemed to be north. I was beginning to feel that nothing was certain on this strange, misty day. A huge chasm in front of me separated me from Dan. The AT curved eastward around this part of the valley, and Dan was on the north side of the curve, facing south and yelling back toward me. There might have been less than half a mile between us as the crow flies, but I couldn't see him. I yelled to let him know that I heard him. He immediately yelled again, which meant he heard me, but I couldn't tell what he was saying. It sounded like, "John! Head for the cairn!" or "John! Head for the camp!" But it just as easily could have been, "Mom, bed for a carp." I yelled "What?" a few times, and Dan repeated the same indecipherable message. We gave up after a few more attempts.

I wondered what Dan might possibly have been saying. Of course I was headed for the cairn *and* the camp! Where else was I going to go? I dismissed it and kept walking hard toward the cairn. At least we both knew that the other was alive.

I got to the cairn very quickly, but Dan wasn't there. I didn't see the note I had given Tory to give to Dan either. I didn't see any obvious sign at all, such as sticks or rocks laid out on the trail in a pattern. The ground was spongy going up the side of the mountain, just as it had been where I had gone off trail, and I could see tracks in the turf. It looked as if the prints had been walked over more than once, but I couldn't tell how many times. Were these just Tory's prints going up and coming down? Or had Dan gone up and down here too? I wasn't sure if there were any dog tracks or not, but it didn't look like it. Another mystery on a day of mysteries.

I had another choice to make, but it was really no choice at all. I had to follow the pink ribbons up to the top. This didn't look as if it had ever been a trail, but the ribbons and the cairn made this the most likely spot. If this was Mount Guyot, I wasn't going to miss it.

Once again, I started up toward what I hoped was the summit of Guyot. Again, the terrain was steep and the soil was soft. Pine needles and humus quickly found their way into my boots. The mountainside was thick with trees. I muscled my way through the tight spots and climbed over fallen trees. At one point, I grabbed onto a fair-sized, standing dead tree to pull myself over a downed tree trunk, and the standing tree cracked. The thought occurred to me to pull the tree down so that it pointed downhill toward where I had come in. I wrapped both hands around the dead tree and put my 235 pounds into it. It broke with a satisfying crack and came down, pointing roughly the right direction.

I followed the pink ribbons up the mountain. I was more determined to get to the top this time, having failed just an hour earlier. The spacing of the ribbons grew farther and farther apart, and just as Tory had said, they soon disappeared altogether. The side of the mountain up ahead was carpeted with a swath of dead trees, all lying down and facing in roughly the same direction. It looked as if a big gust of wind had knocked them down. But the most remarkable sight was the crest of the mountain just 50 yards up ahead of me! *Guyot at last! The white whale.* I could clearly see the ground at the top of the ridge covered with downed trees, just as Ahab's whale had been covered with scars and broken harpoons.

Then it hit me—the trees were dead! I had seen the highest point earlier in the day, and it hadn't been covered with dead trees. This couldn't be Guyot. The top was further south along the AT, maybe closer to where I had gone up through the bush an hour earlier.

Again, I stood frozen, unsure what to do. I considered picking my way through the swath of downed trees simply to be able to say that I stood on the ridge line, but what was the point? The thought of slipping down between two tree trunks and snapping a leg bone flashed through my mind. At this point, no one had any idea where I was. *Damn Dan!* I rationalized that I was within sight of it, looking at the very crest of the ridge, and that would have to be enough. I was certain that I wasn't on the right mountain anyway, so I turned around and started back down.

I followed the pink ribbons and my downed tree marker back to the AT and came out exactly where I had gone in. I was more angry than disappointed this time. I was mad at Dan and mad at myself and even mad at the damned mountain. How in the hell could it be so hard to find a mountain? The hard part was supposed to be *climbing* the mountain. *Finding* the mountain was supposed to be easy. But I had I come all this long, long way, and I was still trying to find Mount Guyot.

I vented my frustration by power-walking north along the AT. I figured I'd catch up with Dan pretty quickly and then I'd find out what the hell had happened. Who could tell with him?

I yelled to Dan, directing my voice up the trail, but I didn't hear a response.

I quick-marched the five remaining miles back down to our camp, expecting to overtake Dan and the dog every time I rounded a corner. Every once in a while, I'd stop and yell again, but I never heard anything. I grew more and more worried. My mind conjured up every possible horrible accident. I wondered if he had been the one who had snapped his leg somewhere off the trail and then passed out. It was even possible that a bear, a boar, or a snake had gotten him.

It was also possible that he was merely out ahead of me on the trail. My last hope was that Dan and Mollie would be waiting for me in camp. When I rounded the final bend and came within sight of our tent, I yelled "Ho, in the camp!" as I had learned to do in my prospector days in California. My heart sank like a stone when I saw that the camp was still. My worst-case scenario was coming true.

I felt very alone. Not frightened, just alone. I sat down on a big tree trunk near the cold fire pit and logically, legalistically went through every course of action open to me. I could almost see myself in court, accused of negligence in the mysterious disappearance of Dan Rafferty and Mollie the dog.

One option was to hike out to the ranger station at Cosby and get help. Cosby was almost seven miles away, so there was no way I could get there before dark. Even if I did go there, there probably wouldn't be a ranger on duty. And if by some miracle I did find a ranger, I knew from my experience over at Newfound Gap that the rangers didn't mount rescue missions late in the afternoon. They would wait until morning.

Another option was to go back up to the first trail intersection and wait for Dan there. Maybe he had gotten confused without a map and was wandering around on the wrong trail. At least I would have a flashlight to help him get back to camp if it was dark. But that meant hiking back up the steep mile and a half and probably coming back down again in the dark. I had just finished hiking close to fifteen miles at high elevations, and my thigh muscles were pulsing and thrumming as I sat and rested. I didn't know if my legs had any more uphill miles left. I decided that leaving the camp to go anywhere was not a smart idea. The last thing we needed was two guys wandering around lost in the dark. One of the rules of rescue was to make sure you didn't become a victim yourself.

The only remaining option was to stay put until morning. I could build a big fire that Dan would see if he came in after dark, and I could keep it going late into the night. In the morning, if he still wasn't back, I would hike out to Cosby at first light and try to get help. What would I tell the rangers? I lost my buddy and his dog (that was in the park illegally) on the AT somewhere around one o'clock on the previous day. We had been looking for Mount Guyot, but we hadn't been able to find it. I hiked back down on the only trail that led to our camp, but I hadn't seen a trace of him. He was wearing a muscle T-shirt and shorts, and all he had was a canteen, a camera, and two snack bars. No map, no compass, no light, no knife. The rangers would laugh their asses off, but I decided it would be the best thing to do.

I started getting camp ready for the night. Every so often, I would yell "DAN!" up in the direction I had come from, but I heard nothing. I hung out the sleeping bags to dry. I gathered some firewood, but I held off on making supper because I knew Dan would appreciate a hot meal if—*when*, I told myself, not *if*—he got back to camp. I was truly sick with worry.

The shadows in the little valley started getting long. I yelled up toward the trail again, and to my surprise I got a response. I couldn't tell what was said, but it was definitely a human voice. The seconds dragged on interminably, but finally I saw a figure come around the bend in the trail. I yelled, "Yee-ha, you yay-hoo!" because that was one of Dan's favorite mountain greetings, but the figure didn't respond. It wasn't Dan. For about the tenth time that day, my heart sank.

When I saw that the hiker on the trail wasn't Dan, I ran from our end of the campsite up to the trail. The running turned out to be unnecessary because the guy veered off the main trail to come into the camp. He was a tattooed, stocky guy probably in his early twenties.

I said, "Sorry I called you a yay-hoo. I thought you were my buddy." He didn't respond to that, maybe because he didn't know what a yay-hoo was. I said, "Did you pass a guy with a dog?"

He said he hadn't. He told me he had come up the Snake Den Ridge Trail from the Cosby parking lot. "Dude," he rolled his eyes, "it was a bitch."

I told him briefly how I had lost my friend somewhere. This tattooed guy seemed about as interested in my story as I had been in his, so our conversation wasn't long. I went back to the far end of the campsite.

After five or ten minutes, another hiker came around the corner. Again, my hopes rose for a moment and then fell when I saw that this second guy wasn't Dan either. This guy was slimmer and sported fewer tattoos. He came into camp and greeted his friend, "Dude, we totally conquered that mountain!" I would have laughed out loud if I hadn't been so worried. I wanted to tell them that mountains were never conquered.

A few minutes later, the heavily-tattooed guy came down to my end of the camp and said that his friend had heard someone out on the trail somewhere. The friend had been yelling to see how far behind he was, and the friend had heard someone yell in response. I was somewhat encouraged by this news, but it really didn't tell me anything. I thanked the tattooed guy anyway.

The forest was slowly turning to sepia tones like an old-time movie. In another half hour or so it would be dark. I thought about starting the fire to cook some dinner, but I had no appetite. At that moment, another figure came around the corner. I yelled again, "Yee ha, you yay-hoo!," and even from that distance, I could see the smile on Dan's face.

Dan strode down to our end of the camp. Still smiling, he said, "What the hell? Where's dinner? Didn't I give you enough time to cook?"

"What happened to you, man? I thought you were dead!"

Touched by my concern, Dan reached out to put a friendly hand on my shoulder, but I brushed it away. Now that I knew he was alright, I was angry. "I was worried sick all afternoon! You don't just take off on someone in the mountains, man!"

"I didn't 'take off.' I told you where I was going."

"Yeah? Well, you didn't leave much room for discussion." I decided to change my tone a little. After all, I *was* happy to see my friend alive. "Dan, you don't know how glad I am to see you. All afternoon I was thinking you were dead or lost or something."

"What happened to *you*? That's what I wanna know."

"Did you talk to Tory? Did he give you my note?"

Dan reached into his nearly empty pockets and pulled out a crumpled piece of notebook paper. He scoffed, "He gave me this," and tossed the ball of paper at me. I opened it up, but I could barely read my own chicken scratches. It was pretty much gobbledygook.

"So I'm not the best writer in the world. It does say 'wait for me'." That underlined portion of the note was fairly legible.

"Johnny, I *did* wait! But you never showed up! I didn't know what happened to you!"

374

As Dan fed a hungry Mollie, he recalled his afternoon on Mount Guyot. "When we split up, I was tired of talking. I knew we needed to get to the cairn, so I just kept walking. To be honest, I was kind of hoping you guys would follow me. When I got to the cairn, I saw the pink ribbons Tory was talking about, so I followed them up to the top." He paused for effect. "Johnny, I got to the top of Mount Guyot!"

Instinctively, I said, "So did I." My mind wouldn't allow the possibility that Dan had made it when I hadn't.

He looked at me suspiciously. "What's at the top?"

"A bunch of dead trees." For the moment, I set aside my belief that the dead trees weren't the peak of Mount Guyot.

"Did you see the marker?"

"No," I admitted. I had always been a lousy liar. "I *saw* the top, but I didn't go to the very peak. I stopped about thirty yards away. What marker?"

Dan smiled triumphantly. "There's one of those brass plates in the ground up there that shows the elevation. You know. Like the one on Mount Sterling." I wasn't sure if I believed him, so I said nothing. I don't know what emotion he saw cross my face, but he continued, "You didn't see me at the top? How close did you get?"

"I told you. I was about thirty yards away. I could see it plain as day."

"I don't know where you went up, but I followed the pink ribbons up to the top and sat down on the ridge for a while and had a snack."

"I didn't see where the pink ribbons went all the way to the top," I said.

"Well, they were spaced out further apart toward the top. Did you see the dead trees?"

"I just told you I did. That's kind of why I stopped. The footing looked pretty treacherous."

"I know," Dan said. "I stopped for a minute when I got to the dead trees, too. But the ribbons curved around to the left, and there was a little bit of a path there, and it went to the top."

I was trying to remember if I had yelled Dan's name at any point while I was up there. It made sense that I would have, but I wasn't absolutely certain that I had. However, I knew for a fact that I had snapped that standing dead tree, so I said, "And you didn't hear me coming up? Hell, I broke a tree on my way up that you had to hear! Or Mollie had to hear it anyway."

"Mollie heard something, but I hushed her up. I didn't know what it was."

That made no sense to me at all. Dan would have been hoping I would show up and would have yelled out to me if he heard anything at all. And if he was worried that it was a bear, he would have yelled at the bear too. The best way to avoid bears was to let them know you were there.

One other thing occurred to me. "How long did you sit up there? Were you up there all afternoon?"

"I went up and found the top and then I came back down to wait for you guys. That's when I saw Tory and he gave me your note. So I waited a while for you to show up and then I went back to the top. I figured you would get to the cairn at some point and come up. I just relaxed up there for a while. I actually fell asleep for a little bit. Then I woke up and figured I better get back to camp."

"C'mon, Dan. You went up and down *twice*? That doesn't make any sense."

Dan eyes flamed with anger. "I'll take you up there right now, Johnny!"

The atmosphere in camp was tense after that. We wolfed down our supper in silence as night fully descended. We found enough wood for a good fire. After the misery of the previous two nights, sitting by a fire seemed like a night at the Ritz.

Finding Mount Guyot

A little warmth and full bellies eased the tension and got us talking about the events of the day. I might never find out what had happened to Dan that afternoon, but our friendship had survived worse moments, including times when the stupidity had been all mine. The October air was cold, but the fire made it pleasant. The stars were magnificent, and the city lights that I had glimpsed out to the northwest were now in full view at the open end of our valley. We couldn't have chosen a more beautiful night to rest in the bosom of Mount Guyot.

All evening, we stayed away from the other group in the camp—the tattooed guy, his buddy, and a girl who had wandered into camp shortly after Dan. Apparently, she was the girlfriend of one of the guys. They had made their camp up near the main trail at least fifty yards from ours. We could see their campfire and hear them laugh occasionally. We assumed they were drinking or getting stoned like we used to do.

As we sat quietly by our fire, the tattooed guy stepped through the darkness and cautiously approached our campfire. "Hey," he nodded toward me, "I see you found your friend."

"I keep trying to ditch him, but he keeps finding his way back."

The usual backpacker conversation ensued. The tattooed guy and his friends had driven down from Michigan. This was the first time in the Smokies for all three of them and their first serious backpacking trip.

We told him we were from Ohio but had been coming down to the Smokies for years. "My first time down here was in 1977," I boasted.

Dan said, "And my first trip was a year before that."

The tattooed guy took a drag off his cigarette and said, "Dudes, I was *born* in '84." We all laughed at that one, but it made me feel old just the same. We made small talk until the guy's smoke was done, and then he went back to his friends.

"That was us, Dan, a long time ago," I said after the tattooed guy walked away.

Dan shook his head. "We were a lot wilder than that, Johnny. These kids now aren't nearly as wild as we were. We were fucked up, doing acid and T and all that stupid shit."

I said, "Never in a million years did I think I could ever be out here without a drink or a smoke or some dope and still have a good time. I'm so glad I made it to this."

"You know what else surprises me?" Dan asked. "I'm not afraid in the least any more. To tell you the truth, I used to be a little scared out here at night, even when we were all fucked up."

I grunted in agreement.

"Now," Dan continued, "I'm sober and I sleep like a baby out here."

We might have slept like babies, but we woke up like old men. Both of us had stiff backs and sore legs from all the miles we had covered. "You know what's really funny?" Dan said as he did his morning back stretches. "The other guys think we're in good shape. Hee hee! We're the fittest ones out of the whole bunch!"

"That's not saying much, really," I muttered. I tried to unkink my back as well. After three nights on the hard ground, I was looking forward to a real bed.

Since my thighs had healed up so well, I decided to wear my kilt and sporran again. As we walked through camp up to the main trail, the three young hikers from Michigan were still drinking their morning coffee. "Morning!" Dan said brightly. "Can one of you guys take our picture?" The tattooed guy took the camera, and Dan and I posed side by side for a shot. I noticed the other guy, the thinner one, sitting on a log with his head down and his hand over his mouth. The girl had her head down too. Their heads were bobbing up and down slightly, and I realized that they were laughing at my kilt. Once I noticed them, I noticed that the tattooed guy was trying not to laugh either.

""This is a kilt, you guys, not a skirt," I said. "It's just a joke." Dan took a few steps away from me.

"Dude," the thinner guy exploded, "I was trying so hard not to laugh!"

The girl spoke for the first time. "That's a really bad look for you."

I laughed myself. "But you know what? You guys are going to remember me for the rest of your lives now. Every time you think about your first trip to the Smokies, you'll think about a bald guy wearing a kilt."

"A skirt," Dan corrected me.

"Whatever."

We had our picture taken, said our goodbyes, and headed toward home. Once we got to the Snake Den Ridge Trail, the path turned steeply downhill for five rocky, unrelenting miles. The young guy from Michigan had been right; the Snake Den Ridge Trail was a bitch.

Mollie stopped at one point to investigate some fresh bear crap in the middle of the trail. For some unfathomable dingo reason, she decided to take a ladylike nibble of the sloppy mess.

"Mollie!" Dan scolded. "Stop it!" He grabbed her collar and dragged her a few yards away.

"Dan," I laughed, "you have to feed this poor dog more food! She's eating paper and egg shells and bear shit, man!" I had also seen her eat an apple core and few snails along the way.

"You think she's too skinny?" he asked me seriously, but I didn't bother to answer.

My thighs were starting to get raw again, so I decided to change into my pants. I dropped my pack and started changing right there in the middle of the trail. Out of the blue, Dan asked, "If I wasn't on Mount Guyot, Johnny, what was that marker I saw on top of that mountain?"

I was surprised that Dan was bringing up that sensitive topic again, but I wasn't going to change my opinion. I said, "Dan, when we were looking at Mount Guyot from a distance, the highest peak had living trees on it, remember? The peak next to it, the one a little bit to the north, was the one with the bare trees on it."

Dan grunted noncommittally.

"I think you were on that other peak. Tory had a good map, and it showed a mountain called Old Black just north of Guyot. I think that's where those pink ribbons were. You probably saw the marker for Old Black." Dan didn't say anything else, and neither did I. Some things between old friends were best left alone.

Eventually, the trail became a gravel road. We came to a metal gate that was there to keep the machines of civilization out. Mollie absolutely freaked when she saw the gate. She whined and turned in circles and refused to go within fifty feet of it. We guessed that she was remembering when she had been abandoned by her original owners. I thought about how terrifying it must have been for her to be so lost and alone. Dan had to pick Mollie up and carry her past the gate, and she was fine once she got past it.

Walking through the big Cosby parking lot to Dan's SUV, my thoughts turned back to Tory. "I wonder if Tory made it to the top. Probably not, since we didn't see him heading back south."

"He had to go up and down that trail we just did, right?"

"Yeah. He had about a seventeen-mile hike to do it in one day." I shrugged, "That's not that bad, really." I was thinking that maybe it wasn't as hard to get to Mount Guyot as we made it out to be. Not if you were smart and did it the right way.

Finding Mount Guyot

Dan must have been thinking the same thing. "You know, we probably could've gotten to Mount Guyot years ago if we'd stayed on the trail."

"Yeah," I grinned, "but what would've been the fun of that?" I hitched up my shoulder straps. "And you gotta remember, Dan, we haven't gotten there yet."

Buddha Palguta

13   Going to Mount Guyot: Fifth Attempt

I lived across the street from a garrulous World War Two combat veteran who happened to be the father of Lauren, the woman I had fallen so hard for in 2003, so I couldn't help but see her occasionally. I'd wave to her from time to time, and she'd send me cookies every Christmas. I dated other women, but none of them touched my heart the way Lauren had. Deep in my soul, I prayed for another chance.

I was friends with her father, and I made damn sure he told Lauren that I was sober and not smoking. Then, in the summer of 2008, my friend the old soldier fought his last battle, and they'd call me periodically when they needed help lifting him. Lauren was usually there, and a few times I sat with her in the kitchen, drinking coffee and passing the time.

Not long after the funeral, I found a flimsy excuse to call Lauren, and she found a reason to call me, and soon we were taking long walks in the woods together. Lauren was the one who had jokingly suggested that I try wearing a kilt. Her soft brown eyes often sparkled as if she were keeping a very funny secret, and she was still everything I dreamed of. The first time

382

around, I had blurted out the dreaded words "I love you" far too soon, which had rightly scared the hell out of her. This time around, I was trying to behave more like a normal person, but I was feeling the same mad joy inside.

We day hiked the parks of Ohio, and the following spring we camped out in the cold rain. Little Lauren seemed to me to be as tough or tougher, pound for pound, than the big men I was used to hiking with. I wanted to take her to the Smokies and up to Mount Guyot, and she agreed to go.

Before we left, I did as much research as I could about the top of Mount Guyot. I looked at USGS topographic maps and even went so far as to call the rangers down in the Great Smoky Mountain National Park. I spoke to a young ranger who didn't know anything about an old side trail to the top of Guyot. All he could tell me was that it wasn't on any of the maps. Finally, the ranger said, "Here. Let me put on the guy who would know. He's the head of the whole backcountry."

"Damn," I said in spite of myself. After all those years of breaking laws and messing with the rangers, I was going to talk to the Trail Boss himself.

An older man's voice came on and said, "This is George. Can I help you?"

I wanted to ask him why there weren't any decent tent spots at the backcountry campsites, but I asked instead about the top of Guyot and the side trail I'd seen there in 1997.

The Trail Boss explained that that side trail hadn't been maintained for many years, but it was still possible to get to the top of Mount Guyot via that route. I could hear him remembering it as he spoke. "The sign is gone. Sometimes it's marked with a cairn, but sometimes not. If you're coming from the north, the path is right after the two springs, and those are marked on the topo maps." I only remembered the one spring, which I had called the highest water in the Smokies, but I didn't interrupt him. "There's a wide spot in the AT," he continued. "The old trail goes off to the left right there. There's a big deadfall of fir trees on the path, but it's passable. Once you get up there, go left at the false top and through a saddle, and then you'll find the top of Guyot."

Thinking of what Dan had said, I asked, "Is there a brass marker at the summit?"

George paused and then answered, "Yeah, there's a marker up there, but it's been several years since I've actually been there." My hopes fell for a moment, thinking that maybe Dan had been to the top after all, but then I remembered that Dan hadn't gone up anywhere near the spring. I had been closer to the top when I went up by myself the first time.

Finally, I asked about the pink ribbons that we had seen off trail. George chuckled, "No, those don't mean anything. Bird watchers put those up sometimes. Ignore them." That simple answer solved a decade-old mystery for me. I could have asked the Trail Boss questions all day, but I didn't want to abuse his kindness, so I thanked him and said goodbye. I looked down at the notes I had scribbled while he had been talking and felt as if those words held the key to Mount Guyot.

I relived the excitement and nervousness of going backpacking for the first time through Lauren. One night at her place, she went through the ritual of packing everything she was going to carry into her brand new backpack. She stood the pack up against the wall and then knelt to put her arms through the shoulder straps. She tried to stand but only managed to fall forward onto her hands and knees. "Oh my God, this is heavy," she said with wide-eyed surprise. She was determined to do it herself though, and she eventually staggered to her feet.

I laughed, "You're gonna have to move faster than that when those hillbillies come after you."

"I'm not afraid of them. I'm just afraid I'm not going to be any good at this."

"You'll do fine," I reassured her, but I *was* worried about taking a novice into the mountains. Lauren was nearly my age, and she was a very petite eighty-nine pounds. Her pack was only eighteen pounds, but proportionally I was asking Lauren to carry nearly as much as I was. I was worried about myself too. I wondered if I was still good enough to get us both to the top.

The night before we went into the mountains, we stayed at a HoJo motel in Kingsport, Tennessee. When we pulled in, the message board on the hotel's road sign read, "Some people are so afraid to die that they never live." It gave me goose bumps. Lauren, who believed very much in portents and signs, said, "See, we're *supposed* to go."

We ordered a pizza and watched a *Man vs. Wild* marathon on the Discovery channel. I tried to imitate the host of the wilderness survival show, a British Special Forces guy named Bear Grylls. With a preposterous accent that sounded more like *Monty Python's Flying Circus*, I told Lauren, "Right, then! Remember that maggots are packed with protein!"

In the morning, when we pulled out of the hotel, Lauren noticed that the reverse side of the hotel sign said, "Cowards die 1,000 deaths. Brave men die only once." Clearly, the manager of the hotel was a kindred spirit with me and Bear Grylls. I hoped the messages were a good omen.

It was Memorial Day weekend, and the Cosby parking lot was overrun with picnickers and day hikers. I said, "You're going to feel like the toughest woman out here when you walk through this lot with that pack on your back," but Lauren didn't respond. Her thoughts were elsewhere. I secretly studied her face, remembering how nervous I had been my first time. She looked focused, but not scared.

At the Gabes Mountain trailhead at the far end of the parking lot, we met the first of a long succession of day hikers.

We were getting a late start, and these go-getters were already coming down out of the mountains. They were a well-dressed couple in their late thirties, sporting high-tech trekking poles in each hand and cutesy day packs that couldn't hold anything more than a water bottle. The woman was wearing perfume and full make-up. We chatted briefly about the trail, and the man told me quite seriously, "It's not the steepness; it's the rockiness that makes it hard." I knew the trail was as wide and smooth as a trail could be in the Smokies. I wished for a moment that this guy was going with me to learn what a rocky trail really was and how it felt even rockier with a fifty-pound pack on your back.

We passed many people on the trail, mostly families coming and going from a tiny waterfall called Hen Wallow Falls. "Maybe we'll have the campsite to ourselves," I told Lauren. "These people are only day hiking."

Just as I hoped, we passed no one else on the trail after we hiked up beyond the falls, but as the trail lengthened, Lauren began to struggle with her pack. She didn't say anything, but several times I watched her bend forward at the waist for a moment of blessed relief from her shoulder straps. I knew what she was going through, so I showed her how to cinch her waist belt tighter to keep the weight off her collarbones.

After many, many breaks, we finally arrived at #34, the same camp where Dan had traumatized the nice young Indian couple the year before. By the time we rolled into camp, Lauren was beyond caring about wet feet. She splashed through the creek at the campsite with her boots on, not even trying to hop the rocks. "I don't care," she muttered. "These boots are waterproof." After five miles of uphill, she was very close to used up. I could see her slender legs quivering. We had spent five hours covering those five miles, which didn't bode well for us making it to the top of Mount Guyot.

I was prepared to see a few people in the camp already, but I wasn't prepared to see fifteen or twenty tents poking up. The place was crawling with people, more than I had ever seen in one place in the backcountry, and every last crooked, rocky tent site was full. I said, "Stay here while I go look around." I cut through somebody's camp and crossed over to the far side of the creek where there were no designated sites. I found a semi-flat spot between some pines and an old fire-ring where someone had evidently camped years ago. The mosquitoes were fierce, but at least we'd have one whole bank of the creek to ourselves while the other people were packed in like sardines. I dropped my pack to claim the spot and went back to fetch Lauren.

"Isn't it against the rules to camp over there?" she asked.

Automatically, I replied, "Yeah, well, rules are for dopes."

Lauren smiled. "You really were born a hundred years too late."

"I know," I said as I grabbed Lauren's pack. "I should've been a cowboy."

After a hasty supper, we pitched our tent in the stand of pines, and one of the trees was only inches away from the door of our tent. I was afraid one of us would get an eye jabbed out if we got up to pee in the night, so I set to work breaking off the pointy low branches of the tree. I was using my hands, and I had to push hard to break off one short, stubborn branch. The instant before it broke, I was thinking, *I should use my knife for this one.* Sure enough, the branch I was leaning into broke where I didn't want it to, and I raked the palm of my left hand across the sharp stub. I could tell right away that it was a deep wound. I looked at my hand as blood welled up quickly. A lot of blood.

My first thought was, *Shit! I'm not going to get to Guyot!* I moved away from the tent to keep the blood smell away from where we would be sleeping. The water in my canteen was clean, bacteria-free city water, so I used that to rinse out the wound and get a good look at it. It was a puncture wound with a gash about an inch and a half long trailing after it, jagged and deep. I couldn't see any bone, but I could see down into the flesh of my hand. I knew from my meat cutting days that it was at least a five- or six-stitcher. And who knew if there was any nerve or tendon damage inside? I wiggled my fingers and they seemed to work alright.

Lauren heard me gasp and ran over to me. She looked at my palm and made a small retching sound. Later, she told me that she thought the trip was over right there. I was thinking the same thing. *Damn! The curse of Guyot. Again!* And it was my own stupid fault. I knew better than to be careless in the mountains. I called myself a dumbass at least a dozen times.

It was getting full dark—a lousy time to be hurt. I told Lauren where to find the first aid kit in my pack. I still had some thirty-year-old gauze rolls and tape from the hospital supply warehouse. "I'm finally going to use this stuff," I laughed. After all the foolish chances I had taken in the Smokies, this was my first real injury.

Lauren helped me bandage my wound. By the light of a flashlight, we applied alcohol and Neosporin and band aids and then wrapped sterile gauze around my hand to hold the band aids in place. The bleeding slowed down to a trickle. Finally, I wrapped an elastic Ace bandage around my hand just to protect the whole thing. Lauren had Amoxicillin capsules in her pack, so I took two to ward off any infection.

"What pisses me off is that I'm going to be handicapped for the whole trip."

"You mean we're not going back in the morning?"

"Let's see how it feels. If it's throbbing and infected, we'll hike out. If not, we'll keep going."

Lauren recalled another TV survival show. "Remember that *Survivorman* episode when he pretended like his arm was

388

broken? This is like that now." The host of this second show, Les Stroud, was maybe tougher than Bear Grylls (if that was even possible) because Stroud carried his own camera gear and went into the wilderness all by himself. Bear Grylls had a camera crew with him and probably stayed at Hojo's after the day's shooting was done. I was secretly pleased to be compared to Survivorman.

I was worried about blood smells as we went to sleep. Predators were attracted to wounded prey. I checked my bandages and saw that a little spot of blood had seeped through all those layers of cloth. My hand was sore from being rammed against a tree, but it wasn't throbbing like an infected wound. Once we were in our sleeping bags, I asked, "Are you scared to be out here with the bears?"

She said, "I'd be terrified by myself, but I feel pretty safe as long as you're here," which made me feel like Bear Grylls and Les Stroud put together.

I awoke at first light and crawled out of the tent. Lauren groaned but stayed asleep. Not a soul in the whole crowded camp was stirring. Only old men got up this early. I crossed the creek, tiptoed through some camps, and retrieved our food bag from the new-fangled food hangers without waking anyone. I enjoyed a few moments of solitude as the forest came alive around me.

As I waited for the water to boil, I gently peeled away the bloody bandages and inspected my wound in the daylight. It still bled a little when I opened up my hand all the way, and I could see half an inch down into the meat of my hand. It definitely needed stitches, but everything seemed to be working properly, and I didn't see or feel any signs of infection. The choice before me was easy. I wanted very badly to get to Mount Guyot.

Buddha Palguta

It took a long time to pack up and get on our way with me working one-handed. The camp was almost empty when we left, except for a group of four young people who looked as if they had been partying hard the night before. They greeted us groggily as we marched past their site. One of them was a girl, and she was reading from a leather-bound book that looked a great deal like Rick's old reference book, the one we called the bible. I had a sudden, strong sense of the shadows of my past flitting by, like ghosts on the periphery of my vision. I was very conscious of all thirty-two years that had passed since I had first come to the Smokies. We said good morning to the four hung-over kids and kept walking.

The Maddron Bald Trail was very steep in spots, but we took frequent breaks and enjoyed the journey. Every time we stopped, Lauren dropped her pack and offered to get out the granola bars. "You have to be hungry by now," she enticed me.

"No, I'm OK for a while."

"C'mon, you're my mule," she nudged. "I have to keep you fed."

I smiled. "I know what you're doing. You just want to lighten your pack."

She didn't deny it. "C'mon. Eat some," she said, and I did.

The stream crossings gave Lauren more trouble than the steep trail. I had forgotten how hard stream crossings were for new hikers. The trail crossed Indian Camp Creek and Copperhead Branch six times, and each crossing was tricky because the water was high. Crossings that Dan and I had made without breaking stride now posed a challenge, especially to a novice. I helped Lauren at some of the crossings by going first and then holding out my ski pole so she could grab on to steady herself. "C'mon, baby, grab my pole," I said salaciously.

Lauren was all concentration. "Shut up" was all she said.

390

One crossing directly upstream from a big hydraulic was so tricky that it even scared me. I went across with my pack first and then came back to carry hers across for her. Lauren decided to try taking off her boots and crossing barefoot. She took three cautious steps into the fast water and went in up to her knees. "Oh my God, it's cold!" she cried as she quickly retreated. After she scurried back to the bank, she said with surprise, "It hurt so bad I wanted to hurl!" After she recovered, she put her boots back on, and I guided her rock by rock across the treacherous crossing.

We saw almost no one all day, and the final leg of the trail seemed long. We caught a few glimpses off to our right of the Appalachian crest we'd be traversing the next day, and I tried to encourage Lauren by pointing out the high peaks. "I can't believe I'm going to walk that far," she sighed. Lauren's legs were spent once again as she trudged the last mile into camp. When she finally stumbled into #29, she said, "You must've planned this trip just right because both days I couldn't have walked another step."

We were the first people to make it to #29 that day, and the sun was still high in the sky. We grabbed the same spot that Dan and I had occupied, back toward the more secluded end of the little valley. Just beyond our site, the ground dropped off steeply to Otter Creek thirty feet below. The first thing I did was collect the left-over wood from all the other tent sites in the camp. We would have a fire this night with very little effort expended.

The sun was out and the afternoon was pleasant, so we decided to wash up before anyone else showed up. I wrapped my injured hand in a plastic bag and jumped into the creek. Lauren was content to do a splash and rinse job. She was amazed that I could submerse my body in the icy water. Significant shrinkage occurred, but it didn't matter. We were cool that way.

391

The groggy foursome we had left at #34 that morning must have been following us all day because they filed in some time later and took the camp site next to us. They got busy right away gathering wood and lighting a big fire. They expended a tremendous amount of energy keeping their fire going from five o'clock on through the rest of the evening, roaming far onto the surrounding hillsides to gather fuel. "They have no clue what they're doing," I whispered to Lauren, but they were polite and respected our space, so we didn't mind them being there.

My father, an old Marine, mentioned to me once that the Marines used to dig "hip trenches" into the ground to make sleeping more comfortable. The Park Service, quite understandably, didn't want people digging little trenches all over the forest, but my back was hurting and I was now a personal friend of the Trail Boss, so I thought I would give digging a hip trench a try. However, as a proud Army veteran, I couldn't bring myself to use a Marine Corps term like "hip trench." "In the Army," I told Lauren, "we call them 'ass holes'."

"The Marines?" she asked innocently.

"No, baby, at least not when they're around."

I measured exactly where my butt would be when we put up the tent and began using a stick one-handed to scratch a shallow trench into the packed, rocky soil. To amuse myself and Lauren, I invented and performed a James Brown song especially for the occasion:

Hah! Dig ma ass hole! Wif ma bad self!

Huh! Dig ma ass ho-o-ole! Gotta be jus' right!

Step back now! Put ma foot in ma ass hole! Ha!

Heyyyy! I feel good!

Just as I was getting to the second verse, one of the guys and the girl from the group of four camped next to us came over. I wasn't sure how much of my performance they had heard, but they had pretty big smiles on their faces. "Hi!" the girl said. "We saw you guys last night and this morning."

"Yeah," I said. "Where you guys from?" Part of me couldn't believe I was starting one of these insipid conversations, but these kids seemed nice. Perhaps I was mellowing with age.

"Chicago," the guy said. "It's our first time here."

The girl said, "We were in the campground Saturday night," she waved a hand vaguely downhill, "and the EMS came through. We heard some guy chopped his hand with a hatchet, and we were wondering if that was you."

I laughed heartily. "No, I wasn't quite that stupid."

"Almost, though," Lauren said brightly.

They told us that they were part of a group of eight, but only these four had been brave enough to venture into the backcountry. The other four were waiting for them down at Cosby campground. "They saw the mountains and said 'no way'," the girl explained. "It didn't help when the people at the store told us that we shouldn't come up here without somebody who's been here before."

I congratulated them on doing so well their first time out. The girl seemed to be the leader of the group, and I asked her about the book I had seen her reading.

She dug into her pack and handed the book to me. "Here. Take a look."

"This is the 'bible'!" I said excitedly. "I've been using that book for thirty years!" Clearly, neither of them had been alive for thirty years, but they didn't come out and say so. Instead, they told us that the day before had been the girl's birthday, and they had packed in some wine to celebrate, which is why they were hurting in the morning.

"Whiskey's lighter," I grinned, and I told them a little about how we used to party in the backcountry in the old days. I heard myself sounding like Quill Rose, the old moonshiner, and it felt surreal to realize that *I* was now the gray-bearded old-timer. We wished them luck on the rest of their trip and kept a friendly distance for the rest of the evening.

We had a nice evening by an economical fire. As we sat gazing into the flames, I remembered how the boys and I used to burn our dirty, ratty clothing rather than carry it out. Without telling Lauren what I had in mind, I went behind the tent and took off the threadbare underpants I had been wearing for two days.

"What's that?" Lauren asked suspiciously as I came back over to the fire holding something behind my back.

"My 'gotchies'!" I said, unveiling the rotten shorts with a flourish. "Gotchies" was the Slovak word for underwear, and the word must have been the same or similar in other Eastern European languages because Lauren's Hungarian grandparents had used the word as well.

Lauren shrank back. "Oh," she said, "I thought it was a bedspread or something."

I ceremoniously laid the underpants onto the flames. "They had a long and full life," I said solemnly. "This is like a Viking funeral for underwear. It doesn't get any better than this for a pair of shorts."

Later, after the last shred of elastic had been incinerated, I went back behind the tent to put on another pair. "I'm puttin' on my lucky ones for Mount Guyot tomorrow, Laur."

"If they're lucky, you should wear them all the time."

"There's only so much magic in one pair of gotchies, baby."

"I know."

As we settled into the tent later that night, I wriggled around a little inside my sleeping bag and said, "I think my ass hole's too far to the left."

My first conscious thought the next morning was *this is the day*. I rolled over and saw that Lauren was already awake. She whispered sweetly, "How'd your ass hole work?"

394

Finding Mount Guyot

The day was cloudy and windswept and cool—perfect for walking hard. When I lowered our food bag down from the bear-proof food hanger, we discovered that mice had gnawed their way in. The mice had evidently climbed across the steel cables or had jumped eight feet through the air from the nearest tree over to the pack. Either way, it was one hell of an accomplishment. Then they chewed right through the rip-stop nylon fabric and two or three layers of plastic bags. They had gone for the trail mix, eating the M&M's and the banana chips but discarding the pretzels. I imagined their little midnight foray as if they were *Hills Have Eyes* mutant mice. "I like fixin' people good!" one would snarl, and the other would growl, "Fat and juicy!"

The food sack featuring the new mouse holes also doubled as my day pack, so I had to work around those holes as I packed it with snacks and emergency gear for the day's hike. Lauren had a day pack of her own, which she packed with a few more things. We hoisted our big packs up the food hangers, left the tent where it was, and trusted that no one would mess with our stuff.

As soon as we got onto the main trail, Lauren said, "Let's say a little prayer." We held hands and bowed our heads, and I said, "Dear Lord, watch over us and keep us safe today, and please help us get to the top of Mount Guyot." I wasn't used to praying out loud, so I felt a little self-conscious. "Not much of a prayer," I said sheepishly.

Lauren squeezed my good hand and whispered, "It was nice. He heard you."

Lauren loved hiking without a pack on. We climbed the steep, final section of the Maddron Bald Trail easily. Most of the huge purple blossoms had already fallen off the rhododendrons, but we saw a few bushes hidden in isolated hollows that were still in bloom. We stopped at the Maddron Bald lookout, and Lauren was awestruck by the 360-degree view of the high peaks. The gray clouds racing over the highest mountaintops only enhanced the wild beauty. I pointed out Mount Guyot, which was wreathed in clouds and could only be seen in fleeting glimpses. "I can't believe we're *walking* there! They still seem so far away," she said, but she sounded excited rather than worried.

I felt confident, but not certain. I had been confident the year before, and I had failed. This time, though, I knew what I was looking at. I could see Old Black with its thorny crown of dead trees to the north of Mount Guyot. As we continued, I was pensive and quiet. I didn't yell "Gee-oohhh!!!" or "talk big" in any way. I respected the mountain this time, knowing all too well that something could still go wrong. I wasn't feeling the wild exuberance I had thought I would. I was carrying the memories of thirty-two years with me, and for some unexpected reason they suddenly felt very heavy.

The trail dipped slightly into an open, grassy saddle. From that vantage point, we had another excellent view of Old Black and Guyot to the south, but, in the time it took to get out a camera, the clouds swept in again and the view disappeared. Mount Guyot remained mysterious and elusive as always. We left the saddle and climbed up to the AT, marking the first time Lauren had ever stood upon that trail. The name of the place was Inadu Knob, "Inadu" being the Cherokee word for "snake."

Soon we came to a section of the AT that ran along an exposed ridge. The trail was completely enclosed on the sides and on top by a tunnel of huge rhododendron. The clouds dropped even lower, and we could see white wisps of vapor blowing through the center of the tunnel like fleeing spirits. It was as foreboding a sight as I'd ever seen in the Smokies. "Welcome," I said melodramatically, "to the Appalachian Trail."

Finding Mount Guyot

A brief description in the bible said that there was a nameless gap from which a faint, rugged trail climbed up to Mount Guyot. That, along with what the Trail Boss had told me, were the only directions we had to go on. I walked slowly and deliberately, checking my compass and my map often. We were as silent as if we were walking into church after the service had begun.

I could see glimpses of the dead trees on the high ground ahead of us and knew that we were approaching Old Black. We came to Dan's cairn on the left side of the trail, and I was almost certain that the piled stones marked the way up to Old Black and not Mount Guyot. I told Lauren, "I have to be sure this isn't it." We climbed up the steep mountainside, Lauren right behind me, and I recognized the major deadfall of trees a hundred yards up. Finally, I knew in my heart that Dan hadn't climbed Mount Guyot at all. It was entirely possible, though, that he had gone to the top here and *thought* that he was at the top of Guyot.

The AT dipped slightly after Old Black and curved southeast. I walked with my compass open in my hand, watching the needle as the trail began to rise again and curve west, and then we saw a mucky pool covering the trail. "This must be the first spring that the Trail Boss was talking about!" I said. I vaguely recalled it being no more than mud the last time. We walked another hundred yards and found the Guyot Spring that I remembered, the one that Mollie had drunk from. It issued out of the hillside and ran steadily across the trail and then down the mountainside toward the Ramsey Cascades far below.

We paused at the Guyot Spring as I collected my thoughts. The top of Guyot seemed to be visible over our left shoulders. The year before, I had been closer to the top here than I had been at any other point. Now, I was close again—so close that I could taste it—but I forced myself to be deliberate. The Trail

Boss said the old path to the top was just past the two springs. We followed the AT as it curved around the peak of the mountain, and within a few hundred yards, I saw the wide spot in the trail that the Trail Boss had told me about, and I started laughing. Lauren was certain I had gone mad. There was no cairn and no pink ribbon. The only marker was a white quartz stone about twelve inches square on the left side of the little clearing—the exact same stone on which I had rested on the previous trip!

The side trail was obvious and not obvious at the same time. The AT widened out, but only for the space of ten feet. The hidden entrance to the path headed roughly north up the mountain. Now, in May, it looked like a thin spot in the vegetation, but in October with the undergrowth full grown, it would have looked like nothing at all. In fact, I recalled that Tory had poked around this place and seen nothing. This time, I studied it more closely, and I spotted the slightest hint of a trail about twenty yards up the slope. "I can't believe Dan and I missed this!" I said. In our haste, we had simply overlooked the white rock and the wide spot in the trail.

I grabbed Lauren and kissed her. "This is really it!" I said maniacally. She looked slightly bewildered. She had no way of truly understanding how long and how hard I had fought to get to this point. In one perfect moment, I felt the elation of discovery and the heart-pounding rush of anticipation.

We plunged into the undergrowth, and Lauren didn't hesitate. She didn't know how lost we could get or how quickly it could happen. I picked my own way up the mountain, occasionally spotting scant traces of the old trail. I was amazed at how much an unmaintained trail could deteriorate in twelve short years. In most places, the trail was completely gone. After a few hundred yards, I realized the way to the top was longer and not as well defined as I had thought it would be. Nonetheless, I knew in my soul that we were going to get there this time, and that knowledge was like a shot of good whiskey spreading happy warmth through my veins.

The terrain was steep and difficult, but not impassable. I churned forward, making sure Lauren stayed with me. The ground was a carpet of pine needles an inch or two deep. The earthy smell we kicked up was sweet incense. Scattered deadfalls barred the way, as the Trail Boss had promised, but they were spaced far enough apart that we could work around them. The underbrush, which was always the real stopper, was just starting to mature for the season. The climb would have been much tougher in high summer or in the fall. We hit a few patches of prickers that we had to work our way out of, but I barely noticed them.

Even from this close, we couldn't see the summit. The low-hanging clouds, the trees, and the slope of the mountain made it impossible to tell exactly where the top was. I realized that I hadn't been looking at the *real* top of the mountain when I scrambled up from the Guyot Spring the last time. The true top was definitely not visible from the AT.

After going three or four hundred yards up, it was clear that we were going to have hard time finding our way back down. Like Hansel and Gretel, we started leaving marks behind us so that we could retrace our steps. Instead of bread crumbs, we used our feet and our walking sticks to scratch large arrows into the pine needle turf marking the direction back down. Not trusting entirely to fairy tales, I took a compass reading too. "I never really understood how those degree things worked," Lauren admitted. I didn't tell her that I really didn't either.

Gradually, after another three or four hundred yards, the slope became less steep, and we approached the summit. I felt more curious than elated. We found a rough tabletop maybe twenty yards wide and forty yards long covered with firs and a heavy blanket of pine needles. We looked around for the saddle and the false top that the Trail Boss had talked about, but we didn't see anything like that, and I was suddenly afraid that I had somehow gone astray again at the very end. I walked around the perimeter to make absolutely sure that there was no higher ground anywhere. There wasn't. Lauren watched as I anxiously searched for the highest spot and any sign of a brass USGS marker. Then, on what appeared to be the highest section of the tabletop, I saw a tiny cairn only five rocks high. It rose only a few inches off the ground. A blue marble with cloudy white streaks in it was perched atop the cairn. It was the top of Mount Guyot.

Even being there, I still wasn't sure I had found it. I poked my ski pole down through the pine needle turf at an angle to assure myself that the brass marker lay beneath the cairn. I couldn't see the brass marker, but I could feel hard bedrock. Standing back from the cairn, though, we could clearly see that it was the highest point on the tabletop. "This has to be it," I said.

"Your friends aren't going to believe you were here," Lauren said. We had talked about getting a photo of the brass marker for evidence, but there was no way I was going to disturb the delicate cairn for a picture.

"That's alright," I murmured. "This is it. Let them find it themselves and they'll see."

And then Mount Guyot didn't matter to me. I had dreamed of this moment, and I couldn't help myself. I took Lauren's hands in mine and I said, "I love you, Laur. I never stopped loving you. I hope it's OK now."

Her soft brown eyes met mine, and for a heartbeat she was silent. I was afraid I had spoken too rashly again, but then she said the words I had waited so, so many years to hear. "Oh, I love you too, John. I think I did all along." Then she smiled her secretive smile and chided me, "It's not like I didn't know. It took you long enough to say it this time!"

I picked her up off the ground and hugged her to my chest. I twirled us around a few times, and nothing else existed, not even the mountain beneath us, and all the positive energy in the universe was rushing toward us, toward our hearts beating a few inches away from each other, and it was light and good and joy. We kissed and hugged and soaked in the moment. It was deep, soulful joy. In recent times, with the trail all but abandoned and so hard to follow, few people ever made it to where we now were.

Slowly, we came back down to earth, and I remembered a surprise down in the bottom of my day pack. I reached in and pulled out the flag of the Slovak Republic: three broad, horizontal stripes of white, blue, and red, emblazoned with a shield showing a white patriarchal cross rising above three blue mountains. I held the flag up with my bandaged hand, standing next to the cairn, and Lauren snapped the photo. "I'm gonna send that picture to the Raffertys," I told Lauren, "and the caption is going to be 'The Slovak has taken Guyot'."

"How 'bout if the Slovak takes me?" Lauren asked coyly, so I laid the flag down on the pine needles and then laid Lauren down on the flag. We were one with each other and one with the mountain. It was cold and slightly prickly, but it was perfect.

Afterwards, we explored the edges of the tabletop some more, but the trees and the heavy clouds blocked any possible views. We could only catch occasional glimpses of Old Black to the north. We sat next to the cairn and picnicked on smoked oysters, beef jerky, and trail mix, eating carefully around the part of the trail mix that the mice had raided. I drank a can of O'Doul's Amber with gusto.

I congratulated Lauren. "You got up here your first time! You know how lucky you are? You did great on that off-trail stuff."

Buddha Palguta

"We used to play down by the cliffs at the edge of the Flats when I was little."

"You're still little," I laughed.

We both had to pee, but Lauren said, "It almost feels like it would be disrespectful though," and I agreed. We decided we could wait until we got back down to the AT.

We put two flat stones on top of the cairn and carefully replaced the blue marble. The mountain had finally welcomed me, but now it was time to bid farewell and leave Mount Guyot to its majestic silence.

We had a much harder time coming down off the summit. We followed the lines we had drawn in the turf easily enough for the first three or four hundred yards, but after our markings ended, we almost immediately got tangled up in thickets of dead trees and pricker bushes. For some reason, I found it much harder to navigate going downhill. I watched my compass and followed a straight course, even when it meant crawling on all fours through deadfalls. Lauren stayed calm even when the going got rough. Eventually, I saw a small clearing in the vegetation and headed toward it. Once we were on top of it, we realized it was the AT. It looked like an eight-lane highway compared to where we'd just been. We ended up only thirty yards from where we had gone in.

We regrouped on the trail, and Lauren asked, "So when you guys were here last time, all you would've had to do was read that red book and you would've known where to go?"

It sounded so painfully simple. "Yeah," I shrugged, "It would've helped a lot." *It's amazing*, I thought, *how accurate that old book turned out to be.*

The rain had held off all day, but not ten minutes after we started back toward camp, it came down in buckets. It broke somewhat as we neared camp, but we experienced periods of drizzle for the rest of the evening. Everything was muddy and soaked at #29, but it didn't matter. Love had shifted our

402

perspective on the world, so the discomforts were inconsequential.

We were sitting around eating our remaining goodies when a good-looking, thirtyish couple marched into camp from the west. He had a neatly trimmed beard and wore a bandana on his head. She was slim and pretty and had some type of tight-fitting short skirt on. Both were carrying heavy packs. One glance told me that all their gear was state-of-the-art and expensive. The guy walked past us, looked over the edge of the drop-off behind us, and barked, "Are there any more campsites down there?"

The only open site was right next to us. "You're welcome to look for yourself," I said, "but there's no room for a tent down there."

He looked, and without taking off his pack, he climbed down the steep and now muddy slope to get a closer look. Lauren asked the girl, who was still up top with us, where they were headed. It turned out that they were doing the same exact route that we were doing, just one day behind us. I asked her if they were going to the very top of Guyot. She said, "If we can," which seemed like an intelligent answer.

A few minutes later, the guy climbed back up and rejoined us. "No room for a tent," he muttered to the girl.

Resuming our conversation, Lauren pointed to me and told the girl, "You guys should talk to him if you want to find the top of Mount Guyot."

"It's not easy to find," I simply said.

The girl said "OK," but the guy chose that moment to walk away from us to continue looking for a tent site that wasn't right next to us. The girl smiled an apologetic half smile and turned to join her man.

As soon as they were out of ear shot, I whispered to Lauren, "I *told* him there was no room for a tent down there."

Buddha Palguta

She whispered back, "I can't believe he went down there with a pack on!" Lauren was grasping the finer points of backpacking very nicely.

We tended to our few chores, but we had plenty of time to watch the other couple set up their camp next to us. I was fascinated by them and all their camping gadgets. The guy was heavily armed with a leather-holstered hunting knife on one hip and a leather-holstered hatchet on the other. The hatchet was useless weight. Any piece of wood dry enough to burn could be broken more easily by slamming it across a big rock. I glanced over to their camp at one point, and the guy had donned a pair of fingerless leather gloves just so he could hoist the steel food-hanger cable into the air. I nearly laughed out loud. There were smooth plastic grips on the cable that made it very easy to hoist a pack up without getting blisters on your delicate palms. Nevertheless, he looked mighty rustic with those gloves on his hands, his weapons at his sides, and his bandana on his head. I suspected that he had grown the beard specifically for the trip.

He kept calling the girl "babe," which reminded us of the yuppie "A-hole" couple on *Saturday Night Live*. In those skits, the A-hole man ended every sentence with "babe," as in, "You want a Hummer or a Beamer, babe?" or "Tell 'em how much I can bench, babe." The A-hole woman on TV had a Coach purse surgically attached to her elbow and sighed "whatever" in a bored voice whenever the guy asked her a question. We dubbed the couple next to us the "A-hole backpackers," which might not have been fair to the girl. She seemed nice enough, although I knew from experience that hiking with a skirt on wasn't the best idea in the Smokies. Maybe her thighs didn't rub together as much as mine did.

Later on, first the girl and then the guy left the camp with a square, blue, plastic article tucked under their arm. "What's that thing they're carrying?" Lauren whispered.

404

I looked at the guy disappearing into the woods fifty yards away. "I don't know. I think it's some kind of folding toilet seat!" In all my days in the backcountry, neither in the Smokies nor on any other mountain or desert or prairie had I ever seen anyone carry a folding stool with a hole in the seat. But the A-hole backpacker had one, and he carried it proudly.

I started wondering whether or not I should tell this guy how to get to the top of Mount Guyot. On one hand, it would be selfish to withhold what I knew. But it felt almost as if I would be betraying the mountain if I helped him just waltz right up to the top. "If they ask how to get there, let me do the talking," I told Lauren. "I'm not going tell them anything. They wouldn't appreciate it anyway."

After supper, the A-hole backpacker guy sauntered over to our camp. "So you made it up to the top of Mount Guyot today?"

"Yeah, we did," I answered. I wasn't going to lie, but I wasn't going to volunteer any information either.

"How long did it take you from here?"

I shrugged. "I don't know." And I truly didn't know. Then I realized I was sounding distinctly unfriendly, so I elaborated. "We don't have a watch." I turned to Lauren. "How long would you say it took?"

She frowned. "Maybe five or six hours. But we had a snack at the top."

"Yeah," I agreed, "no more than six hours."

The bearded wonder woodsman got a sour look on his face, as if he found it distasteful to talk to people who didn't wear watches, but he continued. "How are the views at the top?"

The question seemed superfluous to me, but I answered him the best I could. "We were in a big cloud up there. There were a few breaks in the clouds, but not many."

The guy scratched his beard as if he were thinking about what I just said. "But there are good viewing points up there?"

Viewing points? I wasn't sure what this guy was after, but again I answered to the best of my ability. "There's a lot of pines on top. I don't know, but I don't think the views would be that great even on a clear day." *Shit! You told him there are pines on top! Just shut up!*

"I'll find out tomorrow," he said and then turned and walked away.

What was with this guy? Didn't he know how to say "hello" or "goodbye" or "fuck you" or anything? I was glad he was going away before I gave away any other tidbits of information, but I couldn't resist calling after him, "If it doesn't rain."

He answered back over his shoulder. "Oh, we're going. Rain or shine."

Then I realized that he hadn't even asked me how to get there! Lauren turned to me with this incredulous look on her face, and I knew she realized it too. Once he was out of earshot, I told Lauren, "See, I'm like a secret agent. I didn't tell him anything!" She just rolled her eyes.

THE SAME CONVERSATION FROM THE A-HOLE BACKPACKER'S POINT OF VIEW:

After using my brand new Camper's Comfort Chair (which was a real bargain at $49.99 and totally worth carrying), I went over to the hillbilly backpacker's camp to ask them a few simple questions about Mount Guyot. At least I thought they were simple questions.

The hillbilly guy was wearing saggy, wet cargo pants and a T-shirt that he should have thrown into the fire and burned. He had about a week's worth of salt-and-pepper beard on his face and a ratty, dirty bandage wrapped around his left hand. I was upwind, but I'm sure he stank. Surprisingly, he had all his teeth.

Finding Mount Guyot

The hillbilly chick was either the guy's daughter or his twelve-year-old bride, or maybe both. She was about four feet tall and she probably weighed less than my backpack. She had on a T-shirt that said "cowgirl," and she probably smelled like a cow too. But that really isn't fair to the girl, the poor little thing. She seemed OK. The hillbilly guy had probably dragged her out to the woods to have his way with her, *Deliverance*-style.

I tried to put them at ease by talking like them. "Hello, you-all folks!" I said. "So you-all went to the top of Mount Guyot today?"

The hillbilly guy just said, "Yup," and eyed me suspiciously.

"Well, that's great!" I tried to remain upbeat and friendly. "How long it did it take you-all to get there and back?"

"Don't rightly know. Ain't got no watches or nuthin'," the guy drawled. I couldn't believe it! In the year 2009, there were still people in America who couldn't afford a watch. It made me sad. The guy asked the hillbilly chick how long it had taken them to go to Mount Guyot.

I was surprised that she spoke at all. She kept her head down and mumbled, "Reckon it took five or six hours. But we stopped and ate some vittles at the top." She reminded me of one of the characters in the "Appalachian Emergency Room" skits on *Saturday Night Live*. In fact, we dubbed this couple with the cheap 1980s camping equipment and the ratty clothes the "Appalachian backpackers."

I really didn't want to be anywhere near them. I was afraid that bugs would be leaping off them and landing on me. As I stood there, lice might be burrowing into the beard that I had grown just for the trip. But I wanted to find out about the top of Mount Guyot so I would know what type of lenses to bring for my camera in the morning. I decided to skip the friendly

407

chatter and get right to my point. "How are the views at the top?"

The Appalachian backpacker guy said something about the clouds in the sky, which seemed superfluous to me. I wasn't sure what he was getting at. Maybe his bunions were acting up, and he thought he could predict the weather according to his aches and pains. I tried to rephrase my question in a way he might understand better. "But there are good viewing points up there?"

The guy looked at me as if I had just told him that WWF wrestling was fake, and he didn't say anything for a long time. Finally, after letting the two lonely brain cells in his head fire a few feeble charges toward each other, he said, "There's a lot of trees up yonder. I don't reckon the views would be real good even on a clear day."

Sha-zaam! There are trees on mountains? Thanks for the tip, old timer! Clearly, the Appalachian backpacker guy was trying to cover something up. He was probably cooking meth up there or growing pot. I decided I better leave before this guy shot me or the itching in my beard got any worse.

Forcing myself to keep smiling, I said, "Well, I'll find out tomorrow," and I turned to walk away.

The guy couldn't resist one last attempt to discourage me from going up to Mount Guyot. He called out to me, "If'n it don't rain!"

What was with this guy? Couldn't he see all the high-tech equipment I had? It should have been obvious even to him that I knew what I was doing. A little rain wasn't going to bother us in the least. I couldn't resist a parting shot of my own. "Oh, we're going. Rain or shine," I said.

Later that evening, we sat next to the fire ring in our camp while the A-hole couple sat in their expensive tent no more than fifteen yards away. We saw the A-hole guy come out for a moment in his Spandex sleeping tights, which probably gave his legs the super-power he needed to carry all his high-tech stuff and his toilet seat up and down mountains. We could hear them laughing and enjoying themselves as they settled in for the night.

Lauren and I sat side by side in the gathering gloom on a plastic bag laid over a wet, flat rock, staring into our cold fire pit. We couldn't start a fire because everything was so wet. Even the chunks of Duraflame log that I used as fire-starters wouldn't hold a flame. We were content sipping our hot tea in the gloom. Lauren zipped up her fleece top all the way to keep the chill out. Rain was threatening once again, but we were happy. We had love.

We were having some good laughs of our own. We sat in our camp giggling about them, and they sat in their tent probably giggling about us. Neither camp was exemplifying the spirit of the wilderness, but we were, after all, frail humans.

"You think they'll leave all their stuff here tomorrow like we did today?" Lauren wondered.

It was a good question that I hadn't considered. "Man, I don't know if I would. They've got a lot of expensive gear over there." I hadn't been too worried about our stuff sitting unattended all day because it really wasn't worth much.

"They'll probably try to carry it all the way to the top of Mount Guyot," Lauren laughed.

"Slaves to their possessions," I said.

"It's almost like they have to try to impress people with what they have."

"They'd be better off just being themselves. Man," I shook my head, "if you can't be yourself out here, where can you be?"

Lauren nodded thoughtfully and said, "I think it takes time for some people to learn *how* to be themselves—instead of being what people think they're supposed to be."

I recalled a line from a Beatles' song and softly sang, "'You can learn to be you in time. It's easy.'" Then I chuckled and said, "Except it wasn't easy for me. I think I'm just starting to really be me."

"There's a scary thought."

Then, for the second or third time, I thought I saw movement in the fire pit, so I quickly shined my flashlight on the ring of rocks. Sure enough, our *Hills Have Eyes* mice were back for another raid, drawn by the smells of the food wrappers that we hadn't been able to burn. Lauren said, "Oh, he's a big sucker!"

I borrowed yet another line from the movie and said, "Great big stud."

Lauren wasn't worried about the mouse three feet away from her in the least, and I loved her for that too. She laughed, "Wow! He's a brave little guy, isn't he?"

Later, after we settled in, we heard the sound of big, heavy raindrops hitting our tent. I listened to the steady tapping, wondering if I dared to say "I love you" again, thinking I would somehow break the spell that had been cast up on the mountain. When Lauren leaned over and kissed my head and whispered those magic words to me, I said them back to her.

When I woke up at dawn, it was still raining hard. The two coatings of waterproofing I had sprayed on my old tent had slowed down the water but not stopped it. As soon as I heard Lauren stirring, I said, "I think my ass hole's full of water," but she wasn't laughing. She was listening to the steady downpour.

Lauren got a hardcore introduction to the Smokies that morning. Breaking camp in the sodden Smoky Mountain rain forest was a miserable way to start the day. We pulled on our wet boots and our damp clothes inside the dubious shelter of the tent and ventured outside. We stood dully munching granola bars in the driving rain watching the coffee water heat up. I looked with love at Lauren, who never, ever complained. "Now *this* is a vacation, isn't it, baby?"

Lauren looked at me myopically through foggy, rain-splattered glasses. "You really know how to show a girl a good time." She was ready to go home, and I was too.

When we left #29, we walked right past the A-hole's site, which hadn't shown any signs of life all morning. It was at least eight o'clock, but they still hadn't come out of their tent. If they were waiting for it to stop raining, they would be waiting a long time. I shook my head as we walked by. "There's no way they're getting to the top today," I told Lauren.

"What if they have a GPS?"

I thought of the GPS in Freddie's Ford Condo and laughed. I remembered Freddie insisting that there were high-end GPSs available that could put you within fifty or even thirty feet of any spot on Earth. I told him that there had been many times in my life when I had been within thirty feet of the right place and had still missed it entirely. "I don't care if he has GPS beams shooting out his ass; he's not gonna get to the top. Especially not today. I'd bet money on it!"

"Why not?"

I gave her the logical answer. "A GPS might tell him where the top is, but it won't show him the right way to get there. When he gets to the place where the AT runs closest to the top, he'll start fighting uphill through the deadfalls just like I did last time, thinking he can see the top right there in front of him, and he'll still be a long way off. He'll never even see the right path." But the real answer, the answer that went beyond mere logic, was that Mount Guyot couldn't be found unless you approached it with the proper spirit, a spirit of humility and quiet courage.

I stepped around a long puddle in the trail and continued, "That's if he even bothers getting out of his tent and hauling all his fancy stuff up there."

"Sure you're not just jealous?"

I had to admit that I felt a twinge of jealousy toward guys like the A-hole backpacker, who had apparently grabbed life by the wallet and was squeezing out every last nickel. I shrugged inside my poncho. "Some of that stuff I wouldn't mind having. But a crack dealer could buy all that stuff too, and he'd still be scum."

"But that's what people see," Lauren observed, "and that's how they judge you."

"Maybe that's why I like being out here."

Early on, something in me had rebelled against the sham and drudgery of a life spent accumulating things and toeing the line. In my mind, allowing someone else's expectations to determine the course of your own life was a sad, timid choice. Taking the person you became by default and molding that into the person you aspired to be was, I now knew, the work of a lifetime. Most never traveled that path because of the hardship it entailed, but there was joy in it too. Like backpacking, it was the yin and the yang of perpetual striving and true happiness.

The Snake Den Ridge Trail that brought us out was a slippery, torturous riverbed all the way back to Cosby. After hours of slogging downhill on slick rocks covered with running water, we saw the trail getting flatter and entering into a river valley. The trail crossed over a huge, single-log bridge. "We're almost there," I said. "They don't put these bridges in the backcountry." On the other side of the bridge, the trail turned into crushed gravel and there was a nice, hewn-log bench next to the stream, marking the outer limits of civilization and the border of the backcountry.

Lauren wistfully said, "Is this where the bus picks you up?"

We sat on the bench for a minute. The rain had stopped and woods were dripping and solemn. I whispered, "This is the last tranquil moment."

Lauren sighed, "I know this was hard and I'm tired right now, but part of me still hates to go back."

We passed the graveyard of one of the old families of settlers who had lived in the Smokies before it became a national park. We dropped our packs and took a moment to walk amongst the headstones. The newest one was for a woman who had died in 1983. Her headstone proclaimed her "The Poet Laureate of the Smokies." I tried to remember her name, thinking that maybe someday I'd read her poems, but I knew that I'd be disappointed. No poetry or painting or book could capture the essence of what it meant to be deep in the Smoky Mountains. The mountains were too vast and beautiful and ancient.

We finally came to the Cosby campground. On a rainy Wednesday, the campground was virtually deserted. The first thing we saw was a tent site with a raised bed of finely crushed gravel spread out in a nice, level square and retained by brand new 12x12 treated lumber. I couldn't contain my disdain for such softness. "Look at that!" I scowled. "Why don't they just put feather beds out here?"

Lauren said with feeling, "Yeah! Kiss my ass!" and I hugged her because she was a true backcountry backpacker now.

We used the rest rooms in the parking lot to change into the dry clothes we had waiting in the car. I peeled the wet bandages off my left hand. The wound was still open, and the skin around the edges was fish-belly white, as if I'd been swimming for twelve hours straight. I didn't see any signs of infection though, and I counted my blessings for that.

As we were loading our wet gear into the trunk of our car, a beat-up Toyota pulled into the parking lot, and three scruffy-looking young guys in their late teens or early twenties got out. They pulled their backpacks out of the trunk and went through the ritual of getting ready to go into the backcountry. They talked excitedly and laughed a lot. One kid poured something concealed in a brown paper bag into a plastic bottle and then stuffed the bottle into his pack.

They hoisted their sloppy-looking packs onto their backs and walked off toward the far end of the parking lot. The one kid didn't even have his sleeping bag wrapped in anything. The bag was exposed to the wet air and ready to brush up against every wet bush or tree. He was in for a tough night, I knew. But the thing that struck me the most was that one of the guys had a cooking pot tied to the back of his pack, Hop Sing-style. I watched the cooking pot sway back and forth as the kid walked, and I felt as if I were looking thirty years into the past.

As I stood there lost in that reverie, the kid who had driven suddenly turned around and started walking back toward us. The other two guys laughed heartily. When he got to his car, he saw me looking at him, so he said, "Forgot my car keys! Good thing the door doesn't lock!" He opened the driver's door, retrieved his keys, and banged the door shut again.

The kid saw me still watching, so he said, "Anybody could take this car if they wanted to."

I grinned, "I think it'll be here for you when you come out."

The kid chuckled and nodded. I wanted to say something more—to make some connection to this shadow from my past—so I asked him, "Where you guys headed?"

"We're going up to #34 and then #29. We're just going out to have fun."

The kid started walking back to rejoin his friends, but then he stopped and turned back to me again. "Hey, mister. You know if this is the right way?"

"Yeah," I said, "it is. Just keep going and you'll find it."

After we went home, Lauren and I were happy together. Sometimes she called me her mountain man, which always made me smile. With her encouragement, I finally started to write my book.

The cut I got going to Mount Guyot healed up, leaving a jagged, pale scar across the palm of my left hand. Gypsy fortune tellers say that the palm of the left hand reveals the truth about a person while the right hand only shows what that person wishes were true. My right hand is almost unblemished, but my left hand bears many scars, most of them from self-inflicted wounds. Of all those scars, the only one I'm really proud of is the scar I got finding Mount Guyot.

Buddha Palguta

Read on for a peek into Johnny Reznick's gold-mining adventures in the Sierra Nevada.

An excerpt from *Finding Eldorado*

We were awakened at dawn the next day by gun shots from somewhere downstream. "Somebody must've pissed off Smoky Moe," I said.

Tony scratched himself and said, "It wouldn't take much."

Rick yawned and stretched in his sleeping bag. "We really should've brought a gun."

A few minutes later, we heard a man yell, "Ho, in the camp!" We scrambled out of our tent and saw three men standing at the downstream end of our camp. Again one of them yelled out, "Ho, in the camp. Can we come through?"

I said, "Yeah, come on in," and we watched apprehensively as they walked into our camp.

In such a situation, men instinctively size each other up as potential opponents. These guys were about our age, and all smaller than us, but the long guns slung on their shoulders tipped the advantage to them. One of them had two dead birds dangling from his hand, and another was carrying a hefty dead snake. My assessment was that they looked like pretty rough customers.

The guy holding the birds spoke first. He had short blondish hair, and by gold miners' standards, he was clean-cut, meaning he had apparently shaven sometime in the last two weeks. He said, "My name's Jake. This is Red and that's Dwayne." Red and Dwayne nodded but didn't smile. "You setting up camp here?"

Rick squared his shoulders and straightened to his full height. He had that malevolent look on his face. "Yeah, we're gonna camp here for a while. Is that a problem?"

Jake smiled disarmingly. "Naw, it ain't no thing, man. Relax."

Red spoke up. True to his name, he had red hair and an unkempt red beard. "We're working on the Yuba down past the bridge. We just come up here huntin'. If you don't bother us, we won't bother you."

"Fair enough," I said. I introduced us and then asked, "Where you guys from?"

"Around here. Grass Valley. Red's from Yuba City."

"What about you?" the one called Dwayne asked. "You sound like you're from New York City." I noticed that Dwayne talked with his mouth closed to conceal some truly bad teeth.

We laughed and Tony replied, "No, we're from Cleveland. Land of the free and the home of the Browns."

They looked surprised. "What, are you out here visiting somebody?"

"No," I answered, "we came out here looking for gold."

It was the Californians' turn to laugh. Jake said, "I don't know how much you know about finding color, but it ain't all that easy."

"Tell us about it!" Rick said. "We've been out here two weeks and we haven't found jack shit."

"But we were out here last year too," I added. "We knew it wouldn't be easy." Rick looked at me curiously but didn't say anything.

"You got a dredge?" Dwayne asked.

"No," I gestured toward the General Lee, "just the sluice box."

"Well," Jake said, "you got your work cut out for you."

Red looked around our encampment and said, "You came out here without guns? You got balls, I'll give you that."

Rick stiffened. "Why's that?"

"For one thing, there's mountain lions out here," Jake answered.

Red flourished the snake in his hand. "And rattlesnakes."

Dwayne added, "Can't always be sure about the people out here neither."

Jake smiled. "Have you met your neighbors from upstream yet?"

Dwayne pretended he was coughing but clearly barked out the word, "Convicts!"

"What do you mean?" I was beginning to wonder if these locals were for real, or if they were just trying to run us off.

Red answered, "There's two guys camped upstream a ways and we're thinking they just got out of prison. We don't know if it's true or not."

"Decent enough guys, though," Jake shrugged. "They haven't bothered us."

Tony tried to sound nonchalant. "Some of the best people I know have done time."

I joined in. "Hell, your mom was in prison for a while, wasn't she, Tony?"

"Just six months," he answered. "Nothing worth bragging about."

It was the Californians' turn to wonder about us. I figured it was good to leave them guessing about how desperate a bunch we were.

ABOUT THE AUTHOR

Buddha Palguta lives with his wife, Raputa, in northeast Ohio and spends a lot of time wondering why he's not in the mountains. *Finding Mount Guyot* is his first book worth reading. *Finding Eldorado* is his second. Both are available on Amazon.com.

If you like these books, please write a review!

To find out more or to join his e-mail list, go to BuddhaPalguta.com.

Johnny Rez definitely has another story to tell....

Printed in Great Britain
by Amazon

36446192R00243